CW01337242

# A Dictionary of English and Folk-names of British Birds; With Their History, Meaning, and First Usage, and the Folk-lore, Weather-lore, Legends, Etc., Relating to the More Familiar Species

A DICTIONARY OF ENGLISH AND
FOLK-NAMES OF BRITISH BIRDS

A DICTIONARY

OF

ENGLISH AND FOLK-NAMES

OF

BRITISH BIRDS

With their History, Meaning and first usage:
and the Folk-lore, Weather-lore, Legends, etc,
relating to the more familiar species.

BY

H. KIRKE SWANN

WITHERBY & CO.
326 HIGH HOLBORN LONDON W.C.
1913

QL677
S93
BIOLOGY
LIBRARY
G

PREFACE.

THE idea and general scheme of this work were first entertained by me as far back as 1895, and from time to time since then I have worked at gathering up and piecing together the materials until during the past year the work had grown to such proportions and approached so nearly towards completion that I deemed it worthy of publication. To say that even as now published it is complete, would be claiming too much for it, since with such a vast field open to research, both in literature and dialect, the possibilities of addition and correction are still very great.

The first work approaching the scheme of the present volume was Swainson's "Folklore and Provincial Names of British Birds," published in 1886, which contains nearly 2,000 local and other English names, but the author did not attempt to deal with the important matter of book-names of species, and moreover the work, useful as it is, suffers somewhat from not being arranged in the form of a dictionary. Compared to Swainson's work, Newton's ' Dictionary of Birds " (1893-6) contains a great many less names, as might be expected from the scope of the book, which was too wide to allow the author to direct much of his great talent and research upon this limited subject. Mr. Hett, in 1898, issued a short list of names in his " Call Notes of Birds," and in 1902 he published a much more extended list, containing nearly 3,000 names, although it comprises merely a list of names with the species they refer to and includes many mere variations and mis-spellings. In the present " Dictionary " I have assembled, including variations of spelling, nearly 5,000 names. Of course there are also partial or local lists of names to be found in various ornithological works and periodicals of all kinds. The labour of collecting, collating and working up these names from a hundred or more different sources, it may be judged, has been enormous, and carefully as it has been done, omissions have probably been made which I shall be glad to have pointed out to me.

I have attempted to combine in this volume the English *book*-names from past authors, giving the history and first usage of the *accepted* names of species, and also the provincial, local and dialect names in use now or formerly in the British Islands, indicating the locality and meaning where possible. The Welsh, Gaelic, Cornish and some of the Irish names have been added, but in the case of the Irish names my available information is deficient. Under the accepted name generally have also been added what folk-lore, legends, weather-lore, etc., I have been able to collect regarding each species.

A list of the principal works made use of has been prefixed, and it should be stated that the copy of Turner on Birds (1544) used, is the reprint edited by Mr. A. H. Evans. This work may be said to contain the earliest series of English names of British birds, an honour generally claimed for the list in Merrett's "Pinax" (1666-7). The copy I have used of the latter work is the second edition of 1667, which, however, hardly differs in any respect in its contents from the 1666 edition. The copy of Willughby and Ray's "Ornithology" (generally quoted as "Willughby") used, is the English edition of 1678, as being not only the one more commonly in use, but also because owing to its emendations and enlargement it is preferable to the Latin edition of 1676. This work forms the first great basis of modern British ornithology, and comparatively little advance was made after it, only three or four works of note appearing until the time of Pennant's "Zoology" (1766), after which date various books on British birds began by degrees to appear; yet the English nomenclature, always confused and changing, through such popular works as those of Lewin, Bewick, Montagu, Latham, Donovan, Fleming, Selby, Macgillivray and others, resolved itself but little until the time of Yarrell (1st ed., 1843), whose English names have been followed, with but few exceptions in the later editions of his work as well as by quite the majority of writers to the present day. Of the enormous mass of ornithological literature issued since Yarrell's day, I have availed myself by gleaning where anything may be gleaned for my purpose, and if any of the works thus consulted are not included in the Bibliography it is because I have felt it necessary to restrict the list to the principal and most interesting.

In conclusion I have to thank a number of past and present correspondents and friends who have obliged me with names or information for this book, and to beg their indulgence for not detailing more specifically the help they have given me. I must also add a word of thanks to Mr. H. F. Witherby for his kindly suggestions, and the interest he has shown in the publication of the work.

H. KIRKE SWANN.

38, Great Queen Street, Kingsway,
London, W.C.,
December 12*th*, 1912.

BIBLIOGRAPHY

Of principal works referred to, arranged chronologically

CHAUCER'S WORKS. Tyrwhitt's ed.
TURNER, W. "Avium Præcipuarum Historia" (1544), reprint ed, A. H Evans, 1903. [Contains 132 species, nearly all British, of which 112 have the English names affixed]
GESNER, C. "Historiæ Animalium," liber III, qui est de Avium Natura, *Tiguri*, 1555.
CAIUS, J. "Britanni, de Rariorum Animalium," etc. (1570), translated in part by A. H. Evans in App, "Turner on Birds," 1903
ALDROVANDUS, U. "Ornithologiæ, hoc est de Avibus historiæ," 1599.
CAREW, R. "Survey of Cornwall," 1602.
DRAYTON, M. "Polyolbion, or a Chorographical Description of Great Britain," 1613.
SPENSER'S WORKS. Ed 5 vols, 1845.
SHAKESPEARE'S WORKS. Ed. Staunton.
WITHERINGS, J "Order, Lawes and Ancient Customes of Swannes," 1632.
BROWNE, SIR THOMAS, Notes and Letters on the Natural History of Norfolk (1662-8) ; ed. by T. Southwell, 1902.
MERRETT, C. "Pinax, rerum Naturalium Britannicarum," etc, 1667. [This is the 2nd ed., the first being dated 1666, and it contains at pp. 170-84 what is usually cited as the earliest list of British Birds, comprising 170 species, for many of which, however, no English name is given]
CHARLETON, W. "Onomasticon Zoicon," 1668.
PLOT, R. "The Natural History of Oxfordshire," 1677.
WILLUGHBY, F. "Ornithology, in Three Books, wherein all the Birds hitherto known, being reduced into a Method suitable to their natures, are accurately described, translated into English, and enlarged, by John Ray," 1678. [Originally published in Latin in 1676, but the English ed has been used for the present work.]
SIBBALD, R. "Scotia Illustrata, sive Prodromus Historiæ Naturalis," etc., 1684.
MORTON J "Natural History of Northamptonshire," 1712
RAY, J. "Synopsis Methodica Avium et Piscium," 1713.

ALBIN, E. "Natural History of Birds," 3 vols., 1738 [The majority of the 308 plates are of British Birds, the Author stating that he has been particularly industrious to procure all the English birds he could.]
EDWARDS, G. "Natural History of Uncommon Birds," etc., 4 vols., 1743-51; *id.*, "Gleanings of Natural History," 3 vols., 1753-64.
MARTIN, M. "A Late Voyage to St. Kilda," 4th ed., 1753.
BORLASE, W. "Natural History of Cornwall," 1758.
PENNANT, T. "British Zoology," original fo. ed. (132 plates, 1766); *ib.*, 4th ed., 4 vols. 8vo, 1776-7; *ib.*, new ed., 4 vols. 8vo, 1812.
WALLIS, J. "Natural History and Antiquities of Northumberland," 1769.
TUNSTALL, M. "Ornithologia Britannica," original fo. ed., 1771.
RUTTY, J. "An Essay towards a Natural History of Co. Dublin," 1772.
HAYES, W. "Natural History of British Birds," 1775.
LATHAM, J. "A General Synopsis of Birds," 3 vols. in 6, and two Supps., 1781-90.
PENNANT, T. "Arctic Zoology," vol. II. (Birds), 1785.
WALCOTT, J. "Synopsis of British Birds," 1789.
WHITE, G. "Natural History and Antiquities of Selborne," 1st ed., 1789.
LORD, T. "Entire New System of Ornithology, or Œcumenical History of British Birds," 1791-6.
DONOVAN, E. "Natural History of British Birds," 10 vols., 1794-1819.
LEWIN, W. "Birds of Great Britain," 8 vols. (2nd ed.), 1795-1801.
WHITE, G. "Naturalists' Calendar," 1795.
BEWICK, T. "History of British Birds," 1st ed., 2 vols., 1797-1804. [The text of vol. I. was by Beilby and of vol. II. by Bewick, but Major Mullens says that Rev. Mr. Cotes of Bedlington assisted with this latter volume.]
MONTAGU, G. "Ornithological Dictionary," 1st ed., 2 vols., 1802, and Supp., 1813.
[FORSTER, T.] "Observations on Brumal retreat of Swallow," by "Philochelidon," 1808.
GRAVES, G. "British Ornithology," 3 vols, 1811-21.
LOW, G. "Fauna Orcadensis," 1813.
HUNT, J. "British Ornithology," 3 vols. (vol. 3 unfinished), 1815-22.
BULLOCK. "History of the Isle of Man," 1816.

SELBY, P. J. "Illustrations of British Ornithology," text. 2 vols, 1825-33.
FLEMING, J "History of British Animals," 1828, 2nd ed, 1842.
GOULD, J. "Birds of Europe," 5 vols., 1832-7.
JESSE, E. "Gleanings in Natural History," 3rd ser., 1832-5.
COTTON, J. "Resident Song Birds of Great Britain," 2 pts. 1835-6.
JENYNS, L. "Manual of British Vertebrate Animals," 1835
DALYELL, J. G. "Darker Superstitions of Scotland," 1835
DUNN, R. "Ornithologist's Guide to the Islands of Orkney and Shetland," 1837.
MACGILLIVRAY, W "History of British Birds," 5 vols, 1837-52
YARRELL, W "History of British Birds," 1st ed, 3 vols, 1843; id Supp. 1, 1845, Supp. 2, 1856.
THOMPSON, W. "Natural History of Ireland—Birds," 3 vols, 1849.
HOWITT, M. "Pictorial Calendar of the Seasons," 1854
STEVENSON, H., and SOUTHWELL, T. "The Birds of Norfolk," 3 vols., 1866-90
INWARDS, R. "Weather Lore," 1869
CHAMBERS. "Popular Rhymes of Scotland," 1870.
GREY, R "Birds of West of Scotland, including the Outer Hebrides," 1871.
HARTING, J. E "The Ornithology of Shakespeare," 1871.
YARRELL, W. "History of British Birds," 4th ed., edited by Newton and Saunders, 4 vols., 1871-85.
HARTING, J. E. "Handbook of British Birds," 1872; ib, new ed., 1901.
HARLAND and WILKINSON. "Lancashire Legends and Traditions," 1873
SAXBY, H. L. "Birds of Shetland," 1874
RODD, E. H. "The Birds of Cornwall," edited by J. E. Harting, 1880
SMITH, C. "The Birds of Wiltshire," 1881.
BRITISH ORNITHOLOGISTS' UNION. "List of British Birds," compiled by a Committee of the B O.U, 1883
DYER, T. F. THISELTON "English Folk Lore," 1884.
MITCHELL, F. S. "Birds of Lancashire," 1885.
SWAINSON, Rev. C "The Folk Lore and Provincial Names of British Birds," 1886.
SAUNDERS, H. "Illustrated Manual of British Birds," 1st ed., 1889; 2nd ed., 1899.
MUIRHEAD, G "The Birds of Berwickshire," 2 vols, 1889

GRAHAM, H. D. "The Birds of Iona and Mull," edited by J. A. Harvie-Brown, 1890.
CHRISTY, MILLER. "The Birds of Essex," 1890.
BORRER, W. "The Birds of Sussex," 1891.
HARVIE-BROWN, J. A. and BUCKLEY, T. E. "A Vertebrate Fauna of the Orkney Islands," 1891.
NEWTON, A. "Dictionary of Birds," 1893-6.
BUCKNILL, J. A. "The Birds of Surrey," 1900.
HETT, C. L. "Glossary of Popular, Local and Old-fashioned Names of British Birds," 1902.
NELSON, T. H., and CLARKE, W. E. "Birds of Yorkshire," 2 vols., 1907.
FORREST, H. E. "Vertebrate Fauna of North Wales," 1907.
WHITAKER, J. "Notes on the Birds of Notts.," 1907.
GLADSTONE, H. S. "The Birds of Dumfriesshire," 1910.
COWARD, T. A. "Vertebrate Fauna of Cheshire," 2 vols. (the Birds by Coward and Oldham), 1910.
BOLAM, G. "Birds of Northumberland and the Eastern Borders," 1912.
HARTERT, JOURDAIN, TICEHURST and WITHERBY. "Hand-List of British Birds," 1912.

"Archæological Review."
"Bailey's Universal Etymological Dictionary," 1749.
"British Birds" [Mag.], 1907-12.
"Bulletin" of the British Ornithologists' Club.
Dyche and Pardon's "New General English Dictionary," 2nd ed., 1757.
English Dialect Society's Publications: Glossaries of County Words, etc.
"Field."
"Folklore."
"Folklore Journal."
"Ibis."
Littré, "Hist. de la Langue Française."
Murray's "New English Dictionary," 1884-1912.
"Notes and Queries."
Philological Society's "Transactions."
Skeat's "Etymological Dictionary of the English Language," 1879-80.
Wright's "English Dialect Dictionary," 1896-1905.
"Zoologist."

A DICTIONARY OF ENGLISH AND FOLK-NAMES OF BRITISH BIRDS, Etc.

NOTE —The accepted English names of species are printed in capitals, whilst the numbers inserted in brackets refer to the species as listed in the "Hand-List of British Birds," compiled by Messrs Hartert, Jourdain, Ticehurst and Witherby, 1912, which should be referred to for the scientific nomenclature and distribution of the species The names of introduced or doubtful species are printed in *italics* The Folk-lore, weather-lore, philological and other notes are usually given under the accepted names of species (printed in capitals), to which reference should be made from alternative or local names, printed in small capitals The latter, it should be noted, are given under the first letter of the name without cross-references, i e for "Red-legged Crow" see under "R" Localities or authorities have, where possible, been appended to the equivalents of the less familiar names (in parentheses) Where these immediately follow the name of one species, without an intervening point, it should be understood they refer only to that species

ABERDEEN SANDPIPER. The KNOT. Occurs in Pennant, Montagu, Bewick, etc., as a name for a phase of this species, described as the "Red Sandpiper" by Pennant.

ABERDEVINE, ABERDAVINE, ABADAVINE, or ABERDUVINE. Obsolete names for the SISKIN, first used by Albin (1735) who, however, spells it "Aberduvine" in the text and "Abadavine" on the plate, but in his "Brit. Song-birds" (1737) it is spelt "Aberdevine." It is printed "Aberdavine" in the "New General History of Birds," 1745, and "Abber de Vine" in Rutty's "Nat History of Co. Dublin," 1772. Pennant (1766) spells it "Aberdavine," Montagu (1802) "Aberdevine," as also Cotton (1835), Yarrell (1843) and other later writers; while it occurs in the same form as a local name in Coward and Oldham's "Vert. Fauna of Cheshire," and in Nelson and Clarke's "Birds of Yorkshire," the latter stating that it was known to old bird-catchers about Beverley under that name. The derivation seems to be unknown, but a clue to its usage is given by Pennant, who says that· "It is frequently to be met with in the bird-shops in London, and is known there by the name of *Aberdavine*." Swainson thinks it an equivalent to Alderfinch and synonymous with the German *Erlenzeisig*.

B

2   DICTIONARY OF NAMES OF BRITISH BIRDS.

ABHARARCAN-LUACHRACH or ADHARCAN LUACHRACH. A Gaelic name for the LAPWING; lit. "the horned creature of the rushes."

ACADIAN OWL. A North American species, supposed to have occurred once at Beverley, Yorkshire.

ADEN GWYR: The WAXWING. (North Wales) lit. "wax-wing."

ADERYN ADEIN GOCH: The REDWING. (North Wales) lit. "red-winged bird."

ADERYN BRONFRAITH. A Welsh name for the SONG-THRUSH; lit. "thrush-bird."

ADERYN CYWARCH· The LINNET. (North Wales) lit. "hemp-bird."

ADERYN DU. A Welsh name for the BLACKBIRD; lit "black bird." The female is called Mwyalchen (=hen).

ADERYN DU'R DWR: The DIPPER. (North Wales) lit. "water blackbird."

ADERYN EIRA· The SNOW-BUNTING. (North Wales) lit. "snow bird."

ADERYN Y BWN. A Welsh name for the BITTERN; lit. "boom bird."

ADERYN-Y-CYRPH or ADERYN CORPH. A Welsh name for the TAWNY OWL and the BARN-OWL; lit. "corpse bird."

ADERYN-Y-CYRS. The REED-WARBLER. (North Wales) lit. "reed bird."

ADERYN-Y-DROELL A Welsh name for the NIGHTJAR; lit. "spinning-wheel bird."

ADERYN-YR-EIRA· The FIELDFARE. (North Wales) lit. "snow bird."

ADERYN-Y-TO. A Welsh name for the HOUSE-SPARROW; lit. "thatch bird."

Aery or Aerie. An eagle's nest or a brood of eagles or hawks Occurs as airie, aiery, ayrie, eyery, aeiry, etc., in various authors. Also as eyrie or eyrey, an incorrect form. The derivation of this word is somewhat uncertain. Murray seems to favour Fr. *aire*, fr. Lat. *area*, a floor or space of level ground, which is the view held by Littré; but Skeat thinks the original source is the Icelandic *ari*, an eagle, and hazards that the Fr. *aire* and Low Lat. (not the class. Lat. word) *area* come from a similar source (although he modifies this in his second edition). The Low Lat. *area* is used by Ducange to denote the nest of a bird of prey, and Cotgrave gives *aire* as "an airie or nest of hawkes." Dyche and Pardon have "eyrie or ayrie, among falconers the place or nest where hawks sit and hatch and feed their young" The spelling eyrie or eyrey, used by many authors, seems to be incorrect. Murray says it was first used by Spelman (1664) who was under the misapprehension that the derivation was Saxon, from egg; Willughby and Ray also spell it *eyrie*, Halliwell and Wright think eyrey is the right form, derived from *ey*, Mid-Eng. for egg. The word occurs in most of our early authors: Shakespeare has *ayerie* but the word is printed aery and aiery by most editors, Milton has *eyrie*, Ben Jonson uses *aiery*, but applies it to a brood of kestrels; Browne ("Britan. Past") spells it *eyerie*, and Massinger ("Maid of Honour," I, 2.) has —

> One *airy*, with proportion ne'er discloses
> The eagle and the wren

African Crowned Crane An example obtained in Ayrshire in 1871 is thought to have escaped from captivity.

AFRICAN HERON. The PURPLE HERON is so-called by Latham, Lewin, Montagu, etc. It is a migratory species occurring in Africa, hence the name

AILSA COCK or AILSA PARROT. Local Scots names for the PUFFIN; also used in Antrim (Swainson).

ALAMONTI The STORM-PETREL. (Orkneys.) The Orcadian name "Alamonti" is given by Low, but Macgillivray spells it Alamouti, and this form was sent me by Mr. R. Godfrey as a Shetland name, it is also rendered Allamotti, Jamison thinks it is of Italian extraction from *ala*, a wing and *monte*, to mount.

ALARCH DOF. A Welsh name for the MUTE SWAN; lit. "tame swan"

ALARCH GWYLLT. A Welsh name for the WHOOPER SWAN; lit "wild swan."

ALDROVANDINE OWLET. Macgillivray's name for the SCOPS OWL.

ALEXANDRINE PLOVER The RINGED PLOVER.

ALGERIAN RED-NECKED NIGHTJAR [No. 204]. A bird obtained near Newcastle in 1856 and recorded in most subsequent authors as the "Red-necked Nightjar," is considered by Hartert to belong to the "desert" form inhabiting Algeria and Tunisia, and not to the western or Spanish form; hence the change of name.

ALK : The RAZORBILL; literally signifying auk, being no doubt from Icelandic *alka*, auk (q.v.).

ALLAN. A Scots name for a Skua; generally the ARCTIC SKUA, which in East Scotland is called Dirty Allan or Aulin; in Orkney, Scouty Allan or Aulin, and Weese Allan; Macgillivray spells it "Allen."

ALLECAMPAGNE. The BLUE TITMOUSE is so-called in Cornwall (Swainson).

Allen's Gallinule. A single example, captured off Yarmouth, is thought to have escaped from captivity.

ALP: The BULLFINCH. (Obsolete.) Synonymic with Alph, Awbe, Olp, Olph, Olf and Ulf, but the derivation is unknown. Occurs in Chaucer ("Romaunt of the Rose") and Willughby. Possibly from *Alb* (Mid. Eng. *albe*) a derivate of Lat. *albus* (white), the rump being very conspicuously pure white. Gael. "*Alp*" signifies a high mountain, and does not seem to have any connexion with the present word, although, according to Skeat, connected with Lat. *albus*. Olph appears to be still in local use for the Bullfinch ("Blood-Olph") and Greenfinch ("Green-Olph"). Swainson seems to be in error in supposing Hoop or Hope to be derived from Alp, as Hoop seems to be clearly from the bird's note. Nope and Mwope, however, may be from Alp.

ALPINE ACCENTOR [No. 186]. So-called from its inhabiting the Alps and other mountain ranges of South Europe. The name first appears in Fleming's "Hist. of Brit. Animals" (1828), probably as a translation of Temminck's "Accenteur des Alpes" (1820). Its former generic name of *Accentor*, Lat. *accentum*, Fr. *ad*, to, and *cantus*, singing, was bestowed on account of its song. Also sometimes rendered Alpine Chanter and Alpine Warbler.

Alpine Chough. An accidental visitor of doubtful status on the British List. The name occurs in Latham as "Alpine Crow."

ALPINE RING-OUZEL [No. 163]. An Alpine form of the RING-OUZEL.

ALPINE SWIFT [No. 199]. A native, as its name implies, of the Alps, and other parts of South Europe. The name is found in Selby (1825). It is the White-bellied Swift of Gould.

ALPINE VULTURE : The EGYPTIAN VULTURE. (Bewick.)

AMADAN MOINTICH or AN TAMADAN MOINTICH. A Gaelic name for the DOTTEREL; lit. "the fool of the moor" or peat-bog.

AMERICAN BELTED KINGFISHER: The *Belted Kingfisher*. The prefix "American" to this and other species in the "Hand-List" seems unnecessary, there being no European form to be distinguished.

AMERICAN BITTERN [No 269]. An irregular visitor from America, as the name implies The name first appears in Selby, but the species was first distinguished under the name of Freckled Heron, in 1813, by Montagu ("Orn Dict.," Supp.)

AMERICAN BLACK-BILLED CUCKOO See BLACK-BILLED CUCKOO.

AMERICAN BLUE-WINGED TEAL [No. 291]. An American species of accidental occurrence

AMERICAN CUCKOO: The YELLOW-BILLED CUCKOO (Gould.)

AMERICAN GOLDENEYE. See *Barrow's Goldeneye*.

AMERICAN GOLDEN PLOVER [No. 363]. A casual visitor from Arctic North America.

American Goshawk. A North American species, said to have been twice obtained in our islands.

AMERICAN GREEN-WINGED TEAL [No 290]. Another accidental visitor from America

AMERICAN HAWK-OWL [No. 221]. An occasional visitor from America The name Hawk-Owl first occurs in Gould's "Birds of Europe" (pt. x). It is the Canada Owl of Jenyns.

AMERICAN HOODED MERGANSER See HOODED MERGANSER.

American Kestrel A North American representative of the KESTREL, said to have occurred in our Islands

AMERICAN PECTORAL SANDPIPER. See PECTORAL SANDPIPER.

American Purple Martin. Included by Yarrell (1843) on the strength of one said to have been shot in Ireland

AMERICAN QUAIL. The *Virginian Colin*. (Montagu)

American Scaup. An American species, also called RING-NECKED DUCK, said to have been obtained here

AMERICAN STINT [No 376] A casual visitor from America.

American Trumpeter Swan An American species, said to have been obtained in our Islands

AMERICAN WATER-PIPIT [No. 71]. This species, first figured by Edwards ("Gleanings," p. 297) as the "Lark from Pennsylvania," is also called AMERICAN PIPIT or AMERICAN TIT-LARK.

American White-winged Crossbill. The name is found in Gould and in Yarrell (1st ed.).

AMERICAN WIGEON [No. 294]. The name seems to occur first in Wilson's "American Ornithology." It is found in Yarrell (1st ed.), the species having been recorded for Britain by Blyth in 1838.

AMERICAN YELLOW-BILLED CUCKOO. See YELLOW-BILLED CUCKOO.

AMMER or EMMER GOOSE: The GREAT NORTHERN DIVER. (Aberdeen and East Lothian.) Ammer appears to be a corruption of Immer (q.v.).

AMZEL or AMSEL. This is another form of Ouzel, and is cognate with German *Amsel*. It appears to be applied to both the BLACKBIRD and RING-OUZEL. Montagu gives Amsel as a provincial name for the BLACKBIRD.

Andalucian Hemipode. A south European species recorded on two or three occasions (probably introduced birds). The name is also written Andalusian. It occurs first as Andalucian Hemipode in Yarrell ("Brit. Birds," Suppl. 1, 1845). Latham calls it Andalusian Quail, and Gould Andalusian Turnix.

ANNET: The KITTIWAKE GULL. (Yorkshire). Found in Graves's "Cleveland," 1808; it is a feminine diminutive; also applied in Northumberland to the COMMON GULL, according to Swainson.

ANT-EUN FIORM. A Gaelic name for the HEN-HARRIER.

APPLE-BIRD: The CHAFFINCH. (Cornwall.) No doubt akin to "Shell-apple."

APPLE-SHEALER or APPLE-SHEILER. Northumbrian names for the CHAFFINCH. Bolam, who spells it "shealer," thinks it is from the bird's habits among the buds of fruit trees; but see "Shell-Apple."

AQUATIC WARBLER [No. 140]. A casual visitor, in habits resembling the SEDGE-WARBLER, whence its name.

ARBOUR-BIRD: The CHIFFCHAFF (?). Perhaps from the shape of its nest.

ARCTIC BIRD or ARCTIC GULL: The ARCTIC SKUA.

ARCTIC JAGER: The LONG-TAILED SKUA. (Eyton.)

ARCTIC PUFFIN: The PUFFIN.

ARCTIC SKUA [No. 441]. Commonly known as Richardson's Skua—a rather more appropriate name, as the name Arctic Skua is sometimes applied to the LONG-TAILED SKUA; both are Arctic species. Skua is from the note which sounds like *skui*. The name Arctic Skua seems to occur first in Fleming (1828), it is the Arctic Gull and Black-toed Gull of Pennant, while the name Richardson's Skua is first found in Jenyns (1835), and was adopted by Yarrell in his first edition.

Arctic Tern [No. 420] A more northern species in our Islands than the COMMON TERN It was first distinguished by Brunnich in 1764, but was not noticed by our British ornithologists until well into the 19th century It is mentioned by Fleming (2nd ed 1840), but he considered it only a variety of the Common Tern, and the bird seems to be first admitted under the name of Arctic Tern by Yarrell in 1843. For derivation of Tern, see COMMON TERN.

Arling or Arlyng The WHEATEAR. Occurs in Turner (1544), in Gesner and in Merrett.

Arnt, Arent Given by Aldrovandus as English names for an Eagle, no doubt equivalent to "Erne."

Arran ake The RED-THROATED DIVER The "ake" is equivalent to auk. Swainson says it is so-called "about Luss in Dumbarton"

Arsfoot The GREAT CRESTED GREBE. (Merrett, Willughby.) The LITTLE GREBE is the Small Arsfoot of Willughby. Cognate with Dutch *arsvoote*, from the backward position of the legs.

Asau, Ausa. Gaelic names for the GANNET, the former is used in the western isles, and the latter on the mainland (Graham).

Asgell-arian. A Welsh name for the CHAFFINCH; lit. "silver wing."

Asgell-hir The SWIFT (North Wales) lit. "long wing."

Ash-coloured Buzzard, or Falcon, or Harrier See MONTAGU'S HARRIER. It is the Ash-coloured Falcon of Montagu, formerly supposed to be the discoverer of the species.

Ash-coloured Heron, or Hern, or Hernshaw The COMMON HERON. (Merrett) Hett applies the first name to the NIGHT-HERON, but Merrett's bird is obviously the COMMON HERON.

Ash-coloured Loon. The GREAT-CRESTED GREBE. (Willughby.)

Ash-coloured Sandpiper The KNOT in winter-plumage was separated under this name by Pennant and other writers up to Montagu (1804), who however remarked that he doubted its distinctness from the KNOT. Swainson gives it as an Irish provincial name.

ASH-COLOURED SHRIKE: The GREAT GREY SHRIKE. Bewick (1st ed.) calls it the Great Ash-coloured Shrike.

ASH-COLOURED SWAN: The GREAT CRESTED GREBE. (Swainson.)

ASHY-HEADED WAGTAIL [No. 77] A South European form recorded on two occasions.

ASIATIC GOLDEN PLOVER [No. 364]. A subspecies of the AMERICAN GOLDEN PLOVER, breeding in eastern Arctic Asia, hence its name

ASIATIC HOUBARA. See MACQUEEN'S BUSTARD.

ASSILAG: The STORM-PETREL. (St. Kilda—Martin; also Hebrides—Swainson). Derived from Gael. *easchal*, a storm.

Associations of Birds (*terms denoting*). Curlews: a "flock"— Wild Geese · a "string" or a "skein"—Grouse. a "pack" —Partridges. a "covey," also a "brace" (two)—Quail: a "bevy"—Rooks: a "congregation"—Snipe. a "whisp" —Starlings: a "gathering" or "murmuration" (many together)—Teal: a "flock"—Wigeon · a "company" (many together), a "bunch" or "trip" (30 or 40)—or a "little knot" (10 or 12).

ASTRACANNET: The VELVET SCOTER and also the GREAT NORTHERN DIVER (Northumberland).

ATHENIAN OWL · A name for the EAGLE-OWL (Macgillivray.)

ATTAGEN. The Attagen of the Ancients has been identified by old authors with various species, i.e. the WOODCOCK, female BLACK GROUSE, Godwit, etc. Turner favours the Heather-Hen or the Godwit, while Merrett gives the name to the latter. Willughby says the Attagen of Gesner is the Hazel-Grouse. The Attagen of Brisson, however, seems to be the RED GROUSE.

ATTEAL, ATTEILE, or ATTILE. An ancient Scottish name, occurring also in the Orkney dialect, for a kind of Duck, supposed by Baikie and Heddle to be the COMMON POCHARD, but Professor Newton was inclined to think it to be the TEAL.

AUER-CALZE. The CAPERCAILLIE was so called north of Inverness according to Pennant; and it appears under this name in Hector Boethius (1526).

AUK · The GREAT AUK; also the RAZORBILL (Yorkshire coast). Occurs also as "Alk." From Icel *alka*, an auk; thence also Lat. *alca*. The word seems to have no certain connection with *awkward*, or *aukward*, signifying unhandy or contraryward, the prefix *auk* or *awk* being from the Icel. *afig* or *ofg*. The name Auk appears formerly to have more properly belonged to the RAZORBILL, Willughby gives it as the North of England name for that species, and Sibbald mentions the RAZORBILL by the name of Auk (see GREAT AUK), as also does Pennant (1766). Swainson gives Auk as an Orkney name for the COMMON GUILLEMOT

Australian Gallinule. Examples of this species recorded as British are regarded as escaped birds

AUSTRIAN PRATINCOLE The PRATINCOLE (Montagu.)

AVOCET [No. 401] Also spelt Avoset Der. from the Ferrarese *Avosetta* or *Avocetta*, probably literally a graceful bird (dim. of Lat. *avis*) The name occurs in Willughby (1678) as the "Avosetta of the Italians" It is called Scooper (q v) by Charleton (1668), Avosetta by Pennant (1766), while Montagu and others call it Scooping Avoset; Yarrell also calls it Avoset

AWL-BIRD The AVOCET. So called from the shape of the bill, resembling an awl. From A Sax. *awel*, Mid-Eng *aul*, *eawl*, an awl or pointed instrument for piercing Also applied to the GREEN WOODPECKER, Montagu gives it as a provincial name for that species.

BAAGIE or BAIGIE A Shetland name for the GREAT BLACK-BACKED GULL

BABBLER The GREAT REED-WARBLER. From its noisy song.

BABBLING WARBLER A provincial name for the LESSER WHITETHROAT (Macgillivray)

BABILLARD The LESSER WHITETHROAT (Montagu, "Orn. Dict.," ed. Rennie, 1831) Rennie adapted the name from the French, as pointed out by Newton and it does not seem to have been in use colloquially, although given by Macgillivray as a provincial name.

BADOCK The ARCTIC SKUA; also GREAT SKUA (Swainson).

BAD WILLY The COMMON GUILLEMOT.

Baer's Duck An East Siberian species, named by Radde in honour of K E. von Baer.

BAG The LONG-TAILED TITMOUSE. (Northants) In allusion to the shape of its nest.

BAILLON'S CRAKE [No. 458]. The name seems to occur first in Selby. This is the *P bailloni* of Vieillot, hence the name.

BAIRD'S SANDPIPER [No. 380]. A North American species named by Coues in honour of Spencer F. Baird, the well-known American ornithologist.

BAKIE. A Shetland name for the BLACK-HEADED GULL.

BALBUSHARD: The MARSH-HARRIER. Occurs in Turner (1544) and is an equivalent of Bald Buzzard. In Aldrovandus and Gesner it is applied to the Osprey.

BALD BUZZARD. Properly the MARSH-HARRIER (from its whitish cap) but also applied to the OSPREY. Willughby (1678) appears to have confused the MARSH-HARRIER and OSPREY together in his account (p. 69) of this bird, and he confuses the Sea-Eagle and OSPREY also. Other authors of his day in like manner confused the OSPREY with the WHITE-TAILED or Sea-EAGLE. Merrett mentions the "Bald Buzzard or *Kite*." Montagu gives the name to the OSPREY, while Swainson gives it as an Essex name for the MARSH-HARRIER.

BALD COOT. The COOT (Albin and Macgillivray). Montagu gives it as a provincial name, and it occurs in Rutty's "Nat. Hist. of Dublin." Swainson gives Bald Duck or Bald Coot as a Somerset name, and Nelson and Clarke give Bald Coot and Baldheaded Coot as Yorkshire names. In Scotland it becomes Bell (q.v.)

BALD GOOSE: The WHITE-FRONTED GOOSE. (Scotland.)

BALD KITE: The COMMON BUZZARD. (Provincial.)

BALD PATE: The WIGEON. (Provincial.)

BANKJUG, BANTYJUG, or BANK-BOTTLE. Local names for the CHIFFCHAFF and the WILLOW-WARBLER, on account of the shape of the nest.

BANK LARK: The TREE-PIPIT and MEADOW-PIPIT. (Yorkshire—Cleveland.)

BANK MARTIN, BANK MARTNET, or BANK SWALLOW. The SAND-MARTIN. The name Bank Martnet occurs in Turner (1544) and in Merrett, while Bank Martin or Swallow is still in use provincially. It arises from the bird's habit of excavating its nest in sandstone banks or cuttings.

BANK SPARROW. The WHINCHAT. (Provincial.)

BANK WREN. The WILLOW-WARBLER. (Yorkshire—South Holderness).

BARRALOT. Willughby records this as a Jersey and Guernsey name for the PUFFIN.

Barbary Partridge A North-west African species, of which examples (probably introduced birds) have been taken in Britain. It was added to the British List by Yarrell ("Brit. Birds," Supp , 1845). The name is found in Latham.

BARCUD or BARCUTAN. A Welsh name for the KITE; lit. " swift hawk." In North Wales it is generally applied to the COMMON BUZZARD, according to Coward and Oldham

BARCUD GLÀS A Welsh name for the HEN-HARRIER , lit. " blue kite."

BARDRAKE· The SHELD-DUCK, also the RED-BREASTED MERGANSER. See Bargander. Swainson gives it as an Irish name for the former species

BAREFACED CROW The ROOK. So called from the bare whitish skin surrounding the base of the bill

BARETOED DAY-OWL Macgillivray's name for the LITTLE OWL.

BARFOG (Y). A Welsh name for the BEARDED TITMOUSE.

BARGANDER, BARGANSER, BERGANDER, or BAR-GOOSE The SHELD-DUCK. Etymology uncertain, but most probably from the conspicuous chestnut " bar " or band on the breast. Occurs in Turner, Willughby and Merrett as " Bergander." Evans thinks it should be spelt " Burgander i e Burrow Duck," while Turner suggested " Berg-ander " from its nesting in "holes of lofty rocks " (see SHELD-DUCK). According to Wallis, Bergander is a Northumbrian name, and Bolam says it is pronounced Banganner about Boulmer Swainson also gives Bar-goose as an Essex name for the BARNACLE-GOOSE

BARGEZ A Cornish name for the KITE.

BARK-CREEPER The TREECREEPER. (Provincial)

BARKER The AVOCET Also applied to the BLACK-TAILED GODWIT, while Newton points out that Albin has figured the GREENSHANK under this name, and Montagu, taking the plate to be that of the SPOTTED REDSHANK, has applied the name " Barker " to that bird also. Albin says the decoy-men so called it because it " makes a noise like the barking of a dog."

BARLEY-BIRD. Variously applied locally to the GREY WAGTAIL (Yorks), the YELLOW WAGTAIL (Notts), the NIGHTINGALE (East Anglia), and the WRYNECK (Hants), and also to the COMMON GULL, on account of their appearing at the time of barley-sowing. It has also been applied by Willughby to the SISKIN. The name "Barley-seed Bird" for the YELLOW WAGTAIL is found in Carr's "Craven Dialect," 1828.

BARLEY SNAKE-BIRD: The WRYNECK. (Hants.)

BARNACLE, or BARNACLE GOOSE. The BRENT GOOSE is sometimes so called, especially in Ireland.

BARNACLE-GOOSE [No. 282]. The name Barnacle or Bernacle has been considered to have its origin in the ancient belief that this goose was generated from the shell-fish of that name (*Lepas anatifera*) which are found adhering in clusters to floating timber, etc., the prevalent belief for some centuries being that these shell-fish were the embryo geese which grew upon trees, termed "goose-trees," and as Gerard in his "Herbal" (1597) states, "as it groweth greater, it openeth the shell by degrees till at length it is all come forth and hangeth only by the bill: in short space after, it cometh to full maturitie and falleth into the sea, where it gathereth feathers," etc. Turner, who calls it "Bernicle" ("Avium Præcip. Hist.," 1544), writing from the evidence of a "certain man of upright conduct," confirms the same tale put forth originally by Giraldus Cambrensis (*ca.* 1175) and remarks that no one has seen the Bernicle's nest or egg as evidence of this spontaneous generation. For an interesting account of the fable see Harting's "Birds of Shakespeare," pp. 246-57, 1871. Dr. Murray points out that the oldest known English form of the word is the *Bernekka* (Latinised *Bernaca*) of Giraldus Cambrensis in the reference cited above, and he remarks that the Cirriped took its name from the bird and not the bird from the Cirriped, which of course leaves the derivation of the bird's name still a moot point. Willughby and Ray call it the "Bernacle or Clakis: Bernicla seu Bernacla." It is figured by Lobel, Gerard and many other old authors. Seemingly an allusion to the above fable is to be found in the diary of Peter Suavenius during his mission in these islands (printed in Appdx. to 45th Rept. of Deputy Keeper of Public Records) where it is recorded that "there are trees in Scotland from which birds are produced . . . those birds which fall from the trees into the water become animated, but those which fall to the ground do not: the figures of birds are sometimes found in the heart of the wood of the trees and on the roots: the birds themselves do not generate."

BARN-OWL [No. 227, White-breasted Barn-Owl; No. 228, Dark-breasted Barn-Owl]. This species has been separated into the two forms noted, the White-breasted being the resident species and the Dark-breasted a casual migrant. The name Barn-Owl arises from its predilection for barns and other old buildings it occurs first in Willughby. It is the White Owl of Pennant and other authors, and the "Yellow Owl," "Church Owl," etc., of yet others Yarrell (1st ed) calls it the "White or Barn Owl," and the latter name has generally been adopted by later writers "White Owl" is derived from the white hue of the under-parts · "Yellow Owl" from the tawny yellow upper-parts "Church Owl" from its partiality for churches This and other species of owls were formerly very generally regarded as birds of ill-omen Chaucer, referring obviously to this species, says —

> The owle al nyght aboute the balkes wonde,
> That propheto ys of woo and of myschaunce

An ancient belief that this bird shrieking at a birth portended ill-luck to the infant is alluded to in Shakespeare (Henry VI, pt. III, act v, sc. 6).

> The Owl shrieked at thy birth, an evil sign.

BARN SWALLOW. A common provincial name for the SWALLOW, so called from its nesting on the rafters, etc., of barns and other out-buildings.

BARRED WARBLER [No. 143]. So called from its grey-and-white barred plumage.

BARRED WILLOW WARBLER The YELLOW-BROWED WARBLER.

BARRED WOODPECKER· The LESSER SPOTTED WOOD-PECKER. (Bewick) So called from the black and white of its wings and upper-parts presenting a barred appearance.

BARREL TIT. The LONG-TAILED TITMOUSE. (Provincial)

Barrow's Goldeneye. An American species of which one example is erroneously thought to have occurred in Suffolk.

BAR-TAILED GODWIT [No. 402] The name is found in Fleming (1828) and arises from the dusky bars on the white upper tail-coverts. It occurs in Turner (1544) as "Godwitt or Fedoa," and in Willughby as "Godwit, Yarwhelp, or Yarwip." Pennant calls it Godwit and Montagu the Common Godwit. Godwit is from A.-Sax. *god-wihta* (lit good-eating)

BARTRAM'S SANDPIPER [No. 369]. A rare American visitor, the name being found in Wilson. Also known as Bartram's Tatler.

BASS COCK: The PUFFIN. (Scotland.) From its frequenting the Bass Rock.

BASS GOOSE: The GANNET. (Scotland.) From its being found on the Bass Rock. Swainson also gives Basser as a Forfarshire name.

BASTARD PLOVER· The LAPWING. Occurs in Merrett and Willughby, and Nelson and Clarke cite it as an ancient Hull name for the bird (1560).

BATTY BIRD: The LITTLE EGRET.

BAWKIE, BAUKIE, or BAWKEE. The RAZORBILL. (Orkneys.) An equivalent of Auk.

BAY DUCK: The SHELD-DUCK. (Norfolk.) From the chestnut band on the breast.

BAY IBIS: The GLOSSY IBIS.

BEAM-BIRD. The SPOTTED FLYCATCHER. (South and east England). Perhaps an equivalent of "Rafter-bird" (q.v.).

BEAN-CRAKE: The LAND-RAIL. Montagu gives it as a provincial name; Swainson says Bean-Crake or Bean Cracker is a South Pembroke name for the species.

BEAN-GOOSE [No. 277]. The name is first found in Pennant. It is also called "Corn Goose," a name arising from the bird's partiality to grain and pulse (Swainson). It is the "Wild Goose" of some parts of Scotland and Ireland, and is so called in Fleming and some other authors. According to Yarrell the noise in the air attributed to the Gabriel or Wish Hounds, is really caused by this species (see "Gabble Ratchet").

BEARDED BUSTARD. The GREAT BUSTARD. From the moustache-like tuft on each side of the head.

BEARDED PINNOCK or BEARDED REEDLING: The BEARDED TITMOUSE. (Provincial.)

BEARDED TITMOUSE [No. 105]. The name Bearded Titmouse first appears in Albin. Edwards calls it the Least Butcher-Bird and Pennant in his folio "Brit. Zoology" (1766) follows Edwards and places it with the Shrikes under the name of the "Lest Butcher Bird," but in his later editions he calls it Bearded Titmouse. The name is derived from the tuft of black feathers resembling a moustache running backward from the gape. It is frequently abbreviated to Bearded Tit.

BEARDIE · The WHITETHROAT. (Provincial.) Probably from its habit of puffing out the throat-feathers.

BEARDMANICA   The BEARDED TITMOUSE (Albin.)

BECK   A local Norfolk name for the SHOVELER.

BEE-BIRD   The SPOTTED FLYCATCHER. (Norfolk and Yorkshire.) Also applied to the BLUE TITMOUSE (Hants) and the WHITETHROAT (Devon), the name being derived from their supposed fondness for bees.

BEE-BITER   The GREAT TITMOUSE. (Provincial)

BEECH-FINCH · The CHAFFINCH. So called from its partiality to beech-mast

BEECH-OWL: The TAWNY OWL. (Provincial) From its supposed partiality for these trees.

BEE-EATER [No. 205]. The name Bee-eater (implying its fondness for bees) was first used, according to Prof Newton, in 1668 by Charleton ("Onomasticon," p. 87) as a translation of the Greek *Merops*. It also occurs in Willughby and most subsequent writers, although Macgillivray attempted to substitute "Yellow throated Bee-eater" The bird was long known as a common European species, but according to Montagu its first recorded occurrence in England was one shot from a flock in July, 1794, near Mattishall in Norfolk. and exhibited before the Linnean Society.

BEE-EATER   A local Northumberland name for the GREAT TITMOUSE, which is found sometimes to have a propensity for devouring bees.

BELLCOOT, BELLKITE, or BELLPOOT   The COOT. Corruptions of "Bald Coot" or "Bald Pout." It occurs in Rutty as "Belcoot or Baldcoot," and is found in Scotland as Bellkite (=Baldcoot) and Bellpout (=Bald fowl).

BELLONIUS'S ASH-COLOURED GULL. The KITTIWAKE GULL. (Willughby)

BELLRINGER: The LONG-TAILED TITMOUSE. (Kirkcudbright.)

BELL-THROSTLE: The MISTLE-THRUSH.

BELL WIGEON: The SCAUP-DUCK. (Teesmouth).

Belted Kingfisher. A North American species of doubtful occurrence in the British Isles. The name occurs in Wilson's "Amer Ornith."

BELTIE   The COOT. Probably a corruption of Baldie (see Bellcoot)

BENFELEN (Y): The YELLOW BUNTING. (North Wales); lit. "the yellow head."

Benloyn-fwyaf (Y). A Welsh name for the GREAT TIT-MOUSE; the Benloyn (=blackhead) becomes Penloyn in North Wales.

Benloyn-gynffonhir (Y). A Welsh name for the LONG-TAILED TITMOUSE; lit. "long-tailed blackhead."

Benloyn-lygliw (Y). A Welsh name for the COAL-TIT-MOUSE.

Bent Linnet. The LINNET. (Spurn, Yorks.)

Bergander or Berganser: The SHELD-DUCK. The name Bergander occurs in Willughby (See Bargander)

Bernacle Goose or Bernicle Goose: The BARNACLE-GOOSE (q.v.). Alternative spellings. Pennant says the BRENT GOOSE is also called Bernacle in Ireland.

Berry breaker. A Hampshire name for the HAWFINCH.

Berthuan. A Cornish name for the Screech Owl (BARN-OWL?).

Bessy Blackcap: The REED-BUNTING. (Provincial).

Bessy or Bessie Blakeling · The YELLOW BUNTING. (Westmorland, Yorkshire.)

Bessy Brantail or Katie Brantail: The REDSTART. (Shropshire.)

Bessy Bunting: The YELLOW BUNTING. (Provincial.)

Bessy Doucker or Bessy Ducker: The DIPPER. (Westmorland and other northern counties) From its habit of ducking on entering the water. Also the PIED WAG-TAIL (Huddersfield).

Betty Tit: The BLUE TITMOUSE. (Provincial.)

BEWICK'S SWAN [No. 272]. The characteristics of this species were first pointed out by Yarrell ("Trans. Linn. Soc.," xvi, 2, p. 453, 1830), and it occurs under this name in all subsequently published works.

Bidnewin, Biduen. Cornish names for a hawk.

Big Black-and-White Duck: The VELVET SCOTER. (Yorkshire)

Big Bunting: The CORN-BUNTING (Yorkshire.)

Big Felt. The FIELDFARE. (Ireland.)

Big Hawk. The PEREGRINE FALCON. (Provincial.)

Bighead: The GREENFINCH (Beverley, Yorks); also COMMON POCHARD (Hull).

Big Mavis: The MISTLE-THRUSH. (East Lothian.)

Big Ox-eye: The GREAT TITMOUSE. (East Scotland.)

BIG PEGGY, or BIG PEGGY WHITETHROAT: The WHITE-THROAT. (Nidderdale.)

BIG THROSTLE · The MISTLE-THRUSH (Provincial.) Occurs in Willughby, also still a north country provincial name.

BIG TIT The GREAT TITMOUSE. (Notts.)

BILCOCK The OYSTERCATCHER. (Criccieth, North Wales) lit. "red bill"

BILCOCK The WATER-RAIL. (Yorkshire) Apparently so called from its colour, *bil* being possibly akin to the north country blae (Icel. *blár*, Dan *blaa*) signifying livid or dark blue. Swainson also gives Bilcock or Bilter as a north country name for the MOORHEN.

BILL The PUFFIN. (Galway) From its bill being a prominent feature

BILLY, or BILLY HEDGE-SPARROW. The HEDGE-SPARROW. (Doncaster.)

BILLY-BITER: The BLUE TITMOUSE (Provincial.) Probably from its habit of pecking at the fingers of intruders when sitting on its eggs, but Newton thinks it is a corruption of "Willow-biter." Nelson and Clarke also give it as a Yorkshire name for the GREAT TITMOUSE.

BILLY OWL The BARN-OWL Swainson also gives BILLY HOOTER as a Shropshire name for the TAWNY OWL, but this is perhaps a corruption of Gilly Hooter.

BILLY WHITETHROAT The GARDEN-WARBLER. (East Lothian)

BILLY WIX · The BARN-OWL. (Norfolk.)

Bimaculated Duck: A bird described by Pennant ("Brit. Zool.," II, No 287) as a separate species, but by later authors considered to be a hybrid bird. Pennant stated that his example was taken in a decoy in 1771, while Vigors claimed to have had a pair sent up from a decoy near Maldon, Essex, in the winter of 1812-13. It retained for nearly a century its place in the British List.

BINC (Y): The CHAFFINCH. (North Wales.) From its note

BIRCH-HEN. The female of the BLACK GROUSE.

BIRRL-BIRD: The GRASSHOPPER-WARBLER. (Provincial.) From its curious song

BISTARD The GREAT BUSTARD. (Gesner)

BITING TOM or BITTER TOM. A local name for the BLUE TITMOUSE among boys, from its habit when sitting on its eggs of pecking at their fingers.

BITTER BANK or BITTERIE. Scottish Border names for the SAND-MARTIN, supposed to have arisen from its habit of *biting* the bank as it makes its nesting-tunnel (Bolam).

BITTER, BYTTER, or BITTER BUM: The BITTERN. (Provincial.) Drayton ("Polyolbion") has the "buzzing bitter." Nelson and Clarke cite "Bytter or Bitter" as occurring in "Neville's Marriage Feast," 1526.

BITTERN [No. 268]. This fine species formerly bred commonly in many parts of the British Islands. The name Bittern is from Old English bitoure, bittour, bittourn, bytoure, botor, or buttour, cognate with Fr. *butor*, Low Lat. *butorius*. Dr. Murray says the word is of doubtful origin, but it seems probable that it is from the mediæval name for bitterns, *Botaurus*, which again was no doubt originally derived from the *taurus* of Pliny (bk. x., c. 42), a bird that imitated the lowing of an ox, and was no doubt the Bittern. The name occurs as "Buttour or bittour" in Turner (1544), as "Bittur" in Spenser ("Faerie Queene"), as "Bitter" in Drayton ("Polyolbion") and as "Bittour or Bittern or Mire-drum" in Willughby (1678), who says, "it is called by later writers Butorius and Botaurus because it seems to imitate *boatum tauri*, the bellowing of a bull." He also writes, "They say that it gives always an odd number of bombs at a time, viz. three or five, which in my own observation I have found to be false. It begins to bellow about the beginning of February, and ceases when breeding-time is over. The common people are of opinion that it thrusts its bill into a reed, by the help whereof it makes that lowing or drumming noise. Others say that it thrusts its bill into the water or mud or earth." In Thomson's "Spring" we find this idea expressed:—

> The Bittern knows his time with bill ingulpht
> To shake the surrounding marsh

Burns also expresses the same belief:—

> Ye Bitterns, till the quagmire reels
> Rair for his sake!

Subsequent writers, after Willughby, call it the Bittern. When more common, its flesh was accounted a delicacy, and even in Montagu's day (1802) we are told the poulterers valued it at not less than half-a-guinea.

BITTERN HERON: The BITTERN. (Pennant.)

BITTOUR, BITTOURN, or BITTUR: The BITTERN (formerly). The first name occurs in Turner, the second in Merrett, and the third in Spenser. Montagu gives Bittour as a provincial name for the species. Bittor and Bittoun are also cited as former variants by Nelson and Clarke.

BLACK-AND-BLUE TITMOUSE. The BLUE TITMOUSE. (Rutty.)

BLACK-AND-WHITE AVOCET. Macgillivray's name for the AVOCET

BLACK-AND-WHITE DABCHICK The SLAVONIAN GREBE. Occurs in Edwards as "Black and White Dobchick."

BLACK-AND-WHITE DIVER: The SMEW.

BLACK-AND-WHITE FLIGHTER The AVOCET.

BLACK-AND-WHITE GULL The GREAT BLACK-BACKED GULL. (Yorkshire.)

BLACK-AND-WHITE WAGTAIL The PIED WAGTAIL. (Yorkshire.)

BLACK-AND-WHITE WOODPECKER The GREAT SPOTTED WOODPECKER. (Norfolk.)

BLACK-BACKED EIDER. Macgillivray's name for the KING EIDER.

BLACK-BACKED FALCON. The PEREGRINE FALCON.

BLACK-BACKED GULL or BLACK-BACK The GREAT BLACK-BACKED GULL; Black-back is a common Yorkshire name.

BLACK-BACKED HANNOCK The GREAT BLACK-BACKED GULL. (Bridlington.)

BLACK-BELLIED DIPPER. See DIPPER.

BLACKBERRY-EATER The STONECHAT. (Merrett.)

BLACK-BILLED AUK. The RAZORBILL (in winter). A name first given by Pennant (1766) to a supposed distinct species of Razorbill, which Latham united with the latter species, considering it to be the young.

BLACK-BILLED CUCKOO [No. 217, The American Black-billed Cuckoo.] An American species which has occurred once in the British Islands

BLACK-BILLED EGRET. Macgillivray's name for a supposed variety of the GREAT WHITE HERON (the East Lothian example, June 9th, 1840).

BLACKBIRD. [No. 164.] From A Sax. *blac, blaec*=black, and A Sax *brid*, a bird It occurs in Dame Berners' "Boke of St. Albans'" (1486) as "black bride"; in Turner (1544) as "blak byrd" and "blak osel"; in Merrett (1667) as "black-bird" and "black ousle", in Willughby (1678) as the "Common Blackbird." Bewick (1st ed.) calls it "Black Ouzel." It is also called in literature the "merle." Strange to say, although one of the commonest of our birds, this species figures very little in English folk-lore. Mr. Thiselton Dyer ("English Folklore") in fact finds nothing to say about it, and Swainson hardly anything. The allusion in both Aristotle and Pliny to this bird changing with the season from black to rufous, is evidently based on a misapprehension as to the sexes, the rufous-brown plumage being that of the female. It is a popular belief that when these birds are unusually shrill, or sing much in the morning, rain will follow. Swainson also gives this as an Irish belief, while in Meath it is said that "when the Blackbird sings before Christmas she will cry before Candlemas."

BLACK-BONNET: The REED-BUNTING. (Scotland.) So called from its conspicuous black head. The name seems also to have been applied to the BLACKCAP.

BLACK-BREASTED PLOVER: The GOLDEN PLOVER. (Ireland.)

BLACK-BREASTED REDSTART: The BLACK REDSTART. (Macgillivray.)

BLACK-BREASTED SANDPIPER. The DUNLIN. (Macgillivray.)

BLACK BRENT GOOSE. See BRENT GOOSE.

BLACK-BROWED ALBATROS [No. 335]. An inhabitant of the Southern Seas, which has once been obtained in Cambridgeshire (in 1897). The name *albatros* (according to the English Cyclopædia) is "a word apparently corrupted by Dampier from the Portuguese *alcatraz*, which was applied by the early navigators of that nation to Cormorants and other sea-birds."

BLACKCAP [No. 146]. More often called the Blackcap Warbler. Occurs in Willughby (1678). The name is also applied to many other species which have the cap or summit of the head black, i.e. the COAL-TITMOUSE, MARSH-TITMOUSE, GREAT TITMOUSE, REED-BUNTING, STONECHAT, BULLFINCH and BLACK-HEADED GULL. The present species is the "Atricapilla seu Ficedula" of Aldrovandus.

BLACK-CAPPED BILLY: The GREAT TITMOUSE. (West Riding, Yorks.)

BLACK-CAPPED LOLLY. A North Country name for the GREAT TITMOUSE.

BLACK-CAPPED TITMOUSE: The MARSH-TITMOUSE. (Bewick.)

BLACK-CAPPED WARBLER: The BLACKCAP. (Macgillivray.)

BLACK-CHINNED GREBE: The LITTLE GREBE. Found in Pennant, Latham, Montagu, etc., as a supposed distinct species from the Hebrides. It is also a Berkshire name for the species.

BLACK COCK or BLACK GAME: The BLACK GROUSE. The name Black Cock occurs in Sibbald (1684).

BLACK CORMORANT. The CORMORANT.

BLACK CROW: The CARRION-CROW (Notts.)

BLACK CURLEW: The GLOSSY IBIS.

BLACK CURRE. A Hampshire name for the TUFTED DUCK.

BLACK DIVER. The COMMON SCOTER (Willughby); also the VELVET SCOTER (Northumberland), and sometimes the CORMORANT.

BLACK DUCK. The TUFTED DUCK, COMMON SCOTER, VELVET SCOTER, and also the SCAUP-DUCK. It is used for the COMMON SCOTER in Northumberland, Yorkshire and Cheshire.

BLACK EAGLE. The GOLDEN EAGLE (immature). A fairly general name, derived from its dark plumage. In the Highlands the Gaelic name, *Iolair dhubh* also signifies Black Eagle. Albin's and Pennant's Black Eagle is the same as the Ring-tailed Eagle, for long known to be the immature GOLDEN EAGLE.

BLACK-EARED WHEATEAR [No. 170, Western Black-eared Wheatear; No. 171, Eastern Black-eared Wheatear] This is the Black-throated Wheatear of former authors, the Black-eared and Black-throated Wheatears being now considered dimorphisms of the same species.

BLACK-FACED BERNICLE-GOOSE. Macgillivray's name for the BRENT GOOSE.

BLACK-FOOTED KITTIWAKE. The KITTIWAKE GULL. (Macgillivray.)

BLACK GAME. The BLACK GROUSE. Occurs in Willughby.

BLACK GOOSE. The BRENT GOOSE. (Essex.) It is also a North Country gunner's name for the same species.

BLACK GREBE. The BLACK-NECKED GREBE.

BLACK GROUSE [No. 463]. Occurs first in Willughby (1678), who calls this species the "Heathcock or Black-game or Grous," the first-mentioned name being that of the female, which occurs first in Merrett's list (1667) as "Hasel Hen"; Sibbald calls it Black Cock. It is variously called Black Cock, Black Game or Black Grous by later writers, with Heath Cock, Heath Hen or Hazel Hen for the female. The spelling "Grous" in fact survived to 1835 (Jenyns), but one or two writers and finally Yarrell (1st ed., 1843) adopted the final "e" now invariably used. The word Grouse is of uncertain origin, it first occurs as "Grows" in an ordinance for the regulation of the Royal Household, dated "apud Eltham, mens. Jan. 22, Hen. VIII" (i.e. 1531), and referring, Newton thinks, to the Black Grouse. He thinks the most likely derivation is from Old Fr. *griesche, greoche,* or *griais,* meaning speckled. Cotgrave (1611) has "Poule griesche · a moore-hen, the henne of the *Grice.*"

BLACK GUILLEMOT [No. 447]. The name Black Guillemot is first found in Pennant (1766). Occurs in Willughby and in Albin as the "Greenland Dove or Sea-Turtle." The name is in reference to its chiefly black plumage; Guillemot being from Fr. *guillemot.*

BLACK GULL. The Skuas are sometimes so called from their dark colour, especially the GREAT SKUA.

BLACK HAWK. The MERLIN is sometimes so-called.

BLACK-HEADED BARNACLE. A name for the BRENT GOOSE; given in Macgillivray.

BLACK-HEADED BOB: The GREAT TITMOUSE. (Devon.)

BLACK-HEADED BULLY: The BULLFINCH. (Yorkshire.)

BLACK-HEADED BUNTING [No. 45]. A southern species of casual occurrence. The name is also applied to the REED-BUNTING (a totally distinct indigenous species) which occurs under the name in the first edition of Yarrell and is frequently so called provincially on account of its black head.

BLACK-HEADED BUSHCHAT · The STONECHAT. (Macgillivray.)

BLACK-HEADED DIVER: The male SCAUP-DUCK, so called from its glossy-black head.

BLACK-HEADED FURZECHAT · The STONECHAT. (Provincial.)

BLACK-HEADED GULL [No. 427]. So called from its "black" (really dark brown) cap. Gull (in Old Eng. *mew*) is from Welsh *gwylan,* Fr. *goeland* Occurs in Turner, who calls it "a white semaw, with a black cop," giving it no English name other than the provincial one of "Sea-Cob." He also, without apparent justification, identifies it with the *Fulica* of classical writers, a name now given to the COOT. Willughby and Ray call it the "Pewit or Black-cap, called in some places the Sea-Crow and Mire-Crow." Black-headed Gull appears to be first found in Pennant.

BLACK-HEADED HAY-JACK · The BLACKCAP. (Norfolk.) See Hay-Jack.

BLACK-HEADED PEGGY. The BLACKCAP. (Provincial.)

BLACK-HEADED SNIPE· The SPOTTED REDSHANK. (Provincial)

BLACK-HEADED THISTLEFINCH. Macgillivray's name for the SISKIN.

BLACK-HEADED TOMTIT or TITMOUSE: The GREAT TITMOUSE, also the MARSH-TITMOUSE (Macgillivray).

BLACK-HEADED WAGTAIL [No 78]. A south-east European form of Yellow Wagtail.

BLACK-HEADED WIGEON: The SCAUP-DUCK. (Provincial.)

BLACK IBIS The GLOSSY IBIS Occurs in Willughby.

BLACKIE: The BLACKBIRD (Northumberland, Yorkshire.)

BLACK KITE [No. 251]. The name is found in Sibbald, and in most modern authors

BLACK LARK [No. 58] A West Siberian species first recorded in 1907 for our islands.

BLACK MARSH-TERN. Macgillivray's name for the BLACK TERN.

BLACK MARTIN, MARTLET, SWALLOW, or SWIFT· The SWIFT. Occurs in Merrett (1667) as "Black Martin or Martlet," and in Willughby (1678) as "Black Martin or Swift." As a provincial name it is still in use locally. According to Bolam the MARTIN is also so called "at Wooler, and perhaps in other places, though [the name is] apparently dying out."

BLACK NEB or BLACK-NEBBED Crow· The CARRION-CROW (North Country) The latter form occurs in Bewick (1797); so called from its black bill Nelson and Clarke give "Black Neb" for the HOODED CROW and "Black-nebbed Crow" for the CARRION-CROW in Yorkshire.

BLACK-NECKED GREBE [No 339] This is the Eared Grebe of Pennant and succeeding writers.

BLACK NODDY. The *Noddy Tern.* (Jenyns.)

BLACK OUZEL The BLACKBIRD. (Craven and Cleveland, Yorkshire.) Occurs in Turner as "Blak Osel"

BLACK OX-EYE The COAL-TITMOUSE (Forfar.)

BLACK PHEASANT. An ironical Cleveland name for the CARRION-CROW. (Nelson and Clarke.)

BLACK PLOVER· The LAPWING. (Provincial.)

BLACK POKER or BLACK-HEADED POKER. The TUFTED DUCK. The former is a Norfolk name, "poker" being a common term for species of wild duck in East Anglia. Nelson and Clarke give "Black Pocker" (Poker?) for this species at Beverley, Yorks., and Black Poker Duck for the SCAUP DUCK on the Humber.

BLACK REDSTART [No. 179]. The name is found in Gould's "Birds of Europe," VIII (1834). This species has more black and slate in its plumage than the commoner species, hence its first name. For derivation of the word Redstart, see under REDSTART.

BLACK REDTAIL The BLACK REDSTART. (Jenyns.)

BLACK SANDPIPER· The immature KNOT (provincial); also the immature PURPLE SANDPIPER (Pennant).

BLACK SCAUP· The SCAUP-DUCK. (Humber.)

BLACK SCOTER: The COMMON SCOTER is so called by Selby, Fleming, Jenyns and others.

BLACK SHEARWATER· The SOOTY SHEARWATER. (Flamborough.)

BLACKSMITH. The YELLOW BUNTING. (Salop.)

BLAKSTART: The BLACK REDSTART. An erroneous name, as it signifies "Black tail" (see Redstart), while the tail happens to be red.

BLACK-STEER. The STARLING (Upton-on-Severn, Worcestershire); also called Black Starling in East Lothian.

BLACK STORK [No. 257]. The name first appears in Willughby (1678), who calls it Black Stork to distinguish it from the Common or White Stork, but it seems to be first recorded for our Islands by Colonel Montagu in 1815 in a communication to the Linnean Society.

BLACK SWIFT: Macgillivray's name for the SWIFT.

BLACK-TAILED GODWIT [No. 403] The name is found in Fleming (1828). It is called Red Godwit by Edwards, Pennant, Latham, etc Now only a visitor on migration, but it used to breed with us up to the year 1847. Distinguished from the Bar-tailed Godwit by its tail being black instead of dusky grey with the base white only. It is described by Willughby (1678), who calls it "the second sort of Godwit."

BLACK TERN [No. 412]. A species of Tern which is now only a migrational visitor, although it used to breed in East Anglia up to the year 1858. The plumage is really of a sooty slate-grey, the head only being black. This species is mentioned by Turner (1544) who calls it "*Stern*" and bears witness to its abundance in England in his time, stating that "throughout the whole of summer, at which time it breeds, it makes such an unconscionable noise that by its unrestrained clamour it almost deafens those who live near lakes and marshes." Willughby and Ray (1678) call it " our Black cloven-footed Gull " and give also " Scare-Crow " as a popular name " Black Tern " occurs in Pennant (1766).

BLACK-THROATED DIVER [No 343]. This species is so called from its black chin and throat. The name is first used by Edwards, and is also found in Pennant, Latham and later writers In Benbecula and North Uist the natives compare its cry in dry weather to " Deoch ! deoch ! deoch ! tha'n loch a tras-ghadh "—" drink ! drink ! drink ! the lake is nearly dried up " (Gray).

BLACK-THROATED GROSBEAK. Macgillivray's name for the HAWFINCH.

BLACK-THROATED THRUSH [No. 161] An Asiatic species in which the throat and breast are of a dull black hue.

BLACK-THROATED WAXWING Macgillivray's name for the WAXWING

BLACK-THROATED WHEATEAR The BLACK-EARED WHEAT-EAR.

BLACK-THROATED YELLOW-HAMMER A local name for the CIRL BUNTING.

BLACK THRUSH The BLACKBIRD (Macgillivray.)

BLACK-TOED GULL The ARCTIC SKUA. (Pennant.) It is a local name for this species in Moray, and Swainson also applies it to the GREAT SKUA

BLACK-TOPPIN' DUCK The TUFTED DUCK. (Yorkshire.)

BLACK WHEATEAR [No. 174]. A recent addition to the British List, first recorded in 1909

BLACK WIGEON The female WIGEON. (East Ireland)

BLACK-WINGED GULL. The BLACK-HEADED GULL. (Yarrell.)

BLACK-WINGED HORNED OWL. The EAGLE-OWL.

BLACK-WINGED PRATINCOLE [No. 355] This is the *G melanoptera* of Saunders ("Brit. Birds" [Mag], vol i, 1, p 15), hence the name Black-winged.

BLACK-WINGED STILT [No. 400]. This species was not of quite such rare occurrence in former times. It was known to the older authors from Pennant (1766) to Donovan as " Long-legged Plover." Occurs in Willughby (1678) under the name of Himantopus (ex Pliny and Aldrovandus) Black-winged Stilt is found in Selby (1833) The name Stilt is ascribed by Newton to Rennie in 1831, as a rendering of Brisson's *Echasse* (1760), although according to Wilson used long before in America. I may point out, though, that in Bewick's "Brit. Birds" (1st ed., vol. II, p. 5, 1804) will be found a cut of a sportsman walking in the water on *stilts*, placed as a tail-piece to the account of the "Long-legged Plover," which suggests both the bird's present name and its habits.

BLACK-WINGED STILT-SHANK. Macgillivray's name for the BLACK-WINGED STILT.

Black Woodpecker. This fine North European and Asiatic species has frequently been recorded as British, but no really authentic British examples are known and it is therefore yet denied a place on the British List.

BLACK WREN: The HEDGE-SPARROW. Swainson says it is an Irish name for the species, on account of the dusky plumage.

BLACKY-TOP: The STONECHAT. (Provincial.)

BLAKELING: The YELLOW BUNTING. (Northumberland and Yorkshire.)

BLEATER: The COMMON SNIPE. From the peculiar noise it makes during its love-flight. Also occurs as "Blutter."

BLETHERING TAM: The WHITETHROAT. (Renfrew.)

BLIND DORBIE: The PURPLE SANDPIPER. (North Shetland.)

BLIND DUNNOCK: The HEDGE-SPARROW. (Somerset.) Smith says it is from its stupid blindness in not distinguishing the Cuckoo's egg laid in its nest.

BLOOD HAWK: The KESTREL. (Oxon.)

BLOOD HOOP, BLOOD OLF, or BLOOD ULF: The BULLFINCH (see Alp). The term "blood" is from the salmon-red tint of the under-parts.

BLOOD LARK: The YELLOW BUNTING. (Provincial.) Also the TREE-PIPIT. (Cheshire.)

BLOOD LINNET: The LINNET (Norfolk.) From the crimson of its breast in breeding-plumage.

BLUE-BACK, BLUE-BIRD, BLUE FELT, BLUE RUMP, or BLUE-TAIL. The FIELDFARE is so called in various localities from the blue-grey tint of the lower-back. Blue-tail is noted as used in the Midlands and West Yorkshire, and is a misnomer, as the tail is dark brown; Blue-Back is a Cheshire name.

BLUE-BACKED CROW: The HOODED CROW. (Thirsk, Yorks.)

BLUE-BACKED DOVE   Macgillivray's name for the STOCK-DOVE.

BLUE-BACKED FALCON   The PEREGRINE FALCON. (North England) From the dark blue-grey of the mantle.

BLUE-BACKED MAW   The HERRING-GULL. (Orkney and Shetland) Also occurs in Yorkshire as Blue-backed Gull.

BLUE-BILLED CURRE· The TUFTED DUCK. (West Coast.)

BLUE-BONNET or BLUECAP· The BLUE TITMOUSE. The former is a Scots and Irish and the latter an English provincial name. Nelson and Clarke, however, say Blue Bonnet is used in the West Riding of Yorkshire, but Bluecap elsewhere in the county

BLUE-BREAST : The NORWEGIAN BLUETHROAT.

BLUE DARR or BLUE DAW. The BLACK TERN. (Norfolk.) Johns says Darr is a corruption of Dorr-hawk, a name for the NIGHTJAR, "which it resembles in its mode of flight and also in its food."

BLUE DOVE· The ROCK-DOVE. (North Yorkshire.)

BLUE DUNNOCK or BLUE SPARROW : The HEDGE-SPARROW. From its neck and breast being of a bluish-grey tint. The first is a Cheshire name

BLUE GLED or BLUE KITE   The HEN-HARRIER. (Scotland.) From the blue-grey plumage of the male.

BLUE HAWK. A common name for the SPARROW-HAWK; also the MERLIN (North Yorkshire), the HEN-HARRIER (Bewick) and the PEREGRINE FALCON (Macgillivray).

BLUE-HEADED QUAKETAIL . The BLUE-HEADED WAGTAIL. (Macgillivray.) Macgillivray separated the " Yellow Wagtails " under the name of " Quaketails " from the Black-and-White group or " Wagtails."

BLUE-HEADED WAGTAIL [No 74]. The name occurs in Jenyns (1835) It is sometimes called the Blue-headed Yellow Wagtail, and erroneously the Grey-headed Wagtail, the latter being a distinct form.

BLUE ISAAC or BLUE JIG· The HEDGE-SPARROW. (Provincial.) Isaac is probably a corruption of *Heges-sugge* (see under " Segge ").

BLUE JACKET· MONTAGU'S HARRIER ; from the blue-grey of its mantle (or jacket).

BLUE JAY· The JAY. (Linlithgow, and at Scarcroft, Yorkshire.)

BLUE MAA or MAW· The COMMON GULL. (Shetlands.) Blue Maw is also a Scottish Border name for the species.

BLUE MERLIN. The SPARROW-HAWK. (Perth.)

BLUE MOPE, BLUE THEE, BLUE TIT, BLUE TOMTIT, BLUE TOP, BLUE OX-EYE, BLUE WHAUP, or BLUE YAUP. Provincial names in various localities for the BLUE TITMOUSE.

BLUE-NEB (=BLUE-BILL). A Northumberland gunner's name for several species of ducks, i.e. SCAUP-DUCK, WIGEON, TUFTED DUCK, etc.

BLUE-PIGEON: The FIELDFARE. (Ireland.)

BLUE POKER: The COMMON POCHARD. (Provincial.)

BLUE ROCK. The STOCK-DOVE. (Cheshire and Yorkshire); the ROCK-DOVE (Yorkshire.)

Blue-tailed Bee-eater. An Oriental species said to have been shot at Teesmouth in 1862.

BLUE-THROATED REDSTART, BLUE-THROATED ROBIN, or BLUE-THROATED WARBLER: The NORWEGIAN BLUE-THROAT (commonly known as the Red-spotted Blue-throat). The first name occurs in Edwards (plate 28), the second in Bewick, and the third in Yarrell.

BLUE TITMOUSE [No 89, Continental Blue Titmouse; No. 90, British Blue Titmouse]. So called from the prevailing blue colour of the upper-parts. The name occurs in Willughby (1678). Turner mentions the species, but calls it the Nun, a name derived from its hooded appearance. Titmouse appears for the members of this genus in most old authors, but Yarrell in his first edition shortened the names of these birds to Tit, and has been followed in this by many later writers.

BLUE-WINGED JAY. Macgillivray's name for the JAY. Blue-wing is a Yorkshire provincial name.

BLUE-WINGED SHOVEL-BILL: The SHOVELER (Macgillivray).

BLUE-WINGED SHOVELER or BLUE-WINGED STINT: The SHOVELER. Montagu gives the first as a provincial name.

BLUE-WINGED TEAL. See AMERICAN BLUE-WINGED TEAL.

BLUE WOODPECKER: The NUTHATCH. (Provincial.)

BLUEY · The BLUE TITMOUSE. (Yorkshire)

BLYTH'S REED-WARBLER [No. 138]. An Asiatic species so called in honour of Blyth, who named it in 1849.

BOATSWAIN. A general name for the Skuas. In the Shetlands and north Scotland it is used for the species now called ARCTIC SKUA, while Bo'sun is applied at Flamborough to the GREAT SKUA.

BOBBY WREN: The WREN. (Norfolk) So called from its short tail.

BOB ROBIN The REDBREAST (Stirling.) Also occurs as Bob or Bobbie in Notts.

BOD, BODFFORCHOG, BOD WENNOL, BODA CHWIW Welsh names for the KITE fforchog signifies "fork tailed," wennol "swallow" and chwiw "whistling."

BODA or BODA LLWYD · The COMMON BUZZARD (South Wales.)

BODA GARWGOES. The ROUGH-LEGGED BUZZARD (North Wales)

BOD GLAS The MERLIN (North Wales) lit. "blue hawk"

BODI-GUERIN A Cornish name for a "Buzzard" (MARSH-HARRIER ?).

BOD TEIRCAIL. A Welsh name for the COMMON BUZZARD. (Fleming)

BOD TINWYN. A Welsh name for the HEN-HARRIER; lit. "white-tailed Kite"

BOD Y GWERNI or BOD Y WERN. A Welsh name for the MARSH-HARRIER; lit. "marsh kite"

BOD Y MÊL A Welsh name for the HONEY-BUZZARD, lit. "Honey-Buzzard"

BOG BLEATER · The COMMON SNIPE. (Ireland.)

BOG BLUTTER, BOG BULL, BOG BUMPER, BOG DRUM, BOG JUMPER Provincial names for the BITTERN

BOGEY: The RAZORBILL. (Redcar, Yorkshire.)

BOG GLED. The MARSH-HARRIER. (East Lothian.)

BOG LARK: The MEADOW-PIPIT (Provincial.)

BOG SPARROW. The REED-BUNTING (Provincial)

BOHEMIAN CHATTERER or BOHEMIAN WAXWING. The WAX-WING Occurs in Willughby (1678), in Montagu (1802), and later authors The 18th century writers from Edwards and Pennant to Latham, Lewin and Donovan, called it the Waxen Chatterer Albin (1738) calls it "Bohemian Jay or Chatterer."

BOHEMIAN PHEASANT · A variety of the PHEASANT.

BOLDIE · The CHAFFINCH. (Aberdeen.)

BONAPARTE'S GULL [No. 425] The name is found in Audubon. It is the Bonapartian Gull of Thompson.

BONAPARTE'S SANDPIPER [No. 381]. An American species named in honour of Prince C. L. Bonaparte, the celebrated ornithologist. Formerly called Schinz's Sandpiper.

BONCATH: The COMMON BUZZARD. (North Wales.) Coward and Oldham think it is probably from Boda cath=cat hawk, from its mewing cry.

BONNETIE. The LITTLE GREBE. (Forfar.)

BONXIE. A Shetland name for the GREAT SKUA; said to be used also in the Orkneys.

BOOMER: The BITTERN. From its booming cry.

BOONK: The LITTLE BITTERN. (Montagu.)

BOOTY: The MANX SHEARWATER. Mr. R. Godfrey informs me it goes under this name on the East Coast of Shetland.

BOTHAG. A Gaelic name for the RINGED PLOVER.

BOTTLE-BUMP: The BITTERN. (Yorkshire.)

BOTTLE-JUG. The LONG-TAILED TITMOUSE. (North and East Yorkshire.) From the shape of its nest.

BOTTLE-NOSE: The PUFFIN. From its peculiarly-shaped bill. Willughby records it as so called in South Wales.

BOTTLE TIT or BOTTLE TOM: The LONG-TAILED TITMOUSE. (Provincial.) From the shape of its nest.

BOUGER or BOWGER: The PUFFIN. Bowger occurs in Martin's "Voy. to St. Kilda"; while Bouger, or Bulker, is the Hebrides name.

BRACKEN OWL: The NIGHTJAR. (Longdendale, Cheshire.)

BRACKET: The TURNSTONE. (South Northumberland.)

BRAKE-HOPPER or BRAKE LOCUSTELLE: The GRASSHOPPER-WARBLER. From its habit of frequenting thick underwood.

BRAKE NIGHTINGALE: The NIGHTINGALE. (Macgillivray.)

BRAMBLE COCK: The BRAMBLING. (Cheshire.)

BRAMBLE-FINCH: The BRAMBLING. (Yorkshire and elsewhere.)

BRAMBLING [No. 38]. The name appears in Turner (1544) as "Bramlyng" and in Merrett's list and also Willughby as "Bramble or Brambling." Pennant calls it the Brambling or Mountain Finch. Also applied to the young of the SNOW-BUNTING.

BRAME: The WHIMBREL. (East Suffolk.)

BRAN: The CARRION-CROW. (Cornish.) Mr. Harting also applies it to the Rook.

BRAN or BRAN FAWR: The CARRION-CROW. (North Wales) lit. "crow" or "great crow."

BRAN BIG COCH The CHOUGH. (North Wales) lit "red-beaked crow."

BRANCHER. The GOLDFINCH; also the newly-fledged young of the ROOK and other perching birds In falconry a young Hawk which has left the nest but remains near it, hopping from bough to bough.

BRANDRE. A Cornish name for the ROOK.

BRAND-TAIL: The REDSTART. (North Country.) Sometimes also occurs as Bran-tail, a mere corruption; lit. fire-tail, from A.Sax. *brand, brond*, a burning piece of wood

BRAN GERNYW: The CHOUGH. (North Wales) lit "Cornish Chough."

BRAN HEDLYD, BRAN YR IWERDDON, BRAN LWYD. Welsh names for the HOODED CROW, the first signifies ash-coloured crow, the second Irish crow, and the third grey crow.

BRAN SYDDYN. A Welsh name for the CARRION-CROW; lit. "cottage crow."

BRANT or BRAND GOOSE· The BRENT GOOSE. Occurs in Turner (1544), who makes it identical with the BARNACLE-GOOSE. Brant Goose is a Holy Island name for the BRENT GOOSE, while Brant is a Cheshire name for the same species.

BRAS-Y-CYRS, BRAS PENDDU : The REED-BUNTING (North Wales)

BRAS-Y-DDRUTTAN, BRAS-YR-YD. Welsh names for the CORN-BUNTING; the last name signifies "stout (bird) of the grain"

BRAZILIAN CURLEW or BRAZILIAN WHIMBREL. The immature GLOSSY IBIS

BREAC-AN-T'SIL. A Gaelic name for the PIED WAGTAIL.

BREAD-AND-CHEESE The YELLOW BUNTING. (Salop) From its cry, which has been syllabled "little-bit-of-bread and-no-che-e-s-e."

BRECH Y FUCHES, or BRITH YR OGED. The PIED WAGTAIL (North Wales); also applied to other species; lit. "pied bird of the cowshed," "pied bird of the harrow."

BRENT GOOSE [No 283, Brent Goose; No 284, Pale-breasted Brent Goose, No 284*, Black Brent Goose]. The name occurs as Brent Goose in Willughby and also in Pennant, who says it is called Bernacle in Ireland. Brent is from Welsh *brenig*, a limpet. Goose is from A.Sax. *Gos*, and is properly the female, the male being called Gander, and the young Gosling. Brent Goose is also a Cheshire name for the BARNACLE-GOOSE.

BRIAR BUNTING: The CORN-BUNTING. (North Ireland.)

BRID or BRYD. The original form of Bird in Mid.-Eng. and A.Sax., being derived from A.Sax. *bredan*, to breed. The term was properly applicable to the young only, and seems synonymous with *brood*, A.Sax. *brod*, the proper term for the adult bird being fowl, A.Sax. *fugol*, which has in recent times come to be applied more especially to the barn-door varieties of gallinaceous birds. Shakespeare (Henry IV, act v, sc. 1.) has "that ungentle gull the cuckoo's bird (i.e. young)." Chaucer has "take any *brid* and put it in a cage," etc., also the plural form *briddes*. In the corrupted Northern English it appears to have become early changed to *bird* by the shifting of the "r," although it survived for a time as *brid* or *bryd* in the Wessex, or Southern English, tongue, which was less subject to corrupting influences. According to Poole *brid* still survives in Staffordshire

BRIDLED GUILLEMOT. A supposed variety of the COMMON GUILLEMOT; also known as the *Ringed Guillemot*.

BRIDLED MARROT. A local name for the *Ringed Guillemot* among the fishermen in the West of Scotland (Gray).

BRIDLE DUCK. The SCAUP-DUCK. (Dublin.)

BRIECAN BEATHA. A Gaelic name for the CHAFFINCH.

BRINKER. The RING-OUZEL.

BRISK FINCH, BRISKIE, or BRICHTIE: The CHAFFINCH. (Scotland.) From its smartness of appearance and activity.

BRITH Y FUCHES A South Wales name for the PIED WAGTAIL; lit "pied bird of the cowshed."

BRITH Y FUCHES FELEN. A Welsh name for the YELLOW WAGTAIL; felen signifies "yellow."

BRITH Y FUCHES LWYD. A Welsh name for the GREY WAGTAIL; lwyd signifies "grey."

BRITISH COAL-TITMOUSE. See COAL-TITMOUSE.

BRITISH DIPPER. See DIPPER.

BRITISH GOLDEN-CRESTED WREN. See GOLDEN-CRESTED WREN.

BRITISH GREAT SPOTTED WOODPECKER. See GREAT SPOTTED WOODPECKER.

BRITISH GREAT TITMOUSE. See GREAT TITMOUSE.

BRITISH HEDGE SPARROW. See HEDGE-SPARROW.

BRITISH LONG-TAILED TITMOUSE. See LONG-TAILED TITMOUSE.

BRITISH MARSH-TITMOUSE. See MARSH-TITMOUSE.
BRITISH NUTHATCH. See NUTHATCH
BRITISH REDBREAST. See REDBREAST.
BRITISH SONG-THRUSH. See SONG-THRUSH.
BRITISH WILLOW-TITMOUSE. See WILLOW-TITMOUSE.
BROADBILL or BROAD-BILLED DUCK: The SHOVELER. (Provincially) So called from its spatulate bill.
BROAD-BILLED SANDPIPER [No. 385]. The name is found in Gould's "Birds of Europe" (pt. xvii.).
BROAD-BILLED SCAUP-DUCK. The SCAUP-DUCK. (Macgillivray)
BROINN DEARG. A Gaelic name for the REDBREAST.
BRONGIE The CORMORANT. (Orkney and Shetland.)
BRONRUDDYN or BRONGOCH. The REDBREAST (North Wales); lit. "ruddy breast." and "red breast"
BRONRUDDYN Y MYNYDD. The BRAMBLING. (North Wales)
BRONWEN: The WHITETHROAT. (North Wales) lit "white breast."
BRONWEN LEIAF The LESSER WHITETHROAT. (North Wales) lit. "lesser white breast."
BROOK OUZEL· The WATER-RAIL. (Willughby.) Hett also applies the name to the DIPPER.
BROOK-RUNNER The WATER-RAIL (Provincial.)
BROWN-AND-WHITE GULL· The immature GREAT BLACK-BACKED GULL.
BROWN-BACKED WARBLER [No. 153]. A rare straggler from south-east Europe, first recorded in 1907.
BROWN BEE-HAWK Macgillivray's name for the HONEY-BUZZARD.
BROWN BUZZARD. The COMMON BUZZARD. (Macgillivray)
Brown Crane. A North American species of which a solitary example, probably an escaped bird, has occurred in Ireland
BROWN EAGLE. A name for the GOLDEN EAGLE. (Macgillivray)
BROWN FLYCATCHER [No. 115] An Eastern Siberian species, first recorded in 1909.
BROWN GLED· The female HEN-HARRIER. (Scotland.) From its brown plumage, an English equivalent being Brown Kite; the male is called Blue Gled.
BROWN GULL The GREAT SKUA, also the immature BLACK-HEADED GULL.

BROWN HAWK: The MARSH-HARRIER (Ireland); the KESTREL (Yorkshire).
BROWN-HEADED DUCK · The GOLDENEYE (female).
BROWN-HEADED GULL. The BLACK-HEADED GULL. (Albin.)
BROWN HEN: The female BLACK GROUSE.
BROWN-HOODED MEW. Macgillivray's name for the BLACK-HEADED GULL; the head is really dark brown.
BROWN JERFALCON: The GYR-FALCON. (Latham.)
BROWN LINNET: The LINNET. A common provincial name, properly applicable to the bird in winter-plumage.
BROWN LONGBEAK: The RED-BREASTED SANDPIPER. (Selby.)
BROWN OWL: The TAWNY OWL. (Pennant.) Occurs in Willughby (1678) as the "Common Brown or Ivy Owl." Also commonly called Brown Owl or Brown Hoolet provincially, the names arising from its tawny-brown plumage.
BROWN PHALAROPE: The RED-NECKED PHALAROPE. Occurs in Macgillivray.
BROWN PTARMIGAN: The RED GROUSE. (Macgillivray.)
BROWN SANDPIPER: The LITTLE STINT.
BROWN SNIPE: The RED-BREASTED SANDPIPER in its winter-dress. The name is found in Pennant, Montagu and Yarrell.
BROWN STARLING: The STARLING. (Young.)
BROWN SWALLOW: The SWIFT (Renfrew.)
BROWN TERN · The COMMON TERN (immature). Occurs in Willughby.
BROWN TREE-CREEPER. Macgillivray's name for the TREE-CREEPER.
BROWN WOODPECKER · The TREECREEPER (Provincial.) From its habit of climbing trees like a Woodpecker, and from its brown plumage.
BROWN WOOD-WREN: The CHIFFCHAFF. (Macgillivray.)
BROWN WREN · The WREN. (Provincial.)
BROWN YOGLE: The SHORT-EARED OWL. (Shetlands.)
BRÜNNICH'S GUILLEMOT [No. 446]. The name is found in Fleming, and also Yarrell and succeeding authors.
BUCHARET: The SWIFT. (Forfar.)
BUCKFINCH: The CHAFFINCH. (Provincial.)
BUDAGOCHD. A Gaelic name for the COMMON SNIPE; Graham thought it a corruption of "woodcock" and therefore a misnomer.

Bud-picker, Bud-bird, or Bud-finch The BULLFINCH, from its habit of picking the buds of fruit trees

BUFF-BACKED HERON [No. 264] Also sometimes called Buff-backed Egret. The name Buff-backed Heron is found in Selby (1833). Montagu ("Orn. Dict.," Supp.) described the young as the "Little White Heron." It is the Red-billed Heron of Pennant and the Rufous-backed Heron of Gould. Bewick's Buff-coloured Egret is the SQUACCO HERON.

Buff-breasted Goosander The GOOSANDER. (Macgillivray.)

BUFF-BREASTED SANDPIPER [No 382]. The name is found as Buff-breasted Tringa in Selby and Buff-breasted Sandpiper in Jenyns.

Buff-coloured Egret The SQUACCO HERON. (Bewick.)

BUFFEL-HEADED DUCK [No. 303] The name is found in Audubon, Bonaparte, etc. It is the Buffel-headed Garrot of Jenyns

Buffon's Skua. The LONG-TAILED SKUA. (Yarrell.)

Buidheag bhealaidh A Gaelic name for the YELLOW BUNTING, lit. "the yellowling of the broom." Macgillivray also gives Buidheag Bhuachair.

Bulking Lark. The TREE-PIPIT. (Thirsk, Yorkshire.)

Bullcoot. The COOT.

BULLFINCH [No 30, British Bullfinch; No. 29, Northern Bullfinch] Probably so called from the stoutness of the neck and head (cf. *Bull*dog, etc.), but according to Yarrell, from its largish size in comparison with other finches The name appears in Turner (1544) as "Bulfinche" and "Bulfinc," and in Merrett (1667) as "Bullfinch." Willughby (1678) spells it "Bulfinch" in the text and "Bullfinch" on the plate The British form was first distinguished by Macgillivray ("Hist. Brit. Birds," I, p. 407, 1837) under the name of *Pyrrhula pileata*, but most later writers continued to identify both forms under Vieillot's name *P europœa* For the principal variants of its peculiar provincial names, see under "Alp."

Bullflinch: The BULLFINCH. (Thirsk, Yorkshire.)

Bullhead or Bullseye. Irish local names for the GOLDEN PLOVER and also the GREY PLOVER. The former name is applied by Macgillivray and also Swainson to the GREY PLOVER, and the latter says it is on account of the round shape of its head.

BULL-HEADED WIGEON: The COMMON POCHARD. (North Ireland.)

BULL LINNET: The LESSER REDPOLL.

BULLOCK'S PETREL: LEACH'S FORK-TAILED PETREL; so called from the type-specimen having been in Bullock's collection.

BULL OF THE BOG: The COMMON BITTERN. (Roxburghshire.) From its "booming" cry.

BULL'S-EYE or BULL'S-EYED PLOVER: The DUNLIN; also the RINGED PLOVER (see also under Bullhead). The name is probably from their prominent dark eyes.

BULL SPINK· The BULLFINCH. Occurs in Merrett (1667) as "Bul Spink." The names Bullspink and Bully are also applied in Yorkshire to this species, and the latter (Bully) locally in North Yorkshire to the CHAFFINCH.

BULL THRUSH: The MISTLE-THRUSH. (Hants.) So called from its large size and stout shape.

BULLY or BULLIE: The BULLFINCH. An abbreviation of Bullfinch.

BULWER'S PETREL [No. 333]. The name appears to be first published in Jardine and Selby's "Illus. Orn." (II, pl. 65, 1829).

BUMBARREL: The LONG-TAILED TITMOUSE. (Notts)

BUMBLE: The BITTERN. (Provincial.)

BUMPY-COSS. Montagu gives this as a provincial name for the BITTERN; another and more correct form is BUMPY CORS, the derivation being from the Welsh name *Bwmp y gors*, lit. "Boom of the Marsh."

BUN-BHUACHAILLE. A Gaelic name for the GREAT NORTHERN DIVER. (West Isles of Scotland) lit. "herdsman of the bottom" (Graham).

BUNDIE. An Orkney name for the DUNLIN, and also the COMMON SANDPIPER.

BUNTER: The MEADOW-PIPIT. (Provincial.)

BUNTING: The CORN-BUNTING. An earlier name for the species.

BUNTING CROW: The HOODED CROW. (Montagu.) Swainson says it is an Irish name for the species.

BUNTING LARK: The CORN-BUNTING. Occurs in Montagu as a provincial name; BUNTING or BUNTLING LARK is also given by Swainson as a Scottish name for the species, the name having its origin in the fact that in appearance this bird somewhat resembles a lark.

BURGOMASTER: The GLAUCOUS GULL. Also the immature GREAT BLACK-BACKED GULL. According to Scoresby the name was first given by Dutch mariners to the former species, either from its majestic appearance or masterful ways.

BURRIAN. The RED-THROATED DIVER. (Ballantrae.)

BURROW-DUCK: The SHELD-DUCK Occurs in Willughby. Montagu spells it "Burrough Duck," as also does Bewick; there is no doubt, however, that the name arises from the fact that it makes its nest in a rabbit-burrow or other hole.

BURROW-PIGEON. The STOCK-DOVE. (Sedbergh, Yorkshire.)

BUSH-CHAT: The STONECHAT and the WHINCHAT have been so called. The term was apparently first applied by Macgillivray. For the first-mentioned bird "bush-chat" would be a far more suitable name than "stone-chat," as it is found frequenting furze-covered commons and neglected meadows. Hett applies the name less appropriately to the WHEATEAR.

BUSH-DOVE. The STOCK-DOVE (Provincial.) Somewhat of a misnomer, as it never nests in bushes.

BUSH-LARK. The CORN-BUNTING. (Ireland.)

BUSH-MAGPIE The MAGPIE. A popular supposition is that it is a different variety of the bird that nests in bushes.

BUSH-OVEN: The LONG-TAILED TITMOUSE. (Norfolk.) From the shape and situation of its nest.

BUSH-SPARROW: The HEDGE-SPARROW. (Stirling.)

BUSTARD The GREAT BUSTARD. Also the STONE-CURLEW (Swainson)

BUTCHER-BIRD or MURDERING-BIRD: The GREAT GREY SHRIKE Also applied to the RED-BACKED SHRIKE; from their habit of impaling small birds, mice and insects on thorns. The two names given are applied to the GREAT GREY SHRIKE by Merrett. Willughby and Ray call it the Greater Butcher-bird or Mattagess. Thompson says the MISTLE-THRUSH is called Butcher-bird in a part of Donegal

BUT-FOR-BUT. A Cheshire name for the QUAIL. From its cry.

BUTTAL or BUTTLE: The BITTERN. (Provincial.)

BUTTER BUMP: The BITTERN. Montagu gives it as a provincial name, and Swainson says it is a Yorkshire name for the species.

38 DICTIONARY OF NAMES OF BRITISH BIRDS.

BUTTERFLIP : The AVOCET. Montagu gives it as a provincial name.

BUTTERIE. A Holy Island name for the SAND-MARTIN; perhaps corrupted from Bitterie (q.v.).

BUTTOUR · The BITTERN. (Turner.)

BUZZARD : The COMMON BUZZARD. Swainson gives Buzzard-Hawk as a Forfar name for the species. The name Buzzard is also sometimes applied to the MARSH-HARRIER.

BWMP Y GORS. A Welsh name for the BITTERN ; lit. " Boom of the Marsh."

CACKAREEN : The KITTIWAKE GULL.

CAD CROW : The CARRION-CROW. (East Riding, Yorkshire.)

CADDAW, CADDER, CADDY, CARDER, CAWDAW. East Anglian names for the JACKDAW; Turner (1544) has Caddo.

CAILCHEAG-CHEAN-DUBH. A Gaelic name for the COAL-TITMOUSE.

CAILLEACH-OIDHCHE. A Gaelic name for the TAWNY OWL ; lit. " old woman of the night."

CAILLEACH-OIDHCHE GHEAL. A Gaelic name for the BARN-OWL ; lit. " white old woman of the night."

Calandra Lark. A south European species which has been supposed to have occurred in the British Isles. *Calandra* (written *Calander* by Newton) is from Ital. *Calandra*=Lat. *caliendrum*, a head-dress or ornament of hair. It occurs in Chaucer (" Romaunt of the Rose ") as " Chalaundre " and " Chelaundre." Edwards (" Gleanings of Nat. Hist.," pl. 268) figured it in error as belonging to Carolina. Willughby (1678) mentions the " Calandra, which perchance is no other than the Bunting." This species being common as a cage bird, it is quite likely that the British birds were " escapes."

CALEY TIT . The LONG-TAILED TITMOUSE. (Provincial.)

CALLOO : The LONG-TAILED DUCK. (Orkney and Shetlands.) From its cry. Swainson also gives Calaw as a variant for the same localities. Hett gives Calloo as a name for the CURLEW.

CALMAN-CHOILLE. The Gaelic name for the RING-DOVE ; lit. " wood pigeon."

CALMAN-FIADHAICH. The Gaelic name for the ROCK-DOVE.

CAMBRIDGE GODWIT : The SPOTTED REDSHANK. (Bewick.)

Canada Goose. A North American species, which has been domesticated in this country for more than two centuries,

so that records of examples shot are always open to doubt
The name occurs in Willughby (1678) Jenyns calls it the
Canada Swan. The name Canada Goose is also applied
to the BARNACLE-GOOSE.

CANADA OWL: The AMERICAN HAWK-OWL. (Jenyns)

CANADIAN DIVER: The RED-THROATED DIVER. (Winter-plumage.)

Canary. Originally so called from its having been brought
from the Canary Isles Wild examples of this universal cage-bird have occurred in our islands, but, as the species is
non-migratory, such occurrences have been generally put
down to escaped birds

CANBOTTLE: The LONG-TAILED TITMOUSE. (Staffs. and
Salop) So called from the shape of the nest (see Bottle-tit).
Can occurs in Shakespeare as a kind of cup.

CAOUEN A Cornish name for an Owl.

Cape Pigeon. A species of Petrel inhabiting the Southern
Seas, which is said to have occurred in our islands.

CAPERCAILLIE [No 462] The name accepted since the
date of Yarrell's first edition (1843) for a large species of
Grouse, more often previously known by its English names
of Wood Grouse, or Cock of the Wood, and formerly indi-genous to the northern parts of the British Islands, but
finally extirpated in Scotland and Ireland during the
eighteenth century, and re-introduced in the Highlands
from Sweden in 1837 The Scots name is variously written
Capercaillie, Capercally, Caperkally, Caperkellie, Caper-cailzie, Capercalze and Capercali, and its precise derivation
seems very uncertain Gesner ("Hist. Anim.," 1554,
lib III, p. 159) has, "De capricalca, quam Scoti vulgo
appellunt ane capricalze," and immediately following he
terms it Capercalze, which is the spelling used by Sibbald
(1684) Yarrell states that the form Capercaillie adopted
by him and given also by Fleming (1842) is derived from
the Gaelic *Capullcoille,* lit. "horse of the wood," a dis-tinction intended to refer to size, it being pre-eminently
large in comparison with others of the genus (a similar
example being found in *bull*finch). Rev. Dr. T. Maclauchlan,
as cited by Professor Newton, thinks the derivation is from
Gaelic *Cabhar,* an old man, but by metaphor an old bird,
and *coille,* a wood—"the old bird of the wood" *Cabhar,*
however, may also mean a hawk, and is pronounced
Cavar. Dr. Maclauchlan thinks it not unlikely, however,
to be the origin of the word spelled "Caper." A similar

metaphoric use may be cited in *Cailleach*=an old woman, and *cailleach-oidhche*=an owl, lit. " the old woman of the night." There is however the word *gabhar*=a goat (but this is a feminine noun) and also *capull*=a horse, which although a masculine noun is at the present day limited in its application to a mare. Mr. Harvie-Brown says that in Argyleshire and Lochaber the bird is still known by the name of " Capullcoille," which Macgillivray in 1837 gave as a Gaelic name for the species. This derivation, as given by Yarrell, is supported by many authorities and references. Saunders preferred *gabur*, a goat (with allusion to the elongated chin-feathers of the male and his amorous behaviour in spring) and *coille*, wood. This latter will, of course, suggest Lat. *caper, capri*, a he-goat (cognate with Eng. to caper) and the Gaelic *coille*, and I do not know that the hybrid word would be so very improbable. Gesner's " Capricalca " and " Capricalze " suggest that he derived from the Lat. *capri*, a goat, and *calca* of course suggests a kicking or capering goat. Merrett (1667) has " Capricalca, Capricalze Scotis," which of course is probably copied from Gesner. In any case the metaphorical sense is similar, i.e. " Old man of the wood," " goat of the wood," etc. Other derivations have been suggested, but without so much ground for their accuracy. The Erse name appears to be *Capal coile*, " the Wood Horse, being the chief fowl of the woods " (Shaw, " Hist. Prov." Moray, 1775). Jamieson in his great Scottish Dictionary spells it " Capercailye," a variation which Mr. Harvie-Brown traces to Bellenden in his translation of Hector Boethius, 1553. For further researches into the origin and spelling of this most difficult name see Mr. Harvie-Brown's " Capercaillie in Scotland " (1888). There is no doubt, however, that the best and most correct name for the species, and a good English one to boot, would be " Wood-Grouse," a name moreover sanctioned by its usage in many of the older ornithological works from Pennant (1766) to Montagu and on to Macgillivray (1837). Pennant, however, while calling it Wood-Grouse, states that north of Inverness it is known by the names of " Caper-calze " and " Auer-calze," and Macgillivray in 1837 stated it was known in Scotland by the name of Capercailzie. It appears now to be flourishing in several counties of Scotland, while in ancient times it could never have been particularly common, as most of the references to it in ancient books show. So far back as 1651, as recorded in the " Black Book of Taymouth " (pp. 433-4), we find one sent by the laird of Glenorchy to Charles II. at Perth, "who accepted it weel as a raretie, for he had never seen any of them." As regards the date of its former extinction in Scotland, Pennant records in his first tour in Scotland in 1769, having himself seen a cock-bird, and this seems the latest actual record, although of course the bird doubtless lingered a few years later. As regards Ireland, Rutty records it in co Leitrim in 1710 and Pennant says it was to be found in co Tipperary as late as 1760. Willughby in 1678 calls it "Cock of the Wood" only, and speaks of it as found in Ireland, but does not refer to it as a Scottish species. The name in Welsh is Ceiliog coed, an equivalent of Cock of the Wood

CAPERLINTY · The WHITETHROAT (Jedburgh)

CAPER-LONGTAIL . The LONG-TAILED TITMOUSE.

CAPPED BUZZARD · The HONEY-BUZZARD. Montagu gives it as a provincial name

CAPPED PETREL [No. 331] A species thought now to be extinct.

CAPUL COILLE A Gaelic name for the CAPERCAILLIE (q.v.).

CAR CROW . The CARRION-CROW. (Craven, Yorkshire)

CARFIL BACH The LITTLE AUK. (North Wales) lit. " Little auk."

CARNER CROW or CARENER CROW The CARRION-CROW. (Norfolk)

CAROLINA CRAKE [No 456] A North American species, named by Linnæus *Rallus carolinus*, whence its popular name

CAROLINA CUCKOO The YELLOW-BILLED CUCKOO (Jenyns)

CARPENTER-BIRD : The GREAT TITMOUSE. (Provincial.)

CARR-CROW The BLACK TERN (see Carr-Goose) It occurs as Scare-Crow in Willughby.

CARR-GOOSE or CARGOOSE. An old name for the GREAT CRESTED GREBE · occurs as Cargoose in Charleton (1668). It arises from the bird frequenting the East Coast "carrs," or marshes

CARRION-CROW [No 3]. The name "Carrion Crow" appears in Merrett (1667) and in Willughby (1678) and is found as " Carren Crow " in " A Brief description of Ireland made in this year 1589," by Robert Payne (Irish Archæol. Soc. Tracts). Turner (1544) calls it "crouu" (=crow) simply. Crow is derived from A.Sax. *crawe* (see " Craw ") ;

and the term "Carrion" is applied to this species from its habit of feeding on the flesh of dead animals. Like the Raven this species was formerly very generally regarded as a bird of ill-omen. In parts of Northamptonshire it is believed to be a token of bad luck to see one flying alone. The belief that it is unlucky to shoot a crow is widely spread: Seebohm met with it on the Petchora, and I found it prevalent in eastern Canada regarding the American Crow, a species almost identical with the present. There is a Cornish legend of St. Neotus impounding the crows in an enclosure during Church service to prevent their depredations while the people came to Church (Mitchell, "Paroch. Hist. St. Neots," 1833), this enclosure is said to be still visible Dyer cites as an Essex saying, in connexion with crows flying *towards* one:—

> One's unlucky,
> Two's lucky;
> Three is health,
> Four is wealth,
> Five is sickness,
> And six is death.

It is said when a Crow makes a hoarse, hollow noise it presages foul weather (Bourne). The saying "as a crow flies" refers to the Rook, which flies straight across country on its homeward journey, and not to this species.

CARRION-GULL: The GREAT BLACK-BACKED GULL.

CARR LAG-GOOSE. An old Yorkshire fowler's name for a variety of goose found on the carrs, probably the PINK-FOOTED GOOSE.

CARR-SPARROW: The REED-BUNTING. (Yorkshire.)

CARR-SWALLOW. A former name for the BLACK TERN in Lincolnshire and Cambridgeshire, from its frequenting the "carrs" or marshes. In east Yorkshire it is applied to the BLACK-HEADED GULL.

CASEG EIRA: The FIELDFARE. (North Wales) lit. "snow ball."

CASEG Y DDRYCCIN. A North Wales name for the MISTLE-THRUSH; lit. "Storm-cock." It has also been applied to the FIELDFARE.

CAS GAN LONGWR (Sailor's hatred). The Welsh name for the STORM-PETREL, signifying the sailors' dislike to it as a portent of storms. Swainson gives the name to the BLACK GUILLEMOT, apparently erroneously.

CASPIAN PLOVER [No. 357]. First recorded as occurring in Norfolk by Saunders ("Manual," 2nd. ed., p. 537).

CASPIAN TERN [No. 416]. The name is found in Selby and was adopted by Yarrell and subsequent authors. Macgillivray calls it Caspian Strong-billed Tern.

CASSIAN HERON : The SQUACCO HERON.

CASSIN'S SNOW GOOSE. See SNOW-GOOSE.

CASTANEOUS DUCK : The FERRUGINOUS DUCK. (Bewick.)

CASUR CLOCH : The WHEATEAR. (Tipperary.) Signifies " stone-hammer."

CAT GULL : The HERRING-GULL. (Kirkcudbright.)

CATHAG. A Gaelic name for the JACKDAW ; probably imitative of its cry.

CATOGLE : The EAGLE-OWL. (Orkneys.) From Norw. *Katugl*, from its similarity in habits and appearance to a cat (Swainson). Saxby gives Catyogle as a Shetland name for both the SNOWY-OWL and EAGLE-OWL. Cat Owl is also applied to the LONG-EARED OWL.

CAWDAW : The JACKDAW. (Suffolk.) From its note.

CAWDY MAWDY : The HOODED CROW ; also the CURLEW. (North Country.)

CEANN DEARG. A Gaelic name for the REDSTART.

CEARC FRAOICH : The female RED GROUSE. (Gaelic) lit. " heather hen."

CEARC LIATH : The female BLACK GROUSE. (Gaelic) lit. " grey hen."

CEARC-THOMAIN. A Gaelic name for the PARTRIDGE.

CEILIOG COED. The former Welsh name for the CAPERCAILLIE ; lit. " cock of the wood."

CEILIOG DDU. A Welsh name for the BLACK GROUSE ; lit. " black cock."

CEILIOG Y GOED : The PHEASANT. (North Wales) lit. " cock of the wood."

CEILIOG Y MYNYDD. A Welsh name for the male RED GROUSE and BLACK GROUSE ; lit. " cock of the mountain " ; the female is termed iar (hen) in place of ceiliog.

CETHLYTH (Y). A Welsh poetical name for the CUCKOO ; lit. " the songster."

CETTI'S WARBLER [No. 130]. Named *Sylvia cetti* by Marmora in 1820, in honour of the Italian ornithologist, hence the English name ; but its first occurrence in our islands was in 1904.

CHACK, CHACKER, or CHECKS : The WHEATEAR. From its cry. The first and last are Orkney names. It is also known in some parts as Check or Check-bird.

CHAFFIE, CHAFFY, CHAFFER, or CHAFFIN: The CHAFFINCH. Popular contractions.

CHAFFINCH [No. 37]. The name appears in Turner (1544) as "Chaffinche" and in Merrett (1667) as "Chaffinch," also in Willughby (1678) by the latter name. "So called because it delights in chaff" (Kersey's Dict., 2nd ed., 1715); the bird being a frequenter of barn-yards, etc. Other derivations are, however, possible, i.e. from Mid.-Eng. *chaufen*, to warm, indicating the reddish or "warm" breast of the male. Finch is A.Sax. *finc*=finch; Modern German *fink*, Old High German *fincho*. From the same root as the Welsh *pinc*=finch, but also applied to anything smart or gay. Newton thinks it is from the *spink* or *pink* note of the Chaffinch originally. The Welsh name for the Chaffinch is *Winc*, also from the note. Jesse says that in Scotland it is known as "drunken sow" because the song has been construed into "Drink, drink till you're fou, wee drunken sowie." Chambers says that in Scotland and the North of England the plaintive note of this bird is taken as a sign of rain, and that when the boys hear it they imitate the note and its consequences thus · "Weet! weet! Dreep, dreep!" A West of England belief is that about the 25th of March this bird always cries "Pay your rent—pay your rent—pay your rent."

CHAIT: The SPOTTED FLYCATCHER. (Worcestershire.) From its note.

CHALDER, CHALDRICK, CHOLDRICK: The OYSTERCATCHER. (Orkneys.)

CHANCHIDER. The SPOTTED FLYCATCHER. (Montagu.) Swainson renders it Chancider, and also gives Chamcider as a Hampshire name for the SEDGE-WARBLER.

CHANGELESS SWAN. Macgillivray's name for the *Polish Swan*.

CHANNEL GOOSE: The GANNET. (North Devon.)

CHARBOB · The CHAFFINCH. (Derbyshire.)

CHARLIE MUFTIE. A common Scots name for the WHITE-THROAT, from its habit of puffing out the feathers of the throat.

CHASER: The ARCTIC SKUA. (Redcar, Yorkshire.) From its habit of pursuing other species.

CHAT: The SEDGE-WARBLER (Thames Valley); also the WHEATEAR (Northants.)

CHATTERER: The WAXWING. Occurs in Pennant (fo. ed., 1766), but in the later editions it is called Waxen Chatterer.

It is really a rather silent bird. The Chatterers are properly the *Cotingidæ*.

CHATTERPIE: The MAGPIE. (Staffs. and Norfolk.) It is proverbially a noisy bird.

CHAUK or CHAUK DAW: The CHOUGH. (Scotland.) From its cry.

CHEAT: The GRASSHOPPER-WARBLER. (Upton-on-Severn.)

CHEEPER, GREY CHEEPER, or MOSS CHEEPER. Common Border names for the MEADOW-PIPIT.

CHEESER: The YELLOW BUNTING. (Northants.) From the drawn-out termination of its song.

CHEETER: The RED-BACKED SHRIKE. (Provincial.)

CHEPSTER: The STARLING. A modification of Shepster (=Sheep-stare). Chep-Starling is found in Tunstall, while Ship-Starling and Sheep-Starling are Yorkshire provincial names.

CHEQUER BIRD: The WHIMBREL.

CHERCOCK: The MISTLE-THRUSH. (Westmorland.) Probably a corruption of Shercock. "Churcock" is also applied to the same species in Yorkshire.

CHERRY CHIRPER: The SNOW-BUNTING (?). (Rutty.)

CHERRY CHOPPER, CHERRY SUCKER, CHERRY SNIPE: The SPOTTED FLYCATCHER. (Provincial.) Whether this species is ever destructive to cherries is very doubtful, although it has been known to eat berries, such as those of the mountain ash.

CHERRY FINCH: The HAWFINCH. (Swaledale, Yorkshire.) From its fondness for cherry-stones.

CHERUBIM: The BARN-OWL.

CHESTNUT-BACKED THRUSH: The FIELDFARE. (Macgillivray.)

CHEVEREL or CHEVIL. A bird-fancier's term for a variety of the GOLDFINCH having a red patch on the throat. Skeat, as cited by Newton, thought it to be from Old Eng. *chefle*, or *chefelen*, to talk idly or chatter, hence "cheveller," a chatterer. Nelson and Clarke give the name as in use in Yorkshire, and make it synonymous with the so-called "Pear-tree Goldfinch."

CHEVVY LINNET or CHIVEY LINNET: The LESSER RED-POLL. (Yorkshire.)

CHICKELL or CHICKER: The WHEATEAR.

CHICKSTONE: The STONECHAT. (Cleveland, Yorkshire.) In the same district "Chetstone" is applied to the WHEATEAR.

CHIFFCHAFF [No. 119, Chiffchaff ; No. 120, Scandinavian Chiffchaff ; No. 121, Siberian Chiffchaff]. This species was the Lesser Pettychaps or Least Willow Wren of eighteenth-century authors. The name Chiffchaff is an imitation of its song and is first found as "smallest willow wren or chiffchaf" in Gilbert White's "Naturalists' Calendar and Observations" (p. 77), published in 1795 by Aiken. The Scandinavian Chiffchaff is a closely-allied form, of which some few examples have been recorded. The other sub-species, the Siberian Chiffchaff, is now known as a regular autumn visitor to Fair Isle.

CHIKEREL. A local name for the WHIMBREL in the Poole district. (Hawker.)

CHIMNEY SWALLOW : The SWALLOW. The species occurs under this name in Pennant and other authors to Montagu, and also Macgillivray.

Chinese Goose. A species not entitled to a place on the British List.

CHINK · The REED-BUNTING. (Provincial.)

CHINK CHAFFEY, CHINK CHAWDY, CHINK CHINK, or CHINKY : The CHAFFINCH. (Provincial.) From its sharp "spink" note.

CHIP-CHOP· The CHIFFCHAFF. From its song. Macgillivray gives it as a provincial name.

CHIPPET LINNET : The LESSER REDPOLL. (Doncaster.)

CHIT-LARK : The MEADOW-PIPIT. (Skelmanthorpe, Yorkshire)

CHIT-PERL . The LITTLE TERN.

CHITTER CHAT : The SEDGE-WARBLER. (Northumberland.)

CHITTIE, CHITTY, or CHIT . The MEADOW-PIPIT and also the TREE-PIPIT. (Lancashire and North of England.) Der. from A.Sax. *cidh*, a sprout, child or offspring, and meaning a small bird, or lit. a small thing. The MEADOW-PIPIT and the SEDGE-WARBLER are also known as "Chitty prat," and at Sedbergh, Yorkshire, the WREN is called Chitty.

CHITTY, CHADDY, JITTY : The LESSER REDPOLL (Cheshire). Probably in allusion to its small size.

CHITTY WREN. Thompson says the WREN· is so called in Ireland on account of its call *chit* when alarmed by a cat.

CHOGH. Given by Aldrovandus as an English name for the CHOUGHS; Turner spells it "Choghe."

Choice and Cheap The CHIFFCHAFF. Swainson gives it as a local name in the neighbourhood of Totnes, Devon.

Choldrick: The OYSTERCATCHER (Orkney and Shetland.)

CHOUGH [No. 12]. This name is now used to denote a mountain-bird of the Crow kind distinguished chiefly by its curved red bill and red feet. It is chiefly found on our Western coasts, hence its frequent name of Cornish Chough. Turner, in fact, gives "Cornish Choghe" as the English name for the species. The name Chough alone was at one time in use for the JACKDAW, which is so called in Turner, in Merrett's list, and also in Shakespeare. Willughby, Merrett and Albin called the present species the Cornish Chough, but succeeding writers up to the time of Montagu generally called it the Red-legged Crow. A Cornish legend is to the effect that King Arthur's spirit entered into this bird after death (Hawker, "Echoes from Old Cornwall").

Chub Lark. The CORN-BUNTING (Yorkshire) Perhaps from its stout, or "chubby" appearance.

Chuck or Chock· The WHEATEAR From its note.

Chuffer· The CHAFFINCH. A corruption of Chaffer

Church Martnet. The SWIFT. (Merrett.)

Church Owl: The BARN-OWL. Occurs in Sibbald, and is also in use as a provincial name in Yorkshire and elsewhere.

Churn The LONG-TAILED TITMOUSE. (Cheshire.)

Churn Owl. The NIGHTJAR. Found in Willughby (1678), and White gives it as a Hampshire name. Swainson gives Churr Owl as an Aberdeen name.

Churr or Churr Muffit· The WHITETHROAT. (Provincial.) Churr is from its harsh note, and Muffit from its habit of puffing out the throat-feathers.

Churre The DUNLIN in winter-plumage. (Norfolk)

Chwilgorn y Mynydd, or Cornicyll y Mynydd: The GOLDEN PLOVER. (North Wales) lit "mountain plover."

Chwilog· The COMMON GUILLEMOT. (North Wales.)

Chwiw or Chwiwell Welsh names for the WIGEON. Probably from its call-note.

Chwybanydd or Chwibanydd. A Welsh name for the BULLFINCH; lit. "whistler."

Ciach fawr: The GREAT SNIPE. (North Wales) lit. "great snipe."

CIGFRAN or GIGFRAN FAWR. Welsh names for the RAVEN. The former signifying "flesh crow" and the latter "great flesh crow."

CIGYDD CEFN-GOCH. A Welsh name for the RED-BACKED SHRIKE; signifying "red-backed butcher."

CIGYDD MAWR A Welsh name for the GREAT GREY SHRIKE; lit. "great butcher."

CINEREOUS BUTCHER-BIRD, or SHRIKE: The GREAT GREY SHRIKE. (Montagu.)

CINEREOUS EAGLE The name employed by Pennant, Lewin, Latham, and Montagu for the WHITE-TAILED EAGLE.

CINEREOUS GODWIT: The GREENSHANK. (Pennant.) Also young BAR-TAILED GODWIT.

CINEREOUS SHEARWATER: The GREAT SHEARWATER. (Selby.)

CINEREOUS WAGTAIL: The WHITE WAGTAIL. (Stephens in Shaw's "Zoology.")

CIRL BUNTING [No. 47]. This species was first ascertained to be a British bird by Montagu in the winter of 1800 near Kingsbridge. The name Cirl Bunting appears to be found first in Latham ("Synopsis," III, p. 190). Swainson says the name is equivalent to "Cheeper" and it seems to be from the German *Zirl-ammer.*

CITRIL FINCH [No. 26]. "Citril" was the name under which Ray and Willughby in 1663 became acquainted with it in Vienna.

CLABITTER. A Cornish name for the BITTERN.

CLACHARAN or CLOCHARET. Gaelic names for the WHEATEAR. lit. "little mason," from its cry, resembling the knocking together of two stones.

CLAKIS or CLAIKIS: The BARNACLE-GOOSE. (Scotland.) It occurs in Willughby, and is also met with as CLAIK GOOSE.

CLAMHAN. A Gaelic name for the COMMON BUZZARD according to Fleming. Clamhan, it should be noted, signifies both a Hawk and a Kite.

CLAMHAN GABHLACH or CLAMHAN GODHLACH. A Gaelic name for the KITE.

CLAMHAN LUCH: The HEN-HARRIER. (Hebrides.) From *clamhan*, a hawk, and *luch*, a mouse.

CLAMHAN RUADH. A Gaelic name for the KESTREL; lit. "red-hawk."

CLATTER-DOVE: The RING-DOVE (Yorkshire.)

CLATTERGOOSE : The BRENT GOOSE. Occurs in Montagu, and Swainson gives it as an East Lothian name ; it is derived from the noisy cry.

CLEE : THE REDSHANK. From its cry.

CLEP Y GARREG : The STONECHAT. (North Wales) lit. " stone gossip."

CLEP YR EITHIN : The WHINCHAT. (North Wales) lit. " gorse-gossip."

CLETT : The COMMON TERN.

CLIFF DAW : The CHOUGH. (Kerry.) A cliff frequenter.

CLIFF HAWK : The PEREGRINE FALCON. From its nesting-resorts.

CLIFF PIGEON : The ROCK-DOVE. (Yorkshire.)

CLINKER : The AVOCET. (Norfolk.)

CLOCHDER Y CERRIG or CLOCHDAR CERRIG. A Welsh name for the STONECHAT, signifying " chirper of the crag."

CLOCHDER Y MYNYDD. A Welsh name for the PIED FLY-CATCHER.

CLOCHDER YR EITHEN or CLOCHDAR EITHEN. A Welsh name for the WHINCHAT. It signifies gorse-chirper.

CLOIBHREAN CLOICH. An Irish name (north and west) for the WHEATEAR.

CLOD BIRD : The WHEATEAR. (See " Clotbird.")

CLOD-HOPPER : The WHEATEAR. From its habit of frequenting the newly-turned-up clods.

CLOICHEARAN. A Gaelic name for the WHEATEAR.

CLOT-BIRD : The WHEATEAR. (Merrett.) Occurs also in Turner as " Clotburd." It is the modern " clod-bird " from its habit of sitting upon the turned-up clods. Hett also gives Clod-bird as a name for the CORN-BUNTING.

CLOVEN-FOOTED GULL : The BLACK TERN. (Albin.) Montagu gives it as a provincial name.

CLUCKING DUCK. A name for the BIMACULATED DUCK.

CNOCELL BRITH : The GREAT SPOTTED WOODPECKER. (North Wales) lit. " spotted pecker."

CNOCELL BRITH BACH : The LESSER SPOTTED WOODPECKER. (North Wales) lit. " lesser spotted pecker."

CNOCELL Y CNAU : The NUTHATCH. (North Wales.) Signifies " nut knocker."

CNOCELL Y COED. A Welsh name for the GREEN WOODPECKER ; lit. " knocker of the wood."

CNUT : The KNOT. (North Wales.)

COAL and CANDLE-LIGHT· The LONG-TAILED DUCK. (Orkneys.) Also COL-CANDLE-WICK (Fife).

COAL GOOSE· The CORMORANT (Kent.)

COAL HOOD, COAL HOODEN, or COAILY HOOD· The BULL FINCH. Scottish provincial names, the first two being in use on the Scottish Border.

COALMOUSE or COLEMOUSE· The COAL-TITMOUSE. The former occurs in Merrett and the latter in Pennant and later authors.

COAL TIT The COAL-TITMOUSE. A common abbreviation.

COAL TITMOUSE [No. 91, Continental Coal-Titmouse; No. 92, British Coal-Titmouse; No. 93, Irish Coal-Titmouse]. Occurs in Merrett's list (1667) as Coalmouse, and in many later writers as Colemouse. Cole Titmouse is found in Bewick (1797). The birds occurring in the British Islands are now separated into three geographical races.

COALY HOOD The COAL-TITMOUSE. (Scotland.) Also the REED-BUNTING. (Scotland.)

COATHAM CROW· The HOODED CROW. (Loftus, Yorkshire.)

COB· Properly the BLACK-HEADED GULL; but also any large Gull. (Newton.) Montagu applied it to the GREAT BLACK-BACKED GULL, while Bolam gives Cob Gull as a Northumberland name for the same species.

COB : The male of the MUTE SWAN ; the female being termed Pen. Newton was in error in supposing no authority could be found for Yarrell's statement that these were the former names for the sexes of the Swans. In that curious old work entitled, "The Order, Lawes and Ancient Customes of the Swannes, caused to be printed by John Witherings, Esquire, Master and Governour of the Royal Game of Swans and Cygnets throughout England" (1632), are to be found these names for the sexes.

COBB or SEA COBB : The COMMON GULL. (South-east coasts.)

COBBLE. A provincial name for the young of both the GREAT NORTHERN and RED-THROATED DIVERS. Occurs in Montagu.

COBBLER'S AWL. The AVOCET (vide "Awl-Bird.") Montagu gives it as a provincial name.

COBLE. The HAWFINCH. (Norfolk—Sir Thomas Browne.)

COBLYN LLEIAF : The LESSER SPOTTED WOODPECKER. (North Wales.) lit. "lesser pecker."

COBLYN MWYAF: The GREAT SPOTTED WOODPECKER. (North Wales) lit. "greater pecker."

COBLYN-Y-COED: The GREEN WOODPECKER. (North Wales) lit. "woodpecker." Other local names are Tarady-coed ("wood-auger") and Tyllwr-y-coed ("wood-borer").

COBWEB: The SPOTTED FLYCATCHER. Occurs in Morton's "Northants." (p. 426). From its use of spiders' webs in the construction of its nest.

COCH DAN ADEN: The REDWING. (North Wales.) Signifies "red under wing."

COCH Y BERLLAN: The BULLFINCH. (North Wales) lit. "red of the orchard."

COCH Y GRUG or COCHIAD: The RED GROUSE. (North Wales.)

COCK: The WOODCOCK is sometimes so called.

COCKANDY: The PUFFIN. Sibbald gives it as a Fifeshire name of the species.

COCKATHRODON: The MANX SHEARWATER. (Scilly Isles.)

COCK OF THE MOUNTAIN: The CAPERCAILLIE. Occurs in Willughby (1678).

COCK O' THE NORTH: The BRAMBLING. (East and south Scotland.)

COCK OF THE WOOD: The CAPERCAILLIE. Occurs in Merrett (1667), who notes the species as occurring in Ireland ("in Hibernia occurrit"). Willughby and Ray (1678) also mention this as an Irish name for the bird, which they say is not found in England, while they strangely enough omit to mention Scotland as a habitat. Pennant (1766) gives Cock of the Wood as the name of this bird, and he further calls the female, Hen of the Wood.

COCK OUZEL: The BLACKBIRD.

COCK THROSTLE: The MISTLE-THRUSH.

COCK WINDER: The WIGEON. (Norfolk.)

CODDY-MODDY: The COMMON GULL (immature). Willughby and Ray give it as a Cambridgeshire name.

COEGFRAN. A Welsh name for the JACKDAW; lit. "sham crow."

COEG GYLFINHIR. A Welsh name for the WHIMBREL; signifies "sham curlew."

COESGOCH: The REDSHANK. (North Wales) lit. "redshank."

COESWERDD : The GREENSHANK. (North Wales) lit. "Greenshank."

CÒG   A Welsh name for the CUCKOO; from its cry.

COILEACH COILLE. A Gaelic name for the WOODCOCK; lit. cock of the wood. Macgillivray gives it as a name for the CAPERCAILLIE.

COILEACH DUBH. A Gaelic name for the BLACK GROUSE, lit. "black cock;" the Grey Hen is called *Cearc liath*.

COILEACH FRAOICH. A Gaelic name for the RED GROUSE, lit. Heather Cock; the female being called *Cearc fraoich*, or Heather Hen.

COILEACH RUADH. A Gaelic name for the RED GROUSE: *ruadh* signifying red or reddish.

COISTREL · The KESTREL. (Shakespeare.) From Fr. *cresserelle, cristel*.

COIT. A Cornish name for the GREEN WOODPECKER.

COLDFINCH · The PIED FLYCATCHER. The name occurs in Willughby, who describes a "bird called Coldfinch by the Germans." It is figured by Pennant (1766) under this name and by Edwards; Swainson also renders it Colefinch, and gives Coldfinch as a Shropshire name for the YELLOW BUNTING.

COLDIE : The LONG-TAILED DUCK. (Forfar.)

COLE-GOOSE . The CORMORANT.

COLE-MOUSE : The COAL-TITMOUSE   Occurs in Willughby. Also met with as Cole Titmouse.

COLIN BLACKHEAD : The REED-BUNTING   (Renfrew.)

COLISHEEN : The PUFFIN. (Galway) lit. "an old woman."

COLK : The COMMON EIDER. Occurs in Martin's "Description of the Western Isles."

COLLARED BLACKIE : The RING-OUZEL. (Staithes, Yorkshire.)

COLLARED DUCK : The RUDDY SHELD-DUCK.

COLLARED FLYCATCHER [No. 117]. This Continental species was recorded as British for the first time in 1911.

COLLARED PETREL [No. 332]. A Pacific species of which one example was obtained in Wales in 1889.

COLLARED PRATINCOLE : The PRATINCOLE. (Selby, Yarrell, etc.)

COLLARED STARE : The ALPINE ACCENTOR.

Collared Turnstone: The TURNSTONE.

Collier, or Collierjack · The CURLEW. (Cheshire.) Collier is also applied to the HOUSE-SPARROW and the SWIFT in Yorkshire.

Collochan Gull: The BLACK-HEADED GULL. (Kirkcudbright.) From a loch so called.

Colomen. The Welsh name for the wild pigeons. In North Wales the RING-DOVE is called Colomen wyllt (wild pigeon) or Colomen goed (wood pigeon); the STOCK-DOVE Colomen ddof (tame pigeon); the ROCK-DOVE Colomen y graig (rock pigeon); and the TURTLE-DOVE Colomen fair (St. Mary's dove.)

Colly: The BLACKBIRD. (Provincial.) Der. from A.Sax. *col*=coal, and meaning literally, " sooty " or " coal-like."

Colmorn: The CORMORANT; also the SHAG (Hett).

Common Auk: The RAZORBILL.

Common Avocet. See AVOCET.

Common Bee-eater. See BEE-EATER.

Common Bittern. See BITTERN.

Common Brown or Ivy Owl: The TAWNY OWL. (Willughby.

Common Bullfinch. See BULLFINCH.

Common Bunting: The CORN-BUNTING.

Common Bustard: The GREAT BUSTARD.

COMMON BUZZARD [No. 243]. The name Common Buzzard occurs in Willughby (1678). Turner (1544) and Merrett (1667) call it the Buzzard only, as do succeeding writers to the time of Pennant (1766), who calls it the Common Buzzard. The derivation is from Lat. *Buteo*, through Fr. *Busard*.

Common Coot: The COOT. Occurs in most of the old authors from Willughby to Montagu.

Common Cormorant: The CORMORANT. (Yarrell.)

Common Crane. See CRANE.

Common Creeper. A former appellation for the TREE-CREEPER, to be found in most of the older authors from Albin to Montagu.

COMMON CROSSBILL [No. 33, Common Crossbill; No. 34, Scottish Crossbill.] Occurs in Willughby (1678) as Cross-bill, and as Crossbill in most succeeding authors. The first full account of the habits of feeding of this bird is given by Yarrell ("Zool. Journ.," IV, pp. 459-65). The legend of this bird having acquired its twisted beak by striving to draw the nails that held Christ to the Cross is familiar to many. Longfellow, in his "Legend of the Crossbill," from the German of Julius Mosen, alludes not to the twisted bill but to the plumage "covered all with blood so clear." This supposed origin of a ruddy plumage is elsewhere attributed to the Robin (q.v). Hartert has separated the form inhabiting Scotland from that inhabiting England and Wales under the name of Scottish Crossbill.

COMMON CROW. The CARRION-CROW. (Merrett, Willughby.)

COMMON CUCKOO: The CUCKOO. Most of our older authors use the prefix "Common" for this species.

COMMON CURLEW [No. 404]. The name is imitative of its whistling note resembling *cur-lew*. In Fr *Courlis* or *Corlieu*. Occurs in Barlow's plates (1655) as "Curlew" and in Merrett's list as "Curliew." Willughby and many later writers down to Montagu call it the Common Curlew, whilst others of the nineteenth century drop the prefix "Common" It has always been esteemed for the delicate flavour of its flesh. Willughby gives the following as an old Suffolk saying:—

> A Curlew, be she white, be she black,
> She carries twelve pence on her back

COMMON DIPPER· The DIPPER. (Yarrell)

COMMON DUCK: The MALLARD. (Montagu.)

COMMON EIDER [No. 307]. From the Norweg. *Ejdar*, Icel. *Ædur*. Willughby calls it "Cuthbert-Duck; Anas S. Cuthberti seu Farnensis," and also Wormius's Eider. The Cuthbert is an allusion to St. Cuthbert, who lived on Farne Island, where the birds breed Pennant (1766) calls it "Eider Duck," while Montagu terms it the "Eider Duck or Edder." It is the "Great Black and White Duck" of Edwards.

COMMON EUROPEAN CROSSBILL. Macgillivray's name for the COMMON CROSSBILL.

COMMON GALLINULE: The MOORHEN. (Pennant, Montagu, etc.)

COMMON GANNET. See GANNET.

COMMON GODWIT: The BAR-TAILED GODWIT. (Pennant, Montagu.)

COMMON GROSBEAK· The HAWFINCH. (Albin.)

COMMON GUILLEMOT [No. 445]. The name occurs in Yarrell (1st ed.) as Common Guillemot. Derived from Fr. *Guillemot*. Willughby describes it as "The Bird called by the Welsh and Manksmen a Guillem; by those of Northumberland and Durham, a Guillemot or Sea-hen; in Yorkshire about Scarburgh, a Skout; by the Cornish, a Kiddaw." Albin calls it "Guillemot or Sea-Hen," and Pennant and Montagu Foolish Guillemot. Gray says its Gaelic name in the Hebrides is *Eun an t'a Sgadan* or Herring-bird. In Welsh it is Gwilym or Gwylog.

COMMON GULL [No. 430]. It occurs in Willughby as the Common Sea-Mall and in Pennant (1766) as Common Gull. It is said in Scotland that when they appear in the fields, a storm from the south-east generally follows, and when the storm begins to abate they fly back to the shore. A popular rhyme is :—

> Sea-gull, sea-gull, sit on the sand;
> It's never good weather when you're on the land.

COMMON HAWFINCH: The PINE-GROSBEAK. (Fleming.) The HAWFINCH occurs in the same author as Common Grosbeak.

COMMON HERON [No. 260]. From Fr. *Héron*, which is apparently from Gr. ερωδιος. The name occurs as Heron in Turner (who also calls the species *Pella* after Aristotle), also in Willughby as the "common Heron or Heronshaw." Turner relates that it "routs Eagles or Hawks, if they attack it suddenly, by very liquid mutings of the belly, and thereby defends itself." Swainson says it is a belief in the South of Ireland that small eels pass through the intestines of a Heron alive, a belief also found in Pontoppidan's "Norway." Jamieson gives an Angus superstition to the effect that this bird waxes and wanes with the moon, being plump when it is full and so lean at the change that it can scarcely raise itself. In the "Booke of St. Alban's" it is stated that "The Heron, or Hernsew, is a fowl that liveth about waters, and yet she doth so abhor raine and tempests that she seeketh to avoid them by flying on high. She hath her nest in very loftie trees and sheweth as it were a natural hatred against the Gossehawk and other kind of hawks, and so likewise doth the hawk seek her destruction continually." The old saying as to a person not knowing "a hawk from a handsaw" dates back to the days of falconry, and occurs in "Hamlet": the "handsaw," however, is corrupted from "Hernshaw." A country belief is, that when the Heron flies low the air is heavy and thickening into showers.

COMMON HOOPOE: The HOOPOE. (Montagu.)

COMMON KINGFISHER. See KINGFISHER.

Common Kite. See KITE.

Common Lapwing. See LAPWING.

Common Lark. The SKY-LARK. Macgillivray gives it as a provincial name.

Common Linnet. See LINNET.

Common Magpie. See MAGPIE.

Common Nuthatch. See NUTHATCH.

COMMON PARTRIDGE [No. 467]. The name first appears as "Common Partridge" in Willughby (1678). Turner (1544) calls it the "Pertrige," while Merrett (1667) has "Partridge." It appears variously as Partridge or Common Partridge in subsequent authors.

Common Pheasant. See PHEASANT.

Common Pigeon. The STOCK-DOVE. (Pennant.)

COMMON POCHARD [No. 298]. The name occurs as Pochard in Turner and also in Willughby and Ray, the latter authors calling it "Poker or Pochard." Pronounced Pō-chard, the *o* long and the *ch* hard. Akin to Fr. *pocher*, Low Ger. *poken*, to poke. Littre gives *pochard* as Fr. for a drunkard. "Poker" occurs in Willughby. The female is known as "Dunbird."

Common Ptarmigan. See PTARMIGAN.

Common Quail: The QUAIL. (Selby.)

Common Rail: The WATER-RAIL. (Selby.)

Common Redpole: The LESSER REDPOLL.

Common Redshank Tatler. Macgillivray's name for the REDSHANK.

Common Sanderling. The SANDERLING.

COMMON SANDPIPER [No. 387]. The name is found in Pennant (1766) as Sandpiper, and in the later editions as Common Sandpiper. According to Willughby, Sandpiper was originally a Yorkshire local name.

COMMON SCOTER [No. 309]. The name appears in Pennant (1766) as Scoter. Common Scoter seems to appear first in Yarrell (1843). The word Scoter is of doubtful origin. Willughby (1678) calls it "Black Diver."

Common Scraber: The BLACK GUILLEMOT.

Common Sea-Mall, Maw or Mew: The COMMON GULL. The first name occurs in Willughby.

Common Shelldrake: The SHELD-DUCK. (Yarrell.)

Common Shoveler. See SHOVELER.

Common Skua: The GREAT SKUA. (Yarrell.)

COMMON SNIPE [No. 409]. The name occurs in Merrett's list (1667) as "Snipe or Snite," also in the same words in Willughby. Turner does not mention any species of Snipe. Derived from A.Sax. *Snite*, Ice. *snipa*, Dan. *sneppe*, a snipe; properly a "Snapper" from Old Dan. *snabbe*, a bird's bill, which is also the derivation of the English "snap." Inwards says that the "drumming" of the Snipe in the air and the call of the Partridge indicate dry weather and frost at night to the shepherds of Garrow in Scotland.

COMMON STARE: The STARLING.

COMMON STARLING: The STARLING. (Yarrell.)

COMMON SWALLOW: The SWALLOW. (Willughby.)

COMMON SWIFT: The SWIFT. (Selby.)

COMMON TEAL: See TEAL.

COMMON TERN [No. 419]. This is the Sea-Swallow of old authors. Pennant (1766) calls it the "Greater Tern," and in his later editions Common or Greater Tern; and succeeding authors all call it Common Tern. Willughby and Ray call it the Sea-Swallow and state that "In the island of Caldey, adjacent to the southern shore of Wales, they call them *Spurres*: and that little Islet where they build *Spurre* Island. In other places of England they are called *Scrays*, a name, I conceive, framed in imitation of their cry, for they are extraordinarily clamorous. In the northern parts they call them *Terns*, whence Turner calls them in Latin *Sternæ*, because they frequent lakes and great pools of water, which in the north of England are called *Tarns*." In Norweg. *Taerne*; Sw. *Tarna*; Dutch, *Stern*; Dan. *Terne*.

COMMON THICKNEE: The STONE-CURLEW. (Fleming.)

COMMON THRUSH: The SONG-THRUSH. Occurs in Macgillivray.

COMMON TITMOUSE: The GREAT TITMOUSE. (Merrett.)

COMMON TURNSTONE. See TURNSTONE.

COMMON WHITETHROAT. See WHITETHROAT.

COMMON WIGEON. See WIGEON.

COMMON WILD DOVE or PIGEON: The ROCK-DOVE. (Willughby.)

COMMON WILD GOOSE: The GREY LAG-GOOSE. (Willughby.)

COMMON WREN. See WREN.

COMMON WRYNECK. See WRYNECK.

CONEY-CHUCK. The WHEATEAR; locally so called on account of its frequenting rabbit burrows, and from its note.

CONTINENTAL COAL-TITMOUSE   See COAL-TITMOUSE.
CONTINENTAL GOLDEN-CRESTED WREN. See GOLDEN-CRESTED WREN.
CONTINENTAL GREAT TITMOUSE   See GREAT TITMOUSE
CONTINENTAL HEDGE-SPARROW. See HEDGE-SPARROW.
CONTINENTAL REDBREAST. See REDBREAST.
CONTINENTAL SONG-THRUSH. See SONG-THRUSH.
COO-DOO : The COMMON EIDER. (Berwickshire and East Lothian.) From its crooning note (Bolam).
COOPER · The WHEATEAR. (South Pembroke.)
COOSCOT or·COOSHOUT · The RING-DOVE (Craven and Teesdale) ; from A.S. *cusccote*, a wild pigeon (see Cushat).
COOT [No 461]. The name occurs as "Cout" in Turner (1544) and as Coot in Merrett (1667). The derivation seems to be from the Welsh name *Cwta-iar*, lit. "short-tailed hen," from its very short tail. Newton observes it is in some parts pronounced "Cute" or "Scute," and thinks it is perhaps cognate with Scout or Scoter. Most of our eighteenth century writers from Pennant to Montagu call it the "Common Coot." Col. Hawker observes that "if a gentleman wishes to have plenty of wild-fowl on his pond, let him preserve the Coots, and keep no tame Swans The reason that all wild-fowl seek the company of the Coots is because these birds are such good sentries to give the alarm by day, when the fowl generally sleep. But the Mute Swans will attack every fresh bird that dares to appear within reach of them—not so with the 'hoopers'—*they* are the peaceful monarchs of the lake." According to Thompson the MOORHEN is called Coot in some parts of Ireland, where "Bald Coot" is then the distinctive appellation of the COOT. Coward and Oldham also give Coot as a Cheshire name for the Moorhen.
COOT-FOOTED TRINGA. Edwards's name for the Phalaropes, the GREY PHALAROPE being termed Great Coot-footed Tringa and the RED-NECKED PHALAROPE being termed Cock Coot-footed Tringa and Red Coot-footed Tringa (female).
COPOG · The HOOPOE ; signifying "crested." (North Wales.)
COPPED WREN : The GOLDEN-CRESTED WREN   (Rutty.)
COPPER FINCH : The CHAFFINCH. (Devon. and Cornwall.) From the colour of the breast in the male.
COPPER HEAD . The TREE-SPARROW. (Cheshire.) From the colour of the cap.

CORBIE or CORBY : The RAVEN. (Scotland, generally, and also the north of England.) Mr. R. Godfrey writes that in Shetland " corbyin' " is applied to the speech of a person who is unable to pronounce the letter *r* aright : he is supposed to resemble the " corby " or Raven in this respect. The name is also applied in Scotland to the CARRION- and HOODED CROWS.

CORBIE CROW or CORBIE CRAW : The CARRION-CROW. (North Country.) The second form is a common Yorkshire name.

CORCAN-COILLE. A Gaelic name for the BULLFINCH.

CORFRAN, COEGFRAN : The JACKDAW. (North Wales.) The former signifies " dwarf crow," and the latter " sham crow."

CORGWALCH. A Welsh name for the MERLIN ; lit. " dwarf hawk," from its small size.

CORHEDYDD : The MEADOW-PIPIT. (North Wales) lit. " dwarf lark."

CORHWYADEN : The TEAL. (North Wales) lit. "dwarf duck."

COR-IAR. A Welsh name for the PARTRIDGE ; lit. " little hen."

CORIAR YR ALBIN. A Welsh name for the PTARMIGAN (Fleming) lit. " little hen of Scotland."

CORMORANT [No. 316]. Derived from the Fr. *cormoran*, Spanish *cuervo marino*=Lat. *corvus marinus*, hence meaning literally " Sea Raven." The name Cormorant occurs in Turner (1544), also in Merrett and Willughby. Later writers such as Pennant, Latham, Lewin and Montagu spelt it " Corvorant." Milton (" Paradise Lost," bk. IV, 247-68) introduces Satan in the form of a cormorant who perches upon the Tree of Life and beholds the beautiful region spread out before him. It does not seem, however, that evil associations have been properly connected with this bird, as they have with the true *Corvinæ*.

In olden times this bird was frequently trained to fish, in fact the " Master of the Cormorants " was one of the officers of the Royal Household. The bird was carried by its keeper hooded, after the fashion of a hawk, to keep it quiet until its services were required. The practice has survived until recent times in Europe, as well as in the East.

CORMOREL. A name for the CORMORANT, according to Hett.

CORN BIRD : The CORN-BUNTING. (Ireland.)

CORN-BUNTING [No. 42]. This species is also commonly known as the Common Bunting—rather a misnomer, as in many localities it is not "common." It is called "Bunting" simply by the older writers from Willughby to Donovan, Montagu (1802) being the first to name it Common Bunting. The word Bunting (Old Eng. "buntyle," Scots "buntlin") is of uncertain origin. Skeat suggests a connexion with *bunten*=to butt; he also cites Scottish *buntin*=short and thick or plump, which Newton, however, thinks likely to have been derived from the bird. Graham ("Birds of Iona and Mull") has suggested Scots *bunt*=gay, lively, or brisk.

CORNCRAKE. An alternative name for the LAND-RAIL. Rutty spells it "Corn-Creek," while it becomes Corn-drake in North Yorkshire, Corn-rake at Hawes, Yorkshire, and Corn-scrack in Aberdeen.

CORN GOOSE: The BEAN-GOOSE. From its partiality to grain.

CORNICYLL, CORNICYLL Y GORS, CORNICYLL Y WAEN, CORN Y WICH, or CORNOR Y GWENNYDD. Welsh names for the LAPWING; Cornicyll=Plover.

CORNICYLL CADWYNOG, CWTYN MODEWYOG: The RINGED PLOVER. (North Wales.) Both names signify "ringed plover."

CORNICYLL LLWYD: The GREY PLOVER. (North Wales.)

CORNISH CHOUGH: The CHOUGH. Occurs in Turner (1544) as "Cornish Choghe," and in Merrett, Willughby and Pennant as "Cornish Chough." The prefix Cornish was formerly necessary on account of the name Chough being also applied not infrequently to the JACKDAW, which is so called by Turner and by Merrett.

CORNISH DAW: The CHOUGH (Montagu and Rutty), also occurs as Cornish Jack.

CORNISH GANNET: The GREAT SKUA. (Willughby.)

CORNISH PHEASANT: The MAGPIE. (Cornwall.)

CORNWALL KAE. The CHOUGH. (Sibbald.)

CORNWILLEN: The LAPWING. (Cornwall.)

CORNY KEEVOR: The MISTLE-THRUSH. So called about Belfast (Thompson).

CORRA RIATHACH. A Gaelic name for the COMMON HERON.

CORS HWYAD. A Welsh name for the MALLARD; lit. "marsh duck."

CORSHWYAD DDU: The COOT. (North Wales) lit. "black marsh-duck."

CORSICAN WOODCHAT SHRIKE [No. 110]. A Mediterranean form, recorded once for the British Isles.

CORVORANT: The CORMORANT. Appears to have first been so spelled by Pennant (1766), the succeeding writers up to Montagu adopting the same spelling.

COTTON HEAP: The CORMORANT and SHAG. (Hett.)

COUES'S REDPOLL [No. 25]. A Circumpolar ally of HORNEMANN'S REDPOLL, named in honour of Dr. Coues, the well-known American ornithologist.

COULTERNEB: The PUFFIN. (Northumberland). Willughby records it as so called at the Farn Islands It is so termed from the likeness of its bill (or "neb") to the coulter of a plough. Bolam says in Northumberland it is also applied to the RAZORBILL.

COURLAND SNIPE: The SPOTTED REDSHANK.

COUSHOT and COWSCOT: The RING-DOVE. See Cushat.

COVIE or COVEY DUCK: The SCAUP-DUCK. (Northumberland.)

COW-BIRD, COW KLOOT, or COW KLIT: The YELLOW WAGTAIL. From its habit of frequenting grazing-meadows for insects.

COWBOY: The RING-OUZEL. (Tipperary.)

COWE'EN ELDERS: The CORMORANT. (Kirkcudbright.) Swainson says the name is derived from Colvend, a coast parish in that county.

COWPRISE. A North Country name for the RING-DOVE.

CRAA MAA: The KITTIWAKE GULL. (Shetlands.)

CRACKER: The PINTAIL. (Willughby.) Cracker or Craker is also a North Country name for the LAND-RAIL.

CRACKIL: The WREN. (North Devon.) Swainson says it is from its cry.

CRAFF: The HOUSE-SPARROW. (Cumberland.)

CRAG OUZEL: The RING-OUZEL. (Craven.) From its haunts.

CRAIGAG: The SHELD-DUCK. (Iona and Mull.) From Gael. *craig* and *geadh*=rock-goose.

CRAIG DOO: The STOCK-DOVE. (Northumberland.) From its sometimes nesting in crags.

CRAIGIE-EASLIN: The RING-OUZEL. (Scotland.)

CRAIGIE HERON: The COMMON HERON. (Scotland.) Swainson says it is from *craig*=throat.

CRAKE: The LAND-RAIL generally; also a North Country name for the CARRION-CROW. From its hoarse cry.

CRAKE GALLINULE : The LAND-RAIL. (So called by writers from Pennant to Montagu.)

CRAKLE : The MISTLE-THRUSH. (Provincial.)

CRANE [No. 453]. Derived from Dutch, *Kraan*; Old German, *Kraen*. The name occurs in Turner (1544), in Barlow (1655), and in Merrett (1667). Willughby and most of our eighteenth century authors call it the "Common Crane." Now chiefly known as a straggler on migration in the Orkneys and Shetlands, etc., but very rarely occurring in England. According to Saunders the Crane used to breed until 1590 in the fens of East Anglia, but there is no record of its having done so later. Willughby in 1678 writes: "They come often to us in England, and in the Fen-Countries in Lincolnshire and Cambridgeshire there are great flocks of them, but whether or no they breed in England (as Aldrovandus writes, he was told by a certain Englishman who said he had often seen their young ones) I cannot certainly determine, either of my own knowledge or from the relation of any credible person." Turner (writing in 1544) says: "Cranes, moreover, breed in England in marshy places. I myself have very often seen their pipers (i.e. young) though some people born away from England urge that this is false." Aristotle credits the Crane with weather-wisdom, for he writes: "The Grues furthermore do many things with prudence, for they seek for their convenience distant places, and fly high that they may look out far, and if they have seen clouds or a storm, betake themselves to earth, and take rest upon the ground." According to Inwards, if Cranes appear in autumn early, a severe winter is expected. Hesiod says that the voice of the Crane uttering its annual cry both bring the signal for ploughing and indicates rainy weather. Cicero ("De Nat. Deor.," II, 49) states that Cranes in their long flights on migration assume the form of a triangle, the apex of which keeps off the wind from those birds in the flanks, making their course through the air easier, the leader being now and again replaced by one of the latter birds, which are said to be able to rest in their flight by placing their heads on the backs of those in front of them. Martial also alludes to the supposition that Cranes fly in a V shape ("Ep.," XIII, 75), and he says the ranks are disturbed and the letter broken if you destroy a single bird.

CRANE. The COMMON HERON is often popularly so misnamed. The numerous place-names derived from Crane refer obviously in most cases to the Heron, e.g. Cranbrook

Park on the Roding in Essex, which adjoined a large heronry. Willughby also gives Crane as a name for the SHAG in the north of England.

CRANE SWALLOW or CRAN SWALLOW: The SWIFT. (East Lothian.)

CRANK-BIRD: A Gloucestershire name for the LESSER SPOTTED WOODPECKER. (Montagu.) Probably from its cry resembling the creaking produced by the turning of a windlass (Swainson).

CRANN LACH: The TEAL. (Iona and Mull.) Signifying "tree duck."

CRANN-TACH: The CURLEW. (Iona and Mull.) Signifying "one with a long bill."

CRATTICK: The COMMON EIDER. (East Lothian.)

CRAVAT GOOSE: The *Canada Goose.* Occurs in Macgillivray.

CRAW: The CARRION- and HOODED CROWS. (Scotland generally, also Yorkshire.) Sometimes written "Cra."

CREAM-COLOURED COURSER [No. 353]. The name is found in Montagu as Cream-coloured Plover, Cream-coloured Courser occurring in Fleming, while Selby calls it the Cream-coloured Swiftfoot.

CREAM-COLOURED GULL: The immature GLAUCOUS and ICELAND GULLS. (Yorkshire coast.)

CREAM-COLOURED OWL: The BARN-OWL.

CRECER: The SONG-THRUSH. (North Wales.) It signifies "chatterer."

CRECK. A North Country name for the LAND-RAIL.

CREC Y GARREG, CREC PENDDU'R EITHIN: The STONECHAT. (North Wales.) The first signifies "stonechat" and the second "black-headed gorse-chat."

CREC YR EITHIN: The WHINCHAT. (North Wales) lit. "gorse-chat."

CREEPER: The TREECREEPER. Occurs in Turner as "Creper," and in Willughby as "Creeper." Merrett applies the name to the WALLCREEPER.

CREEPIE: The HEDGE-SPARROW. (Kirkcudbright.)

CREEP TREE: The TREECREEPER. (Norfolk.) Also CREEPY-TREE (Barnsley, Yorks.).

CRESHAWK: The KESTREL. (Cornwall.) Probably a corruption of Cristel-hawk (q.v.).

CRESTED CORMORANT or CRESTED CORVORANT. Applied in different localities to both the SHAG and the CORMORANT, but more applicable to the former.

CRESTED DIVER : The TUFTED DUCK. (Ireland.)

CRESTED GREBE : The GREAT CRESTED GREBE. Albin calls it Crested Diver.

CRESTED HERON : The COMMON HERON. (Provincial.)

CRESTED or GREEN LAPWING : The LAPWING. (Selby).

CRESTED LARK [No. 60]. So named from its very distinct and pointed crest. The name Crested Lark occurs first in Willughby (1678). It was added to the British List by Yarrell in 1845 (" Brit. Birds," Suppl.) The bird was formerly considered to be of medicinal value. Willughby observes that " Dioscorides prescribes this bird to be eaten roasted, Galen in some places of his works roasted, in some places boiled, to assuage Colic pains. Marcellus Virgilius prefers the powder of it, put in an earthen pot, and dried or burnt in an oven, taken in water to the quantity of two or three spoonfuls, before all other medicines for the Colic."

CRESTED PURPLE HERON : The PURPLE HERON. (Selby.)

CRESTED SHAG · The SHAG. (Montagu.)

CRESTED TITMOUSE [No. 94, Scottish Crested Titmouse; No. 95, Northern Crested Titmouse; No 96, Central European Crested Titmouse]. Occurs first under this name in Willughby (1678) Since the time of Macgillivray and Yarrell it has been commonly abbreviated to "Crested Tit "

CREUMHACH. A Gaelic name for the ROOK.

CREW . The MANX SHEARWATER. (Scilly Isles.)

CREYR GLAS . The COMMON HERON. (North Wales) lit. " blue crier." Another name is CRECHYDD (screamer).

CRICKALEEL : The GARGANEY (?). Occurs in Merrett (see Cricket Teal).

CRICKET BIRD : The GRASSHOPPER-WARBLER. (Norfolk.)

CRICKET TEAL · The GARGANEY. From its cry. Hett also gives Crick as a name for the species.

CRISTEL-HAWK · The KESTREL. Derived from Fr. *cristel*= kestrel.

CROCKER : The BRENT GOOSE. Also the BLACK-HEADED GULL.

CROMAN COILLTEACH . The WOODCOCK. (Iona and Mull) lit. " crookbill of the woods."

CROMAN LOCHAIDH. A Gaelic name for the KITE. Croman is used in Iona and Mull, according to Graham, not only for the KITE, but other large hawks.

CROMAN LOIN. A Gaelic name for the COMMON SNIPE.

CROM NAR ANILEAG : The WOODCOCK. (Iona and Mull) lit. "crooked thing of the leaves."

CROOKED BILL : The AVOCET. Montagu gives it as a provincial name.

CROPIEDYDD : The TREECREEPER. (North Wales) lit. "creeper."

CROSSBILL. See COMMON CROSSBILL.

CROTCHET-TAILED PUTTOCK : The KITE. Occurs in Macgillivray. Swainson gives "Crotch tail" as an Essex name for the species. Crotchet-tailed=fork-tailed.

CROUPY CRAW. A North Country name for the RAVEN. (Swainson.) Croupy would be from its harsh cry, and craw=crow.

CROW : The CARRION-CROW is often so termed without the prefix. Pennant (1766) calls the species "Crow" simply. The name is also applied popularly to the ROOK.

CRUCHET: The RING-DOVE. Chiefly North of England or Scotland ; probably a variant of "Cushat."

CRYEL HERON or DWARF HERON. Turner's name for a species of Heron, which I take to be the LITTLE EGRET.

CUACH. A Gaelic name for the CUCKOO. (Iona and Mull.) Imitative of its cry.

CUCKEE : The MANX SHEARWATER.

CUCKOO [No. 214]. The name is onomapoetic, and is such a well received example of a sound-name, that the bird has very few provincial names. This is also the case with its name in most ancient and modern languages, i.e. Gr. *coccys*, Lat. *cuculus*, Fr. *coucou*, Ger. *kuckuck*, Welsh *cwccw* and *Cog*, Gaelic *Cuthag*, Sanskrit *kokila*, etc. In Old and Middle English it occurs as *coccou, cuccu, cukkow, cocow*; later it occurs as Cuckow. Chaucer spells it "Cuckowe"; Turner (1544) has "cukkouu" and "gouke." Merrett (1667) has "Cuckoe or Guckoe." The spelling "Cuckoo" is found in Barlow's plates (1655). A "Cuckoo Song" of the thirteenth century (from the Harleian MS., 978) commencing : —

> Somer is icumen in
> Lhude sing cuccu.

will be found in the "Trans. Philolog. Soc.," 1868-9.

There exist many rhyming allusions to the Cuckoo's time of arrival in country-side lore, as for instance :—

> When the cuckoo comes to the bare thorn,
> Sell your cow and buy your corn :
> But if she sits on a green bough,
> Sell your corn and buy a cow.

Another rendering is :—

> When the cuckoo comes to the bare thorn,
> Sell your cow and buy your corn.
> But when she comes to the full bit,
> Sell your corn and buy your sheep

the inference being that a late spring is bad for cattle and an early spring bad for corn.

Another saying akin to this is recorded in "Notes and Queries" (ser. III, 5, p. 450) —

> Cuckoo oats and woodcock hay
> Make a farmer run away.

the meaning being that if the spring is so backward that oats cannot be sown until the Cuckoo is heard, or the autumn so wet that the aftermath cannot be gathered until the Woodcock comes, the farmer is sure to suffer.

In some parts, April 14th is called "Cuckoo Day," it being thought that the Cuckoo's song is first heard about this day. The date, however, varies in different parts of the country, and according to Dyer it is believed at Tenbury in Worcestershire, that it is never heard till Tenbury Fair-day (April 20th), or after Pershore Fair-day (June 26th). In Wales it is considered unlucky to hear the Cuckoo before the 6th of April, but " you will have prosperity for the whole of the year if you first hear it on the 28th."

There are several variants of the following allusion to the time of the familar cuckoo-song, which is, of course, heard at its best during the breeding-period :—

> In April the cuckoo shows his bill,
> In May he sings all night and day;
> In June he changes his tune;
> In July away will he fly;
> In August go he must.

Another version of this last that I have heard is as follows :—

> In flowery May he singeth all the day
> In leafy June he altereth his tune;
> In hot July away he'll fly;
> In August go he must

Mr. Dyer says that among the Gloucestershire peasants it is :—

> The Cuckoo comes in April,
> Sings a song in May;
> Then in June another tune,
> And then she flies away.

while a Lancashire saying is, "The first cock of hay frights the Cuckoo away"— a reference to the time of it departure. In Northants. April 15th is called "Cuckoo Day." Concerning the note Heywood has :—

> In April the koocoo can sing her song by rote,
> In June of tune she cannot sing a note,
> At first koocoo, koocoo sing still she can do,
> At last kooke, kooke, six kookes to one koo.

The attribution of the song to the female here, must not, of course, be taken literally, as the female does not sing. A Yorkshire custom with children was to sing round a cherry tree :—

> Cuckoo, cherry tree,
> Come down and tell me
> How many years afore I dee.

Each child then shook the tree and the number of cherries falling stood for the years of its life.

The "Cuckoo-penners" of Somerset, who believed they could prolong the summer by caging cuckoos, are alluded to by De Kay ("Bird Gods of Ancient Europe," p. 84).

An Irish superstition is that unmarried persons, on first hearing the cuckoo, should search the ground at their feet, and are certain to find a hair there which will be the same colour as that of the man or woman they will marry. In England in former times this belief varied somewhat, the custom being for a young woman to go into the fields in the early morning to hear the Cuckoo, when, if she pulled off her left shoe she would find in it a hair of the exact colour of her future husband's. This is alluded to by Gay in the Fourth Pastoral of the "Shepherd's Week" :—

> Upon a rising bank I sat adown
> And doffed my shoe, and by my troth I swear
> Therein I spied this yellow frizzled hair.

A more widely-spread custom on first hearing the call is to turn the money in one's pocket, which is supposed to ensure its increase. Evidently akin to this is the belief in the north of England, that it is an unfortunate omen for anyone to have no money in his pocket on first hearing the Cuckoo, great care being usually taken to avoid such an occurrence. Howitt records a Norfolk belief that whatever one is doing on first hearing the Cuckoo, that one will do most frequently during the year. In Scotland it is said to be unlucky, and a sign of coming misfortune, to hear the Cuckoo for the first time before eating a meal. In Hampshire it is considered unlucky to kill a Cuckoo, and this belief also prevails in other localities, as in Connemara, where this bird is, moreover, held in veneration. In Cornwall it is regarded as lucky to hear the Cuckoo first on the right hand and in front, but unlucky from the left. In Shropshire in former times the labourers used on first hearing the Cuckoo to cease work and devote themselves to merry-making and drinking the "Cuckoo Ale."

For some reason not very obvious the Cuckoo is universally believed to be a foolish bird, hence it has long and very generally been the custom to call a foolish person a cuckoo. In Scotland (as also in North Ireland) this becomes "gowk" (q.v.), and the victim of All Fools' Day jokes is invariably termed a gowk. He is usually the bearer on his fool's errand of a missive containing this couplet:—

> This is the first of Aprile,
> Hunt the gowk another mile.

The knowledge of the Cuckoo's singular breeding-economy is as old as Aristotle, who says that it makes no nest and sometimes lays its eggs in the nests of small birds and devours their eggs. He says that some say the young Cuckoo ejects from the nest the other young birds; others that the foster-parent kills her young ones and feeds the young Cuckoo with their flesh; and some again that the old Cuckoo comes and devours them. Cuckold is the name applied from early times down to the present day to the husband of an unfaithful wife. The word is of Scandinavian origin, and occurs in Mid. Eng as *cukeweald*.

An old belief that Cuckoos become SPARROW-HAWKS in winter should be mentioned. It can be traced to Aristotle, who says that the Cuckoo is said by some to be a changed hawk, because the hawk which it resembles disappears when the Cuckoo comes. The late Canon Tristram records that on remonstrating with a man for killing a Cuckoo the defence was that it was "well-known that Sparrow-hawks turned into Cuckoos in summer." Regarding the old belief in the hibernation of migratory birds, Willughby says: "What becomes of the Cuckow in the Winter-time, whether hiding herself in hollow trees, or other holes and caverns, she lies torpid, and at the return of spring revives again, or rather at the approach of winter, being impatient of cold, shifts place and departs into hot countrys, is not as yet to me certainly known." He proceeds to give—second hand—an alleged instance of "some old, dry, rotten Willows" being cast into the stove when a Cuckoo was heard to sing three times, and being taken out, was kept alive two years. The story, however, occurs in Aldrovandus and elsewhere, and Willughby himself appears to be rather less credible on the subject than his editor, Ray.

Cuckoo's Maid : The RED-BACKED SHRIKE. (Hereford.) Because it feeds the young Cuckoo. (Swainson.)

Cuckoo's mate or Cuckoo's messenger : The WRYNECK. (Provincial.) So-called from its arrival generally preceding that of the Cuckoo by a few days. It is also known as Cuckoo's footman or Cuckoo's fool in Gloucestershire and as Cuckoo's leader in Norfolk, while Swainson gives Cuckoo's marrow (i.e. companion) as a name in the Midlands, and Tunstall (1784) called it Cuckoo's Maiden.

Cuckoo's Sandie : The MEADOW-PIPIT. (Northumberland.) The meaning is synonymous with " Gowk's Fool " (q.v.). Swainson also gives Cuckoo's Titling as a Durham name.

Cudberduce : The COMMON EIDER. (Northumberland.) A corruption of St. Cuthbert's Duck.

Cuddan : The RING-DOVE. (North Wales) lit. " cooing bird."

Cuddy : The HEDGE-SPARROW. (Yorkshire.) The TREE-CREEPER. (Northants.) Also the MOORHEN ; probably a corruption of Cutty (q.v.).

Cudgie : The HEDGE-SPARROW. (Notts.) Also probably from Cutty.

Cudon. A Cornish name for the RING-DOVE.

Cudyll coch : The KESTREL. (South Wales.) Signifies " red kestrel."

Cudyll glas : The PEREGRINE FALCON. (North Wales) lit. " blue kestrel."

Cudyll glas bach : The MERLIN. (North Wales) lit. " little blue kestrel."

Cudyll y gwynt : The KESTREL. (North Wales) lit. " windhover."

Culver : The RING-DOVE. (Dorsetshire.) It is an old English name for a pigeon or dove, occurring in Spenser and also in Chaucer as *colver*. Derived from A.Sax. *culfre*, which apparently is only a corruption of Lat. *columba* (Skeat).

Culvert or Culver Duck : The COMMON EIDER. (Northumberland.) A contraction of St. Cuthbert's Duck.

Cumhachag. A Gaelic name for the TAWNY OWL.

CUNEATE-TAILED GULL: The WEDGE-TAILED GULL. (Richardson and Swainson.)

CUR or CURRE. Applied to the diving ducks generally, but more especially to the SCAUP-DUCK. (See also Pied Curre, Grey-backed Curre, etc.)

CURCAG or CUROCHDAG. Gaelic names for the LAPWING.

CURLEW. See COMMON CURLEW.

CURLEW-HELP. An obsolete Lancashire name for the CURLEW (Swainson.)

CURLEW-JACK   The WHIMBREL. An equivalent to Jack-Curlew and Half-Curlew

CURLEW-KNAVE: The WHIMBREL. Occurs in the "Household book" of Lord William of Naworth (Cumberland), 1612-40; lit. small or half curlew, from A Sax. *cnafa, cnapa*= a boy, the application of knave to a rascal or dishonest person being much more recent. An equivalent to Jack-Curlew, Half-Curlew, etc. (q.v.).

CURLEW-KNOT: The WHIMBREL. (Spalding.)

CURLEW-SANDPIPER [No. 374]. Formerly described as the Pigmy Curlew, from its resemblance to a miniature Curlew, the name being apparently first used by Montagu (1802) as a translation of Latham's name *Numenius pigmeus*, based on Gmelin's *Scolopax pygmea*. The name Curlew-Sandpiper is found in Yarrell (1st ed.).

CURLEW-WHELP: The BAR-TAILED GODWIT. (Humber foreshores.)

CURLIEW: The COMMON CURLEW   (Merrett)

CURRE-WIGEON: The TUFTED DUCK. (Somersetshire.)

CURWILLET The SANDERLING. Willughby says it is so called "about Pensance in Cornwall." It is said to be derived from its cry.

CUSHAT The RING-DOVE. Said to be from Lat. *Questus* (see also Quecst), but much more probably from A.Sax. *cusccote*, a wild pigeon. Used in Westmorland, Yorkshire, Cheshire, Berks., Bucks., also throughout Western Scotland (Gray). It occurs in Turner (1544) as "Coushot," and as "Cowshot" in Ray (1691), while Coward and Oldham give both Cowshat and Cushat for Cheshire, and Nelson and Clarke give Cooshat, Cushat, Cushard, Cowscot, Cooshout for Yorkshire. Swainson thinks it is derived from its cooing note, and he gives Cushat as a Northamptonshire name for the STOCK-DOVE.

CUSHIE DOO: The RING-DOVE. (Scottish Borders) lit. Cushat Dove.

CUSTEEN-FAY-CLOUGH. (Properly coistin faoi cloich.) A Kerry name for the WHEATEAR, signifying "the cunning little old man under the stone" (Thompson).

CUTBILL. A North Country name for the GREEN WOODPECKER.

CUTE. A name for the COOT. (Macgillivray.)

CUTHAG. The Gaelic name for the CUCKOO; imitative of its note.

CUTHBERT DUCK: The COMMON EIDER. Occurs in Willughby. Properly St. Cuthbert's Duck.

CUT STRAW: The WHITETHROAT. (Cheshire.)

CUT-THROAT: The WHITETHROAT. Bolam thinks it is from the bird's habit of raising its crest and puffing out the feathers on its chin while it sings.

CUTTY, CUT, or CUTTY WREN. Provincial names for the WREN. Cutty is from Welsh *cwta* = " short-tailed, from *cwt* which signifies literally anything short, e.g. as in "cutty," a short clay pipe, originally applied as a distinction from the long "churchwarden" pipe. The name is in use in some parts of the north and south-west of England, and also as "Cutty Wren" in south-west Scotland. Swainson gives Cutteley Wren as a Somersetshire name.

CUTWATER: The GREAT SHEARWATER and the MANX SHEARWATER.

CWTIAR or CWTAIAR. A Welsh name for the COOT; lit. Short or Bob-tailed Hen. Also applied to the WATER-RAIL.

CWTYN LLWYD: The GREAT PLOVER. (North Wales.)

CWTYN YR AUR, CWTYN AUR, or CWTIAD AUR. Welsh names for the GOLDEN PLOVER. Cwtyn ddu ("black plover") is applied to the BLACK-TAILED GODWIT in North Wales.

CYFFYLOG. A Welsh name for the WOODCOCK; lit. "woodcock."

CYFFYLOG Y MOR: The BAR-TAILED GODWIT. (North Wales) lit. "sea woodcock."

CYGNET. The young of a Swan (properly the MUTE SWAN).

CYLIONYDD: The SPOTTED FLYCATCHER. (North Wales) lit. "insect catcher."

CYNFFONWEN: The WHEATEAR. (North Wales.) Signifies "white rump."

DABBER: The LITTLE GREBE. (Berks. and Bucks.)

DABCHICK : The LITTLE GREBE. Occurs in Merrett (1667). Willughby has "Dobchick." The name is also applied to the MOORHEN in Shropshire (Swainson), and in Cheshire (Coward and Oldham).

DAFFINCH : The CHAFFINCH. (North Devon.)

DAKER-HEN : The LAND-RAIL. (Yorkshire, Cheshire.) Occurs in Turner, Merrett and Willughby. It refers, it has been suggested, to the unsteady flight of the bird. Cordeaux says that the word to "Dacker," meaning to stagger or totter, is a well-known word in Lincolnshire. Another suggested derivation is "t'acre-hen "=the acre or land hen.

DALMATIAN REGULUS : The YELLOW-BROWED WARBLER. (Gould.) Also occurs as Dalmatian Wren.

DANISH CROW · The HOODED CROW. From the supposition that they visit us from Denmark.

DARBY : The HEDGE-SPARROW (Provincial.)

DARCOCK The WATER-RAIL. (Provincial.) Perhaps "dark cock" from its sombre colour.

DARK-FOOTED PETTYCHAPS · The CHIFFCHAFF.

DARR : The COMMON TERN. (Norfolk.)

DARTFORD WARBLER [No. 151]. Takes its name from the locality where the first examples were obtained in 1773 (Bexley Heath, near Dartford); described by Pennant in 1776 The name is found in Pennant, Montagu and other old authors, but Macgillivray in 1839 attempted to substitute "Provence Furzeling."

DAUP, DAUP CROW, or DAUPEE The CARRION-CROW. (Yorkshire)

DAW : The JACKDAW. The name under which it appears in Shakespeare. Newton says it is "doubtless from the bird's cry, as seems also to be the nickname 'Jack' commonly prefixed." This latter assumption, however, seems erroneous, the term Jack more probably having reference to its small size (see Jack).

DDREINIOG. A Welsh name for the SISKIN, also spelt "Dreiniog" (q.v.).

DEARGAN-CHOILLE A Gaelic name for the BULLFINCH.

DELOR FRAITH. A Welsh name for the GREAT SPOTTED WOODPECKER; lit. "spotted pecker."

DELOR FRAITH LEIAF. A Welsh name for the LESSER SPOTTED WOODPECKER; lit. "lesser spotted pecker."

DELOR Y CNAU · The NUTHATCH (North Wales.) Signifies nut-pecker."

DELOR Y DREW. A Welsh name for the GREEN WOOD-PECKER; lit. "oak pecker" (?).

Demoiselle Crane. This beautiful species cannot properly be included as a British bird. The name Demoiselle (a young lady) is borrowed from the French, by whom it is also applied to several other birds

DENMARK CROW   The HOODED CROW. (Humber district.)

DERYN COCH Y FFLAM · The REDSTART. (North Wales) lit. "red fire-bird."

DERYN DU'R LLAN   The SWIFT. (North Wales) lit. "black bird of the church."

DESERT-WHEATEAR [No 168, Western Desert Wheatear, No. 169, Eastern Desert Wheatear] The Western form of this species is confined to the African Sahara, while the eastern form is Asiatic, hence the necessity for distinguishing the two races.

DEVIL · The SWIFT   (Berks)

DEVIL-BIRD, DEVIL-SCREAMER, DEVIL-SHRIEKER, DEVIL SQUEAKER, DEVIL-SCREW. Yorkshire names for the SWIFT. Devil-Screamer is also a Hampshire name for the species, and Devil-screecher a Devonshire name.

DEVILING   The SWIFT. (Bewick) It is in use as a provincial name in Nottinghamshire, Lancashire Westmorland and East Anglia   Devilin' or Dicky Devlin' are also north and west Yorkshire names.

DEVIL'S BIRD   The PIED WAGTAIL (Ireland), also the YELLOW BUNTING (Scotland). because, says Macgillivray, its song is interpreted as signifying, "Deil, deil, deil take ye." that is, the cruel nesters   Devil-bird and Devil's-Bitch are also among the Yorkshire names of the SWIFT.

DEVIL SWALLOW   The SWIFT   (Provincial.)

DICK DUNNOCK or DICKY DUNNOCK   The HEDGE-SPARROW. (Provincial) See Dunnock.

DICKIE-DI-DEE   The COMMON SANDPIPER   (Lancashire.)

DICKY PUG   The WREN   (Cheshire)

DIDAPPER or DIEDAPPER · The LITTLE GREBE (Dorsetshire, Hampshire, Yorkshire, Norfolk) A corruption of Divedapper   Nares says it signifies "Little Diver."   Occurs as Didapper in Willughby and Ray.

DIKE SMOULER   The HEDGE-SPARROW. Occurs in Turner, who says it signifies a bird that hides itself in hedges.

DINBOETH (Y) ·   The REDSTART   (North Wales) lit "hot-rump."

DINNICK : The WRYNECK. (Devonshire.) Swainson says the name is given it on account of its brown plumage.

DIP EARS : The LITTLE TERN. (Norfolk.)

DIPPER [No. 192, Black-bellied Dipper ; No. 193, British Dipper ; No. 194, Irish Dipper]. The name is first given by Tunstall in 1771 as Water Ouzel or Dipper. It is given as a provincial name by Bewick (1804) under the heading of "Water Ouzel," and he observes that it may be seen perched on the top of a stone in the midst of the torrent, in a continual dipping motion or short curtsey, often repeated ; and the name is therefore probably not (as is commonly supposed) derived from its habit of entering the water in search of its food. I find no earlier use than Tunstall's of this name, and therefore the derivation sometimes given from A.Sax. *dippan* or *dyppan* to dip or dive, is inaccurate. Selby calls it the "European Dipper," and Fleming the "Dipper," from which time on the name superseded the older one of Water Ouzel. The species is correctly described under the heading of *Alcedo* by Turner (1544), who calls it the "Water craw," and thinks it akin to the KINGFISHER. His "Cinclus" however, does not refer to the DIPPER. Evans thought it to be the COMMON SANDPIPER, but the description does not correspond at all with the latter species. Willughby calls the present bird "Water Crake," but most subsequent authors call it the "Water Ouzel." Swainson gives Dipper as a Shropshire name for the KINGFISHER. The Black-bellied Dipper is the Scandinavian and North European form, which sometimes visits our eastern counties in winter. Dr. Hartert has lately separated the Irish race from the race resident in Great Britain ; and it must now be called Irish Dipper.

DIPPER or DIPPER DUCK : The LITTLE GREBE. (Yorkshire.) The name is also applied to this species by Willughby and by Montagu.

DIPPURL : The COMMON TERN. (Norfolk.)

DIRSH : The SONG-THRUSH. (Somerset.)

DIRTY ALLEN, DIRTY AULIN, or DIRT BIRD : The ARCTIC SKUA. (East Scotland.)

DISHWASHER, PEGGY DISHWASHER, MOLLY WASHDISH, POLLY WASHDISH, NANNY WASHTAIL, MOLL WASHER, WASHERWOMAN, DISHLICK. English provincial names for the PIED WAGTAIL ; from the bird's habit of frequenting the water's edge and holding its tail above the water to prevent wetting it.

Ditch Blackie   The RING-OUZEL   (East Lothian.)
Ditch Lark   The MEADOW-PIPIT.   (Skipton, Yorkshire.)
Dive-Dapper · The GREAT CRESTED GREBE (Merrett);
also the LITTLE GREBE (see " Didapper "), said to be in use in Lincolnshire. The name occurs in Shakespeare (" Venus and Adonis "), but it is doubtful for which species:
> Like a dive-dapper peering through a wave,
> Who, being looked on, ducks as quickly in

Swainson gives Dive an' dop and Divy Duck as Norfolk names for the LITTLE GREBE.

Diver · The COMMON POCHARD and the GOLDENEYE. (Roxburgh.)
Diving Duck   The GOLDENEYE.   (Shetland Isles.)
Diving Pigeon : The BLACK GUILLEMOT   (Farn Isles.)
Dob, Doup, Doupe, Dowp, or Dowk   The CARRION-CROW. (Yorkshire, Westmorland.)
Dobchick   The LITTLE GREBE   (Provincial.) It occurs in Willughby, and is an equivalent of Dabchick. Dobber is said to be a casual form of the name in Yorkshire.
Dog-tail · The LONG-TAILED TITMOUSE   (Cheshire.)
Dollpopper   A provincial name for the MOORHEN, according to Hett.
Doney : The HEDGE-SPARROW.   (Lancashire.)
Dorbie   The DUNLIN.   (Banff.)
Dor-hawk or Dorr-hawk   The NIGHTJAR; from its feeding on the mischievous " Dor-beetle." It occurs in Charleton (1668), and is still in use in Cornwall and East Suffolk apparently. Hett also gives Dog-hawk, perhaps a misspelling.
Dot Plover · The DOTTEREL.   (Norfolk.)
DOTTEREL [No. 356]. According to Newton, the word is a diminutive of dolt. The name appears as Doterell in Caius (or Kay), who also calls it *morinellus*, its present specific name. Drayton (1613) has " Dotterell." It occurs in Merrett's list (1667) as Dotterel; Willughby has " Dottrel," as have also most of the later writers up to Montagu (1802). Kay remarks that it is a very foolish bird, and is taken in the night time, by the light of a candle, by imitating the gestures of the fowler, for if he stretches out an arm the bird also stretches out a wing, if he a foot the bird likewise a foot ; in brief, whatever the fowler does, the bird does the same, and so being intent upon the man's gestures it is deceived, and covered with the net spread for it. The

same actions are earlier described by Drayton ("Polyolbion," 1613). Kay also accounts for its name by saying that we call a foolish, dull person a Doterell, and "on this account our people also call it Doterell, as if they were to say doating with folly." The Gaelic name for the bird, *An tamadan mointich*, also signifies "the fool of the peat bog," or moor. Willughby relates that in Norfolk the bird was caught by several persons carrying stones in each hand, which they struck against one another and so drove the birds into the net. A Scottish saying is —

> When dotterel do fast appear,
> It shows that frost is very near,
> But when the dotterel do go,
> Then you may look for heavy snow.

DOUBLE SCOTER. The VELVET SCOTER. (Bewick.)

DOUBLE SNIPE. The GREAT SNIPE. So called from its being of superior size to the COMMON SNIPE.

DOUCKER SCOTER: The VELVET SCOTER. (Hett.)

DOUK: The DIPPER. (Settle; Yorkshire.)

DOUKER or DOUCKER. The LITTLE GREBE. (Cheshire.) Willughby calls it the "small Doucker." while Turner gives Douker as a general name for the Grebes. The word signifies literally "ducker" and is cognate with Dutch *duycker*. It is a local name for the TUFTED DUCK and COMMON POCHARD, and according to Hawker Doucker is a gunner's name for the immature GOLDENEYE in Scotland.

DOVE. A general term for the species of wild pigeons; in Scotland it becomes "Doo."

DOVE-COLOURED FALCON. The HEN-HARRIER. (Bewick.) Dove-Hawk is also an old local name for the species, and probably refers to its blue-grey colour.

DOVEKEE or DOVEKY (also written Dovekie). The whalers' name for the BLACK GUILLEMOT; but sometimes misapplied to the LITTLE AUK.

DOVVER: The TUFTED DUCK. (East Coast.)

DOW FULFAR (Dove Fieldfare). The FIELDFARE.

Downy Woodpecker. An American species said—but on insufficient evidence—to have been obtained in England.

DRAIN SWALLOW: The GREEN SANDPIPER. (Spurn, Yorkshire.)

DRAKE HEN or DRAKER HEN. Yorkshire names for the LAND-RAIL.

DRAW-WATER. A name given to the GOLDFINCH, which in captivity learns the trick of pulling a small bucket or cup of water from a reservoir placed below its cage.

DREINIOG. The SISKIN. (North Wales) lit. "urchin," perhaps from its small size. Also spelt Ddreiniog.

DREOLLAN, DREATHAN. Gaelic names for the WREN, the former signifying a silly person or fool.

DREYDWEN, or DRUDWEN. Welsh names for the STARLING; signifying the same.

DRINGEDYDD BACH or DRINGWR BACH The TREECREEPER. (North Wales) lit "little climber"

DRINK-A-PENNY The LITTLE GREBE. (Lough Strangford.)

DRUID, or TRUID (pron. trootch). A Gaelic name for the STARLING; the word means to close or shut up (perhaps in reference to the bill)

DRUMSTICK. The CHAFFINCH. (Frodsham, Cheshire—Holland's "Glossary.")

DRYDWY (Y) The STARLING. (North Wales) lit. "the chatterer."

DRYW or DRYW BACH. Welsh names for the WREN; the former signifies "Wren" and the latter "little Wren."

DRYW BACH Y COED. The GOLDEN-CRESTED WREN. (North Wales) lit. "little wood wren."

DRYW BACH Y DDAEAR: The WILLOW-WARBLER. (North Wales) lit. "little ground wren."

DRYW BEN AUR The GOLDEN-CRESTED WREN. (North Wales) lit "golden-headed wren."

DRYW BEN FELEN· The GOLDEN-CRESTED WREN (North Wales) lit. "yellow-headed wren"

DRYW FELEN The CHIFFCHAFF, the WILLOW-WARBLER and the WOOD-WARBLER. (North Wales) lit. "yellow wren."

DRYW'R COED The WOOD-WARBLER. (North Wales) lit. "wood wren."

DRYW'R DDAEAR The WOOD-WARBLER. (North Wales) lit. "ground wren."

DRY'WR DRYSNI: The WHITETHROAT. (North Wales) lit. "thicket wren."

DRYW'R HELYG· The WILLOW-WARBLER. (North Wales) lit "willow wren."

DRYW'R HESG· The SEDGE-WARBLER. (North Wales) lit. "sedge wren."

DRYW WEN: The WHITETHROAT and the GARDEN WARBLER. (North Wales) lit. "white wren."

DUBH CHRAIGE. A Gaelic name for the RING-OUZEL.

DUCKER. A provincial name for the DIPPER, according to Macgillivray (see also "Douker").

DUCK HAWK: The NORTH AMERICAN PEREGRINE is usually so called; also applied to the PEREGRINE FALCON (Montagu) and the MARSH-HARRIER (Bewick).

DULWILLY. A local name for the RINGED PLOVER. Skeat says it signifies dull of will or stupid.

DUN: The KNOT. (Cheshire.) See also DUNNE.

DUNBIRD. A general name formerly applied by decoy-men and gunners to the smaller species of ducks, especially the COMMON POCHARD. Montagu gives it as a provincial name for this bird, while Bolam also gives it as a Northumberland name, and Nelson and Clarke as a Yorkshire name for the same species. Nelson and Clarke also mention DUNPOCKER (Dun poker, or Dun Pochard) as a name on the river Hull.

DUN-CROW: The HOODED CROW. Montagu gives it as a provincial name, and Swainson says it is a Craven name for the species.

DUN CURRE: The COMMON POCHARD. (Provincial.)

DUN DIVER· The immature or female GOOSANDER and RED-BREASTED MERGANSER. (Yorkshire.) Occurs in Willughby for the former.

DUNG-BIRD: The HOOPOE. (Charleton.)

DUNG-HUNTER. The immature GREAT BLACK-BACKED GULL. (Pennant) Dung-bird is also applied to the ARCTIC SKUA (Bewick). Pennant says the former pursues the lesser Gulls until they void their excrement from fear, which it catches up and swallows. What really happens is that the pursued disgorge the fish they have recently swallowed.

DUNLIN [No. 373]. So called from the colour of its plumage, from A.Sax. *dunn*—dark or obscure, lit. a little "dun" bird, *lin* (=*ling*) being a diminutive. Mr. Harting has argued that this name should be spelled "Dunling" (see "Field," Jan. 12th, 1884, and "Brit. Birds," Jan., 1912). He quotes the name as occurring in the "Durham Household Book" containing the accounts of the Monastery of Durham A.D. 1530-34, as "Dunling," but the change, even though countenanced by Prof. Newton, seems unnecessary, as if strict rules or precedents were to be followed in the spelling of popular names of birds, an enormous number of changes would be entailed, usage rather than precedent being the rule at present. The name Dunlin appears originally to have been the name for the species in the North of England. Willughby speaks of the "North Country Dunlin of Mr. Johnson," while his "Stint, Sea-Lark or Purre" is also the Dunlin. In eighteenth century authors the name Dunlin was generally applied to the bird in summer-plumage, while in winter-dress it was called "Purre."

DUNLIN SNIPE: The GREAT SNIPE.

DUNNE. A name for the KNOT in winter-plumage about Belfast Lough.

DUNNOCK. A widely-used provincial name for the HEDGE-SPARROW. Thought to be a corruption of "dunn-cock," i.e. a cock or bird of a dark or obscure colour, from A.Sax. *dunn* dark; but more probably signifying a little *dun* thing or bird, "ock" being a well-known diminutive.

DUN PICKLE. An obsolete Wilts. name for the MARSH-HARRIER.

DUNTER. A Scots name for the COMMON EIDER. It is in use in Mid-Lothian and the Shetland Isles, and in other parts of Scotland. Sibbald's "Dunter Goose" seems to refer to this species.

DUSKY DUCK: The COMMON EIDER. (Provincial.)

DUSKY and SPOTTED DUCK: The HARLEQUIN-DUCK. (Edwards.)

DUSKY GODWIT: The SPOTTED REDSHANK, also called DUSKY REDSHANK and DUSKY SNIPE.

DUSKY GREBE: The SLAVONIAN GREBE. (Bewick.)

DUSKY LARK: The ROCK-PIPIT. (Pennant.)

DUSKY PETREL: The LITTLE DUSKY SHEARWATER. (Gould.)

DUSKY REDSHANK TATLER: The SPOTTED REDSHANK. (Macgillivray.)

DUSKY SANDPIPER: The SPOTTED REDSHANK. (Selby.)

DUSKY SHEARWATER. See LITTLE DUSKY SHEARWATER. Eyton also applies the name to the GREAT SHEARWATER.

DUSKY THRUSH [No. 160]. A Siberian species first obtained on our shores in 1905. It is the *T. fuscatus* of Pallas, hence its name. Dusky Thrush has also been applied to the young of the STARLING.

DUTCH CROW : The HOODED CROW. (Ackworth, Yorkshire.)
DWARF AUK : The LITTLE AUK. (Flamborough.)
DWARF HERON : The LITTLE EGRET (?). Occurs in Turner. Hett gives the name to the SQUACCO HERON.
DWARF RAIL : The LITTLE CRAKE.
DYKE HOPPER : The WHEATEAR. (Stirling.)
DYKE SPARROW : The HEDGE-SPARROW. (Provincial.)
DYLLUAN FAWR. A Welsh name for the EAGLE-OWL; lit. "great owl."
DYLLUAN FRECH, DYLLUAN FELYNDDU, DYLLUAN FIG, DYLLUAN RUDD, DYLLUAN Y COED. Welsh names for the TAWNY OWL, signifying (1) spotted, (2) yellow-black, (3) hooting, (4) ruddy, and (5) wood-owl.
DYLLUAN GLUSTIOG. A Welsh name for the SHORT-EARED OWL, signifying "eared owl."
DYLLUAN GORNIOG. A Welsh name for the LONG-EARED OWL, signifying "horned owl."
DYLLUAN WEN. A Welsh name for the BARN-OWL, signifying "white owl."
EAGLE FISHER The OSPREY. (Scotland.)
EAGLE-OWL [No. 223]. So called from its pre-eminent size and supposed resemblance to an eagle. The name occurs in Willughby (1678).
EALA. A Gaelic name for the WHOOPER SWAN. (Western Isles.)
EAQUAL, ECALL, ECCLE, or ECLE. The GREEN WOODPECKER (see Stockeekle). The first two are Shropshire names, and the third is an Oxfordshire one
EARED DOBCHICK : The BLACK-NECKED GREBE. (Edwards.) Also occurs as Eared Dabchick.
EARED GREBE. A former name for the BLACK-NECKED GREBE. Occurs in most authors from Pennant onwards to Yarrell.
EARED OWL : The LONG-EARED OWL.
EARL DUCK : The RED-BREASTED MERGANSER. (East Lothian.) In Northumberland it becomes Yearel (Witherby). No doubt corruptions of Harle Duck, the Orkney name.
EARTH TITLING : The MEADOW-PIPIT. (East Lothian.)
EASING SPARROW : The HOUSE-SPARROW. (Shropshire.) From its nesting in the eaves, or easing, of houses (Swainson).

EASING SWALLOW or EAVES SWALLOW   The MARTIN. (Craven.) See Easing Sparrow.

EASTERLING.   A name for the WIGEON.   Rutty ("N.H. Co. Dublin") gives Easterling for the male and Lady fowl for the female, and Latham says they were sold in London under these names.

EASTERN GOLDEN PLOVER   The ASIATIC GOLDEN PLOVER.

EASTERN RUFOUS TURTLE-DOVE [No 349].   An East Asian species, recorded as occurring once near Scarborough.

EASTERN SKY-LARK [No. 63].   A Western Asiatic form of the Sky-lark.

EAST SIBERIAN MEADOW-BUNTING [No. 50].   An Eastern Asiatic species which has once reached our shores.

EAVE SPARROW.   The HOUSE-SPARROW.   (Notts.)

EAVE SWALLOW.   The MARTIN   (Notts)

EBB.   The COMMON BUNTING.   Montagu gives it as a provincial name.

EBB-SLEEPER   The DUNLIN.   (Orkney and Shetland.)

EDDER.   The COMMON EIDER.   (Montagu)

EGLE   Given by Aldrovandus as English name for an EAGLE

EGRET   The LITTLE EGRET.   (Montagu.)

EGRET HERON   The LITTLE EGRET   (Pennant)

Egyptian Goose.   An introduced species, of which examples are not infrequently shot, but without any evidence that they are genuine visitors   It is included by Yarrell (1st ed.) and others of our earlier authors.   Macgillivray calls it Egyptian Fox-Goose

EGYPTIAN NIGHTJAR [No. 203]   This species so-called because Lichtenstein's type-example came from Egypt, ranges from the latter country to Afghanistan.

EGYPTIAN VULTURE [No 255]   The name is first found in Latham ("Syn.," I, p. 13).   It is the Alpine Vulture of Bewick (1832) and other authors.   Egyptian Vulture is derived either from its inhabiting Egypt and other parts of Africa, or else from Egypt being the locality of Linnæus's type.

EIDER-DUCK.   The more general name for the COMMON EIDER

EHEDYDD   The SKY-LARK.   (North Wales) lit. "a flier."

EHEDYDD BACH ·   The MEADOW-PIPIT and the ROCK-PIPIT. (North Wales) lit. "little lark."

EHEDYDD Y COED · The WOOD-LARK and the TREE-PIPIT. (North Wales) lit. "wood lark."

ELCYSEN : The BARNACLE-GOOSE. (North Wales.)

ELERCH. A Cornish name for the wild Swan (the WHOOPER).

ELIGUY · The COMMON GUILLEMOT. (South Pembroke.)

ELK. An east Yorkshire and Northumberland name for the WHOOPER SWAN. Occurs in Willughby, Edwards and other writers. It is cognate with the Icelandic *Alft*.

ELM-TREE GOLDFINCH The GOLDFINCH. ("Rather small size, supposed to have been bred in an elm tree."—HETT.)

ELRCK. A Welsh name for a wild Swan (the WHOOPER).

EMBER GOOSE or IMMER GOOSE : The GREAT NORTHERN DIVER. (Orkney and Shetland.) Swainson gives Ammer or Emmer Goose as Aberdeen and East Lothian names. (See Immer.)

EMMET-HUNTER. This name for the WRYNECK is found in Charleton (1668), and still survives as a provincial name; it is derived from the bird's partiality to ants.

ENGLISH HECKLE : The WRYNECK. (Provincial.)

ENGLISH ORTOLAN . The WHEATEAR. Perhaps from its gastronomical qualities.

ENTERMEWERS. A falconer's term for Hawks of the second year, after they have moulted their immature-plumage.

EOIN RUA. A Gaelic name for the RED GROUSE. (Western Islands) lit. "red bird."

EOS. A Welsh name for the NIGHTINGALE ; lit. "nightingale."

EPICURIAN WARBLER : The PIED FLYCATCHER. (Hett.)

EQUESTRIAN SANDPIPER : The RUFF. (Provincial.)

ER. A Cornish name for an Eagle.

ERN BLEATER . The COMMON SNIPE.

ERNE : The WHITE-TAILED EAGLE. From A.Sax. *Earn*. It appears to have been formerly a falconer's term for the male to distinguish it from the larger female, called Eagle. Occurs in Turner (1544) and Sibbald (1684) ; now chiefly used in the Orkneys and Shetlands, and perhaps other parts of Scotland. Scott has —

Upon her eyrie nods the Erne.—LADY OF THE LAKE

The name was sometimes spelt iron, according to Colonel Thornton.

ERYR CYNFFON WEN, ERYR TINWYN, or MOR ERYR Welsh names for the WHITE-TAILED EAGLE ; the first two names signify "White-tailed Eagle," and the third "Sea-eagle"

ERYR EURAIDD or ERYR MELYN: The GOLDEN EAGLE. (North Wales.) The former signifies "golden eagle" and the latter "yellow eagle."

ERYR Y DWR (water eagle) or ERYR Y MOR (sea eagle). The OSPREY. (North Wales.)

ESKIMO-CURLEW [No. 406] The name occurs in Pennant's "Arctic Zoology" (1792), as Esquimaux Curlew

ESS COCK The DIPPER. (Aberdeen.) Ess is Gaelic for waterfall.

ESS FEANNAG A Gaelic name for the DIPPER; signifying "Crow of the Waterfall" (Bolam)

ETWALL The GREEN WOODPECKER. (Cheshire.)

EUN DU' NA SGADAIN. A Gaelic name for the COMMON GUILLEMOT. (Western Isles) lit the "black herring bird."

EUN-T-SNEACHDAIDB A Gaelic name for the SNOW-BUNTING; lit "snow bird"

EUROPEAN DIPPER. The DIPPER. (Macgillivray.)

EUROPEAN GOATSUCKER. The NIGHTJAR (Montagu.)

EUROPEAN HAWK-OWL [No 219]. So-called in contradistinction from the AMERICAN HAWK-OWL

EUROPEAN NUTHATCH The NUTHATCH (Montagu.)

EUROPEAN SCREECH-OWL. Macgillivray's name for the BARN-OWL

EUROPEAN WHITE-WINGED CROSSBILL: The TWO-BARRED CROSSBILL (Thompson) "Whitewinged Crossbill" is found in Latham

EVE CHURR. The NIGHTJAR. (Provincial) From the vibrating *churr* or jarring note emitted while the bird is stationary.

EVE JAR The NIGHTJAR. (Hants.)

EVENING JAR. The NIGHTJAR. (Cheshire.) Like the last name, this is derived from the jarring note.

EVERSMANN'S WARBLER [No. 126] Of this Arctic species of *Phylloscopus* two examples have been obtained in the Orkneys and Shetlands.

EYASS or EIASSE HAWKS. A falconer's ancient term for nestling-hawks taken from the nest and brought up by hand (a corruption of "Nias," q.v)

FAAKIN HAWK: The PEREGRINE FALCON. (Aberdeen.) A corruption of "Falcon Hawk."

FAIRY BIRD: The LITTLE TERN. (Galway.)

FALCON: The PEREGRINE was formerly simply designated Falcon by falconers. The species occurs in Barlow (1655), as Falcon, and in Merrett as Faulcon. The name is derived from Lat. *Falco*. Newton says the earliest use of this word (*Falco*), which is unknown to classical writers, is said to be by Servius Honoratus (*ca*. 390-480 A.D.) in his notes on "Æneid," lib x, v, 145. It seems to be possibly the Latinised form of the Teutonic *Falk*, though *falx* is commonly accounted its root.

FALCON GENTLE or GENTILE FALCON. The female PEREGRINE FALCON. It occurs in Willughby (1678) and also in Albin. The term Falcon or Falcon Gentle appears from the days of falconry to have always been given to the female bird, the former name from her superior size and excellence, while Gentle is from Fr. *gentil*, signifying neat or handsome, but perhaps also denoting the more noble nature of the bird as compared with the Hawks. Linnæus's *Falco gentilis* was based upon Albin's description, but is without doubt the immature GOSHAWK. In the Isle of Skye and other of the western islands of Scotland, ever since the days of falconry, the larger and stronger female was designated the "Falcon" simply, the male being known here, as elsewhere, as the Tiercel or Tiercel Gentle (q.v.).

FALK or FAIK · The RAZORBILL. (Hebrides.) An equivalent of Auk.

FALLER · The HEN-HARRIER.

FALLOW-CHAT: The WHEATEAR. (Provincial.) On account of its partiality for the clods on fallow land Swainson also gives Fallow-finch and Fallow-lunch as provincial names.

FALLOW-SMICH: The WHEATEAR. (Willughby.) Merrett gives "Fallow-Smiters" as a Warwickshire name for the species.

FAMILIAR CREEPER: The TREECREEPER. (Pennant, 1812.)

FANNER-HAWK. A West Sussex (Arundel) name for the KESTREL. Somewhat synonymous with Windhover (q.v.), the name no doubt arising from the fan-like movement at intervals when hovering. Also occurs as Fan Hawk.

FANTAIL WARBLER: The SEDGE-WARBLER.

FAOILEANN. A Gaelic name for the HERRING-GULL. (Western Isles.)

FASCEDDAR: The ARCTIC SKUA. (Newton.) From Gaelic *fasgadair*, a squeezer.

FAUVETTE. Properly the female of the ORPHEAN WARBLER. Used by Buffon ("Hist Nat.," Ois, vol v, p 117). It has also been applied to other species by various writers, the Fauvette of some of the old English writers being the GARDEN-WARBLER, while the Winter Fauvette of Bewick is the HEDGE-SPARROW, and his Fauvette and Lesser Fauvette the GARDEN-WARBLER.

FEADAG. A Gaelic name for the GOLDEN PLOVER, and also the REDSHANK. (Western Isles) lit. "the little whistler"

FEASER: The ARCTIC SKUA. (Bewick.)

FEATHER-POKE. A common Provincial name for the curious nest (poke pocket) of the LONG-TAILED TITMOUSE, but commonly used for the bird. It is a general Yorkshire name also for the CHIFFCHAFF, while in north and west Yorkshire the WILLOW-WARBLER is called Feather-poke, and in east Yorkshire the LONG-TAILED TIT-MOUSE Feather-bed is an Oxfordshire name for the WILLOW-WARBLER, from its lining its nest with feathers. Swainson says Feather-bird is a Northants. name for the WHITETHROAT, which, however, does not use feathers. Bolam says in Northumberland it is also applied to the CHIFFCHAFF and WILLOW-WARBLER, while Coward and Oldham apply it in Cheshire to the latter species.

FEDOA. Occurs in Turner for a species of Godwit. Newton says the species it was intended for cannot be discovered.

FELDFARE, FELDYFAR, FELDEFARE, FELTYFARE, FELDY, or FELFER. Common provincial names for the FIELDFARE. Occurs in Merrett as "Feldefare," and as "Felde" in Chaucer.

FELL BLACKIE (Fell Blackbird): The RING-OUZEL (Sedbergh, Yorkshire.)

FELT or FELTIE · The FIELDFARE. (Staffordshire, Notts., Northumberland, Berwick, Northants.) In Ireland the MISTLE-THRUSH is called Big Felt, and Thompson says the REDWING is also known as Felt or Small Felt while in Yorkshire the latter species is called Felfer and in South Scotland Feltie is applied to the MISTLE-THRUSH These names are corruptions or abbreviations of "feldefare" (see Fieldfare).

FELTY FLEE'ER or FELTIE FLIER. The MISTLE-THRUSH is so called in south-west Scotland. The FIELDFARE might seem to be intended, but not necessarily, for the term (i.e. "field-flyer") would well fit the MISTLE-THRUSH.

FENDY-FARE: The FIELDFARE. (Northumberland.) Also applied to the MISTLE-THRUSH, with which it is confused in Northumberland.

FEN EAGLE: The WHITE-TAILED EAGLE. (Provincial.)

FEN GOOSE: The GREY LAG-GOOSE. Montagu gives it as a provincial name.

FEN REEDLING: The REED-WARBLER. (Provincial.)

FEN THRUSH: The MISTLE-THRUSH. (Northants.)

FERN OWL· The NIGHTJAR. Found in Willughby (1678): from its frequenting bracken. It is in use locally in Hampshire, Cheshire, Shropshire, and East Lothian.

FERRUGINOUS DUCK [No 299]. The name occurs in Pennant (1776), probably translated from Gmelin's *Anas ferruginea*. It is also the "Red Duck" of the same author's "Arctic Zoology," and the White-eyed Duck of many authors.

FFESANT A Welsh name for the PHEASANT.

FFESONT. A Cornish name for the PHEASANT.

FFIGYSOG. A Welsh name for the GARDEN-WARBLER.

FIACH. An Irish name for the RAVEN.

FIDDLER: The COMMON SANDPIPER. (Hebrides.) Swainson says the name is derived from the manner in which it continually vibrates its body, as if on a pivot.

FIELD DUCK: The LITTLE BUSTARD. (Albin)

FIELDFARE [No. 155]. Newton says the name is derived from A Sax. *Fealo-for* (=Fallow-farer). The name appears in Turner (1544) as "feldfare" and "feldefare," and as late as 1667 in Merrett's list also as "feldefare" Willughby (1678) has "Fieldfare" and Sibbald (1684) "Fieldfare." Various corruptions are prevalent in the provinces, i e. Felfit, Felfer, Felfaw, Fildifire, etc., while in Wiltshire it becomes Velverd. This species usually arrives from its northern breeding-grounds in September. In the north it is considered that an earlier arrival than usual indicates an early and severe winter.

FIELDIE: The FIELDFARE; an abbreviation.

FIELD LARK: The TREE-PIPIT. So called in Pennant and other writers to Montagu, the species of Pipits being confused with the Larks. Fleming also describes the SKYLARK under this name.

FIELD SPARROW: The HEDGE-SPARROW. (Roxburgh.) Sometimes abbreviated to Fieldie.

FIELD TITLING: The TREE-PIPIT. (Fleming.)

FIERY BRANTAIL or FIERY REDTAIL: The REDSTART. (Shropshire.) "Brantail" signifies fiery tail (Dan. *brand*, firebrand or fire), in allusion to its red tail and coverts.

FIG-EATER or FIG-BIRD. Properly the GARDEN-WARBLER, the *Beccafigo* of the Italians (but also sometimes applied to the SPOTTED FLYCATCHER). It occurs in Willughby (1678) and in Pennant (1766).

FIGHTING RUFF: The RUFF. From the pugnacious habits of the male.

FIONNAG or FEANNAG. A Gaelic name for the HOODED CROW; lit. a "skinner" or "flayer."

FIRECREST: The FIRE-CRESTED WREN.

FIRE-CRESTED WREN [No. 104]. This name is first found in Eyton (1836). Occurs in Jenyns (1835) and Yarrell (1st ed.) as Fire-crested Regulus. Also sometimes known as the FIRE-CRESTED or FIRE-CROWNED KINGLET.

FIRE-CROWN: The GOLDEN-CRESTED WREN. (Yorkshire.)

FIRE-EYED CHAT: The DARTFORD WARBLER. (Provincial.)

FIRE-FLIRT: The REDSTART. (Provincial.) Probably from the red upper tail-coverts and tail, and the frequent quick jerks of the latter. A.Sax. *fleard* (=flirt) properly signifies a piece of foolishness or trifling (i.e. coquetry).

FIRETAIL. A common provincial name for the REDSTART; from the colour of the tail and coverts.

FISHER: The KINGFISHER. (West Riding, Yorkshire.)

FISHING HAWK: The OSPREY. (Scotland.) Properly a name for the American Osprey. It is first found in Catesby's Carolina, but is quoted by Pennant ("Brit. Zool.," 1766), and Montagu gives Fishing Hawk and Fishing Eagle as provincial names.

FISHING OSPREY. Macgillivray's name for the OSPREY.

FITHEACH, FIDHEACH, or BIADHTACH. Gaelic names for the RAVEN; the last form is that given by Macgillivray.

FLACKIE: The CHAFFINCH. (Cheshire.)

FLAMBOROUGH HEAD PILOT: The PUFFIN. (Flamborough.)

FLAMINGO [No. 270]. The name *Flamingo* is Portuguese, in Spanish it is *Flamenco*. It occurs in Willughby as "Flammant or Phœnicopter," and he says "the French call it Flambant or Flammant, rather from the flammeous colour of its wings and feet, than because it comes from

Flanders in the winter time to the coasts of Languedoc. For I believe there was scarce ever seen about Flanders a bird of this kind." The ancients reckoned the tongue of this bird among the choicest dainties. The belief that the Flamingo stands against its conically-shaped nest, with its rump covering the eggs, instead of sitting on the nest, appears to date from Dampier's observations of the American species in Curaçao in the latter part of the seventeenth century. It is not until recent times that it has been conclusively settled that they sit with the legs folded under the body in the usual manner.

FLAMMANT: The FLAMINGO (q v.).

FLAPPER. The young of the MALLARD before taking wing, after which they are called Wild Ducks. The term is also applied to the young of other wild species of duck.

FLAT-BILLED SANDPIPER. Macgillivray's name for the BROAD-BILLED SANDPIPER.

FLAT FINCH. The BRAMBLING. (Cheshire.)

FLAX. The WHITETHROAT. (Shropshire.)

FLAX-FINCH: The CHAFFINCH (Tunstall, 1784). " Fleck Linnet" is still in use in South Holderness

FLEINGALL· The KESTREL. (Provincial.) Swainson makes it an equivalent of Windhover (i.e. " Fly in Gale ").

FLESH CROW. The CARRION-CROW. (Yorkshire.) From its fondness for carrion.

FLIRT-TAIL· The REDSTART. (Ackworth, Yorkshire)

FLITTERCHACK. The RING-OUZEL. (Orkneys.)

FLUSHER: The RED-BACKED SHRIKE. (Obsolete) Willughby (1678) records it as a Yorkshire name. Newton thinks it should be " Flesher," a common North Country word for butcher, and it is also sometimes spelt " Flasher "

FLYCATCHER: The SPOTTED FLYCATCHER. (Pennant.)

FOLK: The RAZORBILL. Occurs in Martin's " Voyage to St. Kilda."

FOOLISH DOTTEREL: The DOTTEREL. For explanation of the term "foolish," see under DOTTEREL.

FOOLISH GUILLEMOT: The COMMON GUILLEMOT. (Fleming.) From the indifference to the approach of man when breeding.

FOOLISH SPARROW· The HEDGE-SPARROW. From its so frequently being made the dupe of the CUCKOO.

FOOL'S COAT: The GOLDFINCH. According to Sir Thomas Browne this was an old name of the species, the inference being that its gaudily-coloured plumage suggested a jester's parti-coloured coat.

FOOT-ARSE or FOOT-IN-ARSE   The LITTLE GREBE. (Cheshire.)

FOR HWYAD DDU (Y)   A Welsh name for the COMMON SCOTER; lit "black sea-duck."

FORK-TAILED KITE: The KITE (Merrett.) Also formerly occurred as Forked Kite (Thornton) and Fork-tail (Yorkshire)

FORK-TAILED PETREL   LEACH'S FORK-TAILED PETREL. (Fleming, Yarrell, etc)

FORK-TAILED STORM PETREL. LEACH'S FORK-TAILED PETREL. (Selby.)

FRANK   The COMMON HERON   (Suffolk, Essex, Stirling.) From its cry

FRAO   A Cornish name for the SHORT-EARED OWL

FRECKLED HERON. The AMERICAN BITTERN was first described under this name by Col. Montagu in 1813 in the Supplement to his "Ornithological Dictionary."

FRECKLED SANDPIPER ·   The KNOT (when changing to summer-plumage).

FRENCH BIRD. The FIELDFARE is so called at Wirral, Cheshire, according to Coward and Oldham.

FRENCH GALLEY-BIRD   The LESSER SPOTTED WOOD-PECKER. (Sussex.) "Galley-bird" signifies merry or laughing bird, in allusion to its loud call, being derived from A Sax *gal* =merry. For the significance of "French," see French Magpie

FRENCH HECKLE · The LESSER SPOTTED WOODPECKER. See above, and also "Heckle"

FRENCH HERON   The BITTERN. (Provincial.)

FRENCH LINNET   The LESSER REDPOLL   (Yorkshire) The CHAFFINCH (South Holderness), the BRAMBLING (North Yorkshire)

FRENCH MAGPIE or FRENCH PIE. Names often given to the GREAT SPOTTED WOODPECKER in the southern counties of England, while Garner gives the first form also as a Staffordshire name for this bird and Swainson the second form as a Leicestershire name   It is also locally used for the GREAT GREY SHRIKE, which is referred to in Walton's "Angler" as French Pie · and in each case implies a stranger or foreigner, it being a common practice to designate an uncommon bird by the name of its supposed country of origin. It occurs also sometimes in falconry books for this species. Swainson also applies French Magpie to the RED-BACKED SHRIKE (Sussex) and the LONG-TAILED TITMOUSE.

FRENCH PARTRIDGE: The RED-LEGGED PARTRIDGE. In Nottinghamshire "Frenchman" is a local name for this species, but at Bridlington it is applied to the BLACK TERN.

FRENCH PIEFINCH· The BRAMBLING. (Provincial.)

FRENCH PIGEON. The LAPWING. (Provincial.)

FRENCH SPARROW· The TREE-SPARROW. (Provincial.) Also the SNOW-BUNTING. (North Riding, Yorkshire)

FRENCH WOODPECKER. The GREAT SPOTTED WOODPECKER (Provincial.)

FRENCH YELLOW HAMMER: The CIRL BUNTING. (Devonshire.)

FRESHWATER SANDLARK: The COMMON SANDPIPER. (Ireland.)

FRESHWATER WIGEON· The COMMON POCHARD. (North Ireland) Also the GOLDENEYE (Strangford Lough).

FRIGATE-PETREL [No. 323]. This well-known bird, first described by Latham in 1790, is now ascertained to be a very rare straggler to our shores from the Southern Ocean.

FRONFRAITH· The SONG-THRUSH. (North Wales) lit. "mottle-breast."

FRONFRAITH FAWR. The MISTLE-THRUSH. (North Wales) lit. "great mottle-breast"

FROSTY-BACK WIGEON· The SCAUP-DUCK. (Provincial.)

FUFFIT: The LONG-TAILED TITMOUSE. (East Lothian.)

FULFRAN LEIAF. A Welsh name for the SHAG; lit. "lesser crow."

FULL CURLEW The CURLEW, in contradistinction to the WHIMBREL (or "Half-Curlew"). The COMMON SNIPE is also sometimes termed Full Snipe to distinguish it from the JACK (or Half) SNIPE.

FULMAR PETREL [No. 334]. The name Fulmar is found in Pennant (fo. ed., 1766) and is used by all succeeding authors except Montagu, who spells it Fulmer, the added word Petrel being seldom used, although found in Yarrell (1843) and others The name is said to be derived from the Gaelic *Fulmair*, but Mr. Harvie-Brown ("Zoologist," Oct., 1912) decides that the Gaelic is derived from the English and not the English from the Gaelic. The English name is of uncertain derivation : Swainson thought it akin to *Foumart*, a polecat, meaning a foul martin, from the peculiar and disagreeable odour of the bird, owing to the oil which it emits and the rankness of its food. The oil vomited by this bird when caught, is highly valued by the natives of St. Kilda as a cure for all diseases (Gray) A bit of weather-lore in the same island, as recorded by Inwards, is that if the Fulmar seeks land it is a sign to the inhabitants that the West wind is far off. The species was formerly known as the Mallemucke or Mallemuck (q.v.).

FULVOUS GRIFFON or FULVOUS VULTURE. The GRIFFON-VULTURE. The first name is found in Harvey's "Fauna of Cork"; the second in Willughby and in Latham and others.

FURZE-CHAT · The WHINCAT Found in Rutty and Montagu. Swainson gives FURR-CHUCK as a Norfolk name.

FURZE CHEQUER : The MEADOW-PIPIT. (Provincial)

FURZE CHIRPER or FURZE-CHUCKER The BRAMBLING. (Provincial)

FURZE-CHITTER The STONECHAT. (Cornwall)

FURZE-HACKER The WHINCHAT and the STONECHAT. (Hants)

FURZE KITE An old name for the HEN-HARRIER.

FURZE LINNET The LINNET. (Oxfordshire)

FURZE WREN The DARTFORD WARBLER. (Provincial)

GABBLE-RATCHET A name applied to one or other species of wild geese when flying by night and crying as they fly, although Swainson (quoting Macquoid's "About Yorkshire," p 143) gives the name to the NIGHTJAR. Newton observes that "In many parts of England, but especially in Yorkshire, the cries of some kind of Wild Goose [presumably the BRENT, but according to Yarrell the BEAN-GOOSE] when flying by night, are heard with dismay by those who do not know the cause of them, and are attributed to 'Gabriel's Hounds,' an expression equivalent to 'Gabble ratchet,' a term often used for them, as in this sense *gabble* is said to be a corruption of *Gabriel*, and that, according to some mediæval glossaries, is connected with *gabbara* or *gabares*, a word meaning a corpse [cf. Way, 'Promptorium Parvulorum,' p. 302, *sub voce* Lyche]; while *ratchet* is undoubtedly the same as the Anglo-Saxon *raecc* and Mid. Eng. *racche* or *rache*, a dog that hunts by scent and gives tongue. Hence the expression would originally mean 'corpse-hounds' and possibly has to do with legends such as that of the 'Wild Huntsman.'" Macquoid, as cited above, says that in Nidderdale the country people say that the Nightjars embody the souls of unbaptised infants doomed to wander for ever in the air, and call them "gabble-ratchets," i.e. "corpse hounds." The Cheshire and Shropshire name for the same species, "lich fowl," also signifies "corpse-fowl." Nelson and Clarke ("Birds of Yorkshire"), while repeating the Nidderdale legend, say that in the Thirsk district the bird is called "Gabble-ratch," because it ratches (hoots) on the gables of houses. For an article on the etymology of the name, see "Notes and Queries," series IV, vii, p. 439

GABHAR-ADHEIR A Gaelic name for the COMMON SNIPE. (Western Isles.)

GADDEL: The GADWALL. (Merrett.)

GADWALL [No. 288]. Occurs first in Merrett's list (1667) as "Gaddel," a name which is probably a corruption of Gadwall, inasmuch as Merrett says it is called Gaddel by the bird-dealers. Willughby and Ray call it the "Gadwall or Gray." The latter term is of course an allusion to its dull colour, but the derivation of the former is apparently unknown. Macgillivray calls it Gadwall Teal. The young or female PINTAILS are also called "Gadwall" on the Northumberland coast (Bolam).

GAE. The JAY. (Scotland.)

GAFR Y GORS. The COMMON SNIPE. (North Wales) lit. "goat of the marsh"

GAIR-FOWL. See Gare-fowl.

GALLEY-BIRD or GALLY-BIRD: The GREEN WOODPECKER; lit. merry or laughing bird (see French Galley-bird).

GALLINULE: The MOORHEN.

GALLINULE CRAKE. The LAND-RAIL. Possibly a reversal of Crake Gallinule.

GALRUSH: The RED-THROATED DIVER. (Dublin Bay.)

GAMBET SANDPIPER: The immature REDSHANK. Pennant, Montagu, etc, described it as a separate species.

GAMBO GOOSE The *Egyptian Goose* (Hawker), the *Spur-winged Goose* (Macgillivray).

GAME HAWK: The PEREGRINE FALCON. (Scotland.)

GAN or GANS. A Welsh name for the GANNET, with the same significance.

GANNET [No. 318]. This species is mentioned by Turner (1544) who calls it "Goose of the Bass," and says it nests upon the lofty cliffs of the Bass Isle "and nowhere else in all Britain." The name Gannet occurs first in Merrett (1667), as "Ganet," and in Pennant as "Gannet." Willughby calls it the "Soland Goose, Anser bassanus." It was formally generally called Solan Goose, and in early days was classed with the Geese, hence its present name Gannet, i e. Little Goose. This latter name however is of great antiquity: it is the A Sax *ganot*, the plural "ganotes" occurring in the Anglo-Saxon Chronicle The name is sometimes met with provincially as "Gant." A valuable article on the history of this species, by Cunningham, will be found in the "Ibis" for 1866 (pp. 1-23).

GANSER or GAMBO GOOSE   The *Egyptian Goose*. (Bewick.)
GARAN.   A Cornish name for the CRANE.
GARAN HWYAD.   A Welsh name for the MALLARD.
GARDEN FAUVET or FAUVETTE : The GARDEN-WARBLER. Given in Macgillivray.
GARDENIAN HERON. The immature NIGHT-HERON is described under this name in Pennant's "Arctic Zoology" (II, No. 355), and also in Latham, Montagu, etc. It was the *Ardea gardeni* of Gmelin
GARDEN OUZEL   The BLACKBIRD
GARDEN THRUSH   The BLACKBIRD, also the SONG-THRUSH.
GARDEN-WARBLER [No 145]. This name, which appears in the 1832 edition of Bewick, seems to have been derived from Gmelin's name *Sylvia hortensis*, which, however, had been wrongly applied to this species, being properly the ORPHEAN WARBLER   The Garden-Warbler is the Fauvette of old English authors.
GARDEN WHITETHROAT   The GARDEN-WARBLER.
GARE-FOWL or GAIR-FOWL · The GREAT AUK. This name has been made familiar by its adoption by the late Prof. Newton, who preferred the name to that of GREAT AUK (a name first applied to the species by Pennant). Gare-fowl is almost undoubtedly derived from the Icel. *Geirfugl* Newton however prefers to derive it from the Hebridean or Gaelic name, which is *Gearbhul* or *Gearrbhul*, meaning "the strong stout bird with the spot " Sibbald mentions the species as "the bird called Gare." Martin ("Voyage to St. Kilda") spells it "Gairfowl."
GARGANEY [No. 292]. The name occurs in Willughby (1678) who derives it from Gesner, and also calls it the Summer Teal, which Newton considers the colloquial name for the

species—Garganey, according to him, being a book name. Macgillivray calls it Garganey Teal.

GARROT. The GOLDENEYE. Newton says it is a French name first used by Griffith in 1829, and probably refers to its rapid flight, "one meaning of garrot being a cross-bow bolt."

GARRULOUS ROLLER: The ROLLER. (Montagu.)

GARTON GREYBACK: The HOODED CROW. (Wold district, Yorkshire.)

GAUNT· The GREAT CRESTED GREBE. (Lincolnshire.) From A.Sax. *ganot*, an equivalent of Gannet.

GAVERHALE· The JACK SNIPE. (Devonshire.)

GAWK: The CUCKOO. (Yorkshire.) Also occurs as GOWK in the same county.

GAWKY: The CUCKOO. (Dorsetshire.)

GAWTHRUSH· The MISTLE-THRUSH. (Northants.)

GEADH BLAR. A Gaelic name for the BARNACLE-GOOSE; signifying "white-faced Goose."

GEALAG BHUACHAIR. A Gaelic name for the CORN-BUNTING.

GEALAN LIN. A Gaelic name for the LESSER REDPOLL.

GEALBHAG. A Gaelic name for the HOUSE-SPARROW.

GEARRADH GORT. A Gaelic name for the LAND-RAIL.

GECK: The CUCKOO.

GED: The JACK SNIPE. (Rutty.)

GEGID. A Welsh name for the GREENFINCH.

GELVINAK. A Cornish name for the CURLEW; from its long bill (=gelvin).

GENTIL FALCON or GENTLE FALCON. The female PEREGRINE FALCON (see Falcon Gentle).

GER CROW: The CARRION-CROW. (Craven.)

GIACH or GIACH MYNIAR: The COMMON SNIPE. (North Wales).

GIBRALTAR QUAIL: The *Andalucian Hemipode*. (Latham.)

GID or GIDD: The JACK SNIPE. The former spelling occurs in Willughby; the latter is given by Hett.

GILLEBRIDE. The OYSTERCATCHER. (West coast of Scotland.) Signifies gilly or servant of St. Bride.

GILL-HOOTER or GILL-HOWTER: The BARN-OWL. From A.Sax. *jil*=noctua (Swainson). In Norfolk Gill-howter: in Staffordshire it becomes "Gill-houter," according to Poole, "houter" being an equivalent of "hooter," and in Cheshire "Gil-hooter," according to Coward and Oldham.

GILLIVER WREN. A Lincolnshire local name for the WREN; Hett also gives "Giller Wren," which would be a contraction.

GILLY-HOWLET or GILLIHOWLET: The BARN-OWL. (Scotland.) Gilly is thought to be a diminutive of Gillian, a proper name.

GINGLING CURRE. A west-country name for the immature GOLDENEYE. (Hawker.)

GIRGIRIK. A Cornish name for the PARTRIDGE. Mr. Harting suggests the name is imitative of its note.

GLADDIE: The YELLOW BUNTING. (Devon and Cornwall.) From A.Sax. *gladde*= bright.

GLADE, GLEÄD, GLED, GLEDE: The KITE. The spelling and derivation seem uncertain, but the name in its several forms is an ancient one in this country. Turner (1544) and Merrett (1667) spell it "Glede," while Willughby (1678) has "Glead" as do various later writers. The derivation is probably from A.Sax. *glida*, from *glidan*, to glide and move smoothly, this latter happening, however, to be from the same root as the modern "glade" (i.e. an open—hence sunny—part, or grassy passage, in a wood). Glade is from A.Sax. *glæd*, Icel. *gladhr*, signifying something bright, smooth or shining, and being in fact the derivation also of our modern word "glad." Glede (according to Poole) is a Staffordshire provincialism for a red-hot cinder, and he thinks the red colour of the plumage may be the origin of its use for the kite. Such references as :—

The cruel ire red as any *glede*.—THE KNIGHT'S TALE.

and,

His armor glitteryde as did a *glede*.—CHEVY CHASE.

may, of course, apply to the red Kite, but are equally applicable to the red-hot cinder.

Both "Gled" and "Glead" were lately still in use for this bird in Lincolnshire; the latter also in West Yorkshire and perhaps other districts. "Fork-tailed Glead" is another provincial name, while Gray ("Birds of West Scotland") gives "Salmon-tailed Gled."

GLAISEAN DARACH. A Gaelic name for the GREENFINCH.

GLASIAN. A Gaelic name for the MEADOW-PIPIT and also the ROCK-PIPIT.

GLAS Y DORLAN. A Welsh name for the KINGFISHER; lit. "blue (bird) of the river bank."

GLAUCOUS GULL [No. 435]. The name occurs in the 1832 edition of Bewick, and was adopted by Yarrell in his first edition. It is the Burgomaster of many authors and the Great Grey Gull of Albin. The name Glaucous is from the white frosted appearance of its feathers.

GLEAD or GLED: The KITE (formerly). Also a Border name for the HEN-HARRIER, while Swainson says it is applied in north Scotland to the BUZZARD.

GLEAD HAWK: The KITE. (Cheshire.)

GLEG HAWK: The SPARROW-HAWK. (Renfrew.) "Gleg" signifies quick-eyed.

GLIMMER GOWK: An Owl.

GLOSSY IBIS [No. 259]. Apparently in former times a not uncommon visitor to our islands. The name "Ibis" occurs in Willughby (1678), who speaks of them in the plural as "Ibes." Glossy Ibis seems to occur in most authors, from Pennant to Yarrell.

GNAT, GNAT SNAP, KNAT, or KNET. Names for the KNOT. Gnat is the same as Knot according to Sir Thomas Browne (see Newton, "Dict.," pp. 364-5).

GNAT HAWK: The NIGHTJAR. (Hants.)

GNAT SNAPPER: The BEE-EATER.

GOAT CHAFFER. The NIGHTJAR. (Scotland.)

GOAT OWL: The NIGHTJAR (Montagu). Swainson says it is a Gloucestershire name.

GOATSUCKER. A common provincial name for the NIGHTJAR. The name occurs in Merrett (1667) and in Willughby. Turner (1544) calls it by the Latin equivalent *Caprimulgus*, and says on hearsay evidence that it sucks the milk of the goats, making them go blind, a tale which occurs in Aristotle, who says that "flying to the udders of she-goats, it sucks them and thus gets its name. They say that the udder withers when it has sucked at it, and that the goat goes blind." Needless to say the story has long been refuted.

GOBHA DHUBH NAN ALLT. A Gaelic name for the DIPPER, signifying "blacksmith of the stream" (Bolam).

GOBHA UISGE or GOBHCHAN UISGE. A Gaelic name for the DIPPER: "uisge" signifies water. From its haunts.

GOBHLAN GAINBHICH. A Gaelic name for the SAND-MARTIN.

GOBHLAN-GAOITHE. A Gaelic name for the SWALLOW.

GODWIT, GODWIT SNIPE, GODWIN, GOODWIN, or GODWYN: The BAR-TAILED and BLACK-TAILED GODWITS. The name Godwit is from A.Sax. *god*=good and *wihta*=an animal, lit. "good eating." Godwit occurs in Turner (1544) and in Merrett (1667) who identifies it with the "Attagen" (q.v.) of older authors and says it occurs in Lincolnshire. The name Godwit Snipe is more especially used to denote the BAR-TAILED GODWIT, I believe. Willughby's "Godwit, Yarwhelp, or Yarwip" is the BAR-TAILED GODWIT, and his "second sort of Godwit" the BLACK-TAILED GODWIT. Godwyn is used by Rutty (1772) and Swainson gives Godwin as an Irish name, while Nelson and Clarke give it as a Redcar name for the BAR-TAILED GODWIT. The Godwit Snipe of Pennant is the BAR-TAILED GODWIT and his Red Godwit Snipe the BLACK-TAILED GODWIT.

GOG, GOK Cornish names for the CUCKOO.

GOLDCREST. The GOLDEN-CRESTED WREN.

GOLDEN AMBER, GOLDFINCH. GOLDIE, GOWDIE. Local Cheshire names for the YELLOW BUNTING. From its yellow plumage.

GOLDEN-COLOURED WREN The GOLDEN-CRESTED WREN.

GOLDEN-CRESTED KINGLET, or REGULUS, or WARBLER The GOLDEN-CRESTED WREN. The word Regulus is from Cuvier's generic name (1800), and is used by Yarrell.

GOLDEN-CRESTED WREN [Nos. 102-103, Continental and British Golden-Crested Wrens] Occurs in Willughby (1678) as the "Golden-crowned Wren," while Pennant (1766) calls it Golden-crested Wren, the crown having a conspicuous recumbent crest, yellow in front and rich orange behind, bordered on either side with black. Turner correctly describes this species under the name of *Tyrannus*, but confuses it with the Shrikes and gives "Nyn Murder" as its English name, which belongs to the latter birds Willughby and Ray remark, "What is spoken of the antipathy and feud between this bird and the Eagle we look upon as an old wives' fable." The legend, so I believe, belongs to the WREN (q v.) and not this species. The British form appears to be a resident, or partially so, with us, while the Continental form is a migrant to our coasts.

GOLDEN CUTTY. The GOLDEN-CRESTED WREN. (Hants.)

GOLDEN EAGLE [No 240]. This name is first found in Willughby and is adopted by succeeding authors. It occurs in Merrett's Pinax (1667) as Aquila, "the Eagle," which is also given as the English name for it by Aldrovandus (p 110) who names it *Chrysœtos*. Merrett states that it migrates here from Ireland, where it is abundant. Turner (1544) has "ἀετὸς, aquila, Anglice an egle," but apparently this is the WHITE-TAILED EAGLE The name arises from the golden tinge of the plumage, especially on the head and neck. From time immemorial the Eagle has figured as the embodiment of courage and strength, and has been chosen from the days of ancient Rome as the emblem of all the great empires of Europe. Trevisa (1495) says "the egle is a foule that selde syttyth abrood and selde hath byrdes." That a good deal of truth lay in this statement is shown in the fact that this species does not lay more than two or three eggs. It was an ancient belief that the Eagle could look at the sun without hurt, and it was furthermore believed that the young Eagle which could not look at the sun without blinking was killed by its parents In the aeries were found stones called "Aëtites" or "eagle stones" which the eagles were thought by some to bring down from the sun to help hatch their eggs and by others from volcanoes, and these stones were formerly greatly prized for their virtues, being thought to cure a variety of ills. In the Welsh Mabinogion tales the Eagle occurs, being deemed to be only outclassed in longevity by the Salmon of Llyn Llyw. Giraldus Cambrensis tells us of the Eagle of Eagle Mountain (now called Snowdon) which was prophetic of war, and "perching on a fatal stone every fifth holiday, in order to satiate her hunger with the carcases of the slain, is said to expect war on that same day and to have almost perforated the stone by cleaning and sharpening her beak." In the story of Llen, son of Arianrhod, also, he flies off when wounded in the shape of an Eagle. Several stories are extant of infants having been borne away by this bird to its aerie, and lack nothing of probability. Montagu mentions that in Orkney a law existed to extirpate this species by entitling any person who killed an Eagle to "a hen out of every house in the parish in which it is killed."

GOLDENEYE [No. 302]. The name occurs in Willughby (1678) and is in reference to the rich yellow colour of the iris.

GOLDEN-EYED DIVER: The SCAUP-DUCK. (Provincial.)

GOLDEN-EYED DUCK, GOLDEN-EYED GARROT, or GOLDEN-EYED POKER: The GOLDENEYE. (Provincial.)

GOLDEN GLADDY: The YELLOW BUNTING. See Gladdy.

GOLDEN HEAD: The WIGEON. (East coast of Ireland.) Also occurs as Golden-headed Wigeon.

GOLDEN MAW: The GLAUCOUS GULL.

GOLDEN ORIOLE [No. 15]. The name is first found in the Appendix to Pennant's "Brit. Zool." (vol. 4). Oriole, Fr. Oriol, from Lat. *aureolus*, is in reference to its golden colouring It is the Golden Thrush of Edwards and the "Yellow bird from Bengal" of Albin. This species is mentioned by Turner under the name of Vireo, and he says that the English name for it is "Witwol," a name given by Willughby to the GREAT SPOTTED WOODPECKER.

GOLDEN PLOVER [No. 362]. Formerly known by all the older authors, from Merrett and Willughby to Pennant (fo. ed), as the "Green Plover" (a term now applied to the LAPWING). Golden Plover is found in the later editions of Pennant, in Montagu, and other writers, and was finally put into use by Yarrell. The term "golden" arises from the yellow markings on the upper-parts in spring-plumage.

GOLDEN THRUSH · The GOLDEN ORIOLE. (Edwards) It is also a local name in Cleveland (Yorkshire) for the MISTLE-THRUSH.

GOLDEN WREN : The GOLDEN-CRESTED WREN. (Albin.) Also the WILLOW-WARBLER (Ireland). Coward and Oldham also give Golden Wren as a local name for the SISKIN in Cheshire on the authority of Lord de Tabley.

GOLDFINCH [No. 18, British Goldfinch]. So called from the bright yellow on the wings and general gayness of its plumage Occurs in Turner (1544) as "Gold finche," in Merrett (1667) as "Gold-finch," and in Willughby as "Goldfinch." The resident British form of this species has been separated by Hartert from the Continental form, hence the change of name Swainson gives Goldfinch as a Shropshire name for the YELLOW BUNTING.

GOLD-HEAD The POCHARD (North Ireland)

GOLDIE, GOOLDIE, GOLDSPINK, GOWDSPINK, or GOLD LINNET. North Country (Yorkshire to Scottish Border) names for the GOLDFINCH. Goldspink is also a name for the species in the North of Ireland. The same names are also applied in parts of Yorkshire to the YELLOW BUNTING.

GOLDIE-WING. A Northumbrian name for the BRAMBLING. Sometimes rendered "Yallawing."

GOLD TIP : The SPARROW-HAWK. (Sedbergh, Yorkshire.)

Gold-vented Thrush. Included by Yarrell on the strength of an example shot near Waterford in 1838, but it cannot be considered British. The name is found in Latham.

GOLFAN. A Welsh name for the HOUSE-SPARROW; lit. "sparrow."

GOLFAN TINGOCH: The TWITE. (North Wales) lit. "red rumped sparrow."

GOLFAN-Y-GORS. A Welsh name for the REED-BUNTING; lit. "marsh sparrow."

GOLFAN-Y-MYNYDD. A Welsh name for the TREE-SPARROW; lit. "mountain sparrow."

GOLFAN-YR-EIRA. A Welsh name for the SNOW-BUNTING; lit. "snow sparrow."

GOLVAN or GYLVAN. Cornish names for the HOUSE-SPARROW.

GOLVAN-GE or GYLVAN-GE. Cornish names for the HEDGE-SPARROW.

GOOLER, GOOLY, or GOOL FINCH: The YELLOW BUNTING. A corruption of Goldfinch, from the bright yellow of its plumage.

GOOL FRENCH: The GOLDFINCH. (Devon.) Apparently a corruption of Goldfinch.

GOOSANDER [No. 312]. The name occurs in Merrett (1667) as Gossander, while Willughby (1678), who spells it Goosander, bases the species on the Merganser of Aldrovandus. The female was formerly described as a separate species (*Mergus castor* of Linnæus), and is the "Dun-diver or Sparkling (now Sparling) Fowl" of eighteenth century authors, the male being termed Goosander or Merganser. Newton derives the word from Old Norse *Gas* and *önd*, literally "goose-duck."

GOOSE GULL: The GREAT BLACK-BACKED GULL. (Ireland.)

GOOSE HAWK: The PEREGRINE FALCON. (Provincial.)

GOPPOG or COPOG. A Welsh name for the HOOPOE; lit. "crested."

GOR-COCK, GOR-HEN: The RED GROUSE. (Staffordshire.) Gorcock for this species occurs in Willughby.

GOR CROW: The CARRION-CROW. (Oxfordshire, Yorkshire.) Montagu gives it as a provincial name. The derivation is from A.Sax. *gor*=carrion.

GORMA: The CORMORANT. Swainson thinks it an equivalent of "Gor Mew," i.e. Carrion Gull (but see Gormer).

GORMER: The CORMORANT. (Northumberland.) Bolam thinks it a contraction of Gormorant: a guttural pronunciation.

GORS DUCK or GURS DUCK. A name for the LAND-RAIL. (Huddersfield.) Swainson spells it Gorse Duck.

GORSE-BIRD, GORSE HATCHER, GORSE THATCHER. Provincial names for the LINNET; on account of its frequenting and nesting in the gorse.

GORSECHAT, GORSE HATCH, or GORSE HOPPER: The WHINCHAT. From its partiality to gorse

GOSHAWK [No. 248]. Literally "Goose-hawk," from A Sax. *Gos*=goose and *hafoc*=hawk. The name Goshawk appears in Merrett (1667) and in Willughby. Merrett calls the bird *Accipiter palumbarius* after Aldrovandus (p. 342), who describes and figures this species under the latter name. Turner (1544) also alludes to *Accipiter palumbarius*, ex Pliny, but erroneously identifies it as the SPARROW-HAWK Linnæus described the species under the names of *Falco gentilis* and *F. palumbarius*, and although the latter has been generally accepted, the name *gentilis*, as standing first, must replace it. In falconry the name Goshawk was applied to the female, the male being termed Tercel or Tiercel (q v.) In Ireland the name is also applied to the BUZZARD and the PEREGRINE FALCON, and in the Shetlands to the latter species.

GOSS LINNET or GORSE LINNET. A Yorkshire bird-catcher's name for a supposed variety of the LINNET, those bred in gorse being considered to sing better than those reared in hedges

GOUDSPINK The GOLDFINCH (Scotland.)

GOURDER. The STORM-PETREL (Smith's "Hist. of Kerry.") Swainson gives Gourder or Gourdal as a Kerry name.

GOW (=Gull) The COMMON GULL. (Aberdeen).

GOWDY DUCK· The GOLDENEYE. (Orkney, Shetland, and East Lothian.)

GO-WEST The LONG-TAILED DUCK. (Redcar, Yorkshire.)

GOWK An old name for the CUCKOO, still very generally used in Scotland and also North Ireland. It occurs in Turner (1544) as "gouke." The derivation seems to be from A Sax. *geac*. Newton, however, gives Norse *gjøk*, Swed. *gok*. According to Saxby the name Gowk is applied in the Shetlands to the COMMON SNIPE.

GOWK'S FOOL. A North Country name for the MEADOW-PIPIT, on account of the frequency with which it is victimised by the CUCKOO.

GRAND DUKE and DUCHESS. Macgillivray gives these as names for the male and female EAGLE-OWL.

GRASS-CHAT: The WHINCHAT. (West Yorkshire.)

GRASS-CRAKE: The LAND-RAIL. (Ackworth, Yorkshire.) Grass Quake (Barnsley) is, perhaps, a corruption.

GRASS DRAKE: The LAND-RAIL. (West Yorkshire.) Gress Drake and Dress Drake are corruptions.

GRASSHOPPER CHIRPER. Macgillivray's name for the GRASSHOPPER-WARBLER

GRASSHOPPER LARK: The GRASSHOPPER-WARBLER. (Pennant.)

GRASSHOPPER-WARBLER [No. 133]. Occurs first as the "Grasshopper Lark" in Pennant's "British Zoology" (1766 ed.), as "Grasshopper Lark Warbler" in his later editions, and as the GRASSHOPPER-WARBLER in Latham's "Synopsis," but is first mentioned by Willughby (1678) as the "Titlark that sings like a Grosshopper" (p. 207).

GRASS MUMRUFFIN: The WILLOW-WARBLER. (Worcestershire.)

GRASS QUAIL: The LAND-RAIL. (Cheshire.)

GRASS WHEW. A Yorkshire name for the female WIGEON. Whew is from the note; Grass probably refers to seagrass (*Zostera*) of which they are very fond (Witherby)

GRASS WREN or GRASS WARBLER. (Cleveland, Yorkshire.) Names for both the WILLOW-WARBLER and the CHIFFCHAFF.

GRAY: The GADWALL. (Willughby.)

GREAT ALLAN or BIG ALLAN: The POMATORHINE SKUA. (Yorkshire coast.)

GREAT ASH-COLOURED BUTCHER BIRD: The GREAT GREY SHRIKE. (Pennant.)

GREAT ASH-COLOURED SHRIKE: The GREAT GREY SHRIKE. (Bewick, 1797.)

GREAT AUK [No. 444]. The present name of this species is not of any antiquity. The older name is Penguin, which occurs in Pennant (1766), but the latter calls it Great Auk in the 1776 edition, as do also Latham, Lewin, Walcott, Montagu, etc. Willughby (1678) calls it "the bird called Penguin by our sea-men." Sibbald (1684) mentions it as "the bird called Gare" (see Gare-fowl). This fine species is thought to have been formerly an inhabitant of the north of Scotland and the Scottish Isles, yet whether it was of more than accidental occurrence elsewhere than in St. Kilda is open to grave doubt. Gould thinks it "doubtless existed, and probably bred, up to the year 1830," on the northern islands of Scotland. But that this is largely an error is proved by the evidence of Low, Bullock and other writers acquainted with those islands The last isolated bird believed to have occurred in St. Kilda was killed about 1840 (see Harvie-Brown and Buckley's "Vertebrate Fauna of Outer Hebrides"). Montagu writing in 1802, says that "it is said to breed in the isle of St. Kilda." In earlier times it appears to have been abundant in the North Atlantic islands, yet Willughby mentions that he only saw it in the collection of the Royal Society, and in Tradescant's Cabinet at Lambeth. Its last known resort as a breeding species was on a practically inaccessible island off the coast of Iceland, where it became extirpated in 1844

GREAT-BILLED SCOTER · The SURF-SCOTER.

GREAT BLACK-AND-WHITE DUCK: The COMMON EIDER. (Edwards)

GREAT BLACK-AND-WHITE GULL. The GREAT BLACK-BACKED GULL. (Willughby.)

GREAT BLACK-AND-WHITE WOODPECKER · The GREAT SPOTTED WOODPECKER.

GREAT BLACK-BACKED GULL [No. 434]. So called from the slate-black of the mantle and its large size. Occurs in Willughby (1678) as Great Black-and-White Gull Pennant (1766) has the same, but in the later editions calls it "Black-backed Gull," as do also Lewin, Walcott, and others. The name GREAT BLACK-BACKED GULL occurs in Montagu (1802), and is used by most later writers.

GREAT BLACK CORMORANT: The CORMORANT.

GREAT BLACK DUCK · The VELVET-SCOTER. (Bewick.)

GREAT BLACK-HEADED GULL [No. 429]. A Mediterranean species, so called from its large size and black head.

GREAT BLACK-HEADED TOMTIT · The GREAT TITMOUSE. (Provincial.)

Great Black Woodpecker. This fine species was added to the British List by Latham, Lewin, Montagu, Donovan and others, on the strength of the statement of Latham that he had been informed that it was sometimes met with in the south, and in particular Devonshire. The name is found in Albin (II, pl. 27), on the plate, the text-name being Black Woodpecker.

GREAT BLUE HAWK: The PEREGRINE FALCON (Northwest Fells, Yorkshire.)

GREAT BUSTARD [No. 450]. Occurs in Turner (1544) as Bustard or Bistard, and in Merrett (1667) as Bistarda or Bustard; he says it is found on Newmarket Heath and Salisbury Plain. Newton says it is a corruption from the Lat. *avis tarda*. Gesner calls it "Otis vel Bistarda." Willughby (1678) has "Bustard—Otis seu tarda avis." Hector Boethius (1526) has "Gustardes," and Sibbald also gives the popular name as "Gustard." Pennant calls it merely "Bustard" in his folio edition (1766), but in the later editions as well as by later British writers it is called Great Bustard. In Montagu's day (1802) this noble bird was still to be found on the Wiltshire plains "where they are become very scarce within these few years" He states that the eggs were sought after for the purpose of hatching under hens. "Half a guinea is no unusual price for an egg, and ten to twelve guineas a pair for young birds."

GREAT BUTCHER BIRD. The GREAT GREY SHRIKE.

GREAT CINEREOUS SHRIKE: The GREAT GREY SHRIKE. (Pennant.)

GREAT COOT-FOOTED TRINGA· The GREY PHALAROPE. (Edwards.)

GREAT CORBIE CROW: The RAVEN. Occurs in Bewick (1797).

GREAT CRESTED GREBE [No. 336] From its prominent size and its crest. Grebe is from Fr. *grèbe*. Occurs in Willughby (1678) as "Greater Loon, Greater Crested or Copped or Horned Doucker." Pennant (1766) calls it GREAT CRESTED GREBE.

GREAT CURLEW. The CURLEW. (Macgillivray.) So called in contradistinction from the WHIMBREL or "Half-Curlew."

GREAT DIVER: The GREAT CRESTED GREBE. (Cheshire)

GREAT DUCKER or GREATER DOUCKER: The GREAT NORTHERN DIVER. The former name occurs in Merrett and the latter in Montagu. Great Doucker appears still to be a local name for the species

GREAT EAGLE OWL· The EAGLE-OWL. (Macgillivray.)

GREAT EARED OWL: The EAGLE-OWL. (Pennant, Montagu, Bewick.)

GREAT EGRET: The GREAT WHITE HERON. (Gould.)

GREATER BRAMBLING: The SNOW-BUNTING (Pennant.)

GREATER BUTCHER BIRD· The GREAT GREY SHRIKE. Occurs in Willughby (1678).

GREATER COOT. A supposed larger northern form of the COOT, described as distinct by Willughby, Pennant, Latham, Montagu and others. It is the *Fulica aterrima* of Linnæus.

GREATER CRESTED or COPPED or HORNED DOUCKER: The GREAT CRESTED GREBE. (Willughby.)

GREATER DABCHICK or DOBCHICK: The GREAT CRESTED GREBE. Greater Dobchick occurs in Edwards.

GREATER LOON: The GREAT CRESTED GREBE. (Willughby.) Also a local name in Norfolk and West Ireland. It is applied to the GREAT NORTHERN DIVER by Hett.

GREAT ERNE: The WHITE-TAILED EAGLE. (Bewick.)

GREATER PETTYCHAPS: The GARDEN-WARBLER. Occurs in Montagu. Latham, Lewin and others call it the Pettychaps, and Willughby and Ray's Pettychaps is also probably this species, as well as Bewick's Fauvette or Pettychaps. Newton says the name was not obsolete near Sheffield in 1873, while Latham records its use in Lancashire. Pennant (fo. ed., 1766) under "Pettychaps" unites both the present bird and the Lesser Pettychaps or CHIFFCHAFF, but separated them in later editions.

GREATER PLOVER: The GREENSHANK (Willughby), the STONE-CURLEW (Macgillivray).

GREATER RED-HEADED LINNET. The LINNET. (Willughby.)

GREATER REDPOLE The LINNET. (Montagu.) Also spelt Greater Redpoll.

GREATER SEA-SWALLOW. The COMMON TERN (Albin.)

GREATER SHEARWATER The GREAT SHEARWATER. (Yarrell.)

GREATER TERN: The COMMON TERN. (Pennant.)

GREATER YELLOWSHANK [No. 393]. A North American species.

GREATEST BULLFINCH: The PINE GROSBEAK. (Edwards.)

GREATEST MARTIN or SWIFT. The WHITE-BELLIED SWIFT. (Edwards.)

GREATEST SPECKLED DIVER or LOON: The GREAT NORTHERN DIVER. (Willughby.)

GREAT GALLINULE: The MOORHEN.

GREAT GREY GULL. (Willughby and Albin.) Apparently the immature GLAUCOUS GULL. Willughby and Ray, however, "take it to be the Cornish Wagel," which latter name is a local name for the GREAT BLACK-BACKED GULL.

GREAT GREY SHRIKE [No. 107]. So called because it is both the largest species of the genus and the larger of the Grey Shrikes. The name GREAT GREY SHRIKE seems to occur first in Yarrell (1843). It is the Greater Butcher Bird of Willughby. The name "Shrike" occurs first in Turner (1544) who remarks that he had seen the bird twice only in England, but more frequently in Germany, and that in England he found no one who knew its name except Sir Francis Lovell. Newton considered the name "Shrike" (A Sax. *Scric*="shrieker," der. of Mid. Eng. "*scriken*," to shriek) probably belonged originally to the MISTLE-THRUSH (see *Shrite* and *Shreitch*), but the employment of the name for the Grey Shrike by Turner and also by Merrett (1667) and by nearly all later writers has confirmed it in usage. Turner gives a lengthy and generally accurate account of this bird and notices its habit of impaling its prey on thorns. Willughby remarks that this species was formerly used by falconers to take small birds. Col. Thornton in his list of Falcons and Hawks used in this country includes "two sorts of French Pie." Yarrell observes that its Latin name of *excubitor*, or watchman, was given it "because fowlers in France fasten it close to the living bird which they use as a lure. When the Shrike sees the hawk it utters a shrill cry of terror and thus gives notice of its enemy's approach, enabling the fowler to draw the string of the net and enclose the falcon, before the latter has time to carry off the bait."

GREAT GROUSE: The CAPERCAILLIE. (Pennant.)

GREAT HARVEST CURLEW: The CURLEW. (Norfolk.) Swainson says they are so called from their size, and because the birds appear in the marshes about harvest-time.

GREAT HEADED POKER or WIGEON: The COMMON POCHARD. (Provincial.)

GREAT HORNED OWL: The EAGLE-OWL. The name occurs in Willughby (1678) as "Great Horn Owl."

GREAT NORTHERN DIVER [No. 341]. This name first appears in Pennant (1766), Willughby having termed it the Greatest Speckled Diver or Loon. Sibbald calls it "the Goose of our country folk called the Ember Goose, which is said to make its nest under the water and also to hatch out its eggs there."

GREAT OWL: The EAGLE-OWL. Montagu gives it as a provincial name.

GREAT OX-EYE: The GREAT TITMOUSE. Occurs in Merrett's list. Turner has "Great Oxei."
GREAT PEGGY: The WHITETHROAT. (Leicestershire.)
GREAT PIED MOUNTAIN FINCH The SNOW-BUNTING.
GREAT PLOVER: The STONE-CURLEW. (Yarrell.)
GREAT PURL The COMMON TERN. (Norfolk.)
GREAT RED-HEADED WIGEON The COMMON POCHARD. Occurs in Willughby.
GREAT REED-WARBLER [No 135]. The name is found in Gould ("Birds of Europe") as Great Sedge Warbler. Yarrell (1st ed) calls it the Thrush-like Warbler.
GREAT SCART or GREAT SCARVE. The CORMORANT. (Provincial.)
GREAT SEDGE WARBLER. The GREAT REED-WARBLER. (Gould.)
GREAT SHEARWATER [No. 325]. The name is found in Yarrell (1st ed.) as Greater Shearwater. It is the Cinereous Shearwater of Selby and the Dusky Shearwater of Eyton.
GREAT SHRIKE The GREAT GREY SHRIKE.
GREAT SKUA [No. 439]. Often called the Common Skua, but it is nowhere very common, breeding only in small protected colonies in the Shetlands and visiting the other parts of our coasts in winter. It appears to be first mentioned by Willughby and Ray, who term it "our Catarracta" and identify it with the "Cornish Gannet" and also Hoier's Skua of Clusius. They remark that "the Cornish Gannet doth constantly accompany the sholes of Pilchards, still hovering over them in the air. It pursues and strikes at these fish with that violence that they catch it with a strange artifice. They fasten a Pilchard to a board, which they fix a little under water. The Gannet, espying the Pilchard, casts himself down from on high upon it with that vehemence that he strikes his bill clear through the board, and dashes out his brains against it, and so comes to be taken." This habit, however, was obviously fastened erroneously on the present species, as it is a trait of the true GANNET. It is called Brown and Ferruginous Gull by Pennant (1766) in the text, but "Skua" simply on the plate, and the writers succeeding him up to Montagu call it "Skua Gull." The name Skua dates from Hoier the correspondent of Clusius, who sent the latter a species from the Færoe Islands under this name It is probably an attempted imitation of the cry of the bird.

GREAT SNIPE [No. 408]. The name first appears in Pennant (1776).

GREAT SPOTTED CUCKOO [No. 215]. The name is found in Edwards ("Gleanings," pl. 5). It was added to the British List by Yarrell in 1845 (Supp. "Brit. Birds ").

GREAT SPOTTED WOODPECKER [No. 211, British Great Spotted Woodpecker; No. 210, Northern Great Spotted Woodpecker]. The name occurs first as Greater Spotted Woodpecker in Willughby (1678) and is also found in Pennant and succeeding authors. Yarrell and others call it Great Spotted Woodpecker. Hartert has separated the British resident-form from the North European form which visits our east coast in autumn.

GREAT SWALLOW · The SWIFT. (Turner.)

GREAT TERN · The COMMON TERN.

GREAT TIT. See GREAT TITMOUSE.

GREAT TITMOUSE [No. 88, British Great Titmouse; No. 87, Continental Great Titmouse]. The name, which arises from its being the largest of the British species, first occurs in Turner (1544), also in Merrett's list and in Willughby. The British resident-form has been separated from the Continental form, which visits our coasts on migration. The "saw-sharpening" note of this bird is said to foretell rain.

Great Whaup: The CURLEW. (Orkney.)

GREAT WHITE EGRET: The GREAT WHITE HERON.

GREAT WHITE HERON [No. 262]. This is a southern species which has never been more than a very rare straggler, at long intervals, to our islands. The name as Great White Heron first occurs in Willughby (1678).

GREAT WHITE OWL: The SNOWY-OWL. (Edwards.)

GREEDY GLEAD or GLED: The KITE. (Provincial.)

Green-backed Gallinule. Examples, probably escaped from captivity, of this species have been taken in our islands.

GREEN-BILLED GULL. A provincial name for the COMMON GULL.

GREEN BIRD or GREEN CHUB: The GREENFINCH. (Provincial.)

GREEN CORMORANT: The SHAG. (Ireland.) From the dark green of its plumage.

GREENEY: The GREENFINCH. (Cumberland, Forfar.)

GREENFINCH [No. 17]. The name originates in the general green colour of its plumage It occurs in Turner (1544) as "Grene finche," and in Merrett and Willughby as "Greenfinch."

GREEN-FOOTED GALLINULE or WATER-HEN. Macgillivray's name for the MOORHEN.

GREEN GROSBEAK · The GREENFINCH. (Tunstall, Bewick.)

GREEN-HEADED BUNTING: The ORTOLAN BUNTING Occurs under this name in Latham and in Brown's "New Illustrations of Zoology." Montagu thought it a variety of the YELLOWHAMMER.

GREEN-HEADED DIVER The SCAUP-DUCK. (Belfast.) From the rich green gloss on the black feathers of the head.

GREEN-HEADED GOOSANDER: The GOOSANDER. (Fleming)

GREEN-HEADED QUAKETAIL. Macgillivray's name for the YELLOW WAGTAIL (see Blue-headed Quaketail).

Green Heron. A North American species said to have occurred once in Cornwall

GREEN IBIS. The GLOSSY IBIS.

GREENICK, GREEN LENNART. Northumbrian names for the GREENFINCH.

GREENISH WARBLER [No. 124]. An East European species which winters in India, where it was first described by Blyth as long ago as 1843.

GREENLAND DOVE: The BLACK GUILLEMOT. Albin says the name is on account of its laying two eggs.

GREENLAND FALCON [No. 232] The white form of the GYR-FALCON inhabiting Greenland.

GREENLAND REDPOLL [No 22] A close ally of the MEALY REDPOLL, which has its summer-quarters in Greenland.

GREENLAND TURTLE · The BLACK GUILLEMOT.

GREENLAND WHEATEAR See WHEATEAR.

GREEN-LEGGED HORSEMAN· The GREENSHANK. (Albin, Bewick.)

GREEN-LEGGED LONGSHANK The GREENSHANK. (Macgillivray.)

GREEN LINNET: The GREENFINCH. (Provincial.) Greeny is also used in parts of Yorkshire.

GREEN OLF. The GREENFINCH. (Norfolk.) Also met with as Green Ulf.

GREEN PEEK: The GREEN WOODPECKER. (Lincoln.)

GREEN PLOVER: The LAPWING generally at the present day, especially in Ireland. Merrett and Willughby both apply it to the Golden Plover, however, as do also Albin and Pennant (1766) and even Fleming (1828).

GREEN SANDPIPER [No. 390]. The name is found in Pennant (1766), and originates in the olive tint of the upper-plumage.

GREEN SCOUT: The SHAG. (Provincial.)

GREENSHANK [No. 396]. So called from the olivaceous colour of the tarsi and feet. The name is found in Pennant (1766) as "Green Shank." Occurs in Willughby as the Greater Plover (ex Aldrovandus).

GREENSHANK SNIPE · The GREENSHANK. Occurs in Macgillivray.

GREEN SNIPE: The KINGFISHER. (Hett.)

GREEN TATLER. Macgillivray's name for the GREEN SANDPIPER.

GREENWICH SANDPIPER: The RUFF (winter), described by Latham as a separate species from an example killed at Greenwich.

GREEN-WINGED TEAL: The AMERICAN GREEN-WINGED TEAL. Also applied to the COMMON TEAL.

GREEN WOODPECKER [No. 209, British Green Woodpecker]. The name is bestowed on account of the green of the upper-parts. It occurs first in Merrett's list (1667) and also in Willughby. Turner (1544), who is not clear as to the several species of Woodpeckers, calls it the "Huhol" (=Hewhole). The legend of the baker's daughter who was turned into an owl by Jesus for having refused Him bread, has been tacked on to this bird by the poet Montgomery, who makes it say:—

    Thus am I ever labouring for my bread.

In some parts this species is known as the "Rain-bird" or "Rainfowl," it being believed that when their cries are much heard rain will follow.

GREEN WREN: The WOOD-WARBLER. (Albin.) From the green upper-plumage.

GREPIANOG. A Welsh name for the TREECREEPER.

GREVE: The RED-NECKED GREBE. (Redcar, Yorkshire.) A corruption of Grebe.

GREW. A Cornish name for the CRANE.

GREY-AND-WHITE WAGTAIL: The WHITE WAGTAIL. (Macgillivray.)

GREY-AND-YELLOW WAGTAIL· The GREY WAGTAIL. (Macgillivray.)

GREYBACK. The HOODED CROW (Northumberland, Yorkshire), from its grey mantle.

GREY BACKED CROW: The HOODED CROW. (Hants.; Yorkshire.)

GREY-BACKED CURRE The SCAUP-DUCK is so called by gunners in parts of the south and west of England.

GREY-BIRD or GREY The LINNET (North Ireland, Westmorland); the SONG-THRUSH (Sussex, Devonshire, Cornwall); the SEDGE-WARBLER (Arkengarthdale, Yorkshire).

GREY BUZZARD· The HEN-HARRIER. (Hants.)

GREY CHEEPER The MEADOW-PIPIT.

GREY CRANE. Macgillivray's name for the CRANE.

GREY CROW or GREY DUN The HOODED CROW. (Provincial.) Grey Crow is a common name in Yorkshire.

GREY CUCKOO The CUCKOO (Macgillivray.)

GREY DIVER: The RED-BREASTED MERGANSER. (Islay.)

GREY DUCK The MALLARD (Yorkshire coast.) Also the GADWALL.

GREY EAGLE A name for the WHITE-TAILED EAGLE. (Macgillivray.)

GREY FALCON The HEN-HARRIER Pennant (1766) also describes a bird under this name, the description and name of which were copied by subsequent authors to Montagu, but afterwards identified with the PEREGRINE FALCON.

GREY FELT. The FIELDFARE (Notts.)

GREY FLYCATCHER· The SPOTTED FLYCATCHER. (Macgillivray) It is also a provincial name in Yorkshire and elsewhere, on account of its greyish plumage

GREY GLEAD. A Scottish Border name for the HEN-HARRIER.

GREY GODWIT· The BAR-TAILED GODWIT. (Lewin.)

GREY GOOSE. The GREY LAG-GOOSE.

GREY HAWK. A name for the PEREGRINE FALCON. (Macgillivray)

GREY-HEADED DUCK· The KING-EIDER (Edwards); also the female GOLDENEYE (Pennant).

GREY-HEADED WAGTAIL [No. 76]. So called from its grey crown. The name occurs in Gould's "Birds of Europe" (1832). Also called Grey-headed Yellow Wagtail.

GREY-HEN. A North Country name for the female of the BLACK GROUSE.

GREY HERON. Macgillivray's name for the COMMON HERON.

GREY KATE or GREY PATE · The young GOLDFINCH. (North and East Yorkshire.)

GREY LAG-GOOSE [No. 274]. The name appears to have arisen from the fact that this was the grey Goose that lagged behind the other species when they betook themselves to their more northern breeding-quarters. Willughby and Ray call it the "common Wild Goose." The name Grey Lag Goose first appears in Pennant (1777). It is the Grey Goose of some authors, and the "Grey-legged Goose" of Yarrell (1st ed.). In Scotland when Wild Geese are seen flying north before the breeding-season, it is looked upon as a sign of fair, settled weather.

GREY LENNART. A Northumbrian name for the LINNET. (Lennart=Linnet.)

GREY LINNET · The LINNET. A common provincial name; also applied to the TWITE in parts of Yorkshire.

GREY LONG-BEAK. The RED-BREASTED SNIPE. (Macgillivray.)

GREY NIGHT-HERON: The NIGHT-HERON. (Macgillivray.)

GREY OWL: The TAWNY OWL. (Willughby.)

GREY PARTRIDGE: The COMMON PARTRIDGE. (Macgillivray.)

GREY PHALAROPE [No. 398]. The name, which originates in its grey-and-white winter-plumage, occurs first in Pennant (1766) as Scallop-toe Sandpiper, but in later editions as Grey Phalarope. It is the "Great Coot-footed Tringa" of Edwards (pl. 308), upon which is based Brisson's genus Phalaropus, whence the name Phalarope.

GREY PLOVER [No. 365]. The name originates in the grey-and-white of the winter-plumage. Occurs first in Merrett's list (1667). Willughby also terms it the "Grey Plover, called at Venice *Squatarola*." The name has also been applied in Ireland to the GOLDEN PLOVER, and in Scotland to the KNOT.

GREY PTARMIGAN: The PTARMIGAN. (Macgillivray.) The name is only appropriate when in summer-plumage, the upper-parts being then freckled with grey and brown.

GREY REDSTART: The REDSTART. (Edwards.)

GREY SANDPIPER: The GREY PLOVER. (Pennant.)

GREY SHRIKE: Properly the GREAT GREY SHRIKE, but also applied to the LESSER GREY SHRIKE.

GREY SKIT: The WATER-RAIL. (Devonshire.) From its stealthy habit of running ("skit "=to slide).

GREY SNIPE: The RED-BREASTED SANDPIPER. (Gould.)

GREY STARLING. The young STARLING. (East Lothian.) From its greyish-brown plumage.

GREY THRUSH· The FIELDFARE. (Scotland.) Also the MISTLE-THRUSH according to Macgillivray, while the SONG-THRUSH is known in parts of England as Grey-bird or Grey Throstle.

GREY WAGTAIL [No 80]. The name originates in the slate-grey of the upper-parts. It occurs first in Willughby (1678). Pennant calls it Grey Water Wagtail

GREY YOGLE: The SHORT-EARED OWL. (Shetlands.) Yogle=Owl.

GRIFFON-VULTURE [No. 254]. This is the Grype or Gryffon of Aldrovandus, from which the name seems to be derived. It is found in Yarrell's First Supp. (1845) as an English species.

GRIGEAR A Cornish name for the PARTRIDGE; also the female BLACK GROUSE

GRISARD: The GLAUCOUS GULL (Bewick.)

GRISELLED SANDPIPER· The KNOT in winter-plumage.

GROSBEAK The HAWFINCH. (Willughby, Pennant, etc.) It is a frequent name for this bird in Yorkshire.

GROUND FEATHERPOKE: The WILLOW-WARBLER. (Doncaster) See "Featherpoke."

GROUND HUCKMUCK, GROUND ISAAC, GROUND OVEN: The WILLOW-WARBLER. English provincial names, in allusion to the structure and materials of its nest (Isaac is a corruption of "hayjack," q v.)

GROUND LARK. The SKY-LARK, generally; also the CORN-BUNTING (Doncaster), and the MEADOW-PIPIT (Cleveland, Yorkshire).

GROUND WREN· The WILLOW-WARBLER (Cheshire, Yorkshire, Scotland), the CHIFFCHAFF (Yorkshire).

GROUS· The RED GROUSE. (Pennant.) This is the ancient form of spelling.

GROUSE The RED GROUSE is frequently termed Grouse simply.

GROVE PETTYCHAPS The WOOD-WARBLER (Provincial.)

GRUGIAR DDU· The BLACK GROUSE. (North Wales) lit. "black heather hen."

I

GRUNDLING : The RINGED PLOVER. (Lancashire.) Swainson thinks it equivalent to Groundling.

GRYPE or GRYFFON. Aldrovandus gives these as names for the GRIFFON-VULTURE.

GUENOL or GUENBOL. A Cornish name for the COMMON WHITETHROAT.

GUERNSEY NIGHTINGALE · The BLACKCAP.

GUERNSEY PARTRIDGE. The RED-LEGGED PARTRIDGE. (Montagu.)

GUGA. An Irish name for the GANNET.

GUILBINN : The CURLEW. (Western Isles of Scotland.) From Gaelic *guil*, wailing, and *binn*, music.

GUILLEMOT. See COMMON GUILLEMOT.

GUINEA-BIRD DIVER : The RED-THROATED DIVER. (East Riding, Yorkshire.) From its speckled back resembling that of a Guinea-fowl.

GUIRENAN. · A Gaelic name for the BRENT GOOSE.

GULDEN-HEAD : The PUFFIN. Willughby records it as so called in South Wales.

GULER. The YELLOW BUNTING. (Norfolk.) From A.Sax *geolu*=yellow.

GULLALLAN. A Northumbrian name for the Skuas.

GULLAN. Cornish for a Gull.

GULL-BILLED TERN [No. 415]. The name occurs in Montagu (Supp. " Orn. Dict.").

GULL-TEASER : The COMMON TERN. Occurs in Montagu.

GUNNER : The GREAT NORTHERN DIVER.

GURADNAN. A Cornish name for the WREN.

GURFEL : The RAZORBILL. (Provincial.)

GUSTARD : The GREAT BUSTARD. (Sibbald.)

GUTTER COCK : The WATER-RAIL. (Cornwall.) From its frequenting ditches.

GUTTER TEETAN The ROCK-PIPIT. (Orkneys.)

GWALCH. The SPARROW-HAWK. (North Wales) lit. " hawk."

GWALCH Y NOS · The NIGHTJAR. (North Wales) lit. " night hawk."

GWALCH Y PENWEIG. A Welsh name for the RAZORBILL ; lit. " herring hawk."

GWALCH Y WEILGI. A Welsh name for the OSPREY, signifying " sea-hawk."

Gwas y gog, Gwddfro. A Welsh name for the WRYNECK and also the MEADOW-PIPIT. It signifies "Cuckoo's knave," i.e. servant.

Gwas y seiri. A Welsh name for the GOLDFINCH; lit. "sheriff's servant."

Gwddfgam or Gwddfro. Welsh names for the WRYNECK, lit. "wryneck."

Gwddfgwyn   A Welsh name for the WHITETHROAT.

Gwennol, Gwenfol. Welsh names for the SWALLOW; lit. "white belly."

Gwennol y bargod, Gwennol y bondo. Welsh names for the MARTIN. The former signifies "eave swallow," the latter "house swallow."

Gwennol-y-Glennydd. A Welsh name for the SAND-MARTIN, lit. "bankside swallow."

Gwennol-y-môr   The COMMON TERN. (North Wales) lit. "sea-swallow."

Gwich hedydd. A Welsh name for the GRASSHOPPER-WARBLER

Gwilym. The COMMON GUILLEMOT. (North Wales) lit. "William."

Gwilym ddu. The BLACK GUILLEMOT. (North Wales) lit. "Black William."

Gwipa, Gwipai, or Gwepia. Welsh names for the SPARROW-HAWK

Gwyach fach   A Welsh name for the LITTLE GREBE, lit. "little grebe"

Gwyach gorniog. A Welsh name for the GREAT CRESTED GREBE; lit. "horned grebe."

Gwybedog. A Welsh name for the SPOTTED FLYCATCHER; lit. "insect catcher"

Gwybedog brith, or Gwybedog ddu a gwyn. The PIED FLYCATCHER   (North Wales) lit. "pied flycatcher."

Gwydd bonar. The BEAN-GOOSE. (North Wales) lit. "bean-goose."

Gwydd dalcen gwyn. The WHITE-FRONTED GOOSE. (North Wales) lit. "white-forehead goose."

Gwydd droed binc   The PINK-FOOTED GOOSE. (North Wales) lit. "pink-footed goose."

Gwydd wyllt. The GREY LAG-GOOSE   (North Wales) lit. "wild goose."

Gwylan benddu: The BLACK-HEADED GULL. (North Wales) lit. "black-headed gull."

GWYLAN BENWEN: The KITTIWAKE. (North Wales) lit. "white-headed gull."

GWYLAN FRECH: The POMATORHINE SKUA. (North Wales) lit. "spotted gull."

GWYLAN GEFNDDU FAWR: The GREAT BLACK-BACKED GULL. (North Wales) lit. the same.

GWYLAN GEFNDDU LEIAF: The LESSER BLACK-BACKED GULL. (North Wales) lit. the same.

GWYLAN GYFFREDIN: The COMMON GULL. (North Wales) lit. "common gull."

GWYLAN GYNFFON HIR: The ARCTIC SKUA. (North Wales) lit. "long-tailed gull."

GWYLAN MANAW The MANX SHEARWATER. (North Wales) lit. "Manx Gull."

GWYLAN WYDD: The GANNET. (North Wales) lit. "gull-goose."

GWYLAN Y PENWEIG: The HERRING-GULL. (North Wales) lit. "herring gull."

GWYLAN Y WEILGI: The STORM-PETREL. (North Wales) lit. "ocean gull."

GWYLOG: The COMMON GUILLEMOT. (North Wales) lit. "guillemot."

GYLFINBRAFF. A Welsh name for the HAWFINCH.

GYLFINGROES (Y). A Welsh name for the COMMON CROSSBILL, lit. "the crossbill."

GYLFINHIR. A Welsh name for the COMMON CURLEW; lit. "long-bill."

GYP STARLING, GYP STARNILL, GYP, or GYPEY: The STARLING. (Yorkshire.)

GYR-FALCON [No. 230]. Anciently often called the Ger-Falcon, and erroneously Jer-Falcon. The name properly belongs to the female, the male being formerly called the Jerkin (either dim. of "Jer" or else from Jerkin, a short coat, hence indicating an inferior size). Willughby spells it "Jer-Falcon" and says it "seems to take its name from the High Dutch word Gyrfalco, i.e. a ravenous Falcon, or Vulturine Falcon" (Gyr=Vulture). Newton thinks the derivation is probably from Low Latin *Gyrofalco*. Originally the three forms of *Falco rusticolus* (the GYR-FALCON, ICELAND FALCON, and GREENLAND FALCON) were confused together under the name of Gyr-Falcon or Jer-Falcon, under which name they will be found in Pennant, Lewin, and other early writers.

GYR FALCON. The PEREGRINE FALCON. (Longdendale, Cheshire.)

HACKBOLT. The GREAT SHEARWATER. (Scilly Isles.)

HACKET or HACKLET. The KITTIWAKE (Provincial.)

HAGDOWN. The GREAT SHEARWATER. (Dungarvan, Isle of Man, and coast of Ireland.)

HAGGARD or HAGGARD FALCON. The PEREGRINE FALCON in adult-plumage. (Willughby.)

HAGGARD HAWK. In falconry, a full-grown hawk, taken in its unreclaimed state.

HAGGISTER or HAGISTER An old Kentish name for the MAGPIE Occurs in Scott's " Discovery of Witchcraft," where it is said that, " to prognosticate that guests approach to your house upon the chattering of pies or haggisters is altogether vanity and superstition."

HAIGRIE The COMMON HERON. (Shetland Isles.)

HAIR-TAIL The GARDEN-WARBLER. (Nidd Valley, Yorkshire.)

Hairy Woodpecker. An American species said by Latham, Montagu and others, without sufficient evidence, to have reached our shores

HALCYON The KINGFISHER. (Poetical.)

HALF-BIRD A fowler's name for the TEAL, COMMON POCHARD, SCAUP-DUCK and other small ducks which bring lesser prices than the larger kinds. It seems to be proper to any kind under the size of the MALLARD. It is used in the Fens, also in Norfolk and elsewhere.

HALF-CURLEW: The WHIMBREL (Norfolk, Yorkshire.) So called from its being a miniature of the COMMON CURLEW (see Half-bird). The name is also applied in Norfolk to the BAR-TAILED GODWIT

HALF NEBB The RED-NECKED PHALAROPE. (Provincial.)

HALF-SNIPE The JACK SNIPE. (Norfolk.) So called from its being much smaller than the COMMON SNIPE.

HALF WHAUP The BAR-TAILED GODWIT. (Forfar) An equivalent of Half-Curlew.

HAMBURG GROSBEAK: The TREE-SPARROW. (Latham.)

HAMBURG TREE-CREEPER The TREE-SPARROW. (Albin.)

HAMMER BLATE (or BLEAT) The COMMON SNIPE. (Provincial.)

HANDSAW: The HERON. A corruption of "Heronseugh." Occurs in Hamlet (act II, sc. 2). "I know a hawk from a handsaw"

HARELD: The LONG-TAILED DUCK. (Orkney.) From *haveld*, the Icelandic name of the species.

HARLAN: The PINTAIL. (Wexford.) In the same county the RED-BREASTED MERGANSER is known as Land Harlan.

HARLE: The GOOSANDER (female or young). Also the RED-BREASTED MERGANSER (Orkneys and Shetlands.) From the Fr. name *Harle*.

HARLEQUIN. According to Hett the BUFFEL-HEADED DUCK is sometimes so called.

HARLEQUIN-DUCK [No. 305]. This name was first given by Pennant ("Arctic Zoology," II, No. 490, 1785). Newton, however, says it was anglicized by Forster in 1791 from Linnæus's *Anas histrionica*. It is the Harlequin Garrot of Selby.

HARLEY: The SWIFT. (Forfar.)

HARPY, HARPY DUCK HAWK, or WHITE-HEADED HARPY: The MARSH-HARRIER.

HARRY DUTCHMAN: The HOODED CROW. From the supposition that the winter-immigrants come from Holland.

HASEL HEN, HAZEL HEN, or HAZEL GROUSE: The female BLACK GROUSE. Occurs in Merrett (1667) as "Hasel Hen" and in Willughby as "Hazel Hen," the latter saying that it is the Attagen of Gesner (see Attagen).

HATCHER: The HEDGE-SPARROW. (Provincial.)

HAWFINCH [No. 16]. The name probably implies a partiality for haw-berries, but can also mean hedge-finch, the original meaning of the word haw being hedge, from A.Sax. *haga*, an enclosure. Occurs first in Willughby (1678). It is the Grosbeak or Haw-Grosbeak of many authors from Pennant to Montagu.

HAW GROSBEAK. See HAWFINCH.

HAWK DAY-OWL. Macgillivray's name for the Hawk-Owls, now separated as AMERICAN HAWK-OWL and EUROPEAN HAWK-OWL.

HAWK OF THE FIRST COAT. A falconer's term for a Hawk of the fourth year, when it has attained its full growth and perfection. A Hawk of the fifth year was moreover called "a hawk of the second coat," and so on.

HAWK-OWL. Montagu gives this as a provincial name for the SHORT-EARED OWL, on account of the smallness of its head, which gives it a somewhat hawk-like appearance, and Saxby gives it as a Shetland name for that species. The name, however, properly belongs to the EUROPEAN and AMERICAN HAWK-OWLS, members of the genus *Surnia*

Hay-bird   The BLACKCAP (Northants.); the WILLOW-WARBLER (a general provincial name); the WOOD-WARBLER (West Yorkshire); and the WHINCHAT (Ryedale, Yorkshire). From the nest being composed principally of dry grass

Hay-Crake. The LAND-RAIL. (Ackworth, Yorkshire.)

Hay-jack. A name applied to several small birds which build nests of hay or bents, such as the WHITETHROAT, BLACKCAP, GARDEN-WARBLER, etc. Also occurs as Haychat (Northants.), Hazeck (Worcestershire) and Hay-sucker (Devonshire). Originally Hey-suck (or Heges-sugge) according to Newton (see "Segge"). The Hay-chat of North and West Yorkshire is the WHINCHAT.

Hay-tit : The WHITETHROAT. (Oxfordshire, Shropshire).

Haz, Hoet, Houz. Cornish names for a Duck

Hazel Linnet · The LESSER WHITETHROAT. (Provincial)

Heathcock : The BLACK GROUSE. (North Country.) Occurs in Willughby. The female or Grey-hen is termed Heath-hen.

Heather-bleat or Heather-bleater. The COMMON SNIPE. (Bewick) Also a provincial name in parts of the North of England and in Scotland and Ireland. From its familiar "drumming."

Heather Lintie or Heather Lintee. A Border name for the TWITE. From its habit of nesting amongst the heather; also applied in Scotland to the LINNET, and in Cumberland, Westmorland, and Yorkshire to the MEADOW-PIPIT; the latter being also known as Heather Cheeper.

Heather Peeper : The COMMON SANDPIPER. (Aberdeen.)

Heath-poult   A New Forest name for the BLACK GROUSE ; lit. Heath-fowl, a name elsewhere applied to the species.

Heath Throstle : The RING-OUZEL. (Provincial)

Heavy Plover. A name for the GREY PLOVER, according to Hett.

Hebog chwyldro. A Welsh name for the GYR-FALCON.

Hebog llwydlâs : The male HEN-HARRIER. (North Wales) lit. " grey-blue hawk."

Hebog dramor. A Welsh name for the PEREGRINE FALCON; lit. "foreign falcon." *Hebog gwlanog* was also formerly applied to the "Lanner" or young Peregrine Falcon.

Hebog marthin. A Welsh name for the GOSHAWK.

HEBOG YR HEDYDD. A Welsh name for the HOBBY; lit. "lark falcon."

HEBRIDAL SANDPIPER: The TURNSTONE. (Pennant.)

HECCO. An obsolete name for the GREEN WOODPECKER. from A.Sax *hicgan*=to try. Occurs in Drayton's "The Owl" as "sharp neb'd hecco."

HECKLE or HEEKLE. The GREEN WOODPECKER. From the same derivation as Hecco.

HECKYMAL, HACKYMAL, HACKMAL, HAGMAL, HICKMAL: The BLUE TITMOUSE. (Cornwall and Devonshire.) From the strong pecks which it deals with its bill, according to Swainson. Heckymal is also a Dartmoor name for the GREAT TITMOUSE.

HEDGE-ACCENTOR Sometimes applied to the HEDGE-SPARROW, on account of its belonging to the former genus *Accentor*, and to avoid the misnomer "Sparrow." The name is found in Selby (1825) and was adopted by Yarrell (1843).

HEDGE-BETTY: The HEDGE-SPARROW. (Provincial.)

HEDGE-CHANTER: The HEDGE-SPARROW. (Macgillivray.) Also a local name in Yorkshire.

HEDGE-CHAT The HEDGE-SPARROW. (Northants)

HEDGE-CHICKEN: The WHITETHROAT. (Provincial.)

HEDGE-CHICKER: The WHEATEAR. (Provincial.)

HEDGE-CREEPER: The HEDGE-SPARROW. (Yorkshire.)

HEDGE-JUG. The HEDGE-SPARROW. (Provincial.) From the shape of the nest.

HEDGE-MIKE: The HEDGE-SPARROW. (Sussex.)

HEDGE-SPARROW [No. 188, British Hedge-Sparrow; No. 187, Continental Hedge-Sparrow]. The name occurs as "Hedge-sparr'w" in Chaucer, and as "Hedge sparrow" in Turner (1544), in Merrett, and in Willughby, and we find it stated in the latter that, "In the nest of this bird the Cuckow is said to lay her egg, which the foolish bird sits upon, hatches and brings up the young one till it be fledg'd and can shift for itself." Chaucer also alludes to the Cuckoo in his "Parliament of Foules" as the "murtherer" of the Hedge-Sparrow that brought it forth. Turner identifies the Troglodytes of Ætius and others with the Hedge-Sparrow, but it is of course the WREN. Hartert has lately separated the resident British form from the Continental form, only a few examples of which have, however, yet been certainly identified here.

HEDGE SPICK : The HEDGE-SPARROW. (Sussex.)

HEDGE WARBLER. The HEDGE-SPARROW. (Bewick.) Also local name in Yorkshire.

HEDGY or HEDGER · The HEDGE-SPARROW. (Provincial.)

HEDYDD, EHEDYDD, or UCHEDYDD. Welsh names for the SKY-LARK; the first two signify a "flier," the third a "high flier."

HEDYDD-Y-COED The Welsh name for the WOOD-LARK; lit. "wood-lark."

HEEDY-CRAW · The HOODED CROW. (Scotland) No doubt a corruption.

HEFFUL, HEFFALD : The GREEN WOODPECKER (Yorkshire.) Probably same as "yaffle."

HEGRIE, HEGRIL'S SKIP, or SKIP HEGRIE · The HERON. (Shetlands.)

HELEGUG The PUFFIN Willughby records it as so called in South Wales.

HELLEJAY The RAZORBILL (Shetlands) Hett also gives "Hellgog" for this species

HEMPIE The HEDGE-SPARROW. (Scotland and Yorkshire)

HEN-DRIVER An occasional name for the HEN-HARRIER (Thornton.)

HEN-HARRIER [No. 24]. Formerly a common species in our islands, but now rare as a breeding species The names Hen-Harrier (male) and Ring-tail (female) both occur in Willughby (1678). Turner (1544) has "Hen harroer," and says, "It gets this name among our countrymen from butchering their fowls" It is related in the "Zoologist" that in the Hebrides it is said of any one, should he be more than ordinarily fortunate on a certain day, that he must have seen the "clamhan luch" or Hen-Harrier.

HEN HARROER The HEN-HARRIER. Occurs in Turner (1544), and is copied from him by Aldrovandus.

HERALD The COMMON HERON (Forfar)

HERALD DUCK or HERALD : The RED-BREASTED MERGANSER. (Shetland Isles, Forfar.)

HERDSMAN The GREAT SKUA. (Orkneys) Because it is believed to protect the young lambs from Eagles (Swainson.)

HERL The adult male RED-BREASTED MERGANSER. (Northumberland)

HERMIT CROW The CHOUGH From its solitary habits

HERN, HERNSHAW, HERNSEUGH, HERNSEW, HARN, HARNSER, HARNSEY: The COMMON HERON. Vulgar contractions of Heronseugh. "Hern or Hernshaw" occurs in Merrett (1667). The first four are North Country, and the last three East Anglian names. Whitaker gives Herring Sue for Nottinghamshire, and Nelson and Clarke give Heronsew, Herring-sew, Heronseugh, Heron-sue, Heronshaw, and Heronshew for the Yorkshire districts.

HERON. See COMMON HERON.

HERONSEUGH. An old English name for the HERON, the precise meaning and derivation of which is doubtful. Some authorities derive it from the Sanskrit *hansa*. It occurs as Heron-sewe in Chaucer, which has led to the supposition that the "sewe" is derived from Old Eng. *sewe*, a dish, in reference to the bird as a table dainty.

HERRING GANT: The GANNET. (Norfolk.)

HERRING-GULL [No. 431]. The name occurs in Willughby, also in Pennant and succeeding writers.

HERRING SPINK: The GOLDEN-CRESTED WREN. (East Suffolk.) So called from being often caught in the rigging of the boats during the North Sea fishing when on migration ("East Anglian," IV, p. 115).

HEW-HOLE: The GREEN WOODPECKER (see Hickwall.) The name occurs in Turner (1544) and in Willughby.

HICKMALL. A provincial name for the BLUE TITMOUSE (see Heckymal.)

HICKWALL: The GREEN WOODPECKER, according to Merrett, but Willughby applies the name to the LESSER SPOTTED WOODPECKER, as do also Yarrell, Bewick, and other authors. Newton derives the name from A.Sax *higera* or *higere*, lit. a laugher; in which case the GREEN WOODPECKER would appear to be the species intended. Another form of the word is Hickway, from which Newton thinks the names Highaw and Hewhole may be corrupted.

HIGH-HOE: The GREEN WOODPECKER. (Shropshire.) Occurs in Willughby (1678). Heigh-hawe and Hayhoe are other forms of the word, which Newton thinks comes from A.Sax *higera* or *higere* (see Hickwall), but it has been thought to refer to the height at which the bird makes its nesting-holes.

HILLAN PIET: The MISTLE-THRUSH. (Aberdeen.) Probably "Highland Pie."

HILL BIRD: The FIELDFARE. (Scotland.)

Hill Blackbird   The RING-OUZEL. (Northumberland.)
Hill Chack   The RING-OUZEL   (Orkneys.)
Hill Hooter · The TAWNY OWL   (Cheshire.)
Hill Lintie : The TWITE. (Orkneys.)
Hill Pigeon . The STOCK-DOVE. (Cheshire.)
Hill Plover : The GOLDEN PLOVER. (Forfarshire.)
Hill Sparrow · The MEADOW-PIPIT. (Orkneys and Shetlands.)
Hissing Owl : The BARN-OWL   (Yorkshire.) From the hissing sound uttered at times.
HOBBY [No. 235]. The name occurs Latinized "hobbia" in Turner (1544), but in English in Willughby (1678), who correctly designates it "*subbuteo* of Aldrovandus," a name applied by Turner to the female HEN-HARRIER, or Ringtail. Willughby remarks that the word Hobby is derived from its French name (which in Old Fr was *Hobé*, Mod. Fr *Hobereau*, or *Hobreau*), but Swainson thinks the Mod. Fr *Hobereau* is from Old Provençal *Alban* (=white, from its light plumage) through Old Fr. *Aubreau*. Aldrovandus spells it "Hobie" In addition to being a favourite species for hawking, this bird was formerly employed in what was called the "Daring of Larks," an ancient usage in fowling, in which a Hobby was let off to prevent the larks from rising while they were being netted. Among falconers Hobby was properly the name of the female, the inferior male being called Jack or Robin. In the Shetlands the name Hobby is applied to the MERLIN according to Saxby.
Hobby Bird. An old Norfolk name for the WRYNECK according to Sir Thomas Browne, "because it comes either with, or a little before, the hobbies in the spring."
Hobby Owl   The BARN-OWL. (Northants.)
Hobigoch Brongoch (Yr). A Welsh name for the REDBREAST.
Hoddy Craw or Huddy Craw · The CARRION-CROW. (South Scotland)
HOLBÖLL'S REDPOLL [No. 22]   A rare vagrant from the Polar regions. Of doubtful distinction from the MEALY REDPOLL.
Holland Duck . The SCAUP-DUCK. (Forfarshire.)
Holland Hawk · The GREAT NORTHERN DIVER. (Ballantrae, Scotland.)

HOLM COCK, HOLM SCREECH, or HOLM THRUSH : The MISTLE-THRUSH (Cornwall, Devonshire, Dorsetshire); in Yorkshire "Hollin-Cock." From its partiality to the berries of the holly or holm (Mid. Eng. *holin*) and from its loud song or its harsh note when taking flight.

HONEY-BUZZARD [No. 252]. Willughby (1678) thought it new and gave it the name of Honey-Buzzard from having found the combs of wasps' nests in its nest. It was however the Boudree of Belon (1555). Its food is the wasps and bees and their larvæ, not their honey, a fact which perhaps accounted for Macgillivray's attempt to change the name to " Brown Bee-Hawk."

HOOD AWL : The GREEN WOODPECKER. (Cornwall.) Perhaps a corruption of Wood Awl, which is possibly again a corruption of Whetile, from A.Sax. *thwitan*=to cut.

HOODED CROW [No. 2] The name Hooded Crow is first used by Pennant. Willughby and Ray call it the Royston Crow; Turner called it the " Winter Crow." The term Hooded is derived from the black head and nape contrasting with the grey of the mantle. For description of a curious ceremony practised by Scottish herdsmen, in which offerings are made to the hooded crow, eagle, etc., to induce them to spare the flocks, see Pennant's " Tour in Scotland," III, pp. 110-11.

> The Guil, the Gordon and the Hooded Craw,
> Were the three worst things Murray ever saw,

is a Morayshire saying (the guile, or gule, being an obnoxious weed). The CARRION-CROW is frequently called Hooded Crow or Hoodie in Scotland, while in the Orkneys and in East Lothian, according to Swainson, the BLACK-HEADED GULL is known as Hooded Crow or Hooded Mew.

HOODED MERGANSER [No. 315, American Hooded Merganser]. The name is found in Selby and also in Yarrell and succeeding authors.

HOODED TERN : The LITTLE TERN. From the black crown and nape.

HOODIE or HUDDIE CRAW : The HOODED CROW. (Scottish Borders.)

HOOLET . The BARN-OWL. (Scottish Lowlands.) Also applied to the TAWNY OWL.

HOOP or COCK HOOP : The BULLFINCH. (Cornwall, Devonshire, Dorsetshire, Somersetshire, and Upton-on-Severn) It seems to be derived from the bird's whistling-note. The name Hoop or Houp is also applied to the HOOPOE (q.v.)

HOOPER or HOOPER SWAN: The WHOOPER SWAN. Yarrell calls it the Hooper.

HOOPOE [No. 206]. The name, which is derived from its note, occurs in Turner (1544) as "Houupe;" in Barlow (1655) as "Hoopoe;" in Merrett (1667) as "Hoopee;" and in Willughby (1678) as "Hoop, or Hoopoe," while in Bailey's Dictionary it is "Houp." Turner says the species is nowhere found in Britain, but Merrett says that it occurs in the New Forest and in Essex, but is rare. Plot (1677) calls it the "Hoopoe or Hooping-bird," and Pennant (1766) the Hoopoe. The French name is Huppe, and Newton observes that although originally onomatopoetic it is now used to denote a crest or tuft, this secondary meaning having arisen from the bird's crest. Houghton says that the Hoopoe is the bird denoted in the Bible by the Hebrew word *dukiphath*, which is rendered "lapwing" in our version (an error arising from the fact that both birds are crested); it occurs only in the list of birds forbidden to be used as food by the ancient Jews. It is also figured on the Egyptian monuments and appears, according to Horapollo, to represent the quality of gratitude, while the Arabs have a superstitious reverence for it, as they believe it to possess marvellous medicinal properties, calling it "the doctor," and also fancy it is able to point out underground wells and fountains. It figures largely in Continental folk-lore, but not in English, on account of its scarcity with us.

HOOT OWL · The TAWNY OWL. (Craven.)

HORNBILL BUNTING: The CORN-BUNTING. (Ireland.)

HORN-COOT · The LONG-EARED OWL. (Swainson.) From the two erectile horn-like tufts of feathers or "ears."

HORNED DOUCKER or HORNED DABCHICK: The GREAT CRESTED GREBE. (Provincial.) The term "horned" is from its crest; Doucker signifies ducker or diver

HORNED GOOSE: The BRENT GOOSE. (Provincial.) An evident misnomer Perhaps a mistake for Horra Goose (q.v.).

HORNED GREBE The SLAVONIAN GREBE (Latham.)

HORNED LARK · The SHORE-LARK. Macgillivray gives it as a provincial name.

HORNEMANN'S REDPOLL [No. 24]. A Greenland species which sometimes strays to our shores.

HORNER · The GOOSANDER (Holderness, Yorkshire.)

HORNEYWINK The LAPWING (Cornwall.) From the long horn-like crest.

HORNFINCH: The STORM-PETREL (Provincial.)
HORNOUL or HORN-OWL. The LONG-EARED OWL. The first name occurs in Turner, the second in Willughby and many subsequent writers up to Bewick. Horned Owl is an English provincial name, and Hornie Oolet or Hornie Hoolet a Scots one for the species.
HORN-PIE: The LAPWING. (Norfolk and Suffolk.) From its erectile crest and its pied plumage.
HORRA GOOSE or HORRIE GOOSE: The BRENT GOOSE. (Shetlands.) From its frequenting the Sound of Horra.
HORSE FINCH: The CHAFFINCH. Montagu gives it as a provincial name. It is also called Horse-dung Finch, from its frequenting the roads.
HORSE GOWK or HORSE GAWK: The COMMON SNIPE. (Orkneys and Shetlands.) Because the "drumming" is supposed to resemble the neighing of a horse (Swainson.) It has also been rendered Hoarse Gowk, which implies another meaning.
HORSE LARK: The CORN-BUNTING. (Cornwall.)
HORSE MASHER or HORSE SMATCH: The WHEATEAR. (Cornwall.)
HORSE THRUSH: The MISTLE-THRUSH. (Northants.)
HORTULON or HORTULANE: The ORTOLAN BUNTING. (Albin.)
HOUSE-MARTIN. The MARTIN. So called from its building under the eaves and porches of houses. Montagu gives it as a provincial name.
HOUSE-SPARROW [No. 40]. Perhaps the most common and well-known of British birds. The name "Sparrow" is of great antiquity, and is the A Sax. *Spearwa*, Goth. *Sparva*, while it is the *Passer* of classical writers, and occurs under this name in Aristotle, who says it is of all birds the most wanton. "House-Sparrow" occurs in Merrett's list (1667) and in Willughby (1678), but Turner (1544) calls it simply "Sparrow," which is now and has generally been the colloquial name for the species. As regards folk-lore I do not find very much relating to this bird. A Yorkshire legend, however, of the Hermit of Lindholme on Hatfield Chase, is to the effect that being left at home when a boy to keep the sparrows from the corn he shut them all up in a barn without a door, and when his parents got home the birds were all found lying dead on the floor, and the only sparrow seen in the place since was a solitary one as white as snow ("Folklore Journal," December, 1883). A similar tale,

however, is related in Monmouthshire of John of Kent. In Wiltshire, the superstition attaching to other birds in some other counties is held of the Sparrow, that if one taps at a window it is said to indicate a death in the family. A popular belief is that if sparrows chirp a great deal wet weather will ensue (Inwards).

House-Swallow   The SWALLOW. Occurs in Merrett and in Willughby.

Hover-Hawk : The KESTREL. (Berks., Bucks, Yorkshire) An equivalent of "Windhover" (q.v.).

Howlet. An Owl (diminutive). Applied by Aldrovandus, who spells it in old fashion "Houulet," to the LITTLE OWL, and also to the BARN-OWL, and by Willughby to the TAWNY OWL.

Howster : The KNOT. (Provincial.)

Huck-Muck · The LONG-TAILED TITMOUSE and the WILLOW-WARBLER Applied to the latter perhaps in allusion to the somewhat slovenly appearance of its nest.

Hufil : The GREEN WOODPECKER. (East Riding, Yorkshire.) Swainson thinks it is from its laughing note.

Hule, Ula. Cornish names for an Owl.

Hullot, Hullart, or Ullet. Local Cheshire names for the BARN-OWL; corruptions of Howlet and Owlet. Hulote or Hullat is also an Orkney name.

Humming-Bird . The GOLDEN-CRESTED WREN. (Redcar, Yorkshire)

Hunting Hawk · The PEREGRINE FALCON. (East Lothian and Cheviot Hills.)

Hutan. A Welsh name for the DOTTEREL; lit. "stupid."

Hutan-y-mor. A Welsh name for the TURNSTONE; lit. "sea dotterel." Also applied to the RINGED PLOVER in North Wales

Hwyad addfain   A Welsh name for the GARGANEY

Hwyaden bengoch or Hwyad bengoch   Welsh names for the POCHARD ; lit. "red-headed duck."

Hwyaden ddan heddog · A Welsh name for the GOOSANDER. lit. "toothed duck."

Hwyaden ddu : The COMMON SCOTER.   (North Wales) lit. "black duck."

Hwyaden gopog or Hwyaden gopynog : The TUFTED DUCK. (North Wales) lit. "crested duck."

HWYADWYDD GYFFREDIN : The GOOSANDER. (North Wales) lit. "common duck-goose."

HWYADEN LOSTFAIN : The PINTAIL. (North Wales) lit. "narrow-tailed duck." Hwyad gynffonfain is also given by Fleming as a Welsh name for this species, and signifies "long-tailed duck."

HWYADEN LYDANBIG : The SHOVELER. (North Wales) lit. "broad-beaked duck."

HWYADEN LYGAD ARIAN : The SCAUP DUCK. (North Wales) lit. "silver-eyed duck."

HWYADEN LYGAD AUR : The GOLDENEYE. (North Wales) lit. "golden-eyed duck."

HWYADEN WYLLT : The MALLARD, or Wild-Duck (North Wales) lit. "wild duck."

HWYADEN YR EITHIN : The COMMON SHELD-DUCK (North Wales) lit. "gorse-duck."

HWYAD FELFEDOG : A Welsh name for the VELVET SCOTER. lit. "velvet duck."

IAN-ANT 'SNEACHD : A Gaelic name for the SNOW-BUNTING.

IAR DDWFR FOEL : A Welsh name for the COOT ; lit "bald water-hen."

IAR DDWR : The MOORHEN. (North Wales) lit. "water-hen."

IAR GOCH : The RED GROUSE. (North Wales) lit. "red hen."

IAR GOED : The PHEASANT. (North Wales) lit. "wood-hen."

IBIS. See GLOSSY IBIS.

ICE BIRD or ICELAND AUK · The LITTLE AUK. The second name is used on the Yorkshire coast.

ICE DUCK · The LONG-TAILED DUCK. (Northumberland.)

ICELAND FALCON [No. 231]. The Icelandic form of the GYR-FALCON, intermediate between the Scandinavian typical form and the GREENLAND FALCON. The name first occurs in Latham's "Synopsis" (I, p. 71)

ICELAND GULL [No. 436]. This name according to Edmonston was the local name in Unst, Shetland Isles, for both this species and the GLAUCOUS GULL, or Burgomaster. He seems to have been the first to publish the name ("Wern. Mem.," IV, p. 506). Yarrell also calls it Lesser White-winged Gull.

ICELAND HAWK · The ICELAND FALCON and GREENLAND FALCON (Shetlands.)

ICELAND SCORIE. The ICELAND GULL and the GLAUCOUS GULL. (Shetlands.)

ICTERINE WARBLER [No. 141]. Occurs in Hewitson, Yarrell, and Gould as Melodious Willow Warbler, and Melodious Willow Wren. The species was named *Sylvia icterina* by Vieillot in 1817, whence its name arises.

ICWELL: The GREEN WOODPECKER. (Northants.) See "Eaqual."

IMBER DIVER. The GREAT NORTHERN DIVER. (Ireland.) See Immer.

IMMER, IMMER DIVER. The GREAT NORTHERN DIVER. (Scotland.) Said to be lit *immerse*, signifying the act of diving, from Lat. *immersus*, to plunge into. Conf. Dan. *Imber*; Sw. *Immer* and *Emmer*, Icel. *Himbrim*. The name was formerly written "Imber Diver" by the older ornithological writers from Willughby and Pennant to Montagu, the last, however, also gives "Immer" as a provincial name. Sibbald calls it the "Ember Goose." Bewick (1804) gives "Imbrim" as a name for the species.

Indian Gallinule. Examples of this species recorded as taken in our islands had no doubt escaped from captivity.

INDIAN STONECHAT [No. 177] This is the Indian race of the STONECHAT, first described by Blyth as long ago as 1847.

IOLAIR BHUIDHE, IOLAIR RIAMHACH. Gaelic names for the WHITE-TAILED EAGLE

IOLAIR DHUBH The Gaelic name for the GOLDEN EAGLE, signifying "Black Eagle"

IOLAIR UISGE. A Gaelic name for the OSPREY; lit "water eagle."

IRISH COAL-TITMOUSE. See COAL-TITMOUSE.

IRISH DIPPER See DIPPER.

IRISH NIGHTINGALE. A name applied to the SEDGE-WARBLER in some parts of Ireland, from its habit of singing at night, and because the true NIGHTINGALE is unknown there.

ISAAC or HAZOCK: The HEDGE-SPARROW (Worcestershire.) A corruption of Old. Eng. *heisugge* (see Blue Isaac).

ISABELLINE WHEATEAR [No 173]. An Asiatic species which takes its name from the isabelline colour of its plumage.

ISLE OF WIGHT PARSON. The CORMORANT. (Hampshire.)

IVORY GULL [No. 438]. The name, arising from the ivory whiteness of its plumage, appears in Bewick (1832) and Selby, and was adopted by Yarrell. It was, however, first called "Snow-bird" by Edmondston and by Fleming.

IVORY WHALE GULL. Macgillivray's name for the IVORY GULL.

Ivy Owl: The TAWNY OWL. (Willughby.) In casual use provincially.

Jack: Properly the JACKDAW. A common provincialism. From its small size as compared with the other *Corvi* (see JACKDAW). In the days of falconry, Jack or Jack Merlin was also the term for the male of the MERLIN, which is of smaller size than the female, as is usual in the birds of prey. The male HOBBY was also in the same way termed Jack or Robin to distinguish it from the female, termed Hobby.

Jack Baker: The RED-BACKED SHRIKE. (Surrey, Sussex, Hants.)

Jack Bird: The FIELDFARE. From its cry.

Jack-Curlew or Curlew Jack: The WHIMBREL. (Rutty.) lit. a small curlew. Curlew Jack is a Yorkshire name for the species. Swainson applies the name, possibly erroneously, to the CURLEW.

JACKDAW [No 5]. Occurs in Merrett (1667). In Shakespeare it is "daw." Willughby has "Jack-daw." Jack (properly a diminution of John) is used in this connection, not as a nickname, but to indicate insignificance or small size (lit. "boy") and is therefore an equivalent of "knave" (q.v.). For other instances, cf. Jack-snipe, Jack-Curlew, etc. Daw (Mid. Eng.) is apparently onomatopoetic. In Lancashire a Jackdaw alighting on the window-sill of a sick-room is considered an ill omen (Harland and Wilkinson). A Norwich saying is:—

> When three daws are seen on St Peter's vane together
> Then we're sure to have bad weather.

Turner, writing in 1534, says of this bird that it is "by the Latins named Monedula, as if it were Monetula, from the Moneta (money) which alone of birds, as Pliny says, it steals ... Moreover, Ovid happily describes its thievish habits in the following lines:—

> Was changed into a bird, which even now loves gold,
> Monedula, the black of foot, in plumage black arrayed."

Jack Doucker: The LITTLE GREBE. (Shropshire.) From its small size and diving propensities.

Jack Hawk. The KESTREL. (Arkengarthdale, Yorkshire.)

Jack Hern or Jack Heron: The HERON. (Sussex.)

Jack Ickle. The GREEN WOODPECKER. (Northants.)

Jackie Foster: The LONG-TAILED DUCK. (Northumberland.)

Jack-in-a-bottle: The LONG-TAILED TITMOUSE. In reference to the shape of its nest.

Jack Merlin: The male of the MERLIN in falconry (see "Jack").

Jack Nicker, Jack-a-Nickas, or Nicker Nocker: The GOLDFINCH. (Cheshire.) The first name is also found in Northants and Shropshire.

Jack Plover: The DUNLIN. (North Riding, Yorkshire.)

Jacksaw: The GREAT TITMOUSE. So called from its note in many parts of Scotland (Gray). It is also applied on the Yorkshire coast to the GOOSANDER, on account of its saw-like bill.

Jack Snipe [No. 410] lit. *boy* or *half* snipe. So called from its being a miniature of the COMMON SNIPE. The name occurs in Merrett (1667), also in Willughby, who calls the species the "Gid or Jack-Snipe, or Judcock," and says he "thought it not to differ from the Snipe in kind, but only in sex, taking it to be the Cock-Snipe. But afterwards being advised by Mr. M. Lister, I found it to differ specifically: for dissecting several of these small ones some proved to be males, some females." Swainson says the same belief is still held in Ireland, the JACK SNIPE being believed to be the male and the COMMON SNIPE the female, on which account it is called Jill Snipe. At Longdendale, Cheshire, the name "Jack Snipe" is also applied to the COMMON SANDPIPER, and in the Shetland Isles to the DUNLIN.

Jack-squealer: The SWIFT. (Upton-on-Severn.)

Jack-straw: The WHITETHROAT (Shropshire); the BLACKCAP (Somerset). In reference to the materials of which the nest is composed.

Jacob. A name for the STARLING. (Near Beverley, Yorkshire.)

Jadreka Snipe· The BLACK-TAILED GODWIT. (Pennant, Latham, Lewin, Montagu, etc.)

Jager: The GREAT SKUA.

Jan-Chochail. A Gaelic name for the LONG-TAILED DUCK. (Hebrides.) From its plaintive cry.

Jar-bird The NUTHATCH. (Hett.)

Jar-owl: The NIGHTJAR. (Provincial) From its jarring note and nocturnal habits.

Jar-peg: The GREEN WOODPECKER. (Northants) Baker says it is "because it stands on an old stump and strikes with its beak on a hard knot or peg, so that the jar is heard at a great distance."

JAY [No. 10, British Jay; No. 9, Continental Jay; No. 11, Irish Jay]. Occurs in Barlow's Plates (1655), in Merrett (1667), and in Willughby. From Fr. *Géai*. Hartert has separated the resident British and Irish forms of the Jay from the Continental form, hence the change of name.

JAY: The MISTLE-THRUSH is so called in many parts of Ireland. (Thompson.)

JAYPIE: The JAY (Notts., Cornwall, Devonshire); the MISTLE-THRUSH (Wilts.).

JAY PIET: The JAY. (Perth, and Sedbergh, Yorkshire.)

JAY TEAL: The TEAL. (Kirkcudbright.) Swainson thinks it is from its colour.

JEDCOCK: The JACK SNIPE. (Provincial.)

JENNIE CUT-THROAT: The WHITETHROAT. (Roxburgh.)

JENNY CROW. A name for the HERON according to Swainson.

JENNY CRUDLE: The WREN. (Provincial.)

JENNY HERON: The HERON. (Kirkcudbright.)

JENNY HOWLET. The BARN-OWL and the TAWNY OWL. (North of England.) Yorkshire variations are Jinny Hullut and Jinny Yewlatt.

JENNY JAY or JINNY JAY: The JAY. (North and west Yorkshire.)

JENNY OWL: The BARN-OWL. (Northumberland.)

JENNY REDTAIL: The REDSTART. (North Yorkshire.) Nelson and Clarke give Jenny Wrentail and Wrenny Redtail as local Yorkshire variations.

JENNY WREN or JENNY. A common provincial name for the WREN. It is in use in Yorkshire, Lincolnshire, Lancashire, and other counties. Johnson ("Zoologist," 1848) also gives "Jenner Hen" as a Yorkshire name, and "Jinties" is said to be used at Barnsley.

JERCOCK or CHERCOCK: The MISTLE-THRUSH. (Westmorland.) Perhaps a corruption of "Shercock" (q.v.), but Swainson thinks it to be from its harsh cry.

JEREMY JOY (=January Joy). A Cleveland name for the MISTLE-THRUSH.

JER-FALCON: The GYR-FALCON. Also probably formerly applied by falconers to the ICELAND FALCON and GREENLAND FALCON. The name occurs in Willughby (1678), and is a corruption of Gerfalcon (or Gyrfalcon).

JERKIN. An old falconer's term for the male of the GYR-FALCON.

JETCOCK : The JACK SNIPE. (Bewick.)
JILL SNIPE   The COMMON SNIPE. (Ireland.) See JACK SNIPE
JINNY WREN : The GOLDCREST. (Teesdale, Yorkshire.) Jenny Wren is a common provincial name for the WREN.
JOBBIN   The NUTHATCH. (Northants.) Apparently akin to Nutjobber.
JOBBLER : The WHEATEAR. (Dorsetshire.)
JOE BEN : The GREAT TITMOUSE (Suffolk); the MARSH-TITMOUSE (East Anglia).
JOURONGS : The ARCTIC TERN. (Galway.) Watters says it signifies a cross and peevish disposition.
JUDCOCK   The JACK SNIPE (Willughby); also occurs as Juddock, a corruption. Perhaps now obsolete; Nelson and Clarke, however, give Judcock as a local Yorkshire name for the DUNLIN.
KAE or KAY : The JACKDAW is so called in many parts of Scotland, from its cry. It occurs as Kae in Sibbald, and as "Ka" in Turner. According to Swainson, Kae is also a Roxburgh name for the JAY.
KAKERA. Hett gives this as a name for the RED-THROATED DIVER.
KASTREL : The KESTREL   (Turner.)
KATABELLA : The HEN-HARRIER. (Orkneys.)
KATE : The BRAMBLING (Kent.) Occurs also in Montagu. Swainson gives it also as a provincial name for the HAWFINCH.
KATIE BRANTAIL or BESSIE BRANTAIL   The REDSTART. (Shropshire.)
KATIE WREN : The WREN. (Provincial.)
KATOGLE   The EAGLE-OWL (see Cat Ogle).
KA WATTIE : The JACKDAW. (North Scotland.) Ka (=Kae) is from its cry.
KAZEK   A Cornish name for the GREEN WOODPECKER.
KEDYDD YR HELVYG. A Welsh name for the SEDGE-WARBLER.
KEELIE : The KESTREL. (Neighbourhood of Edinburgh.) From its loud, shrill cry (Swainson).
KELL-BIRD. The nestling of the COMMON GUILLEMOT. (Flamborough.)
KELNE : The STONE-CURLEW. (East Yorkshire.)

KELTIE : The KITTIWAKE. (Aberdeen.)

KENTISH CROW or KENTISHMAN : The HOODED CROW. (Provincial.)

KENTISH DOTTEREL : The KENTISH PLOVER. (Provincial.)

KENTISH PLOVER [No. 360]. This species was first described by Latham ("Synops.," Supp., p. 316) from examples sent by Dr. Boys which were obtained at Sandwich, Kent, in 1787 and 1791, hence the name. It was distinguished under the name of *Charadrius alexandrinus* by Linnæus in 1758, but even as late as 1842 Fleming was of opinion that it was only a phase of the RINGED PLOVER. Selby, Yarrell, and later writers, however, include it as a good species.

KERHIDH. A Cornish name for the HERON.

KERTLUTOCK. A name for the SHOVELER (Hawker); also rendered "Kirk tullock."

KESTREL [No. 237]. Fr. *Cresserelle, Crécerelle*; Old Fr. *Quercerelle* or *Quercelle*. The name first appears as Kestrel in Willughby (1678). It occurs in Turner (1544) as " a kistrel or a kastrel," and in Merrett (1667) as " a Keshrel or Kastrel." Pennant (1766) spells it "Kestril." In Lancashire it is pronounced *kisstrill*.

KET CROW : The CARRION-CROW. (West Riding, Yorkshire.) "Ket" signifies carrion.

KIDDAW : The COMMON GUILLEMOT. Willughby gives it as a Cornish name for the species. Swainson thinks it is derived from *skite*=to mute.

KILLDEER PLOVER [No. 361]. A North American species. The name is derived from its cry.

KILLIEWEEACK : The KITTIWAKE. (Orkneys.) From its cry.

KILLIGREW : The CHOUGH (Charleton); Montagu also gives it as a provincial name.

KILLILEEPIE : The COMMON SANDPIPER is so called in some parts of Scotland, from its cry. (Gray.) Also rendered Killieleepsie (East Lothian).

KILLOCKDOE : The BLACK GROUSE. (Scotland.)

KING CHARLES : The GREAT TITMOUSE. (Cheshire.)

KING DUCK. See KING-EIDER.

KING-EIDER [No. 308]. The name first appears as "King Duck" in Pennant's "Arctic Zoology," and as King Eider in Fleming. It is the Greyheaded Duck of Edwards.

KINGFISHER [No. 208]. Literally the chief of the fishers; from A Sax *cyning*, a king or chief of the tribe, and *fisher*. The name occurs in Turner (1544) as "kynges fissher"; in Merrett (1667) as "Kings-fisher" and in Willughby as "Kingfisher," as also in most succeeding authors. A celebrated belief among the ancients was that the Halcyon or Kingfisher made its nest of fish-bones and launched it upon the sea, and it was while brooding thus upon its young that the fabled halcyon days were enjoyed, when "God has ordered that the whole ocean should be stayed," as Montaigne gravely observed. This author (Essay LXVIII, on "Cruelty") has given some account of the belief. Pliny remarks that "they breed in winter, at the season called the Halcyon days, wherein the sea is calm and fit for navigation, the Sicilian sea particularly so," and that they "build their nests in the seven days before the winter solstice and hatch out their young in the seven following." Drayton writes.—
    Then came the halcyon whom the sea obeys,
    When she her nest upon the water lays

He makes use of the belief five times, viz in Noah's Flood, the Elegy upon Lady Aston's departure from Spain, England's Heroical Epistles, and twice in the Polyolbion. It is also alluded to by Milton in the "Hymn on Christ's Nativity," and by Dryden. A common belief in England was that a dead Kingfisher, hung by a string, would always turn its bill in the direction from whence the wind blew. Shakespeare (King Lear, act II, sc 1) alludes to this belief in the words —
    . turn their halcyon beaks
    With every gale and vary of their masters.

Marlow also, in his "Jew of Malta," 1633, says —
    But how now stands the wind?
    Into what corner peers my halcyon's bill?

That the belief has lingered to recent times is shown by the fact that a dead Kingfisher thus suspended may still occasionally, it is said, be met with in country cottages. Another country belief sometimes encountered is that when a Kingfisher is seen it is a sign of rain.

KINGFISHER The DIPPER is so called in the Highlands and in parts of Ireland, its flight being supposed to resemble that of the KINGFISHER Also applied to the COMMON TERN at Lough Neagh.

KING HARRY or KING HARRY REDCAP. A provincial name for the GOLDFINCH. (Suffolk, Shropshire, north and east Yorkshire)

King Harry Blackcap: The BLACKCAP. (Norfolk.)
Kinglet: The GOLDEN-CRESTED WREN.
Kio. A Cornish name for the COMMON SNIPE.
Kip: The COMMON TERN. (Provincial.)
Kipp. A local name for the Terns about Dungeness and Lydd.
Kirr-Mew. A local name for the COMMON TERN. Kirr is from the cry, and Mew is Old Eng. for Gull.
Kishiefaik: The KITTIWAKE. (Orkneys.) From its cry.
Kistrel: The KESTREL. (Turner.)
Kit: The FIELDFARE. (Cheshire.)
KITE [No. 250]. The name, of great antiquity, is from the A.Sax *cyta*. It occurs in Turner (1544) as "kyte," in Merrett (1667) as "Fork-tailed Kite," and in Willughby (1678) as "Kite." This well-known species is now of rare occurrence in most parts of our islands and has long ceased to breed except perhaps in a few localities in Wales. Turner says that in his day it was "abundant and remarkably rapacious. This kind is wont to snatch food out of children's hands in our cities and towns." Its former abundance is indeed perhaps best exemplified by the commonness of kite-flying among boys. The employment by this bird of rags and anything else it can possibly steal as material for its nest is by no means a modern trait in its character, and formerly, when the bird was common in England, this predilection appears to have been well-known, as may be gathered from the instance in the speech of Autolycus in the "Winter's Tale" (act IV, sc. 2):—

> When the kite builds, look to the lesser linen

An old popular saying, now perhaps almost beyond verification—in England, at any rate—is that if Kites fly high, fine weather is at hand. The term Royal Kite originated in the fact that only the King's falcons could take it, its powers of flight being beyond those of the lesser kinds of falcons.

Kite. Used erroneously for the MARSH-HARRIER and the COMMON BUZZARD (Ireland); the KESTREL (Shropshire).
Kitti-ake. The KITTIWAKE GULL. (Flamborough.)
Kittie or Kitty: The KITTIWAKE GULL. (East Anglia, Yorkshire, Banffshire.)
Kittie Needie: The COMMON SANDPIPER. (Kirkcudbright.)

KITTIWAKE GULL [No. 437]. Often known as "Kittiwake" simply. The name first appears in Sibbald (1684), but Ray ("Itinerary," 1671) has Cattiwike, derived from an attempted rendering of its cry. Willughby calls it "Bellonius's ash-coloured Gull, called in Cornwall Tarrock," and under the latter name the immature bird was treated of up to the time of Montagu as a supposed distinct species.

KITTY CAREW. The MANX SHEARWATER. (Provincial.)

KITTY COOT. The MOORHEN. (Dorset.)

KITTY WREN or KITTY-ME-WREN. A Border name for the WREN, where according to Bolam it takes the place of the familiar name Jenny Wren. In Yorkshire it occurs also as "Kitty" only.

KNIFE-BILL. The PUFFIN. (Provincial.)

KNOT [No. 371]. The name Knot occurs in Willughby, who remarks that "King Knout" is reported to have been so fond of them that from him they got the name of Kntos or Knouts. The authority for the derivation of the name from Canute appears, however, to rest with Camden (1607) who has "Knotts, 1. Canuti aves." Du Bartas ("Divine Weekes and Wordes," 1633) calls it "Gnat-snap." Sir Thomas Browne has "Gnatts or Knots" (see Newton's "Dict. Bds" on this latter). Buffon calls it *Le Canut*. Drayton ("Polyolbion," 1613) speaks of it as—

 The Knot that called was Canute's Bird of Old.

In winter-plumage it was distinguished by Pennant and other writers under the name of "Ash-coloured Sandpiper."

KNOT. The RINGED PLOVER is so called about Belfast. (Swainson.)

KNOT-CURLEW. A name for the WHIMBREL. (Hett.)

KROCKET: The OYSTERCATCHER. (Aberdeen.)

KRYSSAT. A Cornish name for the KESTREL.

KYTE. The KITE. (Turner, Blome, and others.)

KYVELLAK. A Cornish name for the WOODCOCK.

LABBE. The ARCTIC SKUA. (Bewick.)

LACHA-BHLAR. A Gaelic name for the COOT.

LACHA CHINN NAINE. A Gaelic name for the MALLARD.

LACH CHOLONSA. A Gaelic name for the EIDER Duck (=Colonsay Duck.)

LADY BIRD. The PINTAIL. (Dublin Bay.)

LADY-FOWL. Said to be a name for the WIGEON.

LADY HEN. The SKY-LARK. (Shetlands.) Signifies "Our Lady's Hen."

LADY LENTLY : The GARDEN-WARBLER is so called in some parts of Northumberland. (Bolam.)

LADY SNIPE: The COMMON SNIPE. (Cheshire.)

LADY WITH THE TWELVE FLOUNCES. Swainson gives this as a Shropshire name for the GOLDFINCH.

LANCEOLATED WARBLER [No 134]. A Siberian species which has occurred recently in Great Britain.

LAND BUNTING : The CORN-BUNTING. (Provincial.)

LAND CORMORANT : The GOOSANDER. (Dublin.)

LAND CURLEW : The STONE-CURLEW.

LAND DAW : The CARRION-CROW. (Northants.)

LAND DOTTEREL : The DOTTEREL (Spurn, Yorkshire.)

LAND-DRAKE : The LAND-RAIL. (Shropshire ; Ackworth, Yorkshire.)

LAND HARLAN : The RED-BREASTED MERGANSER. (Wexford.) Harlan is a form of " Harle " (q v.).

LAND HEN : The LAND-RAIL. (Willughby.)

LAND LAVROCK . The COMMON SANDPIPER and the RINGED PLOVER. (Scotland.) Lavrock=Lark.

LAND MAUL · The BLACK-HEADED GULL. (East Yorkshire.)

LAND-RAIL [No. 454]. Commonly known also as the Corn-Crake (q.v.). Occurs in Willughby (1678) as Land Rail, Land-Hen, and Daker Hen. Most subsequent writers from Pennant to Montagu call it the Crake Gallinule. Montagu also gives Land-Rail, but as a provincial name. Rail is from Fr. *Râle*, Germ. *Ralle*, from Low Latin *Rallus*. It is mentioned by Turner, who calls it Crex after Aristotle, and gives " Daker Hen " as the English name for it. He well describes its cry when he says that it " in spring as well as early summer makes no other cry among the corn and flax than crex, crex." In Scotland if its call is frequently heard it is regarded as a sign of rain. A French name is " Roy de Cailles " (=King of the Quails), from an old belief that the Quails selected a Land-Rail to lead their migrations. A Scots belief was that the bird did not migrate, but became torpid in the winter. Newton says, " formerly it seems to have been a popular belief in England that the Land Rail in autumn transformed itself into a Water Rail, resuming its own character in spring." This belief seems to still prevail in Ireland. The Land Rail is considered a lucky bird on the Scottish Borders, where the saying runs :—

> The Lark, the Corn Crake, or the Grouse,
> Will bring good luck to ilka house

LAND SWALLOW: The SAND-MARTIN. (Hett.)

LAND-TRIPPER. The COMMON SANDPIPER (Kirkcudbright.)

LAND WHAAP The WHIMBREL. Whaap=Curlew.

LANG CRANE: The CORMORANT. (Redcar, Yorkshire.)

LANNER and LANNERET· The immature PEREGRINE FALCON, formerly considered a distinct species. Lanner was the name applied to the female, the male being termed Lanneret. From Fr *Lanier*, Lat. *Lanarius*, from *laniare*, to dissever. The old Lanner of falconry appears not to have been the *Falco lanarius* of Linnæus (=*Falco peregrinus*), but a species now called *Falco feldeggi* (Schlegel), found throughout the countries bordering on the Mediterranean. The name occurs as "Lanar" or "Lanaret" in Merrett (1667), who says it is found in Sherwood Forest and Dean Forest, while Willughby (1678) alludes to "the Lanner whose Tarcel is called the Lanneret."

LAPLAND BUNTING [No. 55]. The name is found in Gould's "Birds of Europe" (pt. x, 1834). It is the Lapland Lark-Bunting of Selby.

LAPLAND LARK-BUNTING · The LAPLAND BUNTING. (Selby, Macgillivray.)

LAPLAND LONG-SPUR. The LAPLAND BUNTING. So called from the length of the hind claw.

LAPPINCH or HAPPINCH · The LAPWING. (Cheshire)

LAPWING [No. 367]. From A Sax. *Hleápewince*, signifying "one who turns about in running or flight" (Skeat). Writers of the Middle Ages translated Lat. *Upupa* (=Hoopoe) as Lapwing, being deceived by the crest. The name Lapwing occurs in Turner (1544) and in Merrett, who further calls it Bastard Plover and Pewit. Willughby also calls it the Lapwing or Bastard Plover. A Lapwing is said to have brought assistance by its cries to the wounded founder of the old Lincolnshire family of Tyrwhitt, who assumed three Lapwings as his device in memory of the deliverance. That the story rests upon fact may be safely assumed, as it is the invariable practice of the birds to circle round in the air uttering their "pewit" cry when their haunts are invaded According to Chatto, however, the Lapwing is regarded as an unlucky bird in the south of Scotland, the cause being attributed to the fact that the Covenanters in the reigns of Charles II and James II were "frequently discovered to their pursuers by the flight and screaming of the Lapwing"

LAPWING SANDPIPER: The LAPWING. (Pennant.)
LARGE-BILLED GUILLEMOT: BRÜNNICH'S GUILLEMOT.
LARGER SPOTTED EAGLE. See SPOTTED EAGLE.
LARGEST WILLOW WREN: The WOOD-WARBLER.
LARGE WHITE-WINGED GULL: The GLAUCOUS GULL. (Yarrell.)
LARK: The SKY-LARK. Occurs in Merrett (1667). In Turner it is "Lerk." Lark is from A.Sax. *Láwerce*, Germ. *Lerche*, Dan. *Lærke*.
LARK BUNTING: The CORN-BUNTING. (Somerset.)
LAS AIR-CHOILLE. A Gaelic name for the GOLDFINCH. (Macgillivray) lit. "flame of the wood." Fleming applies it to the GREEN WOODPECKER.
LAUGHING BIRD: The GREEN WOODPECKER. (Shropshire.) from its laughing note.
LAUGHING GOOSE: The WHITE-FRONTED GOOSE. (Yorkshire, Cheshire.) It occurs in Edwards.
LAUGHING GULL: The BLACK-HEADED GULL. (Montagu.) Properly, however, the name for a distinct American species.
LAVEROCK, LAVROCK, LERRUCK, or Learock: The SKY-LARK. An old English name found in Turner (1544.) From the same root as Lark, i.e. A.Sax. *Láwerce*. The species is still known in Scotland by one or other form of the name, and Swainson also gives Learock for Lancashire, while Nelson and Clarke give Laverock as used at Sedbergh, Yorkshire.
LAVY. A local name for the COMMON GUILLEMOT. It occurs in Martin's "Voy. to St Kilda." (Also spelt Lamy.)
LEAAN: The GREAT NORTHERN DIVER and the RED-THROATED DIVER. (Yorkshire.) A Yorkshire dialect rendering of Loon.
LEACH'S FORK-TAILED PETREL [No. 320]. The name Leach's Petrel occurs in Jenyns, and Fork-tailed Petrel in Fleming and in Yarrell (1st ed.). Selby calls it the Fork-tailed Storm Petrel. It was named in honour of Dr. Leach, who acquired the type-specimen at Bullock's sale.
LEAFY WREN. A provincial name for the WREN. (Hett.)
LEARG. A Gaelic name in the Western Isles for the BLACK-THROATED and RED-THROATED DIVERS.
LEAST BUTCHER-BIRD: The BEARDED TITMOUSE. (Edwards.)
LEAST SNIPE: The DUNLIN. Montagu gives it as a provincial name.

LEAST SPOTTED WOODPECKER: The LESSER SPOTTED WOODPECKER.

LEAST TITMOUSE : The LONG-TAILED TITMOUSE. (Merrett.)

LEAST WILLOW-WREN : The CHIFFCHAFF. (Tunstall, Bewick.)

LEG BIRD. A provincial name for the SEDGE-WARBLER. (Swainson.)

LEMON BIRD. The LINNET. (West Yorkshire.)

LENNERT. A North Country name for the LINNET

LESSER ASH-COLOURED HERON : The NIGHT-HERON. (Willughby.)

LESSER BLACK-BACK · The LESSER BLACK-BACKED GULL. (Yorkshire.)

LESSER BLACK-BACKED GULL [No. 433]. The name refers to its smaller size than the GREAT BLACK-BACKED GULL. It first occurs in Montagu (1802) as Less Black-backed Gull. It is the Silvery Gull of Pennant's "Arctic Zoology"

LESSER BRAMBLING · The SNOW-BUNTING (?). Found in Pennant (1766).

LESSER BUSTARD. The LITTLE BUSTARD.

LESSER BUTCHER-BIRD: The RED-BACKED SHRIKE Occurs in Willughby (1678).

LESSER COB : The LESSER BLACK-BACKED GULL. (Provincial.)

LESSER CRESTED GREBE : The BLACK-NECKED GREBE. (Pennant.)

LESSER CRESTED LARK : The TREE-PIPIT. (Willughby, Pennant, etc.)

LESSER DUN DIVER : The RED-BRESTED MERGANSER. (Pennant)

LESSER FAUVETTE The GARDEN-WARBLER. (Bewick, 1797.)

LESSER GODWIT · The BLACK-TAILED GODWIT. (Pennant.)

LESSER GREY SHRIKE [No. 106]. The name is found in Pennant's "Arctic Zoology" and in Latham's "Synopsis."

LESSER GUILLEMOT · The COMMON GUILLEMOT. It was considered a separate species by Pennant.

LESSER IMBER : The BLACK-THROATED DIVER. (Provincial.)

LESSER KESTREL [No. 238]. A close ally of the KESTREL but smaller in size, hence the name.

LESSER MOUNTAIN FINCH or BRAMBLING: The SNOW-BUNTING. (Willughby.)

LESSER PETTYCHAPS: The CHIFFCHAFF. (Pennant and Montagu.)

LESSER RED-HEADED LINNET: The LESSER REDPOLL (Willughby, Pennant); also the TWITE (Rutty).

LESSER REDPOLL [No. 23]. It is found in Montagu (1802). Occurs in Willughby as Lesser Red-headed Linnet. The name has reference to its small size and red crown, or "poll."

LESSER REED-SPARROW: The SEDGE-WARBLER (?). Occurs in Willughby. Montagu ascribes it to the REED-WARBLER.

LESSER SADDLE-BACK: The LESSER BLACK-BACKED GULL. (Yorkshire.) From its dark saddle-shaped mantle.

LESSER SEA-SWALLOW: The LITTLE TERN. Occurs in Willughby and Ray.

LESSER SNOW GOOSE. See SNOW-GOOSE.

Lesser Sooty Tern. A tropical species of which a single example is said, on somewhat imperfect evidence, to have been taken on a lightship at the mouth of the Thames in 1875.

LESSER SPOTTED EAGLE. See SPOTTED EAGLE.

LESSER SPOTTED WATER RAIL: The SPOTTED CRAKE. (Bewick.)

LESSER SPOTTED WOODPECKER [No. 212, British Lesser Spotted Woodpecker]. The name refers to the variegated black-and-white upper-plumage and to its being of less size than the GREAT SPOTTED WOODPECKER. It occurs in Albin (1738). Hartert has separated the resident British race from the Continental forms, hence the change of name.

LESSER TERN: The LITTLE TERN.

LESSER TOOTHED DIVER. A provincial name for the RED-BREASTED MERGANSER. (Montagu.) From its serrated bill and lesser size than the GOOSANDER.

LESSER TREE-LARK: The TREE-PIPIT.

LESSER WATER-SPARROW: The SEDGE-WARBLER.

LESSER WHITE-FRONTED GOOSE [No. 276]. A very rare straggler, closely allied to the WHITE-FRONTED GOOSE, but of smaller size.

LESSER WHITETHROAT [No. 148]. The name occurs first in Latham's "Synopsis" (Supp., p. 185).

LESSER WHITE-WINGED GULL: The ICELAND GULL. (Yarrell.)

LESS TITMOUSE: The BLUE TITMOUSE. (Merrett.) Turner's Less Titmouse is apparently the LONG-TAILED TITMOUSE, as he says it has a long tail. Mr. Evans thought it to be the MARSH- or COAL-TITMOUSE.

LEVANTINE SHEARWATER [No. 329]. A Mediterranean sub-species of the MANX SHEARWATER, which occurs casually on our coasts (see Saunders, "Manual," 2nd ed., pp. 741-2). It is the *Ame damnée* of the Turks, who believe that the souls of the wicked pass into these birds and are doomed to wander for ever over the waters.

LIATH-TROISG. A Gaelic name for the FIELDFARE.

LICH-FOWL: The NIGHTJAR. (Cheshire and Shropshire.) See "Gabble-Ratchet."

LILTIE-COCK or LINTIE-COCK: The CORMORANT. (Staithes, Yorkshire.)

LINBENGOCH or LLINOS BEN GOCH. A Welsh name for the LINNET; lit. "redheaded Linnet." In North Wales the name is applied to the LESSER REDPOLL.

LING-BIRD, LING-TIT, or LINGIE: The MEADOW-PIPIT. (Cumberland, West Yorkshire.)

LING LINNET: The TWITE. (Ribblesdale, Yorkshire.)

LINKS GOOSE: The COMMON SHELD-DUCK. (Orkneys.) Because it frequents the "links" or sandy plains near the sea.

LINNET [No. 27]. So called from its partiality for the seed of flax. Der. of A.Sax. *Linete*=flax and *Linet-wige*=flax-hopper, from the latter of which is derived the northern provincial name of "Lintwhite." The name occurs as "Linot" in Turner (1544) and as "Linet" in Merrett's list. Plot (1677) has "Linnet," while Willughby calls it the "common Linnet," as does also Sibbald. It is also the Greater Red-headed Linnet of Willughby and others, and the Greater Redpole of Montagu. According to Swainson, "Linnet" is a local name for the GOLDFINCH in Shropshire.

LINNET FINCH: The LINNET. (Provincial.)

LINTIE: The LINNET (Scotland); also the TWITE (Orkneys and Shetlands).

LINTWHITE: The LINNET. (Orkneys.) As an older Scottish name it occurs as "Lintquhit," the derivation being also from A.Sax. *Linet-wige* (see under LINNET). According to Swainson Lintwhite is a Suffolk name for the SKY-LARK.

LINTYWHITE. According to Swainson the WOOD-WARBLER is so called " from the pure white of the under parts of the body." Hett gives the name to the CHIFFCHAFF.

LIPWINGLE: The LAPWING. (Bedfordshire.) An equivalent of LAPWING, the derivation being the same, viz. A.Sax. *hleápwince*.

LITTLE AUK [No. 448]. The name Little Auk is first found in Pennant (1766). Willughby calls it the "Small black-and-white Diver."

LITTLE BILLY BLUECAP: The BLUE TITMOUSE. (West Yorkshire.)

LITTLE BITTERN [No. 267]. This tiny species has been known for about a century and a quarter as a casual summer-visitor. The name is found in Pennant as Little Bittern Heron. Latham ("Syn.," v, p. 66) has Little Bittern. It is the Little Heron of Jenyns and the Little Brown Bittern of Edwards (?).

LITTLE BLACK-AND-WHITE DIVER: The LITTLE AUK.

LITTLE BLACK-AND-WHITE WOODPECKER: The LESSER SPOTTED WOODPECKER.

LITTLE BLACKCAP. The COAL-TITMOUSE. (Yorkshire.)

LITTLE BLACK-HEADED TOMTIT: The MARSH-TITMOUSE. (Montagu.)

LITTLE BLUE HAWK: The MERLIN. (Yorkshire.)

LITTLE BLUE ROCK · The STOCK-DOVE. (Notts.)

LITTLE-BREAD-AND-NO-CHEESE: The YELLOW BUNTING. (Devonshire.) Imitative of its song, also rendered "little-bit-of-bread-and-no-cheese."

LITTLE BROWN-AND-WHITE DUCK: The female HARLEQUIN-DUCK. (Edwards.)

LITTLE BUNTING [No. 52]. This irregular visitor is so called from its diminutive size in comparison with other species.

LITTLE BUSTARD [No. 451]. The name refers to its inferiority in size to the GREAT BUSTARD. It is first found in Edwards (pl. 251), and is used by succeeding writers from Pennant to Montagu and onwards. It is the "Field Duck" of Albin.

LITTLE CRAKE [No. 457]. The name occurs in Selby (1833). It is the Little Gallinule and Olivaceous Gallinule of Montagu and others.

LITTLE DARR: The LITTLE TERN. (Norfolk.)

LITTLE DIVER: The LITTLE GREBE. (Cheshire.)

Little Doucker   The LITTLE GREBE   (East Lothian.)

LITTLE DUSKY SHEARWATER [No. 324]. This Petrel is a rare straggler to us from the East Atlantic Islands, only six having been recorded in our islands.

LITTLE EGRET [No. 263]. The name Little Egret appears to have been first used by Pennant in the Appendix to his "British Zoology," and is from the Fr *aigrette.* Selby calls it Little Egret Heron   The tufts of long filiform feathers which spring from the middle and lower part of the bird's back are called after the bird, and have long been esteemed among Eastern nations as an ornament for the turban or head-dress. Such an "egret" was sent by the Sultan to Nelson after the Battle of the Nile, and was much valued by the recipient.

Little Eten Bird · The WRYNECK.   (Hampshire)
Little Feltyfare   The REDWING   (East Lothian.)
Little French Woodpecker · The LESSER SPOTTED WOODPECKER.
Little Gallinule : The LITTLE CRAKE   (Montagu)
Little Godwit. A name for the young STONE-CURLEW. (Hett.)

LITTLE GREBE [No. 340]. The name Little Grebe is found in Pennant (1766). Willughby and Ray call it "Didapper," and also "Dipper or Dobchick, or small Doucker, Loon, or Arsfoot."

Little Grey Owl   The LITTLE OWL.   (Merrett.)
Little Guillemot. A name for the LITTLE AUK.   (Hett.)

LITTLE GULL [No. 426]. The name is found in Montagu ("Orn. Dict." Supp.), it being first described by him from an example shot near Chelsea.

Little Hawk   The MERLIN.   (Cleveland, Yorkshire)
Little Heron   The LITTLE BITTERN   (Jenyns.)
Little Horn-Owl   The SCOPS OWL.   (Willughby)
Little Magpie Diver. A name for the BUFFEL-HEADED DUCK. (Hett)
Little Nack · The LITTLE AUK.   (Northumberland) Nack is a corruption of Auk
Little Night Owl   The LITTLE OWL.   (Selby).

LITTLE OWL [No. 222]   The name appears in Willughby (1678), also Pennant and all later writers

Little Peewit : The TWITE.   (North Yorkshire.) From its call-note.

L

LITTLE PETREL . The STORM-PETREL. (Pennant.)
LITTLE PICKIE : The LITTLE TERN. (Forfarshire.)
LITTLE RED HAWK : The KESTREL. (Yorkshire.)
LITTLE REDPOLE LINNET : The LESSER REDPOLL.
LITTLE RING DOTTRELL : The LITTLE RINGED PLOVER. (Gould.)
LITTLE RINGED PLOVER [No. 359]. The name is found in Jenyns (1835) and also Yarrell (1st ed) and later writers.
LITTLE SANDPIPER : The LITTLE STINT ; also TEMMINCK'S STINT. (Montagu.)
LITTLE SNIPE : The DUNLIN. (Swaledale and Arkengarthdale, Yorkshire)
LITTLE STINT [No. 375]. This name appears in Bewick (1797). It is the Little Sandpiper of Pennant, Montagu, Latham, etc., and the " Minute Tringa " of Selby.
LITTLE TERN [No. 421]. " Little Tern " seems to be first found in Gould's " Birds of Europe " (pt. 8, 1834) Pennant (1766) and succeeding authors to Yarrell (1843) generally call this species " Lesser Tern." It is the Lesser Sea-Swallow of Willughby.
LITTLE WHAUP   The WHIMBREL. (East Lothian) lit. " Little Curlew."
LITTLE WHITE HERON : The LITTLE EGRET (Willughby); also the young BUFF-BACKED HERON (Montagu).
LITTLE WOODCOCK : The GREAT SNIPE. (Ireland.)
LITTLE WOODPECKER: The LESSER SPOTTED WOODPECKER (Yorkshire) ; the TREECREEPER (Marton-in-Cleveland, Yorkshire).
LITTLE WOODPIE · The LESSER SPOTTED WOODPECKER. (Hampshire) The GREAT SPOTTED WOODPECKER is called " Woodpie " in the same county.
LITTLE WREN   The GOLDEN-CRESTED WREN. (Loftus-in-Cleveland, Yorkshire.)
LIVER or LEVER. The species intended by this name seems a matter of uncertainty. Montagu (" Orn. Dict.," Supp., 1813) is the authority for stating that it was an Ibis, called " Liver," and that the conjunction of the name with the " pool " on which it was obtained, gives rise to the name of the city of Liverpool. Newton was of opinion that Lever was the correct spelling and that the SPOONBILL was intended, a bird which of course frequented such places and moreover bred in England in ancient times. Newton cites Randle

Holmes's "Academy of Armory" (1688) as deriving the word "Lever" from *Lepelaer, Leplar,* and *Lefler* (or *Lofflar*) of Low and High Dutch, which are all names of the Spoonbill. The first-mentioned name occurs in Albin, 1738, as Leplaer, Low Dutch for the Spoonbill. According to Baines's "Hist. of Lancaster" the oldest known form of the name Liverpool (temp. Hen. II) is "Lirpul" or "Litherpul."

LLEIAN. A Welsh name for the BLUE TITMOUSE, lit. "Nun."

LLEIAN GYNFFON HIR. The LONG-TAILED TITMOUSE. (North Wales) lit "long-tailed nun"

LLEIAN WEN. The SMEW. (North Wales) lit. "white nun."

LLINOS · The LINNET. (North Wales) lit. "Linnet."

LLINOS BENGOCH LEIF. A Welsh name for the LESSER REDPOLL; lit. "lesser red-headed Linnet"

LLINOS FELEN. A Welsh name for the YELLOW BUNTING; lit. "yellow linnet."

LLINOS Y MYNYDD. A Welsh name for the TWITE; lit. "mountain linnet."

LLOSTRUDDYN. The REDSTART. (North Wales) lit. "redtail."

LLURSEN or LLURS. The RAZORBILL. (North Wales) lit. "razorbill"

LLWYDFRON: The WHITETHROAT (North Wales) lit. "pale breast."

LLWYDFRON FACH · The LESSER WHITETHROAT. (North Wales) lit. "little pale breast"

LLWYD Y GWRYCH, LLWYD Y BERTH, LLWYD BACH. Welsh names for the HEDGE-SPARROW the first two signify "grey (bird) of the hedge," and the third "little grey (bird)"

LLWYD YR HESG, LLWYD Y GORS The SEDGE-WARBLER. (North Wales). First is "grey (bird) of the hedge," and second "grey (bird) of the marsh."

LLWYD Y TYWOD. A Welsh name for the SANDERLING; lit. "grey (bird) of the sand."

LOERING. The adult CORMORANT. (Shetlands.)

LON DUBH: The Gaelic name for the BLACKBIRD.

LONGBILL · The WOODCOCK. (Provincial.) From the length of the bill.

LONG-BILLED CHOUGH · The CHOUGH.

LONG-BILLED GOOSE · The PINK-FOOTED GOOSE. (Yorkshire.)

LONG-EARED OWL [No. 224] The name first occurs in Pennant (1766). It is the "Hornoul" of Turner and the "Horn-Owl" of Willughby and Ray, while Fleming as late as 1842 calls it "Long Horn Owl."

LONG-HORNED ULLAT. The LONG-EARED OWL. (Yorkshire.) "Ullat"=Howlet.

LONG HORN OWL: The LONG-EARED OWL. (Fleming.)

LONGIE: The COMMON GUILLEMOT. (Shetlands.)

LONGIE CRANE. The HERON. (Pembroke.)

LONG-LEGGED PLOVER. The former name for the BLACK-WINGED STILT (q.v.).

LONG-LEGS. A provincial name for the BLACK-WINGED STILT. (Montagu.) Bewick also gives Longshanks.

LONG-NEB (=LONG-BILL): The COMMON SNIPE. (Yorkshire.)

LONG-NECK. The LITTLE BITTERN (Montagu); the PINTAIL (Holy Island); the HERON (Sedbergh, Yorkshire.)

LONG-NECKED HERON. The HERON. (Ireland.)

LONGNIX (LONG-NECK?): The HERON. (Cheshire.)

LONGSHANKS. A name for the BLACK-WINGED STILT. (Hett.)

LONG-TAILED CAPON: The LONG-TAILED TITMOUSE. (Hampshire, Norfolk.)

LONG-TAILED DUCK [No. 304]. The name first occurs in Edwards, and is used by almost all succeeding authors. Selby, however, calls it Long-tailed Hareld. It is the "Sharp-tailed Duck" and also "Swallow-tailed Sheldrake" of Willughby and Ray.

LONG-TAILED HARELD. See LONG-TAILED DUCK.

LONG-TAILED LABBE: The ARCTIC SKUA. (Bewick.)

LONG-TAILED MAG, LONGTAILED MUFFLIN, LONG-TAILED PIE, LONG-TAILED CREEPER, LONG-TAILED CHITTERING, LONG POD, LONG TOM. Provincial names for the LONG-TAILED TITMOUSE.

LONG-TAILED MAG or LONG-TAILED SHELDRAKE: The LONG-TAILED DUCK.

LONG-TAILED SKUA [No. 442]. Often called Buffon's Skua.

LONG-TAILED TITMOUSE [No. 101. British Long-tailed Titmouse]. The name first occurs in Merrett's list (1667); also in Willughby. The resident British form was first distinguished as long ago as 1836 by Blyth.

LONG TONGUE: The WRYNECK. (Provincial.) From its long projectile tongue.

LONGWING or LONGWINGS The SWIFT. (Cheshire, Yorkshire.)

LON UISGE. A Gaelic name for the DIPPER: lit. "water blackbird."

LOOM. An equivalent of Loon.

LOON The Divers and Grebes (various species). From Icel. *Lómr*. The name is applied in Shetland and South Ireland to the RED-THROATED DIVER. Willughby and Ray call the LITTLE GREBE the "Small Loon," their " Greatest Speckled Loon " being the GREAT NORTHERN DIVER. Loom and Lumme are equivalents; the former is applied to BRUNNICH'S GUILLEMOT. Probably signifying one who is clumsy, and perhaps connected with *lame* (Skeat.)

LOUGH DIVER The SMEW. (Willughby.) As a provincial name it seems to belong to the immature male.

LUCHD FAIRGE. A Gaelic name for the STORM-PETREL (Western Isles) lit. "sea mouse."

LULEAN FINCH. A name for the BRAMBLING. (Hett.)

LUMME The BLACK-THROATED DIVER. Occurs in Willughby (see Loon.)

LUNDA The PUFFIN. From Scand. *Lunde*. Newton considered that Lundy Island, a resort of Puffins, derived its name from this species

LYKE FOULE The EAGLE-OWL (Turner) Printed "alyke foule " (?) " a lyke foule." Pliny says it is a fatal bird, of evil omen beyond other sorts, especially at public auguries.

LYMPTWIGG The LAPWING (Exmoor.) An equivalent of "Lapwing." From A Sax. *hleápe-wince*

LYON The GREAT NORTHERN DIVER. (Holy Island.) Also applied to other species.

LYRIE The MANX SHEARWATER. (Shetlands and Orkneys) Lyrie is the usual name on the west coast of Shetland. Mr. Robert Godfrey tells me that in Fethaland " to gan as licht's a lyrie " (i.e to be as easy in one's motion as a Shearwater) is a proverbial saying. Also spelt Lyre.

LYSEOULE The EAGLE-OWL (Aldrovandus.) See also "Lyke foule "

MAA or MAR · The COMMON GULL. (Kirkcudbright.) From A Sax *Mæw*, Icel *Már*, a gull; originally from the bird's cry.

MAALIN. A corruption of MERLIN. (Shetlands) According to Saxby the name is also applied in the Shetlands to the KESTREL and the SPARROW-HAWK.

MACKEREL-BIRD: The WRYNECK is so called in Guernsey (Cecil Smith), because it arrives at the time when mackerel is in season.

MACKEREL-COCK: The MANX SHEARWATER. (Rutty.) It is also a local name at Lleyn Island, North Wales (Forrest) and at Lambay Island, on the east coast of Ireland. It is so-called from its feeding on mackerel-fry.

MACKEREL GANT: The GANNET. (Yorkshire.)

MACKEREL-GULL: The RAZORBILL (Provincial.) The KITTIWAKE GULL. (Humber District.)

MACQUEEN'S BUSTARD [No 452]. A form of the Houbara Bustard, the name of which arises from its having been named *Otis macqueeni*, in honour of Macqueen, by Gray and Hardwicke ("Illustrations Indian Zoology.") It was included as British by Yarrell (1st ed.).

MADDRICK GULL: The BLACK-HEADED GULL. (Cornwall)

MADEIRAN FORK-TAILED PETREL [No. 321]. A very rare straggler. It was first recorded as British by Saunders ("Manual," 2nd ed., p. 731).

MADGE, MAG, MAGGIE, MARGET, or MIGGY. Provincial names for the MAGPIE

MADGE-HOWLET. The TAWNY OWL (Willughby): also the BARN-OWL (Norfolk).

MAGGIE: The COMMON GUILLEMOT. (Forfar.) Swainson says it is from its black-and-white plumage resembling that of a MAGPIE.

MAGGOT. A Lincolnshire name for the MAGPIE, occuring also in Worcestershire as Magget. (See "Magot Pie" and also "Pie.")

MAG LOON: The RED-THROATED DIVER. (Norfolk.) Signifies "Magpie Loon."

MAGOT PIE: The Mid. Eng. name for the MAGPIE, the latter name being a contraction. The name appears to have no reference to the bird's habit of picking maggots from the backs of sheep, being derived from the French *Margot*, a diminutive of *Marguerite*, but also signifying a Magpie, perhaps from its noisy chattering, in which it is popularly supposed to resemble a talkative woman The name occurs in this form in "Macbeth" (act III. sc. 4):—

> Augurs and understood relations have,
> By magot pies, and choughs, and rooks, brought forth,
> The secret'st man of blood.

MAGPIE [No. 6]. From Mag, a diminutive of Margaret, and Fr *Pie*, a Magpie. Found in Barlow's plates (1655) as "Magpye." Occurs in Merrett and also Willughby as Magpie; Albin spells it "Magpy," and Rutty "Magpye" The folk-lore of our islands is tolerably rich in allusions to the Magpie, as are also the still, or recently, existing evidences of totemism or animal-worship. Keary ("Outlines of Primitive Belief") says that in Ireland a Magpie tapping at the window is taken as a death-warning; also that it is unlucky to kill one of these birds; the latter belief is also met with in north-east Scotland (Gregor). Gray mentions a Dunbar bailie who was in the habit of turning back home if he encountered a pair of Magpies on setting out Harland and Wilkinson ("Lancashire Folk Lore") record the belief that it is unlucky to meet a Magpie, and when it is seen the hat is raised in salutation and the cross signed on the breast or made by crossing the thumbs and then spitting over them. Brand ("Popular Antiquities") makes it accounted unlucky in Lancashire to see *two* Magpies together. In Devonshire, according to Dyer, the peasant, on seeing a single Magpie, spits over his right shoulder three times to avert ill-luck, repeating the following words —

> Clean birds by sevens,
> Unclean by twos,
> The dove in the heavens
> Is the one I choose.

In parts of the North of England it is said to be unlucky to see it cross the path in front of one from left to right, but lucky if from right to left. In the north east of Scotland the sight of one is considered lucky in some villages and unlucky in others (Gregor).

A belief in the power of the Magpie to transform itself into human form is recorded as among the superstitions of Clunie, Perthshire, until the end of the eighteenth century (Gomme) The first Magpies that migrated to Ireland are said to have landed in south-east Wexford, where the first English settlement also took place, and whence the Magpies have since spread over the island Smith ("History of Cork") says it was not known in Ireland seventy years before the time at which he wrote, about 1746 An old Irish saying in this connection is that —"Ireland will never be rid of the English while the Magpie remains." Barrett Hamilton ("Zool.," 1891, p 247) thinks Magpies were first seen in Ireland about 1676 when "a parcel" landed in Wexford. Moryson in 1617 states that "Ireland hath neither singing nightingall, nor chattering pye, nor undermining moule."

I have heard a quaint old saying that :
> One's mirth, two's grief,
> Three's a wedding, four's death,
> Five's heaven, six is hell,
> Sen's the devil's ain sel'.

Dyer gives another version of this rhyme as follows :
> One is sorrow, two mirth,
> Three a wedding, four a birth,
> Five heaven, six hell,
> Seven the de'il's ain sell.

According to Dyer, in Morayshire it is believed that Magpies flying near the windows of a house portend a speedy death to some inmate, a belief which is held in other parts in connexion with various species of birds. Dyer says that "an old tradition" explains the origin of the ill-luck attributed to meeting a Magpie, by the supposition that it was the only bird that refused to enter the Ark with Noah, preferring to perch on the roof and jabber over the drowning world ; but of course this is an idle tale and the real reason must be that it is a survival of totemism. Halliwell ("Popular Rhymes") relates a popular legend accounting for the half nest of the Magpie, to the effect that this bird, once upon a time, was the only bird unable to build a nest, and that the other birds undertook to instruct her. In response, however, to every piece of advice the Magpie kept repeating "Ah ! I knew that afore," until their patience being exhausted, they left her to finish it herself, with the result that to this day the Magpie's nest remains incomplete.

A provincial belief, according to Inwards, is that when Magpies fly abroad singly, the weather either is or will soon be stormy, but when both birds are seen together the weather will be mild.

MAGPIE : The LONG-TAILED TITMOUSE is sometimes so called, on account of its long tail.

MAGPIE DIVER : The SMEW. On account of its pied plumage.

MAIDEN DUCK : The SHOVELER. (Wexford.)

MALDUCK : The FULMAR. (Shetlands.) See Mallemuck.

MALE . The KNOT. (Essex.)

MALLARD and WILD DUCK [No. 287, MALLARD]. The names "Mallard" and "Wild Duck" both occur in Barlow's plates (1655), Mallard being the male name (Fr. *malart*) ; the female should be termed Wild Duck. The name occurs in Merrett's list as "Wild Duck" and in Willughby and Ray as the "common wild Duck and Mallard." Most British authors from Pennant onward call it the Wild Duck

MALLEMUCK. An old Dutch-mariner's name for the FULMAR. Now corrupted into "Molly-mawk," and applied to various other species such as the BLACK-BROWED ALBATROSS. "Mallemucke" occurs for the Fulmar in Martin's "Voyage to Spitzbergen," and Bewick (1804) gives "Mallemoke" Mallemock, Mallimoke, Malmock, or Malduck are still Shetland names for the Fulmar, and Mollemoke or Mollemawk Yorkshire names both for that species and the GLAUCOUS GULL.

MAN-OF-WAR BIRD The ARCTIC SKUA. (Provincial.)

MANX SHEARWATER [No. 328] The name first occurs in Selby. Willughby calls it the "Puffin of the Isle of Man," and Edwards the "Manks Puffin." Pennant terms it the Manx Petrel and Montagu simply "Shearwater." Willughby quotes Sir Thomas Browne as saying that it "doth as it were *radere aquam*, shear the water, from whence perhaps it had its name"

MARBLE THRUSH. A name for the MISTLE-THRUSH (Northants); from the marble-like spots on its breast.

MARBURAN. A Cornish name for the RAVEN.

MARCH OWL The SHORT-EARED OWL. (Provincial.)

MARIGOLD BIRD This name is found in Rutty's "Nat Hist. of Co Dublin," 1772, and seems to be the GOLDEN-CRESTED WREN, which is known elsewhere as Marygold Finch, according to Hett

MARIGOLD FINCH· The GOLDEN-CRESTED WREN. (Provincial)

MARIONETTE. A name for the BUFFEL-HEADED DUCK. (Hett.)

MARKET JEW CROW. A Cornish name for the CHOUGH, and also the HOODED CROW, from their frequenting the neighbourhood of Marazion. (Swainson.)

MARROTT: The COMMON GUILLEMOT (South Scotland), also applied to the RAZORBILL in East Lothian and Aberdeen It also occurs as Marrock and is derived from Icel. *Már*, from the cry of the bird. According to Swainson Marrot is also a name for the PUFFIN

MARSH GOOSE The GREY LAG-GOOSE. (Provincial.)

MARSH-HARRIER [No. 245]. This species, so called from its predilection for marshes and bogs, is the Moor-Buzzard of all our earlier writers, from Willughby and Ray up to Fleming (1842). Edwards, however, has Marsh Hawk. Marsh Harrier seems to occur first in Selby (1825.)

MARSH HAWK: The MARSH-HARRIER. (Edwards.)

MARSH HEN: The MOORHEN. (Provincial.)

MARSH OWL: The SHORT-EARED OWL. (Provincial.)

MARSH REEDLING: The REED-WARBLER. (Provincial.)

MARSH-SANDPIPER [No. 397]. An Asiatic species which has been taken four times in England. The name is probably a translation of Bechstein's name for the species (*Totanus stagnatilis.*)

MARSH-TITMOUSE [No. 97, British Marsh-Titmouse]. First occurs in Willughby (1678). This form is now considered to be restricted to England and Wales, its place being taken in Scotland by the WILLOW-TITMOUSE (q.v.), which however also occurs along with it in many localities in England.

MARSH-WARBLER [No. 137]. A scarce and local summer-visitor, so called from the situations it is supposed to frequent, but the name is more or less of a misnomer.

MARTHIN DDU. A Welsh name for the SWIFT; literally "Black Martin."

MARTHIN' PENBWL. A Welsh name for the MARTIN.

MARTIN [No. 197]. From Fr. *Martin*, a proper name. Usually called House-Martin in modern works. The first name, "Martin," occurs in Merrett (1667) and Willughby (1678). Turner (1544) calls this species "rok martinette or chirche martnette."

MARTINET, MARTINETTE, MARTNET, MARTLET: The MARTIN. *Martinet* is Fr. for the SWIFT. "Martlet" occurs in Shakespeare's "Merchant of Venice" (act II, sc 9):—
> Like the martlet
> Builds in the weather on the outward wall.

MARTIN-OIL: The STORM-PETREL is so called in Galway according to Swainson. It seems as though "oil-martin" is intended.

MARTIN SNIPE: The GREEN-SANDPIPER. (Norfolk.) Stevenson says it is from the white upper tail-coverts and rump forming such a contrast to its dark body.

MARTIN SWALLOW: The MARTIN (East Lothian)

MASKED GULL: The BLACK-HEADED GULL. (Fleming.)

MASKED SHRIKE [No 111]. This south-west Asiatic species was first recorded for the British Isles in 1905, by Mr. Nicoll ("Bull B.O C," xvi, p. 22).

MATTAGESS or MATTAGASSE· The GREAT GREY SHRIKE. The name occurs in Willughby (1678), who remarks that it is a name borrowed from the Savoyards. It was formerly used by falconers, who employed this species sometimes

MAVIS· The SONG-THRUSH. From Fr. *Mauvis*. Probably not now much used, although said to be so in Yorkshire; Newton thinks it was perhaps in England originally the *table* name of the bird. It occurs in Turner (1544) and in Spenser, but Shakespeare, who, as Mr. Harting has observed, only mentions this species three times, prefers our English word Throstle. Willughby has "Mavis, Throstle. or Song-thrush." In south-west Scotland it becomes "Mavie," in which form it is still in use.

MAW or MEW An old English name for a Gull, from A.Sax. *mæw* = gull Maw occurs in Turner for the BLACK-HEADED GULL, while it is a local name in Orkney and Shetland for the COMMON GULL.

MAWP. The BULLFINCH (Lancashire) Swainson thinks it is derived from "Alp"

MAY-CHICK. According to Sir Thomas Browne this was a Norfolk name for a bird "a little bigger than a Stint, of fatness beyond any"

MAY-COCK. The GREY PLOVER (Provincial)

MAY-FOWL, MAY-BIRD, or MAY CURLEW· The WHIMBREL. (Ireland chiefly.) So called from the month in which it arrives May-bird is also a Norfolk name.

MAZE FINCH (Maize Finch?)· The CHAFFINCH. (Cornwall.)

MEADOW-BUNTING [No. 49]. A south European species added to the British List in recent years.

MEADOW CRAKE The LAND-RAIL. (Selby)

MEADOW DRAKE The LAND-RAIL (Yorkshire and Notts).

MEADOW LARK The TREE-PIPIT (Montagu); also the MEADOW-PIPIT (Notts. and Hants)

MEADOW-PIPIT [No. 68] The name occurs in Selby (1825). In previous authors it was confused with other species, and occurs under a variety of names. It is the Titlark of Pennant and other authors up to Montagu. The latter author's "Field Lark or Meadow Lark" is the TREE-PIPIT.

MEADOW TITLING: The MEADOW-PIPIT. (Provincial.)

MEALY BIRD: The young LONG-TAILED DUCK. (Norfolk.)

MEALY MILLER'S THUMB or MILLER'S THUMB: The LONG-TAILED TITMOUSE. (Yorkshire.) From its small size.

MEALY-MOUTH. A Craven name for the WILLOW-WARBLER; also the LESSER WHITETHROAT (North Yorkshire).

MEALY REDPOLL [No. 21]. The name is found in Gould's "Birds of Europe" (pt. xi). It also occurs as Mealy Redpole, an incorrect spelling, as the name arises from its red head (or poll).

MEDITERRANEAN BLACK-HEADED GULL [No. 428]. A Mediterranean species of much the same size as the BLACK-HEADED GULL, but with a really black head.

MEDITERRANEAN GREAT SHEARWATER [No. 326]. A species of Petrel confined to the Mediterranean, but of which a single example was picked up at Pevensey Beach, Sussex, in 1906.

MEGGY: The WHITETHROAT. (North Country) An abbreviation of Margaret (?). Also occurs as Muggy.

MELHUEZ A Cornish name for the SKY-LARK. Mr. Harting thinks it the same as Pelhudz="high-flight."

MELODIOUS WARBLER [No. 142]. First recorded as British by Saunders ("Man. Br. Birds," 1899, p. 77).

MELODIOUS WILLOW-WARBLER: The ICTERINE WARBLER. (Hewitson.) Gould calls it Melodious Willow Wren.

MERLE· The BLACKBIRD. Anglicization of Old. F. *merle* "a mearle, owsell. blackbird" (Cotgrave), from Lat. *merula*. Probably obsolete except in poetry, although Swainson gives it as a Scots and Irish provincial name. Canon Atkinson gives it as a Shakespearean name, but probably erroneously, as I find only "ouzel-cock" (Midsummer Night's Dream") and "black ouzel" (Henry IV).

MERLIN [No. 236] In Old. Eng. Marlin and Marlion, from Old Fr. *Esmerillon* or *Smirlon*. The name occurs in Turner (1544) and in Willughby. Sibbald gives Merlin as the name of the female and Jack as the name of the male, and among falconers formerly the latter was generally called Jack-Merlin, Merlin being properly the term for the female bird (see "Jack.")

MERWYS. A poetical Welsh name for the BLACKBIRD.

MEW. An old English name for any species of Gull (see "Maw"). Also occurs as "Mell."

MICHAELMAS BLACKBIRD The RING-OUZEL. (Dorset.) From the time of its autumnal appearance in flocks at Portland.

MIDDEN CROW The CARRION-CROW (Bewick): midden =refuse. "Midden Daup" is a Craven form of the name.

MIDDLE SPOTTED WOODPECKER The young of the GREAT SPOTTED WOODPECKER, described by Linnæus as a separate species, and called Middle Spotted Woodpecker by Pennant and other writers up to Montagu.

MIGRATORY PIGEON The *Passenger-Pigeon* (Eyton.)

MILFRAN The CARRION-CROW. (North Wales) lit. "carrion crow."

MILLER. An old name for the HEN-HARRIER. The name was applied only to the grey male birds. It appears also to be a local name for the WHITETHROAT, and Swainson says it is a Shropshire name for the young SPOTTED FLYCATCHER.

MILLER'S THUMB or TOM THUMB The GOLDEN CRESTED WREN and the WILLOW-WARBLER (Roxburgh); the CHIFFCHAFF, WILLOW-WARBLER and WOOD-WARBLER (Yorkshire) From their small size.

MINUTE TRINGA The LITTLE STINT. (Selby.)

MIRE-CROW. The BLACK-HEADED GULL (Willughby.)

MIRE-DRUM. The BITTERN. (Montagu and others.) Probably now obsolete.

MIRE DRUMBLE The GREAT WHITE HERON. The name occurs in Merrett (1667) who applies it to *Ardea alba* The name "Mire Drum" has also been used for the COMMON BITTERN, while Turner's Mire Drumble appears to be the LITTLE EGRET.

MIRE DUCK: The MALLARD. (Forfar.)

MIRE SNIPE. The COMMON SNIPE. (Aberdeen.)

MIRET. The COMMON TERN. (Cornwall.)

MISSEL-BIRD or MISSEL THRUSH: The MISTLE-THRUSH.

MISSELTOE-THRUSH The MISTLE-THRUSH. (Charleton.)

MISTLE-THRUSH [No. 156]. There seems no doubt that the name of this bird is a contraction of Mistletoe Thrush, and should be spelled "Mistle" in place of "Missel." It is mentioned by Turner, who says it is particularly known as "Thrushe," as distinguished from the Song-thrush, which he calls "Throssel, or Mavis" The name "Mistletoe Thrush" occurs first in Merrett (1667); Charleton (1668) has "Misseltoe-thrush or Shreitch," while Willughby calls it the "Missel-bird or Shrite" That "Missel" however is used by the latter as an equivalent of "Mistle" (or Mistletoe), is evident from the remark (p. 187) that it "feeds in winter upon Holly berries, but feeds the young upon 'Misselto' berries." Aristotle mentions this species also under the name of *viscivorous*, "since it feeds on naught but mistletoe and gum." Albin (1738) spells it "Mizzel-bird," perhaps erroneously. Pennant (1766) says that "the ancients believed that the *misseltoe* could not be propagated but by the berries that had passed through the body of this bird." Newton (Yarrell, 4th ed., I, p. 620) says the bird "derives its name from feeding on Mistletoe berries, a fact known to Aristotle," and says the name should be Mistletoe Thrush, not Missel Thrush. The spelling Missel Thrush seems to be due to a want of knowledge of the mis-spelling of the plant's name. Skeat also says the name is from its feeding on the berries of the mistletoe, which he derives from A.Sax. *mistel*, a dim. of *mist*, and *tan*, a twig, but Lees ("Botanical Looker-out," 1842) suggests Old Eng *mistion*, defined by Johnson as "the state of being mingled," and Old. Eng. *tod* or *toe*, a bush, i.e. "mingled bush," an allusion to its parasitic nature. As is well known, the mistletoe was held sacred by the Druids. Its growth was ascribed to seeds transplanted from one tree to another by this bird. Another derivation is that given by Prior ("Popular Names of Brit. Plants"), who says that it is from "A.Sax. *mistiltan*, from *mistl*, different, and *tan*, twig, being so unlike the tree it grows upon." The Mistle-Thrush is supposed in some localities to sing particularly loud and long before rain (see Storm-cock).

MITEY. A Shetland name for the STORM-PETREL. Mr. Robert Godfrey tells me he has heard it used in Fethaland and thinks it may be a contraction of "Alamouti" (q.v.). Swainson has "Mitty."

MITHER O' THE MAWKINS: The LITTLE GREBE (Stirling), i.e. "Mother o' the hares," signifying a witch or uncanny person, from its diving capabilities (Swainson).

MIZZLY DICK: The MISTLE-THRUSH. (Northumberland.)

MOAT HEN: The MOORHEN (q.v.).

MOCHRUM ELDERS: The CORMORANT. (Wigtown.) From a loch of that name.

MOCK NIGHTINGALE· The BLACKCAP (Norfolk); the SEDGE-WARBLER (North Yorkshire).

MOLENEK. A Cornish name for the GOLDFINCH.

MOLL HERN. The HERON. (Midlands.)

MOLLY MAWK. See Mallemuck.
MOLLY WASH-DISH   The PIED WAGTAIL. (Hampshire, Somerset)
MOLROOKEN · The GREAT CRESTED GREBE. (Lough Neagh.)
MONK   The BULLFINCH (male). An allusion to its black cap or hood
MONTAGU'S HARRIER [No. 246]. The name seems to occur first in Yarrell (1843) perhaps as a translation of Temminck's *Busard montagu* ("Man.," I, p. 76). It is so called in honour of Col. Montagu, as he was for long supposed to be the first describer of the species under the name of Ash-coloured Falcon ("Orn Dict.," I, 1802) He was, however, anticipated by Albin, who in 1738 published a plate of the species which was later used by Linnæus ("Syst Nat," I, p. 89, 1758) in describing the bird under the name of *Falco pygargus*, thus antedating Montagu.
MONTHLY BIRD. The FIELDFARE. (Forfar.) Swainson thought it might stand for mountain bird.
MOONIE   The GOLDEN-CRESTED WREN is said to be so called at Holy Island, while in Roxburghshire it is called "moon" or "muin." It is said that these names are derived from the frequent appearance of the bird during a full "Hunter's Moon" (Bolam). Mr. Witherby tells me "Shiely" is a more frequent Holy-Island name for this bird.
MOOR BIRD   The RED GROUSE is sometimes so called in Yorkshire
MOOR BLACKBIRD   The RING-OUZEL. (Cheshire and North Yorkshire)
MOOR BUZZARD or MORE BUZZARD   The MARSH-HARRIER. (Probably obsolete) Formerly a common indigenous species before the draining of the fens and marshes, from its partiality to which the bird takes its name, the "moor" being equivalent to "mire" or marsh Willughby (1678) calls it the "more-Buzzard," and later writers up to Fleming (1842) call it "Moor-Buzzard"
MOOR COCK or MOOR FOWL: The RED GROUSE. (Sibbald.) Moor-hen is also a name for the female.
MOOR COOT   The MOORHEN. (Provincial)
MOOR CROW: The HOODED CROW. (Nidd Valley, Yorkshire.)
MOOR DOTTEREL: The DOTTEREL. (Whitby, Yorkshire.)

MOOR GAME : The RED GROUSE. (Yorkshire ; and Longdendale, Cheshire.)

MOOR GLEAD. A Border name for the HEN-HARRIER.

MOOR HAWK · The MARSH-HARRIER (formerly).

MOORHEN [No. 460] It is also commonly known as the Water Hen. Moor is from A.Sax. *mór*, and was anciently equivalent to morass or bog, the name having therefore much the same meaning as Water Hen The name Moor Hen occurs in Merrett (1667). Willughby spells it " Morehen." Turner (1544) has " water hen, or Mot hen," and alludes to the bird as generally haunting " Moats which surround the houses of the great " and fish-ponds.

MOOR LINNET or MOOR PEEP : The TWITE. (Cheshire.)

MOOR PEEP : The MEADOW-PIPIT. (Cheshire.)

MOOR PIPIT : The MEADOW-PIPIT. (Northumberland.)

MOOR POUT or MOOR POOT : The young RED GROUSE. (Yorkshire.)

MOOR THRUSH : The RING-OUZEL. (Sedbergh, Yorkshire.)

MOOR-TITLING : The STONECHAT. (Willughby.) Also occurs in Merrett (1667) but mis-printed " Moor-titing." Moor Tit or Titling is still a Cleveland (Yorkshire) name for the species. The name is, perhaps, more often applied to the MEADOW-PIPIT in North England and Scotland.

MORANT : The MOORHEN. (Willughby) Swainson thinks it signifies Moor-ent ?

MORE-COCK : The RED GROUSE. Occurs in Willughby. (Same as Moor-cock.)

MORE-HEN : The MOORHEN. (Willughby.) Same as Moorhen (q v.).

MORHEN : The female BLACK GROUSE (?). (Turner.) Mr. Evans supposed it to be the PTARMIGAN, but Turner says it is the bird he took to be the " Attagen " (q.v.).

MORILLON. A fowler's name for the GOLDENEYE, but applied only to immature or female birds, which were formerly supposed to be of a different species. From Fr. *morillon*.

MORRA · The RAZORBILL. (North Wales.) From its guttural cry.

MORREL HEN . The GREAT SKUA. (See Murrel Hen.)

MORTETTER : The STONECHAT. Occurs in Turner.

MORWENNOL DDU : The BLACK TERN. (North Wales) lit. " black sea-swallow."

Morwennol fach   The LITTLE TERN. (North Wales) lit. "little sea-swallow."

Morwennol y Gogledd   The ARCTIC SKUA. (North Wales) lit. "Arctic sea-swallow."

Moscovian Black Game Cock and Hen.   The CAPERCAILLIE. (Albin, ii, pl 29, 30.)

Moss-cheeper or Moss-cheepuck ·   The MEADOW-PIPIT. (North England and North Ireland)

Moss Duck ·   The MALLARD. (Renfrew and Aberdeen.)

Moss Hen.   A local Yorkshire name for the female RED GROUSE

Moss Owl   The SHORT-EARED OWL. (Yorkshire, Forfar.) Swainson thought it signified Mouse Owl, and it happens that Mouse-hawk is a name for the species; Nelson and Clarke, however, give it as a name for the species on the north-west fells of Yorkshire, and it might well signify its frequenting the mosses.

Mot-hen :   The MOORHEN. Occurs in Turner and signifies "Moat-hen" (see MOORHEN).

Mother Carey's Chicken ·   The STORM-PETREL; also any other small species of Petrel. Yarrell thought the name was given by Capt Carteret's sailors, from some unknown hag of that name.

Moth-Hawk or Moth-hunter : The NIGHTJAR.   (Provincial.)

Moth Owl .   The NIGHTJAR.   (Cheshire)

Mountain Blackbird ·   The RING-OUZEL. (Ireland and Scotland, Yorkshire.)

Mountain Bunting   The SNOW-BUNTING. (Cheshire.) Also occurs as a distinct species in the older writers, from Pennant to Montagu.

Mountain Colley   The RING-OUZEL. (Somerset.) "Colley" is from the white gorget or collar (Fr. *collet*).

Mountain Finch   The SNOW-BUNTING is so called by the bird-stuffers of Brechin and Kirriemuir (Gray). It is also a Border and Nottinghamshire and Yorkshire name for the BRAMBLING.

Mountain Harrier   A name for the HEN-HARRIER.

Mountain Linnet :   The TWITE   (Yorkshire.) Occurs in Willughby, also Pennant, etc.

Mountain Magpie   A name for the GREAT GREY SHRIKE. (Montagu.)

Mountain Ouzel :   The RING-OUZEL   (North Country.)

M

Mountain Partridge. A variety of the COMMON PARTRIDGE.

MOUNTAIN SPARROW. An old name for the TREE-SPARROW. It occurs in Albin, Pennant and Montagu, and is also a local Cheshire name for the species at the present day.

MOUNTAIN THRUSH : The RING-OUZEL. (Kirkcudbright.)

MOUSE FALCON. A name for the KESTREL. (Hett.)

MOUSE-HAWK. A provincial name for the SHORT-EARED OWL (Montagu); also the KESTREL (Loftus-in-Cleveland, and Beverley, Yorkshire).

MUD-DABBER or MUD-STOPPER : The NUTHATCH. (South England.) So called from its habit of plastering round its nesting-hole with mud.

MUD LARK. A name for the ROCK-PIPIT. (Hett.)

MUD PLOVER A name for the GREY PLOVER from its frequenting flats on the sea-shore.

MUFFIE WREN : The WILLOW-WARBLER. (Renfrew.)

MUFFIT : The WHITETHROAT. (Scotland.) Because the feathers of the head and neck stand out so as to suggest a muffler.

MUGGY : The WHITETHROAT. (North Yorkshire.) Newton thinks it is possibly cognate with the latter part of Germ. *Grasmücke* (Grass-Midge), but perhaps it is only a corruption of Meggie, as Nelson and Clarke say both names are in use in the North Riding of Yorkshire.

MUIR DUCK (MOOR DUCK) : The MALLARD. (Stirling.)

MUIR EUN (pron. murr-yan) : The COMMON GUILLEMOT. (Horn Head, Donegal.)

MUIR FOWL or MUIR HEN : The RED GROUSE. (Scotland.)

MULE : The SCAUP DUCK. (Wexford.)

MULFRAN, MORFRAN. Welsh names for the CORMORANT. The first signifies "shy crow," the second "sea-crow."

MULFRAN GOPOG, MORFRAN GOPOG : The SHAG. (North Wales) lit. "crested cormorant."

MULFRAN WEN : The GANNET. (North Wales) lit. "white cormorant."

MULFRAN WERDD, MORFRAN WERDD : The SHAG. (North Wales) lit. "green cormorant."

MULLET. Willughby gives this as a Scarborough name for the PUFFIN.

MULLET HAWK. An old name for the OSPREY.

MUM-RUFFIN : The LONG-TAILED TITMOUSE. (Worcestershire, Shropshire.)

Mur-Bhuachaille. A Gaelic name for the GREAT NORTHERN DIVER. (Mainland) lit. "the herdsman of the sea."

Murdering Pie: The GREAT GREY SHRIKE. From its habit of impaling mice, small birds, beetles, etc., on thorns, and from its pied plumage.

Murre. The RAZORBILL. Willughby gives it as a Cornish name for this bird. It is now more generally applied to the COMMON GUILLEMOT in the south-west of England and south Ireland, as well as on the Yorkshire coast.

Murrel Hen or Morrel Hen: The GREAT SKUA. (Yorkshire.) The first is used at Redcar and the second from Flamborough to Scarborough (Nelson and Clarke).

Musket-Hawk or Musquet-Hawk. An old name for the male SPARROW-HAWK. From Old Fr. *mousquet* or *mouchet*, from *mouche*, a fly, an allusion to its small size. The name of the *musket* appears to have been borrowed from the bird, and alludes to its smaller and more handy size than the cumbrous early matchlock.

Mussel Cracker: The OYSTERCATCHER. (Teesmouth.)

Mussel Crow. A name for the CARRION-CROW. (Hett.)

Mussel Duck. The SCAUP DUCK. (Norfolk and Teesmouth.) The COMMON SCOTER. (Humber.)

Mussel Pecker: The OYSTERCATCHER. (Belfast, Forfar.)

MUTE SWAN [No. 273]. Swan is from A.Sax. *Swan* or *Swon*. The name was formerly often spelt Swanne. It occurs thus in the "Northumberland Household Book" and Witherington's "Order, Lawes and Ancient Customs of Swannes" (1632), etc. Turner (1544) has "Swan," as also has Merrett, Willughby and later writers. The sexes are known respectively as Cob (q.v.) and Pen; the young being called Cygnets. This latter name, however, although now only applied to the young, is the old Norman name for the Swan, as it is also in its original Latin form, i.e. *Cygnus*. "Mute Swan" is a modern name, found in Bewick, Jenyns and Yarrell (1st ed.), but older authors call it the "Tame Swan."

That the Swan was a royal bird until at least 1632 is certain. Nelson ("Laws Concerning Game," 1753) writes "Swan is a Royal bird, and by Stat. 22, Edw. IV, c. 6, None (but the King's Son) shall have any Mark or Game of *Swans* of his own, or to his use, except he have Lands and Tenements of Freehold worth five marks per Annum, besides Reprises; in pain to have them seised by any having lands of that value, to be divided betwixt the King and the Seizor." The eggs also were protected by a separate enactment from those of wild fowl (viz. 11 Hen. VII, c. 17) which states that "None shall take out of the nest any Eggs of Falcon, Goshawk, Lanner or Swan, in pain of a Year and a day's imprisonment, and to incur a fine at the King's pleasure, to be divided between the King and the Owner of the Ground." This latter enactment was superseded by an act (1 Jac. I, c. 27) which reduced the punishment to three months, or a payment of 20s. for each egg to the churchwardens for the use of the poor, while under our later Game Laws the offence was punishable only by a fine not exceeding 5s. for each egg.

The ancient custom of "Swan-upping," or taking up Swans for the purpose of marking them, appears to date from 1483 at least, when the privilege of keeping Swans was granted from the Crown, Swan marks (*cygni notæ*) being created to denote ownership. These marks were notches or nicks on the bill, three for a royal bird, two for a nobleman's bird, etc., and a curious relic of the custom is to be found to-day in the number of country inns bearing the name or sign of the "Swan with two necks" (i.e. *nicks*), etc. These marks of owners were entered in the book or roll of the Master of the Game of Swans and referred to in case of dispute, and from time to time were held "Swanherds' Courts" at which orders were made for the preservation and ordering of Swans. At the present day the custom of marking still survives on the Thames between London Bridge and Henley: the privileged owners being the King, the Vintners' Company and the Dyers' Company, and the practice of marking the birds as soon as the young are sufficiently grown is annually observed, generally about the end of July, by the swanherds of the respective owners, the time occupied being about four days. At the present day the largest "game" of Swans in England is the great swannery of the Fleet on the Dorsetshire coast, the property of Lord Ilchester. For an account of an ancient "Swan-pit" (for fattening these birds for the table) surviving at Norwich see Stevenson and Southwell's "Birds of Norfolk." For an account of the folk-lore and superstitions relating to the Swan see under WHOOPER SWAN.

Formerly, the most extravagant age was attributed to the Swan. Even our sober ornithologists Willughby and Ray remarked that "It is a very long-lived fowl, so that it is thought to attain the age of three hundred years." In Wynkyn de Worde's "Demands Joyous," an English version of an old French riddle-book, as cited by Mr. Harting

('Birds of Shakespeare"), we find the life of a man computed at 81 years, while "the life of a goose is three times that of a man; and the life of a swan is three times that of a goose; and the life of a swallow is three times that of a swan; and the life of an eagle is three times that of a swallow; and the life of a serpent is three times that of an eagle; and the life of a raven is three times that of a serpent; and the life of a hart is three times that of a raven; and an oak groweth 500 years, and fadeth 500 years." This last computation is not so far from the truth, but the others are obviously absurd.

Muzzel Thrush. A corruption of MISTLE-THRUSH.

Mwope: The BULLFINCH. (Dorset.)

Mwyalchen. A Welsh name for the BLACKBIRD, properly applicable to the female, the male being called "Aderyn ddu."

Mwyalchen ddwr. A Welsh name for the DIPPER; lit. "water blackbird."

Mwyalchen y graig A Welsh name for the RING-OUZEL; lit. "rock blackbird."

Myniar Ciaf· The JACK-SNIPE. (North Wales) lit. "lesser peat hen."

Nannie Wagtail The PIED WAGTAIL. (Notts)

Nanny Redtail. The REDSTART. (Cleveland, Yorkshire.)

Nanpie. A Lincolnshire and Yorkshire name for the MAGPIE; in Craven it becomes "nan-piannot." Swainson also gives "Pie nanny" as a Lonsdale name.

Nauk or Nack· The GREAT NORTHERN DIVER. (Holy Island.) A corruption of Auk, also applied to other Divers. Swainson also gives Naak as a Scottish name for the species.

NEEDLE-TAILED SWIFT [No. 201]. This Asiatic species derives its name from the projecting spines at the end of the tail-feathers.

Nettle-bird The WHITETHROAT. (Leicestershire.)

Nettle-creeper or Nettle-monger. Provincial names for the WHITETHROAT, and also the BLACKCAP; and said to be applied to the GARDEN-WARBLER in Craven. The REED-BUNTING also occurs as Nettle-monger in Morton's "Northamptonshire." The name is most appropriate for the first-named bird, which chiefly frequents nettle-beds.

NIAS or NYAS. A falconer's term for nestling-Hawks. Derived from Fr. *niais*, from Low Lat. *Nidax*. In English it is generally found corrupted into "Eyas" or "Eyess"

NICKA-PECKER, NICKER-PECKER, or NICKLE: The GREEN WOODPECKER. (Notts.)

NICOL or JACK NICO: The GOLDFINCH. (North Wales.)

NIGHTBIRD. The MOORHEN. (Sussex.) From its dark plumage. The name is also given to the MANX SHEARWATER about Skellig Island, because it is only seen at night about the rock.

NIGHT-CHURR: The NIGHTJAR. (Provincial.) From its nocturnal habits and the churring noise it utters.

NIGHT-CROW: The NIGHTJAR. (Yorkshire, Northants., Cornwall.)

NIGHT HAWK: The NIGHTJAR. (Fleming, Selby.) It is a common English provincial name for the species.

NIGHT-HERON [No. 266]. The name seems to occur first in Pennant's "Arctic Zoology" (vol. II, No. 356), the young being described in the same work as "Gardenian Heron." This appears to be the bird anciently known as the Night Raven, under which name it is figured in Albin (1738). Willughby, who terms the species the Lesser Ash-Coloured Heron, says it is called by the Germans Night Raven, "because in the night-time it cries with an uncouth voice." The scientific name *Nycticorax* also signifies Night Raven. Under the heading of the "Bittour or Bittern," however, Willughby writes: "This without doubt is that bird our common people call the *Night Raven*, and have such a dread of, imagining its cry portends no less than their death, or the death of some of their near relations · for it flies in the night, answers their description of being like a flagging collar, and hath such a kind of whooping cry as they talk of." Goldsmith ("Animated Nature") confirms this by relating of the Bittern that he remembered "with what terror the bird's note affected the whole village." Spenser also alludes to "the hoarse night raven, trompe of doleful dreere." The reference may, of course, be to the night-like plumage of the RAVEN.

NIGHTINGALE [No. 180]. The name of this prime favourite among song-birds signifies literally "singer of the night," it being the A. Sax. *nihtegale* (fr. *niht*=night and *gale*=a singer). Prof. Skeat says the middle *n* is excrescent. The name is found in Chaucer's "Canterbury Tales": Turner (1544) writes it "Nyghtyngall," while Merrett (1667) and

Willughby (1678) have Nightingale. Shakespeare and many of the other early poets allude to this species as Philomel (which see for an explanation of the classical allusion). It was locally believed, according to Dyer, that there were no Nightingales at Havering-atte-Bower, Essex, because of a legend that Edward the Confessor, being interrupted by them in his meditations, prayed that their song might never be heard again It has also been said that Nightingales have never been heard in Yorkshire, but as a matter of fact the species does occur in that county, although rarely, it being the northernmost limit of its range. Similarly in Devonshire the species is met with in the south-eastern portion of the county, but I think has never been known to occur in the west. Andrew Boord ("Book of Knowledge") relates a curious belief that in the Forest of Saint Leonards in Sussex "there doth never singe nightingale, althoughe the Foreste round about in tyme of the yeare is replenyshed with nightingales; they wyl singe round about the Foreste and never within the precincte of the Foreste." This bird was formerly popularly supposed to arrive with the CUCKOO (with which it is much connected in folk-lore) on the 14th of April.

NIGHTJAR [No. 202]. This name appears to have been fixed for the species through its adoption by Yarrell (1843), although it was previously used by Bewick (1797). The bird occurs in Merrett, Willughby and subsequent authors to Montagu under the name of Goatsucker (q v.). Montagu gives Nightjar as a provincial name. For the popular beliefs regarding this species, see under "Goatsucker" and also "Puckeridge." In Nidderdale the country people say these birds embody the souls of unbaptised infants doomed to wander for ever in the air (according to Macquoid), and call them "Gabble-ratchets" (q.v.).

NIGHT OWL. The LITTLE OWL. (Merrett.)

NIGHT RAVEN: The NIGHT-HERON (q.v.). Also ascribed to the BITTERN.

NIGHT SINGER · The SEDGE-WARBLER. (Ireland; Sedbergh, Yorkshire.) From its singing at night.

NIGHT SPARROW: The SEDGE-WARBLER. (Cheshire)

NIGHT SWALLOW · The NIGHTJAR. From its nocturnal habits, and because it hawks flies like a Swallow.

NIGHT WARBLER: The REED-WARBLER. (Bewick.)

NILE-BIRD: The WRYNECK. (Berks., Bucks.)

NIMBLE-TAILOR: The LONG-TAILED TITMOUSE. (Shropshire.)

NINE-KILLER: The RED-BACKED SHRIKE. According to Willughby, where this name occurs, it is a translation of the German *Neghen-doer* (Mod. Germ. *Neuntödter*), a term applied because it was supposed to kill nine birds or other creatures every day. The name is, however, older than Willughby, for it is found in Turner (1544) as "Nynmurder," and the latter gives the German equivalent as "Nuin mürder" (= *neunmörder*).

NOCTURNAL GOATSUCKER: The NIGHTJAR. (Pennant.)

NODDY: The COMMON GUILLEMOT. (Whitby, Yorkshire.)

Noddy Tern. The name is found in Gould ("Bds. Eur.," pt. 21) and the species was included by Yarrell (1st ed.), it being said, on insufficient evidence, to have occurred in our islands. Noddy is originally a name applied by sailors to the bird on account of its stupid habits; being probably derived from Fr. *nodden*, a sleepy nodding of the head: hence signifying sleepy-headed or foolish, the word "noodle" being akin.

NOPE: The BULLFINCH. (Staffordshire, Shropshire.) Occurs in Drayton's Polyolbion XIII, also in Willughby. Newton thinks it to be a corruption of some form of Alp (q.v.): the original word perhaps being "an ope." In Dorset it becomes "Mwope."

NORFOLK PLOVER: The STONE-CURLEW. Montagu gives it as a provincial name. It appears to have been first used by Pennant (1766) for the species.

NORIE. A Shetland name for the PUFFIN. (Saxby.)

NORMAN GIZER: The MISTLE-THRUSH. (Oxfordshire.) The meaning is uncertain, although Gizer is probably from Gise (Old.Fr. *gister*) signifying a pasturer, from its habit of frequenting fields. Swainson gives Norman Thrush as a Craven name for this species.

NORTH AMERICAN PEREGRINE [No. 234]. This species is almost invariably known in America as the Duck Hawk.

NORTH COCK: The SNOW-BUNTING. (Aberdeen.)

NORTHERN BULLFINCH: The large North European form of the BULLFINCH.

NORTHERN DIVER: The GREAT NORTHERN DIVER. (Pennant.)

NORTHERN DOUCKER: The BLACK-THROATED DIVER. Montagu gives it as a provincial name.

NORTHERN FULMAR: The FULMAR PETREL. (Jenyns.)

NORTHERN GREAT SPOTTED WOODPECKER. See GREAT SPOTTED WOODPECKER.

NORTHERN HARELD · The LONG-TAILED DUCK (Aberdeen.) Hareld is from *haveld*, the Icelandic name of the bird.

NORTHERN LONG-TAILED TITMOUSE [No. 100] The Continental form of the LONG-TAILED TITMOUSE It was formerly called the White-headed Long-tailed Titmouse.

NORTHERN MEALY REDPOLL : COUES'S REDPOLL

NORTHERN PENGUIN . The GREAT AUK. (Edwards.)

NORTHERN WILLOW-TITMOUSE. See WILLOW-TITMOUSE.

NORTHERN WILLOW-WARBLER See WILLOW-WARBLER.

NORWAY BARNACLE The BARNACLE-GOOSE. (Ireland.)

NORWAY CROW The HOODED CROW. (Northumberland, Yorkshire, Norfolk.) From its being supposed they visit us in winter from Norway Northern Crow is also a Craven name for the species.

NORWAY DUCK · The SCAUP DUCK. (Belfast.) Norwegian Teal is also a Banff name for the same species

NORWAY NIGHTINGALE. A name for the REDWING. (Hett.)

NORWEGIAN BLUETHROAT [No 182] Generally known as Red-spotted Bluethroat It is the Blue-throated Redstart of Edwards (pl 28), the Blue-throated Robin of Bewick, and the Blue-throated Warbler of Yarrell and Jenyns.

NUN or WHITE NUN The male SMEW. (Northumberland.) From its black-and-white plumage : Willughby calls it the " White Nun " Also the BLUE TITMOUSE, from its banded head (occurs in Turner and Willughby).

NUTBREAKER The NUTCRACKER. Appears to be the first English name given to this bird and is found in the index to Willughby (1678), no English name being given in the text.

NUT-BROWN BIRD. A name for the PARTRIDGE. (Hett.)

NUTCRACKER [No. 7, Thick-Billed Nutcracker; No. 8, Slender-Billed Nutcracker]. The name Nutcracker seems to be first found in Edwards's Gleanings (plate 240, 1758). The earliest mention of this species appears to be in Turner (1544) who says "besides the said three kinds of Graculi described by Aristotle, I know a fourth, which I have seen upon the Rhætic Alps . . . Now to this the Rhætians have given the name of Nucifraga, from the nuts which it breaks with its bill and eats " The form breeding in Europe is now separated from the form breeding in Siberia and visiting Europe in winter: hence the two names. In Shropshire the name is applied to the NUTHATCH.

NUTHATCH [No. 86, British Nuthatch]. Occurs in Willughby (1678). Turner (1544) has "Nut jobber" and "Nutseeker." Another Old English form is "Nuthack," the name being derived from its habit of hacking or hammering at nuts which it first fixes in the crevice of the bark of a tree. Hartert has separated the British resident form from the Continental form, hence the change of name.

NUTJOBBER or JOBBIN, NUT TAPPER, or NUT TOPPER: The NUTHATCH. (England.) Equivalent of Nuthatch.

NYROCA DUCK. The FERRUGINOUS DUCK. (Selby.) Also called Nyroca Pochard.

OAK JACKDAW. A name for the JAY. (Hett.)

OAT-EAR: The YELLOW WAGTAIL. (Hett.) See Oatseed bird.

OAT-FOWL: The SNOW-BUNTING. (Orkneys.) From its feeding on oats (Swainson).

OATSEED-BIRD: The YELLOW WAGTAIL; or the GREY WAGTAIL in Yorkshire, according to Swainson, who says it is because it makes its appearance about March, and is then more abundant in those elevated parts which are better adapted for the growth of oats than wheat.

OH DEE-AR. Saxby gives this as a Shetland name for the GOLDEN PLOVER.

OKE. The RAZORBILL. A corruption of Auk (Icel. *álka*).

OLD HARDWEATHER. A name for the male GOLDENEYE. Also the Tufted Duck.

OLD MAID: The LAPWING. (Worcestershire.) For a possible explanation of this name, by a Danish belief that the Lapwings are metamorphosed old maids, see "Notes and Queries," ser III, vol. x, p. 49.

OLD MAN: The SPOTTED FLYCATCHER. (Cheshire.)

OLF, OLP, or OLPH: The BULLFINCH. (Suffolk and Norfolk.) A form of "Alp."

OLIVACEOUS GALLINULE: The LITTLE CRAKE. (Montagu.)

OLIVE: The OYSTERCATCHER. (Essex) Mr. Miller Christy thinks it is a corruption of Olaf (or Olave), the name of the Danish King. It is found in Albin as a name for this species.

OOLERT or OWLERD: The BARN-OWL. (Shropshire.) Corruption of Howlet.

OOSSEL: The BLACKBIRD. (North Yorkshire.) A corruption of Ouzel.

ORANGE-LEGGED HOBBY: The RED-FOOTED FALCON. (Selby.)

ORPHEAN WARBLER [No. 144] The name arises from Temminck's name for the species (*Sylvia orphea*) referring to its song. It is found in Gould and also Yarrell ("Supp.," II, 1856) as "Orpheus Warbler."

ORTOLAN BUNTING [No. 48]. From Fr. *Ortolan*; in Old Fr. *Hortolan*. It occurs first in Albin (1738) as Hortulon or Hortulane, and as Ortolan Bunting in Pennant ("Arctic Zoology") and Latham. It is also the Green-headed Bunting of Latham, Brown, Lewin, and Montagu.

OSPREY [No. 253]. The word "Osprey" occurs in Turner (1544), who derives it from Aristotle and gives an accurate account of its habits; and it also occurs in Aldrovandus (p. 191) as the English name of the bird. Willughby and other old authors confuse it with the "Sea-Eagle" or immature WHITE-TAILED EAGLE, Willughby's "Osprey" being the latter species, while his "Baldbusardus anglorum" is the Osprey. From Lat. *ossifragus*, the Sea-Eagle or Osprey—lit. bone-breaker—from the bird's reputed strength and habits. In Holland's translation of Pliny it occurs both as *ospreie* and *orfraie*, the latter being synonymous with Old Fr. *orfraye*, as in Cotgrave. In Shakespeare, where the bird is named twice, it occurs as *aspray* in the old texts, but is rendered osprey in modern editions. In "Coriolanus" (act IV, sc. 7) we get an admirable simile of the Osprey's pre-eminence as a fisher:—

> . . . He'll be to Rome
> As is the Osprey to the fish, who takes it
> By sovereignty of nature.

Indeed, the bird's powers in this direction were so extraordinary as to lead to the belief that it possessed the fabulous power of fascinating the fish. Peele in 1594 ("Battle of Alcazar," act I, sc. 1) alludes to this.—

> I will provide thee of a princely Osprey,
> That, as he flieth over fish in pools,
> The fish shall turn their glistering bellies up,
> And thou shalt take thy liberal choice of all.

Turner also says that "When the Osprey hovers in the air whatever fishes be below turn up and show their whitish bellies." As regards the then abundance of the species he says that "the Osprey is a bird much better known to-day to Englishmen than many who keep fish in stews would wish: for within a short time it bears off every fish."

OTTERLING. A name for the COMMON SANDPIPER. (Hett.)

Our Lady's Hen. An old Scots name for the WREN. (Swainson.)

Ouzel, Ouizle, Uzzle, Ousel, or Ousel Cock: The BLACKBIRD properly (Yorkshire, Lancashire, Cheshire, etc.); but sometimes also applied without prefix to the RING-OUZEL, where that northern species predominates, the Blackbird on the other hand being sometimes designated Black Ousel. Occurs locally as Oossel or Ussel (North Yorkshire), and also Amzel, the latter actually seeming to be the correct form, as the derivation is from A.Sax. *ōsle* (=*amsele*) the long *ō* as Skeat points out standing for *am* or *an*, and being synonymic with Old High Ger. *amsala* and Mod. Ger. *amsel*, a Blackbird. The word occurs in our Mid. Eng. as *osel* and *osul*. Shakespeare ("Midsummer Night's Dream") refers to the "ousel cock, so black of hue, with orange-tawny bill."

Oven-Bird, Oven Tit, or Ground-Oven. Norfolk names for the WILLOW-WARBLER. From the shape of its nest. In the same county the LONG-TAILED TITMOUSE is called Bush-oven, from the position of its nest, while it is known as Oven's-nest in Northamptonshire and Oven-bird or Oven-builder in Scotland (Stirling).

Over-sea Bird or Over-sea Linnet: The SNOW-BUNTING. (Yorkshire.)

Ox-Bird or Ox-Eye: The DUNLIN, and also the SANDERLING (Kent and Essex). Perhaps from the full round eye, like an ox's.

Oxen-and-Kine: The RUFF (obsolete). Appears to have been a name for this species about the end of the sixteenth century. Swainson cites references to it in the introduction to "Expenses of the Judges of Assize, going the Western and Oxford circuits, between 1596 and 1601," reprinted in Vol. XIV, of "Camden Miscellany," 1857, also Carew's "Survey of Cornwall," 1602, p. 108. Mr. Harting in Intro. Rodd's "Birds of Cornwall," p. xvii, cites it (no doubt from Carew) as an old Cornish name "for some unknown small species of wildfowl."

Ox-Eye. A common provincial name for the GREAT TITMOUSE. Occurs in Willughby. Perhaps so called from the large white patch on the side of the head, resembling that sometimes seen on the face of an ox. It is also a Border name for the BLUE TITMOUSE, according to Bolam.

Ox-eye Creeper: The TREECREEPER. Occurs in Merrett (1667) and also Charleton (1668).

OYSTERCATCHER [No. 351]. Occurs in Kay (1570) and in Willughby (1678) under the name of Sea-Pie, and Pennant (1766) uses the same name, but later writers call it the Pied Oyster-catcher. Oyster-Catcher is first used by Catesby ("Nat. Hist Carolina") in 1731 for the American species, which he (probably erroneously) believed to feed on oysters, and was adopted in this country by Pennant.

OYSTER PLOVER. A name for the OYSTERCATCHER. (Swainson.)

PADGE, PUDGE, or PUDGE OWL: The BARN-OWL. (Leicestershire.)

PAL· The PUFFIN. (North Wales) lit. "Polly" (for Sea-parrot).

PALE-BREASTED BRENT GOOSE. See BRENT GOOSE.

PALLAS'S GRASSHOPPER-WARBLER [No 132] A Siberian species named in honour of Pallas

PALLAS'S SAND-GROUSE [No 350] Called after the explorer and naturalist Pallas Sand Grouse is first found in Latham (1783) being a rendering of Pallas's name *Tetrao arenarius*. An irregular migrant from South-east Europe and Central Asia. the first great immigration of which to the British Islands took place in 1863, since when it has frequently visited us.

PALLAS'S WARBLER [No. 128]. A Siberian species of Willow-Warbler, named in honour of Pallas, who first described it in 1827.

PALORES. A Cornish name for the CHOUGH.

PANDLE WHEW: The WIGEON. (Norfolk.) Whew is from its whistling note and pandle seems to mean a shrimp (Swainson). It occurs in Bewick as "Pandled Whew."

PARASITIC GULL· The LONG-TAILED SKUA. (Gould.)

PARKERS. A Fen name for the smaller kinds of wild-ducks.

PARROT or SEA PARROT: The PUFFIN. (Yorkshire) From its bill being supposed to resemble a parrot's.

PARROT-CROSSBILL [No. 35]. So called from the bill being stouter and more parrot-like than that of the common form. It is first noticed by Pennant ("Br. Zool.," ed. 1776) and the name is found in Selby (1825).

PARSON GULL or PARSON MEW. The GREAT BLACK-BACKED GULL. (Cheshire, Sussex, Galway.) From the contrast of its black coat and white under-plumage.

PARTRICK, PARTRIG: The COMMON PARTRIDGE. (Yorkshire.) An equivalent.

174   DICTIONARY OF NAMES OF BRITISH BIRDS.

PARTRIDGE : The general name for the COMMON PARTRIDGE. Old Eng. Pertriche; Scot., Patrick, Paitrick, or Pertrick.

Passenger-Pigeon. An American species, now thought to be extinct, of which five British examples are on record, but which are presumed to have escaped from captivity. The name seems to have been invented by Wilson, the colloquial name in North America having apparently been "Wild Pigeon." On the British side it occurs in Jenyns (1835) and as Passenger Turtle in Selby (1833).

PASSERINE OWL : The LITTLE OWL.

PASSERINE WARBLER : The GARDEN-WARBLER. Found in Bewick (1797).

PATRICK or PERTICK · The COMMON PARTRIDGE. (Scotland.) See Partridge.

PEA-BIRD : The WRYNECK. (Provincial.) Swainson says it is from its sharp utterance of the sound "pea-pea."

PEAR-TREE GOLDFINCH. A bird-fancier's name for a supposed large variety of the GOLDFINCH, reared in pear-trees.

PEASE CROW : The COMMON TERN. (Provincial.)

PEASE WEEP, or PEESEWEEP : The LAPWING. (Scotland and Northumberland.) From its cry. According to Swainson the name has also been applied to the GREENFINCH, because one of its notes resembles that of the Lapwing.

PECTORAL SANDPIPER [No. 378, American Pectoral Sandpiper; No. 379, Siberian Pectoral Sandpiper]. This species is now divided into two forms, of which the Arctic-American race has occurred many times in our islands, but the Asiatic is only known to have occurred once with certainty. The name Pectoral Sandpiper is found in Jenyns, Yarrell (1st ed.) and later authors.

PEEP O' DAY : A name for the LITTLE GREBE. (East Cottingwith, Yorkshire.)

PEEP : The SANDERLING. (Boulmer, Northumberland.) From its note. Also the MEADOW-PIPIT (Forfar).

PEEPY LENNART. A Holy Island name for the TWITE. (Bolam.)

PEERIE WHAUP : The WHIMBREL. (Shetlands.)

PEESNIPS : The LAPWING. (Cheshire.)

PEETLARK : The MEADOW-PIPIT. (Cheshire.)

PEEWIT : The LAPWING. (See Pewit.)

PEEWIT GULL : The BLACK-HEADED GULL. (See Pewit Gull.)

PEGGY or PEGGY WHITETHROAT : The WILLOW-WARBLER. (Cheshire, West Yorkshire, Shropshire.) Peggy is also applied to the WHITETHROAT (Notts. and Yorkshire) and the GARDEN-WARBLER, BLACKCAP, WREN and CHIFFCHAFF (Yorkshire)

PELICAN. Fr. *Pélican* from Lat. *Pelecanus*. This name, now restricted to the genus *Pelecanus*, appears in ancient times to have been applied to several other birds noteworthy on account of their bills, the true Pelican being in fact called Onocrotalus by most ancient writers from Pliny to Turner, while Willughby has "Pelecan, Onocrotalus sive Pelecanus, Aldrov." Thus we find Turner giving Pelecanus as a synonym of the "Shovelard" or SPOONBILL, and he cites Hieronymus's "Pelecani" as being apparently the same. The Pelican of Aristophanes, however, is the Woodpecker, or joiner-bird, which with its bill hewed out the gates of "Cloud-Cuckoo-town." The derivation, in fact, is from Πεγεκαω, signifying "to hew with an axe," and the Woodpecker was so called from its pecking, the Pelican from its large bill, and the Spoonbill from the remarkable shape of its bill. That some other birds were also so called is certain, and to which species to refer the legend of the Pelican feeding its young with its own blood is very uncertain. Houghton ("Natural History of the Ancients," p 191) thinks that the legend refers to a vulture or eagle, and cites the story of Horapollo that the vulture, if it cannot get food for its offspring, opens its thigh and allows them to partake of the blood. He thinks the story was adapted and magnified from the Egyptian fable by the ecclesiastical fathers in their annotations on the Scriptures. Augustine, for instance, says that the male pelicans "are said to kill their young offspring by blows of their beaks, and then to bewail their deaths for the space of three days At length, however, it is said that the mother bird inflicts a severe wound on herself, pouring the flowing blood over the dead young ones, which instantly brings them to life." Many other writers relate the same story, with variations, and in some accounts the fable is that the female bird feeds her living young in this manner, in which may be traced a return to the Egyptian original. Hieronymus, whose Pelican is, as before mentioned, referred by Turner to the Spoonbill, says that "Pelecani, when they find their young killed by a serpent, mourn, and beat themselves upon their sides, and with the blood discharged, they thus bring back to life the bodies of the dead," which of course is another variation of the story. Whitney, in his "Choice of Emblems," gives a woodcut illustration of a bird like an eagle piercing her breast with her hooked bill, surrounded by the young in the nest whose mouths are open to receive the blood; the lines below being:—

> The pellican, for to revive her younge,
> Doth pierce her breast, and geve them of her blood.

This fable in fact served as a symbol of Christ's love to men, and with the substitution of a real Pelican for the bird, it exists to the present day in ecclesiastical art. What species of bird the eagle or vulture of Whitney and other old writers may be is uncertain, but there is little doubt indeed that the substitution of the Pelican for the other bird in the fable is due to the erroneous idea that the name indicated the Pelican and not some other species. In fact attempts have been made to account for the legend by explaining that the Pelican feeds its young with the fish from its pouch, and that during the process the red *nail* or tip of the lower mandible, pressing against the breast, might lead an observer to suppose that the bird was piercing its own breast. Bartlett ("Land and Water," April 3rd, 1869) made an ingenious attempt to lay the origin of the fable upon the Flamingo, which he says disgorges a blood-like fluid. The Pelican is not a British bird, although several doubtful records of the Great White Pelican (*P. onocrotalus*) in our islands are extant.

PELLILE: The REDSHANK. (Aberdeen.) From its cry.

PEN: The female of the MUTE SWAN. (See Cob.)

PENDDU. A Welsh name for the BLACKCAP; lit. "black head."

PENDEW: The HAWFINCH. (North Wales) lit. "thick head."

PENGOCH: The LESSER REDPOLL. (North Wales) lit. "red poll." Bengoch is an equivalent form.

PENGUIN: The GREAT AUK. Found in Ray's "Synopsis," also in Willughby, Edwards, and other early writers; lit. "Pin-wing." According to Nelson and Clarke "Penwings" is an old Redcar (Yorkshire) name for the species.

PENLOYN: The GREAT TITMOUSE and the COAL-TITMOUSE. (North Wales) lit. "black head."

PENLOYN-Y-GORS. A Welsh name for the MARSH-TITMOUSE; lit. "marsh coal head."

PENNY-BIRD. An Irish name for the LITTLE GREBE. (Lough Morne and Carrickfergus.)

PEN Y LLWYN. A Welsh name for the MISTLE-THRUSH, lit. "chief of the grove."

PERCHER. A young ROOK, after it has left the nest.

PEREGRINE FALCON [No. 233]. Peregrine, from Lat. *peregrinus*=wandering, is sometimes used as the name of the species, but it is an adjective, not a substantive. The name Peregrine Falcon appears in Willughby (1678) being anglicized from the *Falco peregrinus* of Aldrovandus, who gives a good figure of it Ray remarks that it "took its name either from passing out of one country into another, or because it is not known where it builds." In falconry the female used to be called Falcon-gentle and the male Tiercel-, Tassel- or Tercel-gentle (see "Tiercel")

PERRY HAWK · The PEREGRINE FALCON. (Ryedale, Yorkshire.)

PET MAW. A name for the COMMON GULL and the KITTIWAKE at Redcar, Yorkshire.

PETRELL. Pennant gives this as a Flamborough name for the KITTIWAKE GULL.

PETRISEN. A Welsh name for the PARTRIDGE.

PETRISEN GOESGOCH · The RED-LEGGED PARTRIDGE. (North Wales) lit. "red-legged partridge."

PETTYCHAPS. (See Greater and Lesser Pettychaps.)

PEWEEP or PIEWIPE : The LAPWING. (Norfolk.)

PEWIT or PUIT · The LAPWING. A common provincial name, imitative of its cry.

PEWIT or PEWIT GULL . The BLACK-HEADED GULL. From its cry. The first occurs in Willughby and the second in Pennant. It occurs as "Puit" in Fuller's "Worthies" (p. 318) Peewit Gull is a present name for the species in North Wales.

PHALAROE The GREY PHALAROPE. (Yorkshire coast.) A corruption of Phalarope.

PHEASANT [No. 466]. Mid. Eng *Fesaunt* and *Fesaun*, Fr. *Faisan*, from Lat. *Phasianus*. Originally introduced into Europe from the banks of the River Phasis, now Rioni, in Colchis. The name occurs in Turner (1544) as Phesan, and in Barlow's plates (1655) as "Feasant." Pheasant occurs in Merrett (1667), and also Willughby. Plot (1677) spells it "Phesant." As regards its introduction into England nothing definite is known, except that the bird appears to have been known here before the Conquest, and Newton thinks that it must almost certainly have been brought hither by the Romans. It seems to have been early under protection for, according to Dugdale, a licence was granted in the reign of Henry I to the Abbot of Amesbury to kill Hares and Pheasants, and that later they were artificially reared and fattened appears from Upton, who wrote about the middle of the 15th century, while Henry VIII seems from his privy purse expenses to have had in his household in 1532 a French priest as a regular "fesaunt breder," and in the accounts of the Kytsons of Hengrave in Suffolk for 1607, mention is made of wheat to feed Pheasants, Partridges and Quails. In ancient times Pheasants were taken in snares as well as by Hawks. In Barlow's prints (1655) this bird (called "Feasant—Phasianus") is shown being pursued by a Hawk.

PHEASANT DUCK. The PINTAIL. (Beverley, Yorkshire.)

PHILIP or PHIP. The HOUSE-SPARROW. (Provincial.) Swainson says it is from the note. It may originate, however, in Skelton's poem "Philip Sparrow." The names are also applied to the HEDGE-SPARROW.

PHILLIPENE: The LAPWING. (Ireland.)

PHILLIP'S FULMAR: SCHLEGEL'S PETREL. (Godman.)

PHILOMEL: The NIGHTINGALE. The name is frequently met with in poetical and other allusions to this bird, as well as several times in Shakespeare, and arises from the classical tale (to be met with in Ovid's "Metamorphoses," bk. VI, fab. 6) of the transformation of Philomela, daughter of Pandion, King of Athens, into a Nightingale. Philomela, finding herself deceived by Tereus, had her tongue cut out by him to hinder her from revealing the truth; being finally turned by the gods into a Nightingale, whence the name of *Philomela* and the poetic allusion to her supposed sad recapitulation of her wrongs. It was formerly supposed that the bird sang with its breast impaled upon a thorn, thus accentuating "the well-tun'd warble of her nightly sorrow." This popular error is alluded to by Shakespeare in "The Passionate Pilgrim":—

> She, poor bird, as all forlorn,
> Lean'd her breast up-till a thorn,
> And there sung the dolefull'st ditty,
> That to hear it was great pity.

Sir Philip Sidney, also, in one of his sonnets, says that this bird

> Sings out her woes, a thorn her song-book making.

Fletcher and Pomfret, also, among the later poets, allude to it.

PIANET, PIEANNOT, PIANNOT, PINOT, PYNOT, PYENATE, PIANATE or PYANET Provincial names for the MAGPIE (North England), from Lat. *pica*. Pyanet occurs in Merrett (1667) and Pianet in Willughby and later authors (See "Pie")

PIBHINN (pronounced *pee veen*.) A Gaelic name for the LAPWING. (Western Isles.) From its cry.

PIBYDD DDU: The PURPLE SANDPIPER. (North Wales) lit. "black piper."

PIBYDD GWYRDD. The GREEN SANDPIPER. (North Wales) lit. "green piper."

PIBYDD LLEIAF: The LITTLE STINT. (North Wales) lit. "lesser piper."

PIBYDD LLYDANDROED The GREY PHALAROPE. (North Wales) lit. "broad-footed piper."

PIBYDD RHUDDGOCH: The DUNLIN. (North Wales) lit. "ruddy piper."

PIBYDD Y TRAETH. A Welsh name for the COMMON SANDPIPER, and also the SANDERLING (North Wales); lit "piper of the sand." Another name for the first species in North Wales is Pibydd y dorlan (= piper of the streamside).

PICARINI: The AVOCET. Montagu gives it as a provincial name.

PICK: The BAR-TAILED GODWIT. (Norfolk.)

PICKATEE: The BLUE TITMOUSE. (Notts.)

PICK-A-TREE. A Northumberland name for the GREEN WOODPECKER. (Wallis.)

PICKCHEESE· The BLUE TITMOUSE. (Norfolk.)

PICKEREL: The DUNLIN. (Scotland.)

PICKE-TA or PICCATARRY· The ARCTIC TERN. (Orkneys and Shetlands.)

PICKIE: The MISTLE-THRUSH. (Teesdale.)

PICKIE, PICKIE-BURNET, PICKIE-MAW. PICKMAW, PICKMIRE, PICK-SEA, or PICTARNIE Scottish Border names for the BLACK-HEADED GULL.

PICTARNIE: The COMMON TERN. (East Lothian, Fife.) Occurs in Sibbald as "Pictarne."

PIE. A provincial name for the MAGPIE. Occurs in Turner (1544) as "Py," and in Aldrovandus (1599) as "Pie, Pij." Mid. Eng. *pie* or *pye*, from Fr. *pie*, Lat. *pica*, Welsh *pioq*, Scott. *piet*, a Magpie. The name is applied also to many other birds which present more or less of black and white in their plumage. (See "French Pie," etc.)

PIED CHAFFINCH : The SNOW-BUNTING. (Albin.)

PIED CROW : The HOODED CROW. (Provincial.)

PIED CURRE. An old gunner's name for the GOLDENEYE in parts of the South and West of England.

PIED DIVER : The SMEW. (Provincial.)

PIED FINCH, PITEFINCH, or PYDIE : The CHAFFINCH. (Cheshire.) From the pied plumage of the male. Other variants in the Midlands are Pea Finch and Pine Finch.

PIED FLYCATCHER [No. 116]. Appears to be found first in the 4th ed. of Pennant. In the folio edition it is called Coldfinch, as in Willughby and Edwards.

PIED MOUNTAIN FINCH : The SNOW-BUNTING. Occurs in Willughby and in Albin.

PIED OYSTER-CATCHER : The OYSTERCATCHER. So called by Pennant, Montagu and other old writers.

PIED WAGTAIL [No. 81]. It is described by Turner (1544) under the heading of Culicilega of Aristotle, and he gives it the name of "Wagtale" merely. It occurs in most old authors as White Wagtail, Pied Wagtail first appearing in Bewick (1797) although its distinctness from the White Wagtail of the Continent was not pointed out by Gould until 1832. In Gaelic its name, according to Gray, is Breac-an-t'-sil, signifying a plaid, from the resemblance of its plumage to that article. In Cornwall, where it is known as the "tinner," one perching on a window-sill is said to be a sign of a visit from a stranger. Bolam gives it as a Border belief that the bird ought always to wag its tail *nine* times on alighting, and before beginning to run about or feed; should the number be less or more, it is very unlucky for the person who is counting.

PIED WHEATEAR [No. 172]. This Asiatic and South-east European species was first recorded for the British Islands in the " Annals of Scottish Natural Hist.," 1910, p. 2.

PIED WIGEON. A provincial name for the GARGANEY and the GOLDENEYE. (Montagu.)

PIED WOODPECKER : The GREAT SPOTTED WOODPECKER. (Bewick.)

PIE-FINCH : The CHAFFINCH (Upton-on-Severn); the HAW-FINCH (Notts.).

PIE-NANNY : The MAGPIE. (Yorkshire.)

PIENET : The OYSTERCATCHER. (Provincially.) A diminutive of "Pie." Also the MAGPIE (see Pianet).

PIET, PYET, PIOT, or PYOT: The MAGPIE. Turner (1544) has "Piot," and Merrett (1667) has "Pyot." Piet is also applied to the DIPPER. (See "Water-Piet.")

PIE-WYPE or PIE-WIPE. The LAPWING. (See "Wype.")

PIGEON FELT. The FIELDFARE. (Berks, Bucks., Oxon., Cheshire) From the blue-grey lower-back.

PIGEON GULL: The BLACK-HEADED GULL. (Yorkshire coast.)

PIGEON HAWK. The GOSHAWK (Rutty); also the SPARROW-HAWK (Yorkshire). Occurs in Montagu for the latter species.

PIGEON OF THE NORTH. A name for the LITTLE AUK. (Hett.)

PIGEON PLOVER: The GREY PLOVER (Humber district.)

PIGMY CURLEW or PIGMY SANDPIPER: The CURLEW SANDPIPER. So called from its being supposed to resemble a miniature Curlew Montagu includes the species under the name of Pigmy Curlew, which is a Norfolk name for the species.

PIG MYNAWD. A Welsh name for the AVOCET.

PILA GWYRDD. The GREENFINCH. (North Wales) lit. "green finch."

PINE-BUNTING [No. 44]. A bird inhabiting the pine forests of Siberia, which has lately been recorded once from Fair Isle (Shetlands).

PINE-GROSBEAK [No. 32]. So called from its frequenting pine woods. Grosbeak is from Fr. *grosbec* ("great bill"). The name is found in Bewick (1797). It is the Pine Bullfinch of Selby and the Common Hawfinch of Fleming, while Edwards calls it the Greatest Bullfinch.

PINE MAW: The BLACK-HEADED GULL. (Antrim.)

PINK, PINKETY, PINK-TWINK. Provincial names for the CHAFFINCH (England.) From its call-note.

PINK-FOOTED GOOSE [No. 278]. First described and named by Bartlett ("P.Z S," 1839, p. 3), the name being adopted by Yarrell and succeeding authors.

PINNOCK: The HEDGE-SPARROW. (Provincial). From its piping note (Swainson). The BEARDED TITMOUSE is also known as "Bearded Pinnock."

PINTAIL [No. 296]. The name Pintail is first applied by Pennant (1766) who calls it Pintail Duck. Willughby and Ray call it the "Sea Pheasant or Cracker." The name arises from the pointed appearance of the tail, the two middle feathers of which are elongated and finely pointed.

PINUT: The MAGPIE. (Notts., Cheshire) A corruption of Pianet.

PIODEN Y MÔR or PIOGEN Y MÔR: The OYSTERCATCHER. (North Wales) lit. "sea-pie."

PIOGEN, PIODEN, or PIA. Welsh names for the MAGPIE; lit. "Pie."

PIOGEN GOCH, PIOGEN-Y-COED: The JAY. (North Wales.) The first signifies "red magpie," the second "wood magpie."

PIOGHAID. A Gaelic name for the MAGPIE.

PIPE or POPE · The PUFFIN. (Cornwall.)

PIPIT: The MEADOW-PIPIT. Fr. *Pipit* from Lat. *pipio*, lit. a "piper" or nestling; pigeon is from the same root.

PIPIT LARK: The TREE-PIPIT. (Pennant.) Montagu's Pipit Lark is no doubt the MEADOW-PIPIT.

PIRENET or PIRENNET: The SHELD-DUCK. (Scotland.) A corruption of "Pied ent" (Pied Duck).

PIRRE: The COMMON TERN. (Ireland.)

PISAN CUCKOO: The GREAT SPOTTED CUCKOO. (Latham.)

PIT MARTIN: The SAND-MARTIN. (Craven, Yorkshire.)

PIT SPARROW. A local Cheshire name for the SEDGE-WARBLER and also the REED-BUNTING. From their frequenting small ponds locally called pits; Holland also gives Spit Sparrow for the Reed-Bunting in Cheshire.

PLOUGHMAN'S BIRD: The REDBREAST. (Lofthouse, near Wakefield.)

PLOVER. The LAPWING, generally. From Fr. *Pluvier*, Old Fr. *Plovier*, probably from Lat. *pluvia*. rain.

PLOVER'S PAGE: The DUNLIN is so called in parts of Scotland and in the Shetlands (Saxby), from its habit of flying in company with the GOLDEN PLOVER. In the Orkneys the name is given to the JACK SNIPE (Dunn).

PLUM-BIRD or PLUM-BUDDER: The BULLFINCH. (Shropshire.) From its habit of picking the buds of fruit trees.

POCHARD, POCKARD or POKER. See COMMON POCHARD.

POKE PUDDING, POKE BAG, or PUDDING BAG: The LONG-TAILED TITMOUSE. (Gloucestershire, Shropshire, Norfolk.) From the shape of the nest (poke=pocket).

Polish Swan. An aberrant phase of the MUTE SWAN, in which the cygnets are white, instead of dark grey. It was first described by Yarrell ("P.Z.S.," 1838, p. 19) as a separate species.

POLLAIREUN. A Gaelic name for the DUNLIN in the Long Island; signifying "bird of the sand-pits" (Gray).

POMATORHINE SKUA [No. 440]. It is the "Pomerine Skua" of Selby and Yarrell (1st ed.), and the Pomerine Gull of Gould ("Birds of Europe," pt. II, 1832). It is first noticed as a British bird in the "Sale Catalogue of Bullock's Collection" (April, 1819, lot 61, p. 32) where it is referred to as "allied to the Arctic, but greatly superior in size."

POOL SNIPE: The REDSHANK. (Willughby.) Albin calls it the "Poole Snipe," but the derivation is no doubt from the former word (pool, or pond, snipe).

POOR WILLIE: The BAR-TAILED GODWIT. (East Lothian.) Imitative of its call-note. Also called Poor Wren.

POP. A name for the REDWING according to Swainson.

POPE Willughby gives this as a Cornish name for the PUFFIN. The BULLFINCH is also so called in Dorset. Swainson thinks in the latter case it is a derivation of Alp. It is also applied to the RED-BACKED SHRIKE in Hants.

POPELER. An old name for the SPOONBILL.

POPINJAY: The GREEN WOODPECKER. (Provincial.) Dutch *Papegay*. Properly a Parrot, but probably used to denote any brightly plumaged bird. Occurs in Turner as "Popiniay," and in Aldrovandus as "Popiniay" and "Popingay." Shakespeare has: "To be so pestered with a *popinjay*" ("Henry IV, act I, sc 5) which has been held to refer to a parrot, but without any good reason, for the reference is obviously to the human popinjay (i e. an idle fop). He elsewhere ("Cymbeline," act III, sc. 4) speaks of a gaudily-dressed person as a Jay, which is, of course, equally a term of contempt or derision for an over-dressed foppish fellow, in a word, a popinjay. A popinjay was formerly a gaudily-painted bird set up as a target for archers. The name is, or was until recently, in provincial use for the Green Woodpecker, which on the wing presents a clumsy and gaudy appearance

POPPING WIGEON: The GOLDENEYE and the RED-BREASTED MERGANSER (Drogheda Bay.) Because they pop up and down so suddenly (Swainson).

POST-BIRD: The SPOTTED FLYCATCHER (Kent) On account of perching on a post waiting for flies.

POTTERTON HEN: The BLACK-HEADED GULL (Aberdeen.) Swainson says, on the authority of Mr. Harvie-Brown, that it is from a loch of that name, now dried up.

Povey : The BARN-OWL. (Gloucestershire.)

Praheen Cark : The HOODED CROW. (Ireland.) Signifies the "hen crow."

PRATINCOLE [No. 354]. The name first occurs in Pennant (ed. 1776) as a rendering of Kramer's name *Pratincola* (1756).

Pridden pral. A west Cornwall name for the GREAT TITMOUSE and BLUE TITMOUSE; signifies "tree babbler."

Prine · The BAR-TAILED GODWIT. (Essex.) From its habit of probing the mud for food (Swainson).

Prinpriddle : The GREAT TITMOUSE. (Staffordshire.) According to Poole's Glossary Swainson also makes it an equivalent of " Pridden pral " in Cornwall for the LONG-TAILED TITMOUSE.

Proud-tailor : The GOLDFINCH. (Midlands.)

Provence Furzeling. Macgillivray's name for the DARTFORD WARBLER.

PTARMIGAN [No. 465]. The name is from the Gaelic *Tarmachan*. Occurs in Willughby (1678) as "White Game or White Partridge." Sibbald (1684) however called it Ptarmigan, and he is followed by most subsequent authors. According to Inwards it is a Scottish belief that the frequently repeated cry of the Ptarmigan low down on the mountains during frost and snow indicates more snow and continued cold

Puckeridge : The NIGHTJAR. (Hants.) Newton thinks it is possibly connected with A.Sax. *puca*, a goblin or demon. In Gilbert White's "Observations on Birds," published in the "Naturalists' Calendar" (1795), it is related that in Hampshire, where it sometimes goes by this name, "The Country people have a notion that it is very injurious to weanling calves, by inflicting, as it strikes at them, the fatal distemper known to cow-leeches by the name of *puckeridge*" In west Sussex and west Surrey it becomes "Puck-bird"

Puett. An obsolete Cheshire name for the LAPWING. (Holland's " Glossary.")

PUFFIN [No. 449]. The word is apparently a diminutive (=puffing) and was possibly given at first to the young of this bird, which for long was known only by various local names in different parts of the coast. The name would therefore apply to the downy covering of the young birds, e g. a diminutive of "puff" or "puffy." The Welsh name, however, for this bird is *Pwffingen*, but whether derived from the English name or whether it is the origin of the English name needs investigation. It occurs in Kay, or Caius (1570), as the "Puphin or Pupin," and he accounts for the name by remarking that "this bird our people call the Puphin, we say Pupin from its ordinary cry of 'pupin.'" Albin, Edwards, Pennant and later writers call it the Puffin, which spelling is found in Willughby (1678), but that the name was not a general one in the latter writer's day is shown by his referring to it as "the bird called Coulterneb at the Farn Islands; Puffin in North Wales, in South Wales Gulden-head, Bottle-nose and Helegug, at Scarburgh, Mullet, in Cornwall, Pope; at Jersey and Guernsey, Barbalot." Swainson gives Puffin as an Antrim name for the RAZORBILL.

PUFFINET. Albin gives it as a Farn Island name for the BLACK GUILLEMOT.

PUFFIN OF THE ISLE OF MAN. The MANX SHEARWATER. (Willughby.)

PUFFIN OF THE ISLE OF WIGHT. The PUFFIN. (Edwards.)

PUGGY or JUGGY WREN. The WREN. (West Surrey.)

PUIT. The BLACK-HEADED GULL. (Norfolk.) Found in King's "Vale Royall" (1656). From its note (see Pewit Gull). Also the LAPWING (East and South coasts), being a corruption of "Pewit."

PUMP-BORER. The LESSER SPOTTED WOODPECKER. (Shropshire.) "Because the noise it makes is like that produced by boring with an augur through hard wood" (Swainson).

PUPHIN or PUPIN. The PUFFIN (Caius.)

Purple Gallinule. Examples of this exotic species obtained in our islands are usually regarded as escaped birds.

PURPLE HERON [No. 261]. The name is found in Jenyns (1835) and succeeding authors, and is derived from Linnæus's name for the species (*Ardea purpurea*). Latham, Lewin, Walcott, Montagu and other old writers call it the "African Heron." It is the Purple-crested Heron of Bewick and the Crested Purple Heron of Selby.

PURPLE SANDPIPER [No. 385]. The name is derived from the purplish gloss on the upper-parts, and is first found in Montagu (1802). It is the Selninger Sandpiper of Latham and Pennant, and the Purple or Rock Tringa of Selby.

PURRE. An old name for the DUNLIN in winter-plumage (Norfolk, Yorkshire.) Occurs in Willughby.

PURRE MAW: The ROSEATE TERN. (Carrickfergus.) From its hoarse cry. Maw is an equivalent of Gull.

PUTTOCK. The KITE and also the COMMON BUZZARD Turner and Merrett apply it to the former, while Willughby applies it to the latter bird, to which also it was until recently applied in Essex, where half a century ago it was not such a *rara avis* in that county as the Kite. Montagu also gives it as a provincial name of the Common Buzzard, but Bewick, who spells it Puttok, applies it to the Kite. It appears also to have been sometimes applied to the MARSH-HARRIER. It is a contraction of "poot-hawk," lit. "pullet-hawk," *poot* signifying poult or pullet. Also sometimes spelt "Puddock."

PWFFIN. A Welsh name for the PUFFIN, of which it is, perhaps, the original.

PWFFIN MANAW or PWFFINGEN FANAW. Welsh names for the MANX SHEARWATER, lit. "Manx Puffin."

PYGMY CURLEW. See "Pigmy Curlew."

PYSG ERYR. A Welsh name for the OSPREY, signifying "Fish eagle."

PYSGOTWR: The KINGFISHER. (North Wales) lit. "fisher."

QUAIL [No. 468]. From O.Fr. *Quaille* (Mod. Fr. *Caille*). The name occurs in Turner (1544) as "Quale:" Merrett and Willughby have Quail. As instancing the immense migrations of former times it may be related that Pliny credits them with being a danger to sailors, as he says they often settle on the sails, and that always at night, and so sink ships.

QUAILZIE. An old Scots name for the QUAIL.

QUAKETAIL. A name invented by Macgillivray for the group of "yellow" wagtails (Budytes), as distinguished from the PIED WAGTAIL and its congeners which he called "wagtails."

QUEEST, QUEST, QUIST, QUISTY. Provincial names for the RING-DOVE. Occurs in Merrett (1667) as "Quist" and in Montagu as "Quest." It is also found corrupted to Quice, Queeze, or Quease. From Lat. *questus*. (See also Wood Quest.)

QUEET. A name for the COOT. (Swainson.)

QUEEZE: The RING-DOVE. (Cheshire.) (See Queest.)

QUET: The COMMON GUILLEMOT. (Aberdeen.)

QUHAIP. An old Scots form of "Whaup" (CURLEW).

QUICK ME DICK: The QUAIL (Oxfordshire) Imitative of its call-note.

QUICKSTART· The REDSTART. (Ireland.)

QUINK or QUINCK-GOOSE. A fowler's name for the BRENT GOOSE· thought to be from its note.

QUIS The WOODCOCK. (Wiltshire.)

RADDE'S BUSH-WARBLER [No. 129]. An Eastern Siberian species named in honour of Radde, who described it in 1863.

RAFTER or RAFTER BIRD: The SPOTTED FLYCATCHER is so called from its nesting on rafters in old buildings. (Montagu.)

RAIL· The LAND-RAIL. Occurs in Willughby as the "Rail or Daker-hen." Sometimes also used for the WATER-RAIL.

RAIN-BIRD, RAIN-FOWL, or RAIN-PIE· The GREEN WOODPECKER. (Provincial.) "Rayn byrde" is found in Turner, "Rainfowl" occurs in Willughby, and Wallis tells us it was so called in Northumberland. It is still a country belief that when the cry of this bird is much heard rain will follow.

RAIN GOOSE· The RED-THROATED DIVER. (Caithness, Orkneys and Shetlands.) From its cry being thought to foretell rain.

RALPH. A name for the RAVEN. (Swainson.)

RALPHIE The CORMORANT. (Whitby, Yorkshire.)

RAMAGE-HAWK In falconry a young hawk that can fly and prey for itself. Ramage is also used to denote a wild or coy hawk.

RANTOCK: The GOOSANDER. (Orkneys.)

RAT-BIRD, RAT-HEN: The WATER-RAIL. (Sedbergh, Yorkshire.)

RATCH: The LITTLE AUK. (Shetlands.) Probably a corruption of Rotch or Rotchie.

RAT GOOSE: The BRENT-GOOSE. Swainson thought it to be from its note ("rott.")

RATTLE-THRUSH: The MISTLE-THRUSH. (Yorkshire.) From its harsh note.

RATTLE-WINGS. A fowler's name for the GOLDENEYE. (Norfolk.)

RAVEN [No 1]. From A.Sax. *hræfn, hrefn,* a Raven: in Mid. Eng. becoming *raven*, the initial *h* being dropped. Skeat says it is derived from the cry and has no connexion with the word *raven*, to plunder or devour voraciously. The name appears in Turner (1544), also Merrett and all later writers. Turner states that "in places with less space, and where there is not room for many, Ravens dwell only in pairs, and, when their young have just gained power of flight, the parents first banish them from the nest, and later drive them out of the whole neighbourhood." Willughby states, on hearsay, that the Raven was formerly capable of being "reclaimed and trained up for fowling after the manner of a hawk." Kay, or Caius, also says that he saw in the year 1548, two white ravens from the same nest in Cumberland, which were trained for bird-catching just like hawks. The Raven was a sacred bird of the Druids. O'Curry ("Manners and Customs of Ancient Irish") has found that it was domesticated on account of the auguries to be obtained from its croakings. The same belief in its gift of prophecy prevails among the Icelanders. It is also well known as an old Anglo-Saxon emblem. The Raven is a familiar bird in the Norse mythology, as Woden's bird: two Ravens, one black and one white, sit upon his shoulders and tell him all that passes in the world below. In the Welsh "Mabinogion" the hero Owein, son of Urien, is accompanied by an army of Ravens, which attack his enemies. In the Irish legend also Cuchullaind had two magic Ravens which announced to him the coming of his foes It was by the means of this bird that Flokki, in the Norse saga, discovered Iceland. There is a belief among the Cornish fishermen that King Arthur is still living in the form of a Raven, changed by magic into that shape, and that he will some day resume his own form ("Notes and Queries," ser. I, viii). Hawker ("Echoes from Cornwall") has, however, fastened the same belief upon the Chough. An ancient superstition was that the Raven neglected her young after they were hatched. According to Glanville ("De Proprietatibus Rerum," 1483) the young are fed with the "dew of heaven" until they are fledged and have black feathers. Izaak Walton says that the Raven "leaves her young ones to the care of the God of nature, who is said in the Psalms (CXLVII, 9) to feed the young ravens that call upon Him; and they be kept alive and fed by a dew or worms that breed in their nests; or some other ways that we mortals know not." Shakespeare ("Titus Andronicus," act II, sc. 3) alludes to this when he says :—

> Some say that ravens foster forlorn children,
> The whilst their own birds famish in their nests.

Its association with the story of Noah's Ark is known to all. The Romans, who consecrated the Raven to Apollo, regarded it as a foreteller of good or evil. In somewhat later times, it became in England very generally accepted as a bird of ill-omen It is thus frequently alluded to in Shakespeare. In " Othello " (act IV, sc. 1) we find a reference to its flying over a house in which there is sickness being an omen of death—

> As doth the Raven o'er the infectious house,
> Boding to all

Marlowe (" Jew of Malta ") alludes to the same superstition. According to Dyer the belief is still held in Cornwall that the croaking of a Raven over the house bodes evil to some member of the family. Ravens' feathers are said to have been used by witches, and Shakespeare (" Tempest," act I, sc. 2) has —

> As wicked dew as e'er my mother brush'd
> With raven's feather from unwholesome fen

In Rowlands's " More Knaves Yet " (ca. 1613) allusion is made to a curious belief that if a Raven cries just overhead " some in the Towne have lost their virtue." Drayton also alludes to " the black night-raven's throat " as boding ill. According to Inwards it is a popular belief that if Ravens croak three or four times and flap their wings fine weather is expected.

RAVEN or RAVEN CROW. According to Nelson and Clarke the CARRION-CROW is so called in parts of Yorkshire.

RAY'S WAGTAIL. See YELLOW WAGTAIL

RAZORBILL [No. 443]. Occurs first in Merrett (1667). Willughby mentions it as " The bird called Razorbill in the West of England, Auk in the North, Murre in Cornwall." Sibbald calls it the Auk and says it is " the Scout of our country folk " (i.e the Scots).

RAZOR-GRINDER : The NIGHTJAR. (Norfolk.) From its jarring note.

RED-BACKED SHRIKE [No. 112]. The name, which is derived from the bright red-brown mantle, seems to occur first in Pennant (1766) as " Red-back't Butcher Bird," which in later editions is changed to Red-backed Shrike.

RED-BILLED HERON : The BUFF-BACKED HERON. (Pennant.)

REDBREAST [No. 185, British Redbreast, No. 184, Continental Redbreast]. Properly a contraction of the old English name " Robin Redbreast." Modern writers have, however, preferred the name Redbreast to the much more popular name

Robin. In the older name Robin Redbreast (under which it occurs in Turner, Willughby, Sibbald, and other old writers) the word Robin is, it is said, a nickname, but even if so there is no more reason to drop the Robin than to drop the Mag in Magpie, and revert to the old word Pie. Another instance is to be found in Jackdaw, although in this case the Jack is not a nickname as sometimes supposed (see JACKDAW). The name Redbreast alone occurs first in Merrett's list (1667), and although increasingly frequent in books in modern times it has never taken the place of the name Robin colloquially. For other information on the species see under Robin. Dr. Hartert has separated the British resident form from the Continental, which occurs on migration, hence the change of name.

RED-BREASTED DUCK : The FERRUGINOUS DUCK. (Lewin.)

RED-BREASTED FLYCATCHER [No. 118]. So called from the orange-red colour of the throat and breast.

RED-BREASTED GODWIT : The BLACK-TAILED GODWIT. (Bewick.)

RED-BREASTED GOOSANDER : The RED-BREASTED MERGANSER. (Edwards.)

RED-BREASTED GOOSE [No. 281]. The name first occurs in Pennant's "Arctic Zoology" (II, p. 571). It is derived from the chestnut-red of the chest and sides of neck in the adult.

RED-BREASTED LINNET : The LINNET (in spring-plumage). So called from the crimson colour of the breast.

RED-BREASTED MERGANSER [No. 313]. So called from the reddish-brown of the lower-neck and upper-breast. The name occurs in the later editions of Pennant, as also in Montagu, but in the folio edition of Pennant (1766) the species is called "Lesser Dun Diver." Edwards, however, has Red-breasted Goosander. The name Merganser is first found in Gesner ("Hist. Anim.," 1555).

RED-BREASTED MOOR TIT : The STONECHAT. (East Cleveland, Yorkshire.)

RED-BREASTED SANDPIPER [No. 386] So-called from the pale chestnut tint of the under-parts while in breeding-plumage. It is the Red-breasted Snipe of Eyton, and the Brown Snipe of earlier authors.

RED-BREASTED SHOVELER : The SHOVELER. (Bewick.)

RED-BREASTED SNIPE : The RED-BREASTED SANDPIPER ; also the BAR-TAILED GODWIT, in spring-dress. (Montagu, "Orn. Dict.," Supp.)

Red-breasted Snipe-Tattler. The RED-BREASTED SAND-PIPER. So called because it resembles both the snipes and the " tattlers."

Redcap The GOLDFINCH. (North England.) From its red front, also applied to the LINNET when in spring-plumage with red crown, and to the LESSER REDPOLL at Ackworth, Yorkshire.

Red Cock · The RED GROUSE. (Tunstall MS., 1780.)

Red Coot-footed Tringa. The RED-NECKED PHALAROPE (female) is so called by Edwards

Red Craking Reed-Wren. A name for SAVI'S WARBLER.

RED-CRESTED POCHARD [No. 297]. The name is found in Selby It is the Red-crested Whistling Duck of Yarrell (1st ed.) who first recorded the species in 1828 (" Zool. Jnl.," II, p 492). The name arises from the rusty-red colour of the crested head.

Red Duck The FERRUGINOUS DUCK (Pennant.)

Red-eyed Poker The COMMON POCHARD. (Provincial.)

RED-FOOTED FALCON [No 239]. The name, which originates in the bright brownish red of the tarsi and feet, appears in the first edition of Yarrell. It is the Red-legged Falcon of Jenyns and Eyton, and the Orange-legged Hobby of Selby.

Red-fronted Swallow · The SWALLOW (Macgillivray).

Red-fronted Thistle-finch The GOLDFINCH. (Macgillivray.)

Red Game : The RED GROUSE. Occurs in Willughby.

Red Godwit : The BLACK-TAILED GODWIT (Pennant, Montagu), BAR-TAILED GODWIT (Selby)

Red Godwit Snipe The BLACK-TAILED GODWIT, in spring-plumage. (Pennant.)

RED GROUSE [No. 464]. Pennant, in his folio edition, calls it Grous only, but in his later editions " Red Grous," the final *e* being quite modern. Occurs in Willughby (1678) as " Red Game, Gor-cock, More-cock," while Sibbald (1684) calls it " Moor-Cock, or Moor-fowl." It is believed in Scotland that the gathering of Grouse into large flocks indicates snow. Their approach to the farm-yard is a sign of severe weather—frost and snow. When they sit on dykes in the moor, rain only is expected (Inwards).

Red Hawk : The KESTREL. (Stirling and Yorkshire.) From its rufous plumage. Also the PEREGRINE FALCON in first year's plumage.

Red-head . The COMMON POCHARD. (Yorkshire.)

RED-HEADED BUTCHER-BIRD: The WOODCHAT SHRIKE. (Albin.)

RED-HEADED FINCH: The LINNET (Pennant); the LESSER REDPOLL (Swainson).

RED-HEADED POCHARD: The COMMON POCHARD. (Selby.)

RED-HEADED SMEW: The female SMEW. (Pennant.) It is a Holy Island name for the young.

RED-HEADED SPARROW. The TREE-SPARROW. (Albin.) Nelson and Clarke give it as a Linton-on-Ouse (Yorkshire) name.

RED-HEADED WIGEON. The COMMON POCHARD. (Pennant.) In local use in Cheshire and Northumberland.

RED HOOP: The BULLFINCH. (Dorset.)

RED KITE: The KITE. (Macgillivray.)

RED LARK: The AMERICAN WATER-PIPIT. Occurs in Edwards ("Gleanings," pl. 297), Pennant, etc.

RED-LEGGED CROW: The CHOUGH. The name used by Pennant, Lewin, Latham, Walcott, Montagu and other old writers. Nelson and Clarke give Red-legged Daw as a local Yorkshire name.

RED-LEGGED FALCON: The RED-FOOTED FALCON.

RED-LEGGED GODWIT: The SPOTTED REDSHANK. (Bewick.)

RED-LEGGED GULL · The BLACK-HEADED GULL. (Ireland.) Also Red-legged Pigeon Mew in Norfolk.

RED-LEGGED HORSEMAN: The REDSHANK. (Albin.)

RED-LEGGED JACKDAW: The CHOUGH. (North Ireland.)

RED-LEGGED PARTRIDGE [No. 469]. The name first occurs in Willughby (1678). It was not formerly an indigenous species in our islands, having first been introduced in Suffolk about 1770, while it has since spread throughout the south-eastern counties.

RED-LEGGED SANDPIPER or SNIPE: The REDSHANK. (Provincially.) The former name is also applied to the RUFF (without its ruff). Red-leg is also a Norfolk name for the Redshank, and Red-legs a Yorkshire one for the same species.

RED LINNET: The GOLDFINCH (Cheshire); the LINNET (Hampshire, West Yorkshire); the LESSER REDPOLL (West Yorkshire).

RED LOBE-FOOT: The RED-NECKED PHALAROPE. (Selby.)

RED-NECK: The COMMON POCHARD. (Cheshire.)

RED-NECKED BERNICLE-GOOSE: The RED-BREASTED GOOSE. (Macgillivray.)

RED-NECKED GREBE [No. 338] This name, which arises from the red fore-neck, first occurs in Pennant's "Arctic Zoology," and is the name used by most subsequent authors.

RED-NECKED NIGHTJAR. See ALGERIAN RED-NECKED NIGHTJAR.

RED-NECKED PHALAROPE [No 399]. This name seems to occur first in Sowerby's "British Miscellany" (1805); it having been the "Red Phalarope" of the older authors, including Pennant, Latham, Lewin, Walcott and Montagu, and the Red Lobe-foot of Selby Edwards figures both male and female, calling the former "Cock Coot-footed Tringa" and the latter "Red Coot-footed Tringa." The name originates in the red patch on each side of the neck of the adult in summer-plumage

RED-NECKED SANDPIPER The DUNLIN (immature- or winter-plumage). Occurs in Montagu.

RED OWL: The SHORT-EARED OWL. (Dartmoor) From the pale orange of its under plumage (Swainson)

RED PARTRIDGE The RED-LEGGED PARTRIDGE. (Macgillivray.)

RED PTARMIGAN . The RED GROUSE. (Jenyns.)

RED-RUMP The REDSTART. (East Cleveland, Yorkshire.)

RED-RUMPED SWALLOW [No. 196]. So called from its rusty-red lower-back. It was first recorded as British in 1906, when a small party occurred at Fair Isle, Shetlands.

RED SANDPIPER The KNOT. (Pennant, Montagu, etc.) Swainson gives it as an Irish name, and Nelson and Clarke as an obsolete Yorkshire name

REDSHANK [No 394]. The name "Redshank" is found in Willughby, and occurs in Turner (1544) as "Redshane" and in Merrett as "Red Shanks." Turner seeks to identify the species with the Hæmatopodes of Pliny, which is, of course, the OYSTERCATCHER Albin calls it "Totanus or Redlegged Horseman" and "Poole-Snipe."

REDSHANK A name for the FIELDFARE (Swainson)

RED-SHANK GULL The BLACK-HEADED GULL. (Ireland.)

RED-SIDED THRUSH The REDWING. (Macgillivray)

RED-SPOTTED BLUETHROAT. See NORWEGIAN BLUETHROAT. This species seems to occur first in Edwards (pl. 28) as "Blue-throated Redstart." The grounds on which the authors of the "Hand-List" changed the name of this species to "Norwegian Bluethroat" appear to have been to distinguish it from the Lapland and other forms.

REDSTART [No. 178]. From A.Sax. *reád* (red) and *steort* (tail). Turner (1544) calls it "rede tale." The first use of the name Redstart I find is in Merrett's list (1667) and he gives "Red-tail" as an equivalent name. Willughby gives Redstart only, the A.Sax. name having thenceforth taken the place of the later English one.

REDSTER or REDSTARE. Yorkshire names for the REDSTART.

REDTAIL. A Yorkshire name for the REDSTART (q.v.).

RED-THROATED DIVER [No. 344]. So called from the red upper-throat. The name appears in Edwards, in Pennant (8vo ed.), and in most later writers. In the folio edition of Pennant (1766) it is called "Red-necked Diver." It is the Speckled Diver of older authors.

RED-THROATED PIPIT [No. 69]. So called from the pale chestnut of the throat and breast.

RED THRUSH : The REDWING. (Midlands.)

REDWING [No. 159]. So called from the orange-red colour of the sides and under wing-coverts. Macgillivray's name "Red-sided Thrush" would really be more appropriate. Formerly called the Wind Thrush (q.v.). The name Redwing appears first in Willughby (1678); Sibbald (1684) calls it "Red wing or Wind-Thrush." Swainson gives Redwing Mavis as a Forfar name.

Red-winged Starling. A North American species of which examples (no doubt escaped from captivity) have been taken in this country. The name is found in Albin (1738); it is included by Yarrell (1st ed.).

REDWING FELFER or REDWING THROLLY. Yorkshire names for the REDWING.

REED-BUNTING [No. 53]. Frequents streams and rush-covered ground rather than reeds. Occurs in Turner (1544) as "Rede Sparrow" and in Merrett and Willughby as "Reed Sparrow," as also in Pennant (1766). The name Reed-Bunting appears to occur first in Montagu. Yarrell calls it Black-headed Bunting (an unfortunate choice), which has led to confusion with the non-indigenous species so named.

REED BUNTING. Swainson says this was an Essex name for the BEARDED TITMOUSE.

REED CHUCKER. A name for the REED-WARBLER.

REED FAUVETTE : The SEDGE-WARBLER. (Bewick, 1797.)

REEDLING : The BEARDED TITMOUSE. (Norfolk.)

Reed-Pheasant. A Norfolk name for the BEARDED TIT-MOUSE, in allusion to its long tail

Reed-Sparrow. An older name for the REED-BUNTING; still used provincially in Nottinghamshire, Yorkshire and elsewhere.

REED-WARBLER [No. 136]. So called from its frequenting reed-beds. The name appears as Reed Wren in Latham ("Syn.," Supp., p. 184) and as Reed Warbler in Pennant (1812 ed.) It is also sometimes called Reed Tit.

Reefogue An Irish name for the HEDGE-SPARROW.

Reel-Bird or Reeler. Local names for the GRASSHOPPER-WARBLER, from the resemblance of its song to the noise of the reel used by the hand spinners of wool. According to Newton SAVI'S WARBLER (now extinct in the Fens) was formerly also known as the "Night Reel-bird."

REEVE: The female of the RUFF (q.v.) It occurs in Leland's "Collectanea" as "Ree," and in the Northumberland "Household Book" (1512) as "Rey."

Rhegen yddwr. The WATER-RAIL. (North Wales) lit. "water crake", also called Rhegen y Gors, or marsh crake.

Rhegen yr yd A Welsh name for the LAND-RAIL; lit. "corn-crake"

Rhonell coch. A Welsh name for the REDSTART; signifying "red-tail"

Rhostog coch. A Welsh name for the BAR-TAILED GODWIT; signifying "ruddy godwit"

Riabhag-choille. A Gaelic name for the WOOD-LARK.

Richardson's Skua. An alternative name for the ARCTIC SKUA. It seems to occur first in Selby

RICHARD'S PIPIT [No 65] The name is found in Selby (1825). It was first recorded by Vigors from an example taken near London in 1812.

Richel-bird The LITTLE TERN. (Montagu.)

Rind Tabberer. The GREEN WOODPECKER. (Provincial.)

Rine. A Cornish name for the QUAIL

Rine bird The WRYNECK. (West Surrey.) On account of its arriving at the time the oak bark is stripped ("rine" = rind).

Ring Bird, Ring Bunting: The REED-BUNTING. From the white collar

RING-DOVE [No. 345, Wood-Pigeon]. So called from the white patch on each side of the neck. Also known as Wood-Pigeon, but this latter name is inappropriate, having frequently been applied to the STOCK-DOVE, and the attempt to revert to it in the "Hand-List" is therefore unfortunate. Turner (1544) has "Ringged Dove," while Merrett writes it "Ring Dove" as does also Sibbald. Willughby calls it the "Ring Pigeon," Pennant (1766) has "Ring-dove," and this name is used by nearly all subsequent authors. Dyer relates a North Yorkshire belief that once upon a time the Cushat or Ring-dove laid its eggs upon the ground, while the Peewit or Lapwing made its nest on high; but one day they agreed to exchange their localities for building. Hence the Peewit now expresses its disappointment as follows:—

> Peewit, Peewit!
> I coup'd my nest and I rue it.

The Cushat, however, rejoices that she is safe out of the reach of mischievous boys:—

> Coo, coo, come now,
> Little lad
> With thy gad,
> Come not thou

A Suffolk legend is that the Magpie once undertook to teach the Wood-pigeon how to make a more substantial nest, but the latter kept repeating her cry of "Take two, Taffy! take two!" until the Magpie, after insisting that one was enough at a time, finally gave up the attempt in a passion. Pigeons were regarded in former times in England as portents of death, and a sick man who had a desire to eat of one was supposed to foretell his own death (De Kay). Martial says of their flesh that —

> Ringed doves make a man's loins slow and dull,
> Who would be lusty should not eat this bird.

But it is not improbable that he referred to the small Collared Turtle-dove and not our northern species. The Ring-Dove is not so gentle as popular fancy would have it. Montagu relates that he once bred up, to live together "in perfect amity, a common Pigeon, Ring-Dove, White Owl and Sparrow Hawk; of which the Ring-Dove was master."

RINGED BLACKBIRD, RING BLACKBIRD, RINGED THRUSH, or RING THRUSH: The RING-OUZEL. From the white gorget. Macgillivray calls it the Ringed Thrush, and Fleming the Ring-Thrush.

RINGED DOTTEREL or RING DOTTEREL: The RINGED PLOVER. The second form is in use on the Scottish Borders.

Ringed Guillemot A supposed variety of the COMMON GUILLEMOT described in Yarrell (1st ed.) as a separate species It is the Bridled Guillemot of Gould

RINGED PLOVER [No. 358]. So called from its black pectoral band. The name first occurs in Pennant's "British Zoology" (8vo ed.). It is the Sea Lark of Willughby, Albin, Pennant (fo. ed., 1766) and other old writers

RING-EYED SCOUT: The *Ringed Guillemot*. (Yorkshire.)

RINGLESTONES. A name used by Sir Thomas Browne for the RINGED PLOVER Skeat thinks it may refer to the bird's habit of "ranging" the stones for its nest. Swainson refers it to the bird's "white collar."

RING-NECK The RINGED PLOVER. (Yorkshire.)

RING-NECKED DUCK. See *American Scaup*.

RING-NECKED LOON · The GREAT NORTHERN DIVER. (East Lothian, Cork Harbour.)

RING-NECKED PHEASANT. A variety of the PHEASANT.

RING-OUZEL [No. 162]. The name arises from the conspicuous white gorget or crescent on the breast. "Ring-Ouzel" first occurs in Willughby (1678) and was adopted by most succeeding authors.

RING-TAIL or RING-TAILED KITE The female HEN-HARRIER, from the brown-banded tail The former name occurs in Turner and Willughby, and the latter in Merrett. Swainson gives Ring-tail as an East Lothian name. Col. Thornton's "Stangel or Ringtail" is perhaps the KESTREL.

RING-TAILED or RING-TAIL EAGLE The GOLDEN EAGLE (immature). Willughby and Ray describe a "Golden Eagle with a white ring about its tail," which they "take to be specifically the same" as the Golden Eagle It was for long considered a separate species, however, and Linnæus describes it as *Falco fulvus*. Pennant figured it in 1766 ("Brit. Zool.," fo ed.) under the name of Ringtail Eagle, and Montagu in 1802 deemed it a good species.

RING-THRUSH: The RING-OUZEL (see Ringed Blackbird).

RING-WHISTLE. The RING-OUZEL (Teesdale, Yorkshire)

RIPPOCK or RITTOCK. The COMMON TERN. (Orkneys.) Swainson derives it from the Icel. *rit-ur*.

RISING LARK The SKY-LARK. (Northants) From its soaring while singing

RIVER PIE: The DIPPER. (Ireland.) From its haunts and pied plumage.

RIVERSIDE BUNTING . The REED-BUNTING

RIVER SWALLOW: The SAND-MARTIN. (Yorkshire.)
RIXY: The COMMON TERN. (East Suffolk.)
ROAD GOOSE or RHODE GOOSE. The BRENT GOOSE. The latter form is a Yorkshire name. Perhaps from its cry ("rott").
ROARER. Swainson gives this as a Border name for the BARN-OWL.
ROBERD or ROBINET. Names for the CHAFFINCH. (Swainson.)
ROBIN. An alternative name for the REDBREAST, and a contraction of the Old English name "Robin Redbreast" (see Redbreast). The present name is an anglicization of the French Robin, a proper name, in fact a diminutive of Robert. Robin is still in use with us provincially as a Christian name. It is one of the most familiar of English birds, and occurring most frequently in our folk-lore and literature. The most familiar of all rhymes on this bird is, of course, the well-known "Death of Cock Robin." A Derbyshire children's rhyme on the death and resurrection of Cock Robin commences· "Cock Robin is dead and lies in his grave" It is, however, of little value in the Robin cycle ("Folklore Journal," December, 1883). For a note on a Breton song, "Les Noces du Roitelet," narrating the wedding of the Robin and Wren, see the same journal for May, 1883 This song, in which all the birds bring presents or perform services, is similar in many respects to the English rhyme "The Wedding of Cock Robin and Jenny Wren." A couplet still heard at times on the same unscientific union runs. "The Robin and the Wren are God's Cock and Hen." Or, according to Mr. Dyer's version:—

> The Robin and the Wren
> Are God Almighty's Cock and Hen:
> Him that harries their nest,
> Never shall his soul have rest.

An old belief was that the Robin and Wren, and more particularly the former, had a habit of covering, with leaves or moss, unburied bodies, a belief arising no doubt from the old story of the "Babes in the Wood" The supposed habit is, however, alluded to by Drayton and by Webster. The superstitions relating to this bird are many. In some parts of Northamptonshire it is still held in veneration, and its killing is regarded in the light of sacrilege. This aversion to its killing obtains, in fact, in many parts of the country, the feeling being traceable to the bird's attempt, according to one legend, to draw the nails, and according to another, to pluck a spike from the Crown of Thorns at the Crucifixion, and receiving a drop of blood in the effort, from which the red colour of its breast arises. I have found the same reluctance to kill attaching in Canada to the American Robin (or red-breasted Thrush); the superstition having been transferred with the name. Another Northamptonshire belief is that the Robin taps thrice at the window of a room in which a sick person lies before the death of the inmate. The belief in a Robin coming into a house being a sign of death has been recorded from Bath ("Folklore Journal," December, 1894). In Scotland (according to Dalyell), the Robin is considered a lucky token. In Yorkshire it is believed that if a Robin is killed the slayer's cows will give bloody milk. In Cornwall it is thought to be unlucky to hunt the Robin or the Wren. Another belief met with in some parts is that the Robin's song is of ill omen when heard by a sick person, while a curious superstition recorded in Chamber's "Book of Days" (vol I, p. 678) is to the effect that a Robin dying in one's hand causes it to always shake afterwards; this also exists as a Berkshire belief. According to Bolam it is a common Border belief that if the Robin sings from underneath a bush it will rain, but if he mounts to the top of a bush to sing, a fine day may be expected. Swainson says a Suffolk rhyme is:—

> If the Robin sings in the bush,
> Then the weather will be coarse;
> But if the Robin sings on the barn,
> Then the weather will be warm.

ROBIN The male of the HOBBY was formerly so called sometimes by falconers, according to Col. Thornton.

ROBINET The Robin or REDBREAST, lit. "little Robin."

ROBIN GOCH The REDBREAST. (North Wales) lit. "red robin."

ROBIN HAWK. A name for the CROSSBILL. (Hett.)

ROBIN REDBREAST. The old English name of the Robin (see REDBREAST). Saxby says it is also a Shetland name for the WREN.

ROCK BLACKBIRD or ROCK STARLING The RING-OUZEL. (Ireland and Stirling.)

ROCK-DOVE [No 347]. The name arises from its more exclusively frequenting cliffs and caves than its congeners. Willughby calls it the "Common Wild Dove or Pigeon." Montagu (1802), who employs the name Rock Dove for it, unites the STOCK-DOVE with it under the mistaken impression that they were one and the same species. In Northumberland the name is sometimes applied to the Stock-Dove on account of its nesting at times on crags, while Swainson gives Rock Dove as an Irish name for the BLACK GUILLEMOT.

ROCKET-DOVE. The STOCK-DOVE. (Gunnergate-in-Cleveland.) From the rocket-like flight as it leaves the ivy-clad trees (Nelson and Clarke).

ROCK GROUSE   A name for the PTARMIGAN.

ROCK HAWK: The MERLIN. (Provincial.) From its habit of perching on rocks

ROCKIER: The ROCK-DOVE. Montagu gives this as a provincial name for the species. It is also spelt "Rocker."

ROCK LARK. The ROCK-PIPIT. (Montagu.) It is a Bridlington (Yorkshire) name for the species.

ROCK LINTIE: The ROCK-PIPIT. (Aberdeen.)

ROCK-MARTNET· The SWIFT. (Merrett.)

ROCK-OUZEL. The RING-OUZEL. (Lancashire and Yorkshire.) Willughby gives it as a Derbyshire name for the same species. It is applied to the DIPPER at Longdendale, Cheshire.

ROCK-PIGEON. The ROCK-DOVE. (Flamborough and Bempton, Yorkshire.) Nelson and Clarke state that the STOCK-DOVE is there called Rock-Dove.

ROCK-PIPIT [No. 72]. The name is found in Selby (1825). It is the Rock Lark of Montagu, the Dusky Lark of Lewin and Pennant, the Sea Lark of Walcott and the Sea Titling of Fleming.

ROCK PLOVER   The GREY PLOVER. (Wexford.)

ROCK SANDPIPER: The PURPLE SANDPIPER (Northumberland.)

ROCK SPARROW: The TREE-SPARROW. (Cheshire; and Halifax, Yorkshire.)

ROCK STARLING: The RING-OUZEL. (Roxburgh)

ROCK-THRUSH [No. 165]. First described and named by Vigors ("Zool. Jnl," II, p. 396). Its home is in the mountain ranges of South and Middle Europe, hence its name.

ROCK TRINGA: The PURPLE SANDPIPER. (Selby.)

ROCUS.   A Gaelic name for the ROOK.

RODGE.   A name for the GADWALL. (Swainson.)

RODNA-HINLEN.   A Cornish name for the LAPWING.

ROLLER [No. 207] From Fr. *Roller*. The name, which is found in Willughby, appears to originate with Gesner (1555) who says it was so called near Strasburg from its habit of rolling or turning over in its flight.

ROOD GOOSE. The BRENT GOOSE. Swainson thinks it is from its cry ("rott").

ROOK [No. 4] Occurs in Aldrovandus (1599) as "Roock," and in Merrett (1667) and also Willughby as Rook. Turner describes it as probably the *frugilega* of Aristotle, but gives no English name. Shakespeare also mentions it (as a bird of ill-omen) in "Macbeth" (act III, sc. 4). It is probably so named from its colour, rook (A.Sax. *hróc*) being equivalent to smoke-black, rooky is adjectivally used to denote this. It is an equivalent of the German *rauch*, smoke. Some authorities have, with much less reason, preferred *raucus*, from the bird's hoarse note. In some parts of the country, according to Swainson, it is believed that Rooks forsake their home on the downfall of the family, or death of the heir of the estate; this belief prevailing in Northumberland, Rutland and Cornwall. Dyer also says that it is a very prevalent notion in the North of England that "when Rooks desert a rookery which they have tenanted for a number of years, it foretells the coming downfall of the family on whose property it is." It is supposed that in earlier times owners of estates prided themselves on attaching the Rooks to them because they were regarded as "fowls of good omen." The Rook is one of the most commonly believed in as a weather prognosticator among birds. When it hangs about home or flies up and down or especially low, rain or wind may be expected; when it "tumbles" or drops in its flight it is taken as a sure sign of rain. In connexion with this Dr. Jenner's lines may be cited—

> And, see yon rooks how odd their flight,
> They imitate the gliding kite,
> And seem precipitate to fall,
> As if they felt the piercing ball—
> "Twill surely rain—I see with sorrow
> Our jaunt must be put off to-morrow"

If the birds feed busily and hurry over the ground in one direction, and in a compact body, a storm will soon follow. When they sit in rows on dykes and palings wind is looked for; while when going home to roost if they fly high the next day will be fair, and *vice versa* (Inwards). A Devonshire saying is that if Rooks stay at home, or return in the middle of the day, it will rain; if they go far abroad, it will be fine.

ROSEATE TERN [No. 418]. The name is found in Montagu ("Orn. Dict.," Supp.). So called from the pink tinge on the under-parts.

ROSE-COLOURED STARLING [No. 14]. This name is found in the 1832 edition of Bewick. It is generally called Rose-coloured Pastor, from the prevailing colour of its plumage and from Temminck's generic name (*pastor*) for it, and under this name it occurs in Selby (1825). Bewick (1797) has Rose-coloured Ouzel (probably a rendering of Buffon's "*Le Merle couleur de Rose*").

ROSE LINNET: The LESSER REDPOLL (Yorkshire); also the LINNET (in spring-plumage). Occurs in Fleming for the first-named species.

ROSE-LINTIE. A Border name for the LINNET (Lintie=Linnet). Swainson says it is a Lowland name for the LESSER REDPOLL.

ROSS'S GULL or ROSS'S ROSY GULL. See WEDGE-TAILED GULL.

ROSY BULLFINCH. Now called SCARLET GROSBEAK.

ROTCHE, ROTCH, or ROTCHIE: The LITTLE AUK. Rotche is a frequent name for the species, especially among sailors, and originates, apparently, in its cry, which has been syllabled as "rot-tet-tet." According to Gray this species is called Rotchie by the seafaring people on the shores of East Lothian and Fifeshire.

ROTHEROCK. An old Orkney name for the BARNACLE-GOOSE.

ROTT GOOSE: The BRENT GOOSE. From its cry ("rott").

ROUGH-FOOTED EAGLE. See SPOTTED EAGLE. The name occurs in Charleton and in Latham, but belongs to the *Lesser* Spotted Eagle.

ROUGH-LEGGED BUZZARD [No. 242]. The name first appears as Rough-legged Falcon in the Appendix to Pennant's "British Zoology." Fleming and Yarrell have Rough-legged Buzzard.

ROUND-BERRY BIRD: The RING-OUZEL. (Connemara.) From its fondness for the berries of the rowan or mountain ash (Swainson).

ROW-DOW or ROO-DOO: The HOUSE-SPARROW. (Northants.)

ROYSTON CROW. The Old English name for the HOODED CROW, but still in use in the northern counties. It is found in Merrett (1667), and also Willughby, Albin and Pennant (1766 ed.). The latter in later editions calls it

Hooded Crow. Turner (1544) calls it the "Winter Crow." Albin says it is so called from having been seen in numbers in winter about Royston and Newmarket.

Ruby-crowned Wren This American species, of which two examples were said to have been shot near Loch Lomond in 1852, is not considered to have a place on the British List

RUDDOCK · The REDBREAST. (Cornwall and Yorkshire) Occurs in Merrett and Willughby. From A Sax. *rudduc*. Swainson also gives "Reddock" for Dorset.

RUDDY PLOVER The SANDERLING. Adult male in summer-plumage. (Swainson.)

RUDDY SHELD-DUCK [No. 286]. Occurs in Selby (1833), and also in Yarrell (1st ed.) as the Ruddy Shieldrake. It is the Ruddy Goose of Bewick.

RUFF and REEVE [No. 370] Derivation of Reeve is thought to be from A Sax. *gerefa*, literally one in authority, perhaps so called from the pugnacious habits of the males. A wood-reeve was anciently the overseer of a wood. The name is found in Willughby as "The Ruff, whose female is called a Reeve ", in Merrett as "Rough and Reev," perhaps a mere phonetic spelling (but see below). The name Ruff is invariably applied to the male bird, the female being called Reeve. According to Willughby, "They breed in Summer time in the Fens of Lincolnshire about Crowland," but it is, alas, now nearly a thing of the past for them to breed anywhere in England. Newton observes that it is "at present unknown whether the bird was named from the frill (Elizabethan) or the frill from the bird. In the latter case the name should possibly be spelt Rough (*cf* 'rough-footed' as applied to fowls with feathered legs) as in 1666 Merrett ('Pinax,' p. 182) had it."

RUFFED BUSTARD. A name for MACQUEEN'S BUSTARD.

RUFOUS-BACKED EGRET The BUFF-BACKED HERON. (Gould.)

RUFOUS TURTLE-DOVE. An Asiatic ally of our TURTLE-DOVE which has occurred in Yorkshire.

RUFOUS WARBLER [No 152]. The name is found in Latham. ("Syn.," IV, p. 431). It occurs in Gould ("Birds of Europe") and Yarrell ("Supp." II, 1856) as Rufous Sedge Warbler. Derived from the Rufous-brown plumage.

RUNNER · The WATER-RAIL. (Sedbergh, Yorkshire.)

RUNT The WREN. (Near Huddersfield.)

RUSH-WARBLER. A name for the REED-WARBLER.

RUSSET-PATED CHOUGH. Shakespeare mentions ("Midsummer Night's Dream," act III, sc. 2) :—
> Russet pated choughs, many in sort,
> Rising and cawing at the gun's report.

The term "russet-pated" has aroused a good deal of controversy. Mr. Harting considers it to refer to the JACKDAW, and a few years ago in the "Zoologist" he defended at some length his opinion that "russet" might denote the grey nape of this bird. Professor Newton, on the other hand, seems to have preferred to read it "russet-patted" (i.e., red-footed), making the passage refer to the CHOUGH. Mr. Harting has shown (as will be seen in the present work under "Chough") that the word "chough" did not always apply to *Pyrrhocorax graculus*; yet on the other hand he admits that Shakespeare in other cases refers always to the Jackdaw as the "daw."

RUSSET WHEATEAR: The BLACK-EARED WHEATEAR. The name is found in Latham, and it is figured by Edwards (pl. 31). It is also called Russet Chat.

RUSTIC BUNTING [No 51]. The name is an anglicization of Pallas's name *Emberiza rustica*.

SABINE'S GULL [No. 423]. The name is found in Jenyns and was adopted by Yarrell and succeeding authors. It is the Sabine's Xeme of Eyton.

Sabine's Snipe. A melanism of the COMMON SNIPE, for long supposed to be a distinct species. It was first described by Vigors in a communication to the Linnean Society ("Trans.," vol. XIV), from a bird shot in Queen's County, Ireland, in 1822, while many others have been obtained from time to time.

SADCOCK, SEDCOCK, SEDGECOCK, SETTCOCK. Local Cheshire names for the MISTLE-THRUSH. (Coward and Oldham.)

SADDLE-BACK: The GREAT and LESSER BLACK-BACKED GULLS. (Yorkshire.) From the saddle-shape of the dark mantle. Swainson gives Greater Saddle-back as an Irish name for the former.

SAID FOOL. A Shetland name for the LESSER BLACK-BACKED GULL. (Saxby.)

ST. CUTHBERT'S DUCK: The COMMON EIDER (Northumberland.)

ST. GEORGE'S DUCK. The SHELD-DUCK. Occurs in Montagu.

ST. KILDA WREN. See WREN.

SAITH: The MISTLE-THRUSH. The name occurs in Merrett (1667).

SALLYPECKER. The CHIFFCHAFF and also the WILLOW-WARBLER. (Ireland.) "Sally" signifies sallow (=willow.) Swainson says it is also an Irish name for the SEDGE-WARBLER

SAND-BACKIE   The SAND-MARTIN. (Forfar.)

SAND-COCK. The REDSHANK. (Bewick.)

SAND DOTTEREL: The RINGED PLOVER. (Humber.)

SANDERLING [No. 372]. Cognate with Icel. *Sanderla* The name occurs in Willughby (1678) and in most succeeding authors.

SAND LARK, SANDY, or SANDY LAVEROCK. The RINGED PLOVER. (Northumberland.) The last name is also used in the Orkneys and Shetlands. Sand Lark is applied in Scotland to the COMMON SANDPIPER, and in Ireland to the SANDERLING, also at Bridlington to the ROCK-PIPIT.

SANDLARK OF THE SHORE   The DUNLIN. (Ireland.)

SAND-MARTIN [No. 198]   The name occurs in Merrett's list (1667), also in Willughby and most subsequent authors.

SAND MOUSE   The DUNLIN. (Westmorland.)

SAND PIGEON   The STOCK-DOVE. (Cheshire.)

SAND RUNNER. The DUNLIN. Also the RINGED PLOVER and the SANDERLING on the Humber.

SAND SNIPE   The COMMON SANDPIPER. (Cheshire and West Yorkshire.)

SAND or SANDY SWALLOW   The SAND-MARTIN. (Provincial.) Sandy is a Teesdale name.

SAND THRUSH   A name for the DIPPER. (Hett.)

SANDWICH TERN [No. 417]. The name is found in Latham's "Synopsis" (VI, p. 356), it being communicated to him by Boys of Sandwich, whence the name.

SAND WIGEON. The GADWALL. (Essex.)

SANDYHEAD. A name for the COMMON POCHARD.

SANDY LAVEROCK or SANDY LOO. The RINGED PLOVER. (Orkney and Shetland.)

SANDY LAVROCK: The COMMON SANDPIPER. (Scottish Borders.)

SARDINIAN WARBLER [No 149]. Of this South European species an example was obtained near Hastings in June, 1907.

SATIN GREBE. The GREAT CRESTED GREBE. From the silky plumage of the under-parts

SAVI'S WARBLER [No. 131]. This species was first recorded from the Cambridgeshire Fens in 1840 and was known to breed there up to the year 1856. It was named in honour of Savi, the Italian ornithologist, who first described the species in 1824. The name appears in Yarrell (1843).

SAW-BEER: The GOLDEN PLOVER. Mr. Robert Godfrey informs me that this name is used "in one locality lying to the south of the Pentland Hills in this county (Mid-Lothian) and is distinctly an effort to syllable the wail of the bird." It recalls Saxby's version "Oh dee-ar."

SAWBILL. The GOOSANDER and the RED-BREASTED MERGANSER. (Scotland, Yorkshire, and Northumberland.) Also occurs as Saw-neb (Aberdeen) for both species and Sawbill Wigeon (Galway) and Sawbill Duck (Yorkshire) for the RED-BREASTED MERGANSER.

SAWFINCH, SAWFITCH, SAWFILER, SAW-SHARPENER, SAW-WHET: The GREAT TITMOUSE. (Provincial.) So called from its song resembling the sound of saw-sharpening. According to Swainson, in some parts of the country these notes are considered to portend rain, but Bolam says that on the Border the reverse is the belief

SCALD CROW: The HOODED CROW. (Ireland.)

SCALE DRAKE: The SHELD-DUCK. (Orkneys.)

SCALLOP-TOED SANDPIPER: The GREY PHALAROPE. (Pennant, 1766.)

SCAMEL. Occurs in Shakespeare ("The Tempest," act II, sc. 2) and has been erroneously surmised to be intended for "stannel" (the KESTREL), q v. Mr. H. Durrant tells me that in Norfolk the female of the BAR-TAILED GODWIT is known as the "scamel." Swainson gives "Scammel" as a Norfolk name for the Bar-Tailed Godwit. Newton thinks it a misprint for "Seamel" (i.e. Sea-Mew) or "Stannel" (a Kestrel).

SCANDINAVIAN CHIFFCHAFF. See CHIFFCHAFF.

SCANDINAVIAN ROCK-PIPIT [No. 73]. This Scandinavian form of our ROCK-PIPIT is known to occur in our Islands on migration. It was first recorded as British by Booth.

SCARBH (pron. scarrav): The SHAG. (Western Isles of Scotland.)

SCARE-CROW: The BLACK TERN (Willughby); the HOODED CROW (Montagu).

SCARF: The SHAG (Shetlands) and also the CORMORANT. From Gael. *scarbh*, Icel. *Skarfr*. Swainson, however, derives both *Scarf* and *Scart* from A.Sax. *scega*, a beard, derivate of SHAG.

SCARLET GROSBEAK [No. 31]. Formerly known as the Rosy Bullfinch.

SCART or SKART The SHAG. (Orkneys and Shetlands.) From the Gaelic *scarbh*. Also applied to the CORMORANT. (Lancs., Northumberland, North Ireland.)

SCAUP-DUCK [No. 301]. The name occurs in Willughby (1678) and in Pennant and succeeding authors. Montagu observes that " it is supposed to take its name from feeding on broken shells, called scaup." Scalp (Old D *schelpe*, Old Fr *escalope*) signifies a shell It is called Scaup Pochard by Selby.

SCAURIE, SCORIE, or SCOREY · The young of the HERRING-GULL. (Orkneys.) In Shetland applied to any young gull according to Saxby.

SCHINZ'S SANDPIPER : BONAPARTE'S SANDPIPER. (Eyton)

SCHLEGEL'S PETREL [No. 330]. A South Pacific species recently recorded as British (" P.Z S ," 1908, p. 433).

SCISSORS-GRINDER The NIGHTJAR (Norfolk and Suffolk) From its jarring note.

SCLAVONIAN GREBE. See SLAVONIAN GREBE.

SCOBBY · The CHAFFINCH. (Cornwall, North Yorkshire.) Hett also gives " Scoppy." In Staffordshire " cobby " signifies in good form or spirits.

SCOLDER : The OYSTERCATCHER. (Orkney.) From Icel. *Skjoldr*, piebald. Also occurs as " Shelder."

SCOOPER or SCOOPING AVOCET · The AVOCET. Scooper occurs in Charleton (1668). The name Scooping Avocet is first found in Pennant (1776). Montagu has Scooping Avoset. The term " Scooping " is from the bird's habit of scooping its food (marine worms, crustacea, etc.) out of the mud or sand by means of its peculiarly shaped bill.

SCOOT or SCOUT The COMMON GUILLEMOT. (Northumberland, Yorkshire)

SCOPPER-BILL. A local Norfolk name for the SHOVELER

SCOPS OWL [No. 226]. This tiny species was formerly called Scops-eared Owl, under which name it occurs in Latham, etc. It is the " Little Horned Owl " of Montagu (" Orn. Dict.," Supp).

SCORIE or SCOREY. See SCAURIE.

SCOTCH CANARY The YELLOW BUNTING. From its yellow colour.

SCOTCH GOOSE : The BRENT GOOSE. (Flamborough.)

SCOTCH NIGHTINGALE : The SEDGE-WARBLER. From its singing at night.

SCOTCH WREN : The WILLOW-WARBLER. (Pennant.)

SCOTER : The COMMON SCOTER. (Pennant, Montagu, etc.)

SCOTTISH CRESTED TITMOUSE. See CRESTED TITMOUSE.

SCOTTISH CROSSBILL. See COMMON CROSSBILL.

SCOUL A Cornish name for the KITE.

SCOULTON PEWIT or SCOULTON PIE : The BLACK-HEADED GULL. (Norfolk.) From its breeding at Scoulton Mere.

SCOUT. The COMMON GUILLEMOT (Yorkshire and Scotland); also applied to the RAZORBILL (Scotland). Sibbald mentions the latter under the name of Auk, "the Scout of our country folk." Willughby prints it Skout, and gives it as a Yorkshire name. The word as used is of Scandinavian origin and signifies to drive away. Also a Farn Island name for the PUFFIN.

SCOUTIALLIN, SCOUTY-ALLAN, or SCOUTY-AULIN : The ARCTIC SKUA. (Orkney and Shetland.)

SCRABER : The LITTLE AUK. (St. Kilda.) Also the MANX SHEARWATER (Hebrides); and the BLACK GUILLEMOT (Hebrides, East Lothian). Said to be from its Norwegian name, *skrabe*, or scraper, because it scrapes a hole in the sand for its nest.

SCRAYE : The COMMON TERN. From its cry.

SCREAMER, SCREECHER, SCREECH MARTIN, SQUEALER. English provincial names for the SWIFT, from its harsh screaming note.

SCREAMING OWL : The BARN-OWL. (Yorkshire.)

SCRECH Y COED. A Welsh name for the JAY; lit. "wood screech."

SCREECH, or SCREECH THRUSH : The MISTLE-THRUSH. So called from its loud song. Screech-bird or Screech-Thrush is also a Stirling name for the FIELDFARE.

SCREECH HAWK The NIGHTJAR. (Berks. and Bucks.)

SCREECH OWL, SCRICH-OWLE, or SCRITCH-OWL Properly the BARN-OWL. Sibbald applies the name to the TAWNY OWL. The former occurs in Merrett (1667) as the "Screech or Screeching Owl." In old English the name owl occurs as "Oule," "Ouul," or "Ule," the latter being the Saxon name. In Rowland's "More Knaves Yet" (ca. 1613) occurs :—

> Wise Gosling, did but heare the scrich-owle crye,
> And told his wife, and straight a pigge did dye.

Drayton also alludes to the popular belief in the unluckiness of the "scritch-owl's dismal note." That a Screech Owl "hooting" near the house is a sign of death has been recorded as a Berkshire belief ("Folklore," December, 1894), while in Reed's "Old Plays" (VI, p. 357) we find:—
>When Screech-owls croak upon the chimney tops,
>It's certain that you of a corse shall hear

SCREMERSTON CROW· The HOODED CROW. (Roxburgh.) From the large numbers which frequent the sea-shore in the neighbourhood of that place (Swainson)

SCREW or DEVIL SCREW: The SWIFT. (Ackworth, Yorkshire)

SCRIACHAG CHOILLE. A Gaelic name for the JAY; lit. "wood screech"

SCRIBBLING LARK· The YELLOW BUNTING (Cheshire, Yorkshire, Northants) From the scribble-like markings on its eggs. Also occurs as Scribbler.

SCULL. A name for the GREAT SKUA.

SCUTTY A Hampshire and Sussex name for the WREN. Probably for "Cutty." (See "Cutty Wren.")

SEA-AUK· The RAZORBILL (Scarborough.)

SEA-BLUE BIRD OF MARCH The KINGFISHER. (Poetical.)

SEA COCK: The GREY PLOVER. (Waterford.)

SEA CROW. A provincial name for the CORMORANT (Montagu); the RAZORBILL (Orkney and Shetland); the COMMON GULL (Yorkshire), the BLACK-HEADED GULL (Cheshire, Yorkshire); the HOODED CROW (Northumberland, Yorkshire); the CHOUGH (Ireland). According to Swainson the name has also been applied to the GREAT SKUA.

SEA DOTTREL The TURNSTONE. (Willughby.) Bewick gives Sea Dotterel. It is also an obsolete name for the RINGED PLOVER.

SEA-DOVE. A Scots name for the LITTLE AUK.

SEA DOVIE: The BLACK GUILLEMOT. (Forfar)

SEA-EAGLE· The OSPREY; also the WHITE-TAILED EAGLE. The two were much confused by the older authors. Occurs as "Sea Eagle" in Merrett (1667) who says it is notably found in Cornwall, and also in Willughby, but the latter adds the name "Osprey." Pennant and later writers have "Sea Eagle, or Osprey," but their Sea-Eagle is generally the immature White-Tailed Eagle Even Montagu in 1802 describes the Cinereous or White-Tailed Eagle, the Sea Eagle (*Falco ossifragus*, Linn.) and the Osprey. (See WHITE-TAILED EAGLE.)

P

SEA GUL or SEA COB: The COMMON GULL. (Merrett.) Turner (1544) also has "Se-cob or see-gell," and he tells us the species is so named from countrymen likening their cries to the word "cob."

SEA GULL: Properly the COMMON GULL, but loosely applied to any species of Gull. The name occurs as ",Sea Gull" in Barlow's plates (1655).

SEA-GULL HAWK: The HEN-HARRIER. (Connemara.)

SEA HEN: The young or female of the COMMON SCOTER (Northumberland); also the COMMON GUILLEMOT (Northumberland, Durham and East Lothian). Occurs in Albin for the latter species.

SEA KITTIE: The KITTIWAKE GULL. (Norfolk and Suffolk.)

SEA-LARK: The RINGED PLOVER. (Merrett to Pennant.) Still a provincial name. Also applied sometimes to the ROCK-PIPIT; the SHORE-LARK (Yorkshire); the DUNLIN (Cheshire, North Ireland, Scotland); and the SNOW-BUNTING, SANDERLING and the TURNSTONE (Ireland).

SEA LINNET: The SNOW-BUNTING. (Cheshire.)

SEA LINTIE: The ROCK-PIPIT. (East Lothian.)

SEAMAS RUA'. A Gaelic name for the PUFFIN. (Western Isles) lit. "Red James."

SEA MAW or SEA MEW: The HERRING-GULL, the COMMON GULL and the BLACK-HEADED GULL (Scotland); also the COMMON GULL (Yorkshire).

SEA MOUSE: The PURPLE SANDPIPER. (Northumberland.) Bolam says it is an occasional name for the species from the fearless manner in which the bird runs about the weed-covered rocks within a few feet of the intruders. Also a name for the DUNLIN (Lancashire and Dumfries).

SEA NANPIE: The OYSTERCATCHER. (Yorkshire.)

SEA PARROT: The PUFFIN. (Northumberland, Yorkshire, Norfolk.)

SEA PEEK: The DUNLIN. (Forfar.)

SEA PHEASANT: The LONG-TAILED DUCK (Northumberland, Yorkshire); also the PINTAIL (Hampshire, Yorkshire and Dorsetshire). Occurs in Willughby for the latter species.

SEA-PIE: The OYSTERCATCHER was formerly so called, by the older writers from Willughby to Pennant. It is still a common provincial name for the species.

SEA-PIET: The OYSTERCATCHER. (Northumberland.)

Sea Pigeon The BLACK GUILLEMOT. (Holy Island and Ireland.) The name is applied to the ROCK-DOVE in Ireland, and the GREY PLOVER (Yorkshire).

Sea Pilot: The OYSTERCATCHER. Swainson thinks it is a corruption of Sea-piet.

Sea Plover The GREY PLOVER. From its frequenting the sea-shore.

Sea Snipe · The DUNLIN (North England, Scotland); also the KNOT (Dublin).

Sea-Swallow: The COMMON TERN, ARCTIC TERN and LITTLE TERN. (Provincial.) Occurs in Willughby and Ray for the first-named, who also call it *Hirundo marina*. The salmon fishermen in the West of Ireland believe that when the sea-swallows are numerous salmon will also be plentiful. According to Hett, the name is sometimes applied to the STORM-PETREL.

Seathor. A Cornish name for a Diver or Grebe.

Sea Titling The ROCK-PIPIT. (Fleming.)

Sea-Turtle · The BLACK GUILLEMOT. (Willughby.)

Seave-cap: The REED-BUNTING. (Thirsk, Yorkshire.) "Seave"=rush.

Sea-Woodcock The BAR-TAILED GODWIT. (Montagu.) It is a Shetland name for the Godwits.

Sedge-bird or Sedge-Wren · The SEDGE-WARBLER. (Provincial.) Sedge Marine is also a Norfolk name, and Seg-bird a Yorkshire one. Sedge-bird occurs in Albin (1738). Macgillivray calls it Sedge-Reedling.

SEDGE-WARBLER [No. 139]. This species is mentioned by Willughby under the name of Salicaria and is the Willow-Lark of Pennant (ed. 1766), while it is called Sedge Warbler in his "Arctic Zoology" (II, p. 419) and in later authors.

Seed-bird: The COMMON GULL. (Scotland.) From its habit of following the plough Also the PIED WAGTAIL (Yorkshire).

Segge or Heges-sugge. An old name for the HEDGE-SPARROW (and perhaps other small birds) From A.Sax. *Sugge*, Old Eng. *heisugge* Swainson gives it as a Devon name.

Selninger Sandpiper. The PURPLE SANDPIPER. (Latham.)

SEMI-PALMATED SANDPIPER [No. 384]. An Arctic-American species, first recorded for England in 1907.

SENTINEL SHRIKE. A name sometimes given to the GREAT GREY SHRIKE; it exists also in its specific name *excubitor* (i e. a sentinel) and in the names by which this Shrike is known in several countries on the Continent. It originates from the bird's habit of sitting sentinel-wise on an exposed perch, and from its marvellous powers of vision it was commonly made use of in the days of falconry as a sentinel to detect the approach of a wild hawk; it is in fact still so employed in Holland.

SERIN [No. 28]. Sometimes called the Serin Finch. From Fr. *serin*, probably from Lat. *siren*, on account of its song. It occurs in Willughby as the "Serinus of Gesner."

SERULA. A provincial name for the RED-BREASTED MERGANSER. (Montagu.)

SET-HAMMER. A Teesmouth fowler's name for the BAR-TAILED GODWIT.

SEVEN-COLOURED LINNET: The GOLDFINCH. (Shropshire.)

SEVEN WHISTLER: The WHIMBREL; from the clear whistling note, supposed to be repeated about seven times.

SHAD-BIRD: The COMMON SANDPIPER. (Shrewsbury); because before the erection of weirs at Worcester the shad used to ascend the river about the middle of April, the time of the arrival of the Common Sandpiper (Jackson, "Shropshire Word-Book," p. 372).

SHAG [No. 317] Often called the Green Cormorant. The name "Shag" first appears in Merrett, who says Cormorants are so called in Cornwall. Willughby also terms it "the Shag, called in the North of England the Crane." Pennant calls it "Shag Cormorant." From Icel *skegg*=the beard, from *skaga*=to protect; so called on account of the recurved crest of feathers with which the head is adorned in spring-plumage.

SHAGGA: The CORMORANT, also the SHAG. (Cornwall.) See SHAG.

SHAKE: The REDSHANK. (Connemara.) From the constant nodding of its head while on the ground (Swainson).

SHAKING PETTYCHAPS. A name for the WOOD-WARBLER. (Hett.)

SHARPIE: The BLACK-HEADED GULL. (Bridlington, Yorkshire.)

SHARP-SAW: The GREAT TITMOUSE. (Norfolk.) From its "saw-sharpening" notes.

SHARP-TAILED DUCK. Montagu gives this as a provincial name for the LONG-TAILED DUCK.

SHARP-TAILED ISLAND (=Iceland) DUCK: The LONG-TAILED DUCK (Willughby.)

SHEAR-TAIL: The COMMON TERN (Orkneys.)

SHEARWATER: The MANX SHEARWATER. (Montagu.) Also the GREAT SHEARWATER.

SHEELFA, SHILFA, SHEELY. Local names for the CHAFFINCH, supposed by some to be from the variegated plumage of the male (shell, or shield=pied or variegated.) The first two are North England and Scots names, while Sheely is a Northamptonshire and Yorkshire name.

SHEELY, or SHIELY. Mr. Witherby tells me that this is a Holy Island (Northumberland) name for the GOLDEN-CRESTED WREN.

SHEEPRACK: The STARLING. (Northants.)

SHEEP'S GUIDE: The GOLDEN PLOVER. (Longdendale, Cheshire.)

SHEEP'S-HEAD-AND-PLUCK: The RED-THROATED DIVER. (Bridlington.) From a supposed resemblance.

SHELD-DUCK [No. 285] The name (from sheld=particoloured) occurs in Merrett's list (1667) as "Shell Drake"; he gives it as a Norfolk name, but there is no certainty that it was intended for this species. Willughby and Ray call it "Sheldrake or 'Burrough Duck,' called by some Bergander," and observe that "They are called by some Burrow Ducks, because they build in Coney-burroughs; by others Sheldrakes, because they are parti-coloured." They, however, merely cite Bergander as found in Aldrovandus.

SHELDER. The OYSTERCATCHER. (Shetlands.)

SHELD FOWL· The SHELD-DUCK. (Orkneys.)

SHELDRAKE· The SHELD-DUCK. Swainson says it is also a Waterford name for the SHOVELER.

SHELL or SKELL· The SHELD-DUCK. (Yorkshire.)

SHELL-, SHEL-, or SHIELD-APPLE. The CHAFFINCH (Staffordshire and Northumberland) Occurs in Turner (1544) as "Sheld-appel." Swainson thinks the "sheld" means parti-coloured as in SHELD-DUCK, and that the "apple" is a form of Alp (q.v.). Merrett, Willughby, Pennant, Bewick and other authors apply the name, however, to the CROSSBILL, and much more appropriately, as the latter species literally *shells* apples, cf. Carew ("Survey of Cornwall," p 73, 1602) who says. "Not long since there came a flock of birds into Cornwall, about harvest season, in bigness not much exceeding a sparrow, which made a foul spoil of the apples. Their bills were thwarted crosswise at the end, and with these they would cut an apple in two at one snap, eating only the kernels." In this case, of course, the meaning ascribed to the name by Swainson and others is incorrect.

SHELLCOCK, SHERCOCK. Local Cheshire names for the MISTLE-THRUSH. (Coward and Oldham.)

SHELL DUCK. The SHELD-DUCK (Lancashire.) The GOOSANDER is so called on the Shannon.

SHELL-TURNER. A name for the RINGED PLOVER. (Hett.)

SHEP or SHEPPY: The STARLING. (North and West Yorkshire.)

SHEPSTER, SHEPSTARE, or SHEPSTARLING. The STARLING. Equivalent to Sheep-Stare and Sheep-Starling. The first is a Cheshire, Yorkshire, and Northern Counties name, the second and third are Craven (Yorkshire) names.

SHERCOCK. A Lancashire and Yorkshire name for the MISTLE-THRUSH. The etymology is doubtful; it may be, however, that "sher" is a corruption of shire (A.Sax. *scer*) as in *sher*iff, hence the literal signification would be "cock of the shire." Hett gives "Shirley Cock" for the same species.

SHERIFF'S MAN. The GOLDFINCH. (Shropshire.) From its bright plumage. suggesting a showy livery.

SHETLAND WREN. See WREN.

SHEILDRAKE: The SHELD-DUCK (Pennant.)

SHIPSTER, SHIP-STARLING. Yorkshire names for the STARLING; ship is a corruption of sheep.

SHOE-AWL or SHOEING-HORN. The AVOCET. From the shape of its bill.

SHOOI: The ARCTIC SKUA. (Shetlands.) Imitative of its cry.

SHORE-BIRD: The SAND-MARTIN. Occurs in Merrett and also in Willughby.

SHORE-LARK [No. 64]. The name is found in Gould's "Birds of Europe"

SHORE-SANDPIPER: The GREEN SANDPIPER (?) Occurs in Bewick.

SHORE SNIPE: The COMMON SANDPIPER. (Perth.)

SHORE TEETAN: The ROCK-PIPIT. (Orkneys).

SHORT-EARED OWL [No. 225]. The name first occurs in Pennant (1766).

SHORT-HEELED FIELD LARK   The TREE-PIPIT. (Montagu.) Because the hind claw is not so long as the toe itself. Swainson says it is a Scottish provincial name. By inference the SKY-LARK is the Long-heeled species.

SHORT HORN OWL   The SHORT-EARED OWL. (Fleming)

SHORT-TOED LARK [No. 59]. The name is found in Gould's " Birds of Europe " (pt xv, 1835).

SHORT-WINGED WOOD-WREN.   A name for the CHIFFCHAFF. (Macgillivray.)

SHOULFALL   The SNOW-BUNTING. (Sibbald.)

SHOVELARD. An old name for the SPOONBILL   Occurs in Turner (1544) and in Merrett (1667); also occurs as Shovelar and Sholard.

SHOVEL-BILL : The SHOVELER.   From its spatulated bill.

SHOVELER [No 295]   The name arises from the spatulated or spoon-shaped terminal part of the bill. It is found in Willughby and most succeeding authors.

SHRED COCK : The FIELDFARE   (Shropshire)

SHRIEK or SHREEK · The GREAT GREY SHRIKE. An equivalent of Shrike (q v.).

SHRIEKER   The BAR-TAILED GODWIT and BLACK-TAILED GODWIT. (Norfolk.)

SHRIEK OWL : The SWIFT. (Provincial.)

SHRIKE. Usually the GREAT GREY SHRIKE. Occurs in Turner for this species.

SHRILLCOCK   The MISTLE-THRUSH. (Cheshire.) From its loud song

SHRIMP-CATCHER   The LITTLE TERN. (Norfolk.)

SHRITE or SHREITCH : The MISTLE-THRUSH. The first occurs in Willughby (1678), and the second in Charleton (1668) and Sibbald (1684). The former name, at any rate, is a provincialism still in use The derivation appears to be from A Sax. *Scric*, to screech (see Shrike). Swainson spells it " Skrite "

SHUFFLE-WING · The HEDGE-SPARROW (Craven.) So called from its peculiar shake or fluttering of the wings.

SIBERIAN CHIFFCHAFF.   See CHIFFCHAFF.

SIBERIAN GOOSE · The RED-BREASTED GOOSE. (Bewick.)

SIBERIAN PECTORAL SANDPIPER.   See PECTORAL SANDPIPER.

Siberian Ruby-throat   This species is a relative of the well-known " Bluethroats," and of the Nightingales. It is said to have been observed at Westgate-on-Sea, but is not yet admitted to the British List.

SIBILOUS BUSH-HOPPER. A name for the GRASSHOPPER-WARBLER.

SIDANGYNFFON. A Welsh name for the WAXWING.

SIFFSAFF: The CHIFFCHAFF. (North Wales). Imitative of its song.

SIGLDIGWT. A name for the PIED WAGTAIL and WHITE WAGTAIL in South Wales; lit. "shake-tail."

SIGLEN FELEN: The YELLOW WAGTAIL. (North Wales) lit. "yellow wagtail."

SIGLEN LLWYD: The GREY WAGTAIL. (North Wales) lit. "grey wagtail."

SILK TAIL: The WAXWING. It seems to occur first in the "Phil. Trans." for 1685, p. 1161.

SILVER-EYED GUILLEMOT or SILVER-EYED SCOUT: The *Ringed Guillemot*. The latter is a local name among the West of Scotland fishermen (Gray), and is given as a Yorkshire name by Nelson and Clarke.

SILVER GREBE: The RED-THROATED DIVER. (Kent.) According to Swainson.

SILVER OWL: The BARN-OWL. (Forfar.)

SILVER PLOVER: The GREY PLOVER. (Cheshire, Yorkshire, and Scotland.)

SILVER POCHARD: The SCAUP-DUCK. (Yorkshire.)

SILVERY GULL: The LESSER BLACK-BACKED GULL (Pennant); also the HERRING-GULL (Ireland).

SINGING TITLARK. A name for the TREE-PIPIT.

SISKIN [No. 19]. The derivation is probably from the Dan. *Sidsken*, or Swedish *Siska*, a chirper. The name "Siskin" occurs in Turner (1544), also in Merrett and Willughby.

SITHE-BILL: The GLOSSY IBIS. (Willughby.)

SIT-YE-DOWN: The GREAT TITMOUSE. (Provincial.) Imitative of its note.

SKAIT-BIRD: The ARCTIC SKUA. (Old Scots.) Perhaps from *skite*=to mute.

SKEEL DUCK or SKEEL GOOSE: The SHELD-DUCK. (Scotland). Occurs in Sibbald as Skeeling Goose.

SKEER DEVIL or SKIR DEVIL: The SWIFT. (Devonshire, Somersetshire.)

SKELDRAKE: The SHELD-DUCK (Bewick.) Also the OYSTER-CATCHER. (Orkneys) From the parti-coloured plumage.

SKELL DUCK: The SHELD-DUCK. (Northumberland, Yorkshire.)

SKIP-HEGRIE   A name for the HERON. (Montagu.)
SKIRL or SKIRL COCK : The MISTLE-THRUSH. (Derbyshire) An equivalent of Shrill.
SKIRL CRAKE   The TURNSTONE. (Shetlands.) From its shrill cry.
SKIRR . The ARCTIC TERN, COMMON TERN and LITTLE TERN. (Ireland)
SKITE . The YELLOW BUNTING (Aberdeen) Skite=to mute.
SKITTER-BROTTIE . The CORN-BUNTING. (Orkneys.) Swainson thinks it is from its resorting to corn-stacks in winter *skite* being to mute, and *brothies*, the cross-ropes of the roof of a stack.
SKITTY COCK or SKITTY COOT · The WATER-RAIL. (Devonshire, Cornwall, Somersetshire) · from " skit "=to slide. Also the SPOTTED CRAKE (Devonshire) and the MOORHEN (Somersetshire).
SKOOI or SHOOI. The ARCTIC SKUA. (Shetlands.) From its cry.
SKOUT. See Scout.
SKRABE . The MANX SHEARWATER. (Bewick, Montagu) See also Scraber.
SKUA or SKUA GULL . The GREAT SKUA. Also others of the Skuas, from the cry.
SKUTTOCK or SKIDDAW · The COMMON GUILLEMOT. (East Lothian and Northumberland.) From *skite*=to mute.
SKY-LARK [No. 62]   Found in Willughby (1678) who terms it " Skie-Lark," Turner (1544) merely calling it " Lerk." Albin has Sky Lark · Pennant (1766) and later authors call it Skylark. In Mid. Eng. the name lark occurs as larke and laverock : from A.Sax. *láwerce, laverce*, most probably for *lœwwerca*=traitor or guileworker. The reason why one of the most cherished of British birds should have received so bad a name at the hands of our Saxon forefathers seems somewhat obscure. It is considered an auspicious token in Orkney, where it is known as " Our Lady's hen " (Dalyell). It is a popular belief that if larks fly high and sing long, fine weather may be expected (Inwards). Chambers (" Popular Rhymes of Scotland ") gives a curious rhyming version of the lark's song as follows :—

   Up in the lift go we,
   Tehee, tehee, tehee, tehee !
   There's not a shoemaker on the earth
   Can make a shoe to me, to me !
   Why so, why so, why so ?
   Because my heel is as long as my toe.

The reference in the last line is to the bird's long hind claw.

SLAB. A North Country name for the WRYNECK. (Swainson.)

SLATE-BACKED THROSTLE: The FIELDFARE. (Yorkshire.)

SLAVONIAN GREBE [No. 337]. Occurs as "Sclavonian Grebe" in Montagu's "Orn. Dict." (1802) and the name is often so spelt. It is the Horned Grebe of Latham and the "Black-and-white Dobchick" of Edwards.

SLEIGHTHOLME THROSTLE: The SNOW-BUNTING. (Arkengarthdale, Yorkshire.)

SLENDER-BILLED CURLEW [No. 407]. A West Siberian species of which three examples were obtained in Kent in 1910.

SLENDER-BILLED NUTCRACKER. See NUTCRACKER.

SLIGHT FALCON. An old falconer's name for the PEREGRINE FALCON. (Sebright.)

SLY GOOSE: The SHELD-DUCK. (Orkneys.) From its craftiness. Sly Duck is also a Yorkshire name for the species.

SMALL BARRED WOODPECKER: The LESSER SPOTTED WOODPECKER. (Provincial.)

SMALL BROWN GULL. The immature COMMON TERN. (Pennant.)

SMALL CURLEW. A name for the BLACK-TAILED GODWIT; also the ESKIMO-CURLEW.

SMALL DIVER: The SLAVONIAN GREBE. (Humber.)

SMALL DOUCKER· The LITTLE GREBE. (East Lothian.)

SMALL DUCKER· The LITTLE GREBE (Yorkshire)

SMALLER REDPOLL LINNET: The LESSER REDPOLL. (Macgillivray.)

SMALL GREY GOOSE. The BEAN-GOOSE. (Provincial.) Occurs in Montagu.

SMALL MAA The COMMON GULL. (Shetlands.) Maa= Mew or Gull.

SMALL PURL: The LITTLE TERN. (Norfolk)

SMALL SPOTTED WATER-HEN: The SPOTTED CRAKE. (Pennant.)

SMALL-STRAW. A Yorkshire name for the smaller warblers which build nests of dried grass, etc.

SMALL WOOD-PIGEON: The STOCK-DOVE. (Northumberland.)

SMALSTER: The WHITETHROAT. (Cheshire.) Perhaps a corruption of "Small Straw." (See below.)

SMASTRAY (=SMALL STRAW): The GARDEN-WARBLER. (Cheshire.) Small Straw is a name for this bird, as well as the WHITETHROAT and other species, in Yorkshire. From the materials used for the nest.

SMATCH or SMATCHE: The WHEATEAR. Occurs in Turner (1544) and Merrett. Newton says it is an equivalent of Chat.

SMEE DUCK. The SMEW (Norfolk.) Also applied in the same county to the WIGEON and the COMMON POCHARD.

SMEORACH. A Gaelic name for the SONG-THRUSH. Graham thought it to be from *smeòr*, to grease, " probably from the smoothness of its liquid notes "

SMEU, SMEUTH, or SMOOTH The WILLOW-WARBLER. (Stirling.)

SMEW [No. 314]. In Willughby (1678) the name Smew occurs in the text (p. 338), the species being described, however, under the heading of " White Nun," which Newton thinks is the male name, from the hooded appearance of its head, Smew being the female. Pennant, however, gives Smew as the male name, and " Lough Diver " as the female. The name Smew Merganser is also applied to this species

SMOKY The HEDGE-SPARROW. (Northumberland.) " As mild as a Smoky " is a local proverb.

SMOOL. A name for the HEDGE-SPARROW. (Hett.)

SMUDAN A Gaelic name for the RING-DOVE.

SNABBY The CHAFFINCH. (Kirkcudbright.)

SNAITH or SNYTH The COOT. (Orkneys.) From Icel. *Snaud-ur*=bare, in reference to the bare frontal plate.

SNAKE-BIRD The WRYNECK. (Southern English counties.) Perhaps from the hissing noise it makes when disturbed while sitting, or else from its habit of twisting its head and neck

SNAPPER The GREEN WOODPECKER. (Swainson.)

SNENT A Berwick name for the DUNLIN and other small shore-birds a corruption of Stint.

SNIPE The COMMON SNIPE. (Merrett and Willughby.) Also the general colloquial name for the species.

SNIPE-BILLED SANDPIPER: The RED-BREASTED SAND-PIPER

SNIPE HAWK The MARSH-HARRIER. (South of Ireland.)

SNIPEN The COMMON SNIPE. (North Wales.) An equivalent of " Snipe "

SNIPPICK or SNIPPACK. The COMMON SNIPE. (Orkney and Shetland.)

SNORTER. The WHEATEAR. (Dorset.) Swainson thinks it is from its cry.

SNOW-BIRD. A name for the SNOW-BUNTING (North England and Scotland); also the FIELDFARE (Shropshire); and the IVORY GULL (Fleming).

SNOW-BUNTING [No. 56]. From its inhabiting the Polar Regions and its white winter-plumage. Occurs in Sibbald (1684) as "Snowfleck and Shoulfall," and in Edwards as "Snow-bird."

SNOW-CHICK. A name for the PTARMIGAN. (Hett.)

SNOW-FINCH [No. 39]. An Alpine species which has lately occurred in our Islands. The name is found in Latham ("Syn.," III, p. 264).

SNOW-FINCH. The Snow Bunting (Dumfriesshire.)

SNOWFLAKE or SNAW FOWL: The SNOW-BUNTING. (Orkney and Shetland.) The name occurs in Sibbald as Snowfleck. Montagu gives Snow Fowl as a provincial name. Swainson also gives "Snow Flight" as a name for the species. Saxby gives "Snaa Fool" (=Snow Fowl) for the Shetlands.

SNOW-GOOSE [No. 279, Snow-Goose; No. 280, Greater Snow-Goose]. So called from its inhabiting the Arctic Regions and from its white plumage. It was described by Pallas under the name *hyperboreus*, which implies its Arctic habitat. The smaller form is the one which has occurred irregularly in small numbers in Ireland, but the Greater, or Greenland, form has only been obtained once.

SNOW LARK BUNTING: The SNOW-BUNTING. (Macgillivray.)

SNOWY-OWL [No. 218]. This species, so called from its Arctic habitat and its white plumage, occurs in Edwards pl. 61) as the "Great White Owl." Snowy Owl occurs in Pennant's "Arctic Zoology" and in Latham. Macgillivray calls it Snowy Day-Owl.

SNUFF-HEADED WIGEON. A name for the COMMON POCHARD. (Swainson.)

SNYTH: The COOT. (See Snaith.)

SOCAN EIRA. The FIELDFARE. (North Wales) lit. "snow wallower."

SOCIABLE PLOVER [No. 366]. A rare straggler from south Russia and west Asia. The name is derived from the name *gregarius* conferred on it by Pallas in 1771.

SOD. A Forfar name for the ROCK-DOVE. (Swainson.)

SOFLIAR. A Welsh name for the QUAIL; lit. "stubble-hen."

SOLAN GOOSE or SOLAND GOOSE: The GANNET. Occurs in Barlow (1655) and Merrett's list as "Soland Goose," and in Turner (1544) as "Solend Goose." Willughby has

"Soland Goose." The derivation appears to be from the Gaelic *suilear*, meaning quick-sighted, from *Suil*=eye, and *gheur*=sharp. Skeat, however, preferred Icel. *Sula* or *Sulan* (the *n* being the definite article).

SOLITARY SANDPIPER [No. 391]. A North American species, originally described by Wilson, who conferred on it the name *solitarius* from its solitary habits

SOLITARY SNIPE : The GREAT SNIPE. So called from its being commonly met with in this country singly. The name occurs in Bewick (1804)

SOLITARY THRUSH. The STARLING (immature). Occurs in all old authors as a separate species, so called from its greyish-brown plumage, somewhat resembling that of a thrush, and its supposed solitary habits. It will be found described as a British species in the Supp. to Montagu's " Orn. Dict.," 1813.

SONG LINNET. A Yorkshire name for the LINNET.

SONG-THRUSH [No. 158, British Song-Thrush ; No. 157, Continental Song-Thrush] So called from its pre-eminence as a songster. The name was first used by Merrett and also occurs in Willughby and in most modern authors Hartert has recently separated the resident British form from the Continental form, which visits our coast on migration. In " Science Gossip " (vol. III, p 141) a popular belief regarding this bird is referred to, to the effect that it acquires new legs and casts the old ones when about ten years old.

SOOTY SHEARWATER [No 327]. This Petrel, a near ally of the GREAT SHEARWATER, is so called from its sombre plumage.

SOOTY TERN [No. 422]. The name, which originates in the sooty-black of the upper-parts, is found in Jardine's edition of Wilson (vol. III, 1832).

SORE-HAWKS. A falconer's term for hawks of the first year, taken while still retaining immature-plumage. Said to be from Fr. *soret*, signifying a dusky colour, but Newton thinks it akin to " sorrel," and properly applicable to those with reddish plumage.

SOUTHERN SANDPIPER · The KNOT, when changing to summer plumage. (Hett.)

SOUTH EUROPEAN GREY SHRIKE [No. 108]. A southern form of the GREAT GREY SHRIKE.

SPADGE or SPADGER · The HOUSE-SPARROW. (Northern counties.) A vulgar corruption of Sparrow.

SPAR-HAWK or SPUR-HAWK: The SPARROW-HAWK. (Aberdeenshire.)

SPARLIN-FOWL or SPARKLING-FOWL: The GOOSANDER (female). The first form occurs in Willughby and the second in Pennant, Montagu, etc.

SPARROW: The HOUSE-SPARROW. From A.Sax. *Spearwa*, a sparrow. Occurs in Turner, and is the general English name for the species, House-Sparrow being a book-name chiefly.

SPARROW-HAWK [No. 249]. Probably from A.Sax. *Spearwa* (Sparrow) and *Hafoc* (Hawk), Mid. Eng. *Hauk*. The name "Sparrow-Hawk" occurs in Merrett's Pinax (1667), where it is called *Accipiter fringillarius et nisus*, after Aldrovandus (pp. 345-7). Turner's "sparhauc" is the GOSHAWK. In falconry the name Sparrow-Hawk was formerly used to denote the female, the male being termed "Musket" or Musquet Hawk (q.v.).

SPARROW OWL. A name for the LITTLE OWL. (Hett.)

SPARVE: The HEDGE-SPARROW. (West Cornwall.) From A.Sax. *spearwa*, a sparrow.

SPEAR SPARROW. The female REED-BUNTING is so called in Hampshire. (Swainson.)

SPEAR WIGEON. The RED-BREASTED MERGANSER. (co. Kerry.)

SPEASE or SPEETHE: The KNOT. (Holy Island.) Also applied there to the BAR-TAILED GODWIT. It originates from the bird's wheezy note when on the ground.

SPECHT or WODSPECHT. Turner gives this as the English name of a Woodpecker, apparently the LESSER SPOTTED WOODPECKER. (See Speicht.)

SPECKLED DICK: The GOLDFINCH. (Shropshire.)

SPECKLED DIVER or LOON. The RED-THROATED DIVER. Occurs in Pennant, Latham, etc. Given also as a provincial name for the BLACK-THROATED DIVER by Montagu, who, however, misprints it "Speckled Zoon."

SPECTACLED GOOSE: The GANNET. (Provincial.) From the bare circle of skin surrounding the eye.

SPEEL-THE-TREE. A name for the TREECREEPER. (Hett.)

SPEICHT or SPEIGHT (corrupted also to Spite as in Wood-Spite): The GREEN WOODPECKER generally. From Ger. *Specht*.

SPEIKINTARES: The COMMON TERN. (Ross-shire.)

SPEIR SHE'AG. A Gaelic name for the SPARROW-HAWK. The latter word is properly written *seabhag* (=a hawk).

Spence. A Shetland name for the STORM-PETREL. It is in use in the Island of Yell. Swainson gives the name as Spency for the Shetland Isles and the same spelling is given by Montagu, while Saxby prints it Spencie

Speug, Spiug, or Speout. Names for the HOUSE-SPARROW. See also Spug.

Spider-catcher: The WALLCREEPER. Occurs in Willughby.

Spider-diver: The LITTLE GREBE. (Provincial)

Spink. An English provincial name for the CHAFFINCH. From its note. Occurs in Turner (1544). Also applied in Yorkshire to the YELLOW BUNTING.

Spinner · The NIGHTJAR. (Wexford.)

Spirit Duck: The BUFFEL-HEADED DUCK. From its quickness in diving.

Split Straw: The WHITETHROAT. (Cheshire)

Spog-ri-tom The LITTLE GREBE. (Western Isles of Scotland.)

SPOONBILL [No. 258]. Anciently called Popeler, Shovelard, or Shovelar, and perhaps "Liver" (q.v.), the name Spoonbill having been transferred to this species from the Shoveler Duck, the bills of both birds being spatulate at the end. Although now only a scarce and irregular visitor to our shores, the Shovelar or Popeler is recorded as breeding in several places in Norfolk about the year 1300, where it no doubt continued to do so for two or three centuries, while Mr. Harting has shown that in 1523 it is recorded as breeding on the Bishop of London's property at Fulham (" Zool ," 1886, p. 81), and also in 1570 in West Sussex (*ib.*, 1877, p. 425) The latest record of its breeding in England appears to be Sir Thomas Browne's statement that it "now" (*ca.* 1662) bred at Trimley in Suffolk. Turner, however, who calls it merely "Shovelard," says nothing about its breeding with us in his day, and in fact says little about it beyond repeating the legend of Aristotle and Pliny that it devours biggish shell-fish and casts them up again when dead and gaping to pick and eat them He also repeats the tradition of Hieronymus that when they find their young killed by a serpent they " mourn and beat themselves upon their sides, and with the blood discharged they bring back to life the bodies of the dead," which is one of the legends later attributed to the Pelican, owing to the confusion of names, the present species having formerly been so called (see PELICAN.)

SPOONBILL or SPOON-BEAK: The SHOVELER. (Norfolk.) Coward and Oldham give Spoonbill as a local Cheshire name.

SPOONBILL DUCK: The SCAUP-DUCK. (East Lothian.)

SPOTTED CRAKE [No. 455]. The name is found in Yarrell (1st ed.). It occurs as the Small Spotted Water Hen in Pennant (fo. ed. 1766), and as Spotted Gallinule in the later editions. It is the "Wyn-kernel" of Willughby. Bewick calls it the Water Crake, and it is also known as "Spotted Rail" or "Lesser Spotted Water Rail." The names are derived from the small white spots sprinkled over the plumage.

SPOTTED DUCK: The HARLEQUIN-DUCK. (Hett.)

SPOTTED EAGLE [No. 241]. This form (*A. maculatus*) occurs under the name of "Spotted Eagle" in Latham's "Synopsis" (I, p. 13). It is sometimes called the Larger Spotted Eagle. The name "spotted" arises from the buffish spots on the plumage of the *immature* bird. The closely allied Lesser Spotted Eagle does not appear to have occurred in the British Islands.

SPOTTED FALCON. The PEREGRINE FALCON. Occurs in Montagu. Spotted-winged Falcon is a name for the same species found in Latham.

SPOTTED FLYCATCHER [No. 114]. The name Spotted Flycatcher is first given by Pennant (1776) to this species; the word Flycatcher, as an Anglicization of *Muscicapa* dates back, however, to Ray. The name "spotted" originates in the numerous striations on head and under-parts, giving it a spotted appearance.

SPOTTED GUILLEMOT: The BLACK GUILLEMOT (winter).

SPOTTED HERON: The immature NIGHT-HERON. (Latham.)

SPOTTED REDSHANK [No. 395]. The name appears to occur first in Pennant's "British Zoology" (8vo ed., No. 186); in the folio edition he calls it Spotted Sandpiper. It is the Spotted Snipe of Latham and Lewin, and the Dusky Sandpiper of Selby. The names are derived from the general spotted appearance of the plumage.

SPOTTED SANDPIPER [No. 388]. The name is found in Pennant and succeeding authors to Yarrell, and originates in the blackish spots on the under-parts, especially the breast.

SPOTTED SKITTY: The SPOTTED CRAKE. (Devonshire.) Skitty is from *skit*=to slide: from its stealthy habits.

SPOTTED SNIPE The SPOTTED REDSHANK is so called by many old authors
SPOTTED STARLING : The STARLING. (Macgillivray.)
SPOTTED WATER-HEN The SPOTTED CRAKE
SPOWE The WHIMBREL. From Icel. *Spói.* Stevenson gives this as an ancient Norfolk name for the species
SPRAT LOON or SPRAT BORER The RED-THROATED DIVER. (Essex, Yorkshire.) Hett gives Sprat Lumme as a name for the BLACK-THROATED DIVER. Swainson gives Spratoon as a Norfolk name for the former species.
SPRATTER The COMMON GUILLEMOT. (Hampshire.) From its fondness for small fry (Swainson)
SPRIG-TAIL The PINTAIL (Provincial.)
SPRING DOTTEREL The DOTTEREL. (Yorkshire.)
SPRING WAGTAIL The YELLOW WAGTAIL. (Yorkshire.) From its migratory nature
SPRITE The GREEN WOODPECKER. (Suffolk.) Probably a corruption of Specht (q.v.)
SPUG, SPRUG, SPRONG, SPRIG, SPURDIE, SPYNG. The HOUSE-SPARROW. (Scotland.) Spug is also a Nottinghamshire name for the species, Spuggy a Yorkshire, and Sprig and Spug Northumberland names.
SPURRE The COMMON TERN. (North Ireland.) From its cry
Spur-winged Goose. Examples of this tropical African species are sometimes obtained in our islands, but as it has been introduced here they can hardly be genuine visitors. The name is found in Bewick, Yarrell and other authors
SQUACCO HERON [No. 265]. The first mention of the name is to be found in Willughby (1678) who calls it "the Heron which they call Sguacco in the Valleys of Malalbergo," and who derives the species from Aldrovandus. The modern spelling Squacco dates from Latham and is perhaps a misspelling of Sguacco. Montagu ("Orn. Dict.," Supp.) spells it "Sguacco."
SQUAWKING THRUSH. The MISTLE-THRUSH. (Isle of Wight.)
SQUEAK THRUSH The MISTLE-THRUSH. (Wiltshire.)
SQUEALER The SWIFT. (Cheshire.)
STAG : A Norfolk name for the WREN ; also the male RUFF until it acquires its wattles in the second year (Hett).
STANCHEL The KESTREL. (Sibbald.)

Q

STANDGALL: The KESTREL. (Provincial.) An equivalent to "Stannel" (q.v.), not a corruption of "Stand-gale" as has been surmised.

STANDHAWK: The KESTREL. (Provincial) lit. "stone-hawk" (A.Sax. *stan*=stone).

STANECHACKER: The WHEATEAR (Lancashire, Scotland, North Ireland); also the STONECHAT (Craven, Scotland).

STANEPECKER: The TURNSTONE. (Shetlands.) From its habit of turning over small stones in searching for its food. The name is also applied to the PURPLE SANDPIPER.

STANK-HEN or STANKIE: The MOORHEN. (Scottish Borders.) Bolam says Stank is almost an equivalent of *moat* and cites "the Stanks" at Berwick which are parts of the old moat surrounding the town.

STANNEL, STANNEL-HAWK, STANCHEL or STANNYEL: The KESTREL. (Provincial) lit. "stone-yeller," from A.Sax. *stan*=stone and *gellan* (pron *yellan*) to yell. There are many forms of this name occurring in Elizabethan and more recent literature and some are still in use provincially. Probably the original word is "Staniel." "Standgale" appears to be a corruption, as this word has no connexion with the sense of the word "Windhover." (See also Standgall, Steingall, Stonegall.)

STANNIN (Standing?) HAWK: The SPARROW-HAWK. (Halifax.)

STARAG. A Gaelic name for the HOODED CROW.

STARE: The STARLING. (West and North of England; Ireland.) The original name of the bird, from A.Sax. *stær*, Starling being a diminutive. Occurs in Willughby and Merrett, while Pennant (ed. 1766) calls the bird by this name.

STARLING [No. 13]. From A.Sax. *Stær, Stearn* and *Sterlyng*, the latter being a diminutive. The name appears in Merrett and Willughby. Turner (1544) has "Sterlyng." (See also "Stare.") A provincial belief is that if Starlings congregate in large numbers rain may be expected, but Swainson says that in Brittany the belief is that it is a sign of impending cold weather.

STARN. An old Norfolk name for the BLACK TERN. Also a Shetland name for the STARLING.

STARNEL: The STARLING. (Northants.)

STARNIL: The STARLING. (Notts.)

STEENIE POUTER: The COMMON SANDPIPER. (Orkneys.)

STEINGALL : The KESTREL. An equivalent of "stannel" (q.v.). Occurs in Turner (1544) as a name for this species.

STEINKLE : The WHEATEAR. (Shetlands.)

STELLER'S EIDER [No. 306]. The name is found in Yarrell (1843) as Steller's Western Duck. It is the Western Pochard of Selby.

STENOR. An old Cornish name for a Wagtail.

STERLIN The STARLING. (Orkney and Shetland.)

STERN : The BLACK TERN. Turner says that this species, formerly a common bird with us, was so termed in local dialect

STERN COCK. A provincial name (quoted by Jesse) for the MISTLE-THRUSH. Probably an equivalent of "Storm Cock" (q.v.). The A.Sax. *storm* and German *sturm* come from the same root as Lat *sternere* (=to strew or prostrate) and have the same significance.

STILT PLOVER. A name for the BLACK-WINGED STILT.

STINKLIN. A Shetland name for the WHEATEAR. It is a corruption of "stone-clink" (q.v.).

STINT or SNENT. A local term on the coasts of our islands for the DUNLIN, as well as the LITTLE STINT, SANDERLING and other small shore-birds Willughby applies it to the DUNLIN. It occurs as "Stynte" in the Northumberland Household Book, A.D. 1512.

STIX. A Cornish name for a Screech Owl (? BARN-OWL).

STOCK ANNET · The SHELD-DUCK. (East Scotland.) According to Jamieson it signifies Stock *ent* (i e Stock Duck).

STOCK-DOVE [No 346] Said to be so called from its being supposed to be the stock bird from which our domesticated pigeons were derived · it is, however, doubtful whether the name may not refer to the bird's habit of nesting in the "stocks" of trees The name occurs in Turner (1544) as "stocdove," in Barlow (1655) as "Stock-dove," in Merrett (1667) as "Stock-Dove or Wood-Pidgeon," and in Willughby (1678) as "Stock-Dove or Wood-Pigeon." Pennant calls it "Stock Pigeon, or Stock Dove," while Montagu unites it with the ROCK-DOVE and thinks they form one species.

STOCK DUCK. The MALLARD. (Orkney and Shetland.), because it is considered to be the stock from which the tame varieties have sprung.

STOCK-EEKLE or STOCK-EIKLE. The GREEN WOODPECKER. (Staffordshire, Worcestershire.) The word stock (Dan. or Norse *stock*, A.Sax. *stoc*) is in one sense synonymic with *stuck* or *stick* and is thus used (but rarely) to denote a thrust; but more generally it means the trunk or stump of a tree, which seems the correct meaning in this case. The derivation of *eekle* is said to be uncertain. It occurs also as *ecle* and *eaqual*, and is doubtless derived from the Teutonic *hekelen*, to hack or tear asunder. It is, in fact, synonymic with hackle and heckle, the latter word being more generally heard in elections now, but properly denoting the combing of flax. Stock-eekle therefore is literally stump-hacker. Hickwall, another name for the species, appears to be synonymic.

STOCK HAWK : The PEREGRINE FALCON. (Shetlands)

STOCKIE or STOGGIE . The STOCK-DOVE. (Yorkshire.)

STOCK OWL . The EAGLE-OWL. (Orkneys.) Swainson says it is "from its habit of pressing against the stem (stock) of a tree with unruffled feathers, so as to assimilate itself to the stump, and elude notice."

STOCK WHAUP or STOCK WHAAP : The CURLEW. (Provincial.) Occurs in Montagu ; Saxby gives the first form for the Shetlands.

STONECHAT [No. 176, British Stonechat]. The bird occurs in Turner and Merrett as "Stone-chatter" and in Willughby as "Stone-smich or Stone-chatter," the latter form existing as late as Pennant (1766) The species is rather inappropriately named, as it is found inhabiting furze-covered land and neglected meadows. The name is also applied, far more appropriately, to the WHEATEAR (Northumberland, Yorkshire and Cheshire).

STONECHECK or STONE-CHECKER . The WHEATEAR. (Provincial.) The name occurs as Stonecheck in Merrett (1667) and in Turner (1544) as "Steinchek." Dunn gives Stonechecker as a local name in Orkney and Shetland, and Bolam gives it as a Northumbrian name. Stone-check, Stone-chack and Stone-chatter are Yorkshire forms.

STONE-CLINK . The STONECHAT From its note resembling the striking together of two pebbles.

STONE-CURLEW [No. 352] The now accepted name of the species generally styled by eighteenth century writers "Thick-kneed Bustard." Occurs in Merrett's list as "Stone Curlew" and in Willughby as "Stone-Curlew"; the species being based on the *Œdicnemus* of Belon. The name arises from its frequenting stony upland localities.

STONE CURLEW · The BAR-TAILED GODWIT. (Cheshire.) Also applied to the WHIMBREL (Montagu).

STONE-FALCON · The immature MERLIN. (Cheshire, Yorkshire, North Wales, Scotland.) Occurs in Willughby.

STONEGALL: The KESTREL. An equivalent of "stannel" (q.v.). Occurs in Merrett, who calls the species a "Stannel or Stonegall"

STONEHATCH The RINGED PLOVER. (Provincial) So called because it lines the hollow it makes for its eggs with small stones.

STONE-HAWK: The MERLIN (Cheshire, Yorkshire); also the KESTREL (Cheshire).

STONE-PLOVER The BAR-TAILED GODWIT Occurs in Willughby. The Stone Plover of Ray's "Synopsis Avium" (p 105), however, appears to be the BLACK-TAILED GODWIT The name has also been used to denote both the RINGED PLOVER and the STONE-CURLEW (England), also the GREY PLOVER (Ireland).

STONEPRICK or STONEPRICKER The STONECHAT. (Wirral, Cheshire.)

STONE-RAW The TURNSTONE (Armagh.)

STONE-RUNNER The RINGED PLOVER (Norfolk) and the DOTTEREL (Norfolk).

STONE-SMICH or STONE-SMITH · The STONECHAT The latter form occurs in Bewick (1797) and the former in Willughby.

STONE THRUSH The MISTLE-THRUSH. (Cheshire, Dorset)

STORK. See WHITE STORK.

STORM-BIRD The MISTLE-THRUSH (West Sussex) Swainson also gives it as a Norfolk name for the FIELDFARE. (See Storm Cock)

STORM COCK . The MISTLE-THRUSH is known by this name throughout the greater part of England (particularly the Northern and Midland counties) but also locally in Hampshire, Sussex and other Southern counties, because it usually commences to sing in January and continues through the rough weather of February and March; generally, moreover, singing from the topmost wind-rocked branch of a still-leafless tree. Swainson also gives it as a name for the FIELDFARE in Shropshire and Scotland.

STORM-FINCH The STORM-PETREL (Orkneys). Occurs in Bewick.

STORM-GULL. A name for the COMMON GULL. (Hett.)

STORM-PETREL [No 319]. Occurs in Jenyns (1835) as "Storm-Petrel" Pennant in his folio edition (1766) calls it Little Petrel, but in the later editions it is called *Stormy*

Petrel, as also in Montagu. The name Storm or Stormy arises from the belief that its appearance prognosticates stormy weather. The name Petrel is said to be from Fr. *Petrel*, a diminutive of Peter, and alludes to the Apostle Peter walking on the Sea of Galilee. One belief is that if the Storm-Petrel seeks the shore or the wake of a vessel, a storm is imminent.

STRAND PLOVER: The GREY PLOVER. (Cork). From its frequenting the sea-shore.

STRANY. A name for the COMMON GUILLEMOT. (Bewick, Montagu.)

STRAW MOUSE: The WHITETHROAT. (Cheshire.)

STRAW-SMALL: The WHITETHROAT. (West Riding, Yorkshire.) From the nest being composed of dry grass, etc.

STRAW-SMEAR: The GARDEN-WARBLER and the WHITETHROAT. (Westmorland.) Montagu spells it "Strawsmeer."

STREAKED TUFTED-OWL. Macgillivray's name for the SHORT-EARED OWL.

STRIATED WOODPECKER. Macgillivray's name for the LESSER SPOTTED WOODPECKER.

STUBBLE GOOSE: The GREY LAG-GOOSE. (East Lothian.)

STUMPY DICK or STUMPY TODDY. The WREN. (Longdendale, Cheshire.)

SUB-ALPINE WARBLER [No. 150]. The name is derived from Bonelli's name for the species (*Sylvia subalpina*).

SUELLAK. A Cornish name for the FIELDFARE.

SUILEIR. A Gaelic name for the GANNET. (St. Kilda.) From *suil*=eye, and *gheur*=sharp. It is the original of Solan.

SUMMER BIRD: The WRYNECK. (Northumberland.)

SUMMER DUCK: The GARGANEY. (See Summer Teal).

SUMMER SNIPE: The COMMON SANDPIPER. (Northumberland, Yorks, Cheshire, Scotland.) Because seen commonly in summer in those districts to which the true Snipes are chiefly winter-visitors. It is the name adopted by Mr. Dresser for the species. It has also been applied to the GREEN SANDPIPER and the DUNLIN.

SUMMER TEAL: The GARGANEY. (Somerset and Norfolk.) It occurs in Albin. Newton says that it is the colloquial name, Garganey being a book-name

SUMMER WAGTAIL: The YELLOW WAGTAIL. On account of its being a summer-visitor.

SURF-SCOTER [No 311]. The name occurs in Fleming (1828), who recorded it from the Orkneys and Shetlands. Surf-duck, a Scottish name for the COMMON SCOTER (from its habit of diving for food among the breakers) is perhaps the origin of this species' name.

SWABIE. The GREAT BLACK-BACKED GULL. (Orkney and Shetland.) Swainson spells it "Swarbie"

SWALLOW [No. 195]. From A.Sax. *Swalewe*. The name occurs in Turner (1544) as "Swallowe" and in Barlow's plates (1655) as "Swallow" Merrett and Willughby call it the "House-Swallow." This is one of the birds held in veneration in many parts of England, it being usually considered unlucky to kill one, this belief prevailing in Sussex, Hampshire, Yorkshire and other counties, as well as in parts of Scotland, but in some parts of England and more certainly in Ireland we do not find the belief prevailing, in fact the bird is locally called "devil's bird," the belief being that "on everyone's head there is a particular hair which if the Swallow can pluck off dooms the wretched individual to eternal perdition" (Dyer). In connexion with its veneration the Magyar belief may be mentioned that if one is killed the cows' milk will turn to blood, a precisely similar belief prevailing in this country regarding the Robin (q v.). A Cornish custom is to jump on seeing the first Swallow in spring In some parts of England, April 15th is called "Swallow day," because Swallows are thought to appear at that date. The old saying "One Swallow does not make a Summer" was originally a Greek proverb but is found in most European languages. The proverb appears to originate with Aristotle, who says, "One Swallow does not make a Summer, nor one fine day." Willughby, however, uses the expression "One Swallow makes not a Spring," and says the origin appears to lie in the bird being universally regarded as the herald of spring. Swallow-songs to welcome the coming of March and the Swallows still prevail among the children in Greece, where they are of great antiquity. To Aristotle may also be traced the belief, which was formerly very generally held, that Swallows hibernated in hollow places in winter A Cornish belief of comparatively modern times was that they spent the winter in disused tin mines and holes in the cliffs, etc. Gilbert White of Selborne was a strong believer in the hibernation of the Swallow tribe, and Col. Montagu a partial believer. In the Introduction to his celebrated "Ornithological Dictionary" (p. xxvii) he says that "torpidity is probably the state of those summer birds of passage which accident may have detained with us during winter." Willughby says, "What becomes of Swallows in Wintertime, whether they fly into other countries, or lie torpid in hollow trees, and the like places, neither are natural historians agreed, nor indeed can we certainly determine" The notion was actually entertained by Linnæus, by Gilbert White of Selborne, and many others Pliny believed that they retired at the approach of winter to the inmost recesses of rocks and mountains, and there remained in a torpid state till Spring ("Hist. Nat.," lib. xxx, cap IV). Other writers have conjectured that they lie torpid during winter at the bottom of ponds or rivers, and it has been argued that Linnæus was of this opinion, although his reference is not quite lucid. Gilbert White was of opinion that "though they may not retire into that element, yet they may conceal themselves in the banks of pools and rivers during the uncomfortable months of winter." Elsewhere he suggests that during the severe winds that often prevail late in the spring they may retire and sleep away these uncomfortable periods as bats do Forster, writing in 1808, thinks that "Swallows may have *occasionally* been found under water," and suggests their presence there may be due to their having lain in a torpid state at night among the reeds or rushes. He, in fact, credits the occasional records of this kind, as well as their having been found torpid in hollow trees, rocks and under the thatch of houses; but nevertheless he argues that the bulk of the species migrates in the winter. The bird was formerly greatly esteemed for its reputed medicinal value, being considered a remedy for the "falling sickness," "dimness of sight," "blear eyes," etc., their ashes in this latter case being mingled with honey and applied. A Swallow's heart was also eaten to strengthen the memory, or as a cure for the ague, while the blood, particularly when drawn from under the left wing, was thought a specific for the eyes. A stone, called *Chelidonius*, sometimes found in the stomach of young Swallows, was also used as a remedy for the "falling sickness" in children, being hung from the neck or bound to the arm. A popular belief is that when Swallows skim the water, in flying over it, rain is coming. Virgil ("Georgics") alluding to the signs of coming rain, writes "The Swallow skims the river's watr'y face." Dr. Jenner, also, alluding to the low flight before rain, says. "Low o'er the grass the Swallow wings" On the contrary a high

flight signified fine weather Thus Gay in his first
"Pastoral" writes :—
> When Swallows fleet soar high and sport in air,
> He told us that the welkin would be clear.

It is related in "Notes and Queries" that a Swallow alighting upon one's shoulder has been regarded as a sign of death Parker, writing in 1632, in his poem "The Nightingale," relates that it is counted ominous for one to die in one's hand, a belief held also of the Robin

SWALLOW. A Shetland name for the STORM PETREL ; the MARTIN is also sometimes called Swallow.

Swallow-tailed Kite. An American species which has been said to have strayed to our shores. So called from its tail being deeply forked, with the outer feathers somewhat elongated, like the tail of a swallow The name is found in Yarrell (1843) It is the Swallow-tailed Falcon of Catesby and the Swallow-tailed Hawk of Wilson and Audubon

SWALLOW-TAILED SHELDRAKE The LONG-TAILED DUCK. (Willughby.) Also occurs as Swallow-tailed Sheldrake

SWAN See MUTE SWAN.

SWART-BACK : The GREAT BLACK-BACKED GULL. (Orkneys.)

SWAT The REDSHANK (Teesmouth)

SWEET BILLY The CHIFFCHAFF and also the WILLOW-WARBLER. (Nottinghamshire.)

SWEET WILLIAM The GOLDFINCH. From its melodious cry. (Swainson)

SWIFT [No. 200] The name Swift appears first in Willughby and originated in the swiftness of its flight. In the fourth edition of Pennant it is called Swift Swallow. The legend that this bird was unable to use its feet is of remote antiquity, and no doubt arose from the small size of these members, although they are neither weak nor useless. Pliny says these birds, because they cannot use their feet, are called Apodes and live chiefly on the wing, and Aristotle says much the same of the species. In Hampshire it is considered unlucky to kill this bird. A farmer, the owner of seventeen cows, is said to have shot seventeen Swifts in one day, and to have had every one of his cows die within seven weeks ("Folklore Jnl.," Dec., 1883).

SWIFT SWALLOW The SWIFT (Pennant.)

SWINEPIPE. An old English name for the REDWING. (Willughby.) Newton thinks it refers to "the soft inward whistle which the bird often utters, resembling the sound of the pipe used by the swineherds of old when collecting the animals under their charge."

SWING-DEVIL: The SWIFT. (Northumberland.)

SWISS SANDPIPER: The GREY PLOVER. Swainson says it was so called because Reaumur first received specimens from Switzerland.

SYCOCK: The MISTLE-THRUSH. (Notts., Derbyshire.)

SYKES'S WAGTAIL [No. 75]. A West Siberian species first recorded for Britain by Butterfield in the "Zoologist" for 1902, p. 232.

SYWIDER. A Welsh name for the WILLOW-WARBLER.

TABBERER, TAPPERER, or TAPPER: The LESSER SPOTTED WOODPECKER. (Leicestershire.)

TAEL DUIK (=Teal duck): The TEAL. (Scotland.)

TAGGYFINCH· The CHAFFINCH (Upton-on-Severn.)

TAME SWAN: The MUTE SWAN.

TAMMIE HERL: The COMMON HERON. (Perth.)

TAMMIE NORIE: The PUFFIN. (Orkney and Shetland.)

TANGLE-PICKER: The TURNSTONE. (Norfolk.) Tangle is a kind of seaweed.

TANG SPARROW: The ROCK-PIPIT. (Shetlands.) "Tang" signifies seaweed.

TANG-WHAAP or TANG WHAUP: The WHIMBREL. (Orkney and Shetland) lit. "seaweed curlew."

TARAD-Y-KOED. A Cornish name for a WOODPECKER.

TARMACHAN. The Gaelic name for the PTARMIGAN.

TARROCK, TARRET, TARING: The COMMON TERN. (Shetlands.)

TARROCK GULL or TARROCK. Properly the immature KITTIWAKE GULL, but also applied to the young of the COMMON GULL and also to the COMMON GUILLEMOT. It occurs in Willughby for the first-named species. The bird described under this name was formerly considered a distinct species from the Kittiwake Gull

TARRY: The COMMON and ARCTIC TERNS. (Northumberland.)

TARTAN-BACK. A name for the BRAMBLING. (Hett.)

TASTER: The BLACK GUILLEMOT. (Sibbald.) See Tystie.

TATLER: The COMMON SANDPIPER.

TAWNY: The BULLFINCH. (Somerset.)

TAWNY BUNTING : The SNOW-BUNTING. (Young males or females in winter-plumage.) Described as a separate species by the older writers from Pennant to Montagu

TAWNY OWL [No. 229]. So called from its reddish-brown, or tawny colour. The name first occurs in Pennant (1766). Willughby and Ray call it the "Common Brown, or Ivy Owl."

TAWNY PIPIT [No. 66]. So called from its buffish-brown, or tawny, plumage.

TEAL [No 289]. Occurs in Merrett, and in Willughby and Ray. Turner (1544) has "Tele" and Barlow (1655) "Teale."

TEAL-DRAKE : The SCAUP-DUCK is so called by gunners in the North. (Hawker.)

TEARY-EERIE. Bolam gives this as a Northumbrian name for the CORN-BUNTING ; but is uncertain whether it is derived from its song, or is a corruption of "weary-weary" in allusion to its heavy flight.

TEASER · The ARCTIC SKUA. (Provincial.) From its habit of harassing the Gulls and Terns until they disgorge their prey.

TEETAN or TEETING The MEADOW-PIPIT. (Orkneys and Shetlands.) Also the ROCK-PIPIT (Shetlands)

TEETICK or TEETUCK. The ROCK-PIPIT. (Orkneys and Shetland.)

TEEUCK The LAPWING. (Provincial) From its cry.

TEE-WHAAP. A name for the LAPWING. (Hett.)

TELL-PIE, TELL-PIET, TELL-PIENOT The MAGPIE (N. Yorks.).

TEMMINCK'S STINT [No. 377] The name occurs as Temminck's Tringa in Selby and Temminck's Stint in Jenyns, as Temminck's Sandpiper in Eyton. The species was named by Leisler in 1812 in honour of the celebrated ornithologist Temminck.

TENGMALM'S OWL [No 221] The name appears in Jenyns (1825). This little species was named by Gmelin in honour of Tengmalm. hence its English name.

TERCEL The male GOSHAWK. See Tiercel.

TERMAGANT, or TERMIGANT. An old English spelling of the name PTARMIGAN. Newton has shown that the former spelling was used by Taylor (the "water" poet) in 1630, and the latter by James I in 1617.

TERN. The SANDWICH TERN. (Northumberland.) Distinguished locally by its larger size than other species as "the Tern" or "Large Tern" (Bolam).

TEUCHET, TEUCHIT, TEWHIT, TEWET, TEĀFIT, or TEWFIT · The LAPWING· (North country and Scotland.) So called from its cry.

TEUK. The REDSHANK. (Essex.) From its cry.

THACK or THATCH SPARROW: The HOUSE-SPARROW. (Northants., Shropshire.)

THICK-BILL: The BULLFINCH. (Lancashire, Yorks)

THICK-BILLED GUILLEMOT· BRUNNICH'S GUILLEMOT. (Provincial.)

THICK-BILLED NUTCRACKER. See NUTCRACKER.

THICK-KNEED BUSTARD: The STONE-CURLEW. From the thick swollen appearance of the knees when young. Occurs in Pennant (1766) and other writers to Montagu. Also found as Thick-knee.

THIN-NECK The PINTAIL. (Holy Island.)

THIN-THRESHER. A name for the MISTLE-THRUSH. (Hett.)

THIRSTLE: The SONG-THRUSH. (Devonshire, Cornwall, Shropshire.) A corruption of Throstle.

THISTLE-COCK: The CORN-BUNTING. (Orkneys.)

THISTLE FINCH, THISTLE-BIRD, or THISTLE-WARP. The GOLDFINCH (Provincial.) The first name occurs in Willughby.

THOMAS GIERDET. Hett gives this as a name for the REDBREAST.

THORN-GREY. The LINNET. (Ireland) THORN LINNET is a Yorks. name for the same species. Hett gives Thorney-grey as a name for the LESSER REDPOLL.

THORN WARBLER. The SEDGE WARBLER. (E. Cleveland.)

THREE-TOED QUAIL: The *Andalusian Hemipode*.

THREE-TOED SAND-GROUSE PALLAS'S SAND-GROUSE.

THRESHER · The SONG-THRUSH. (Provincial.)

THRICE COCK. A Midland and North of England name for the MISTLE-THRUSH. In use in Cheshire and Shropshire, and Jesse ("Gleanings," 2nd ser.) gives it as a Staffordshire name The literal meaning is "thrush cock," thrice being from A.Sax. *thrysce*=thrush.

THROG, THROGGY, or THROLLIE: The SONG-THRUSH. (Cheshire.) The third form also occurs in North Yorkshire. A corruption of "Throstle" (q.v.).

THROSTLE : The SONG-THRUSH (chiefly in English literature and poetry). Still, however, used provincially (Lancashire, Staffordshire, and other northern counties, also Ireland). Thrustle is a Shropshire form. From A.Sax. *throsle*, apparently a diminutive of A.Sax *thrysce*, a thrush. Shakespeare has "The throstle with his note so true" It occurs in Merrett and in Willughby, while Turner (1544) has "Throssel," and Skelton spells it Threstill. Pennant (1766) gives Throstle as the name for the species.

THROSTLE COCK The MISTLE-THRUSH (Roxburgh)

THRUSFIELD · The SONG-THRUSH. (Shropshire.)

THRUSH. Properly the SONG-THRUSH, although Turner (1544) gives "Thrushe" as the particular name of the MISTLE-THRUSH. From A.Sax. *thrysce*, a thrush. Some authorities refer to Greek στριχειυ=to twitter : Lat. *strix* =a screeching or twittering owl is from the same root. The literal significance would therefore be a singing or twittering bird.

THRUSHEL or THRUSTLE · The SONG-THRUSH. (Shropshire.) A corruption of Throstle.

THRUSHER The SONG-THRUSH (Sussex, Berks , Bucks.), *er* being a Saxon terminal.

THRUSH-LIKE WARBLER The GREAT REED-WARBLER. (Yarrell.)

THRUSH-NIGHTINGALE [No. 181]. This Scandinavian and east European species has been recently added to the British List.

THUMB-BIRD . The GOLDEN-CRESTED WREN. (Hampshire.). From its size, being about that of a thumb. Thummic is also a name for the CHIFFCHAFF.

TIDEE or TIDIFE Old English names for a TITMOUSE (see Tydif).

TIDLEY GOLDFINCH . The GOLDEN-CRESTED WREN is so called in Devonshire. (Montagu.)

TIDLEY or TIDDY WREN The WREN (Essex)

TIERCEL, TERCEL, or TASSAL The male GOSHAWK, and also the male PEREGRINE FALCON. Mr Harting says the term is derived from the male being supposed to be about a *third* smaller than the female , some authorities state, however, that of the three young birds usually found in the nest two are females and the third a male, hence the term tercel. The correct term for the male Peregrine is Tiercel-gentle, in the same way as the female is called

Falcon-gentle (q.v.), the term tercel or tiercel alone properly signifying the male Goshawk. In Merrett's list (1667) the Goshawk is called "Tassal."

TIERCEL-GENTLE: The male PEREGRINE FALCON (see Tiercel). Sibbald gives it as a Ross and Orkneys name, but it was in very general use in falconry, frequently also being spelt Tercel-gentle.

TIETICK: The MEADOW-PIPIT. (Shetlands.)

TIEVES' NICKET or TIEVES GEIT: The LAPWING. (Shetlands.)

TIGER OWL. A name for the SHORT-EARED OWL. (Hett.)

TILE SWALLOW: The SWIFT (Yorks.)

TIMMER DOO: The RING-DOVE in Scots dialect. Timmer= timber, doo=dove.

TINKER: The PURPLE SANDPIPER. (Northumberland.)

TINKERSHERE (Tinker's hue): The COMMON GUILLEMOT. (Provincial.) From its sombre upper-plumage. Hett also gives it for the BLACK GUILLEMOT.

TINNER: The PIED WAGTAIL. (Cornwall.)

TINNOCK: The BLUE TITMOUSE. (Provincial.) Swainson thinks it is from its shrill note.

TINSIGL or TINSIGL Y GWYS. Welsh names for the PIED WAGTAIL: the first signifies Wagtail, while the second (which is given to the WHITE WAGTAIL in North Wales by Coward and Oldham) signifies "Wagtail of the furrow."

TINSIGL FELEN. The YELLOW WAGTAIL (North Wales) lit. "yellow wagtail."

TINSIGL LWYD: The GREY WAGTAIL. (North Wales) lit. "grey wagtail."

TINTIE: The WREN. (Notts.)

TINWEN Y GARN or TINWEN Y GARREG. Welsh names for the WHEATEAR: the first signifies "white rump of the stone-heap," the second "white rump of the crag."

TIPPET GREBE: The GREAT CRESTED GREBE. (Bewick.) From the breast-plumage being used for tippets by furriers.

TIRMA: The OYSTERCATCHER. (Martin's "Voy. St. Kilda.")

TIT. A term applied to individuals of the family *Paridæ*. Equivalent to "titmouse." From Icel. *tittr*, a small bird; lit. anything small.

TITHYS REDSTART: The BLACK REDSTART. Tithys (also the specific name) is from Sansk. *titha*, fire, or Lat. *Titan*, the Sun-god, both capable of allusion to the red tail and tail-coverts. See also REDSTART.

TITLARK. A common provincial name for the MEADOW-PIPIT. Occurs in Merrett, Willughby and many later authors. Has also been applied sometimes to the TREE-PIPIT and the ROCK-PIPIT.

TITLENE. A North Country name for the HEDGE-SPARROW. (Swainson.)

TITLING. A provincial name for the HEDGE-SPARROW Occurs in Montagu (1802). Turner's "Titling," which he wrongly identifies with the "Curuca" of Aristotle, does not appear to be the Hedge-Sparrow, although Aristotle's Curuca no doubt is. The name has been sometimes applied to the MEADOW-PIPIT, for which, however the more general term is Titlark

TITMAL: The BLUE TITMOUSE (Provincial.)

TITMEG, TITEREEN· The WREN. (Hett.)

TITMOUSE Any species of Titmouse Mid Eng *titmose* or *Titmase*, from "tit" (q.v) and A.Sax *mase*, a small bird of no particular species *not* equivalent to "mouse." Plural "titmice" is therefore incorrect and should be titmouses. It usually occurs in old authors as Titmouse, but Macgillivray and Yarrell set the fashion of abbreviating to "Tit."

TITTEREL The WHIMBREL. (Sussex.) Hawker also gives it as a local Dorsetshire name

TITTIMAW or TITMAUPS. Cheshire names for any species of Titmouse, of which name it is a corruption.

TITTY TODGER The WREN (Devonshire) See Titty Wren.

TITTY WREN· The WREN. (Wilts.) "Titty" is from the Icelandic *tittr*—a small bird, or anything small. "Tit" (q.v.) is an equivalent.

TOAD SNATCHER. A name for the REED-BUNTING. (Yorks)

TOD BIRD. The GREAT SKUA. (Yorks.)

TOM HARRY· The GREAT SKUA. (Cornwall.)

TOMMY LOOS. A nickname for species of Divers

TOM NOWP: The BLUE TITMOUSE (Cheshire.) Swainson also gives TOM NOUP as a Shropshire name for the GREAT TITMOUSE. Nowp or Noup seems the same as Nope, a name for the BULLFINCH

TOM PUDDING: The LITTLE GREBE. (Shropshire, Yorks., Antrim.)

TOM PUFFIN: The LITTLE GREBE. (Yorks.)

TOM THUMB· The WILLOW-WARBLER. (Roxburgh.) From its small size.

TOMTIT. A general provincial name for the BLUE TITMOUSE. Swainson also gives it as a Norfolk and Craven name for the WREN, and an Irish name for the TREECREEPER.

TONGUE BIRD or LONG TONGUE. The WRYNECK. (Provincial.) From its long projectile tongue.

TONY HOOP: The BULLFINCH (Somersetshire.) Probably from its whistling note, but Swainson thinks it is from the tawny breast of the female.

TOOK: The REDSHANK. From its note.

TOPE: The WREN. (Cornwall.)

TOR OUZEL: The RING-OUZEL. (Devonshire.)

TORTOISE-SHELL GOOSE: The WHITE-FRONTED GOOSE. (Ireland.) From the mottled markings on the abdomen (Swainson).

TOT-O'ER-SEAS. Newton gives this as a local East Coast name for the GOLDEN-CRESTED WREN, in allusion to its arrival from overseas on the autumnal migration. It seems to be a Suffolk and perhaps a Norfolk name.

TOUNAG A Gaelic name for the MALLARD. (Western Isles.) From *toun*, a wave.

TOWILLY or TOWWILLY The SANDERLING. (Cornwall.) From its cry. Occurs as Towiller in Borlase.

TRANILLYS: The RING-PLOVER (Hett.)

TREE-CLIMBER: The TREECREEPER. (Provincial.) Tree-clipper is an Oxfordshire name.

TREECREEPER [No. 83, British Treecreeper; No. 84, Northern Treecreeper]. Occurs in most of our older authors as "Common Creeper" It is the *Certhia* of Willughby and Ray. Pennant (1766) calls it "Creeper" simply. Ridgway has separated the resident British form from the North European form, examples of which have been identified in Scotland.

TREE FALCON. The HOBBY. (Willughby.)

TREE FINCH. The TREE-SPARROW. (Hett.)

TREE GOOSE: The BARNACLE-GOOSE. (Bewick.) In reference to the old legend. (See BARNACLE-GOOSE.)

TREE HUCK-MUCK: The LONG-TAILED TITMOUSE. (Hett.)

TREE LARK: The TREE-PIPIT. (Notts, Yorks.)

TREE MAGPIE. A supposed variety of the MAGPIE.

TREE-PIPIT [No. 67] The name occurs in Selby (1825) and arises from its more arboreal habits than the MEADOW-PIPIT. It is the "Pipit Lark" of Pennant, and the "Field Lark" of Montagu.

TREE-SPARROW [No. 41]. So called from its habit of nesting chiefly in boles of trees. The name appears to be first found in Montagu (1802). It is the Mountain Sparrow or Finch of many older authors from Albin to Bewick, probably so called from the name *Passer montana,* under which it appears in Willughby and Ray It appears to be the Hamburg Grosbeak of Latham, and the Hamburg Tree-Creeper and Red-headed Sparrow of Albin.

TREE-SPEILER or BARK-SPEILER: The TREECREEPER. (Scotland.) Speiler signifies climber.

TREE-WIDDLE. Occurs in Albin for a species of Stint or Sanderling.

TRESGLEN. A Welsh name for the MISTLE-THRUSH; lit. "screech," from its loud song

TRESGLEN GOCH· The REDWING. (North Wales) lit. "red thrush."

TREUN RE TREUN A Gaelic name for the LAND-RAIL.

TRICKER: The WREN (Thirsk, Yorks)

TRILLACHAN: The OYSTERCATCHER. (Hebrides.) Occurs in Martin's "Voyage to St. Kilda."

TRINGA. The PURPLE SANDPIPER. (Northumberland.) Bolam gives it as a local name at Boulmer.

TRINGA CURLEW: The CURLEW-SANDPIPER.

TRIOLLACHAN TRAIGH. A Gaelic name for any of the smaller shore birds (lit "little quaverers of the shore ").

TROCHWR Y LLYN. A Welsh name for the DIPPER.

TROCHYDD BRONGOCH (Y)· The RED-BREASTED MERGANSER (North Wales) lit. "the red-breasted plunger."

TROCHYDD GWDDGFOCH· The RED-THROATED DIVER. (North Wales) lit. "red-throated diver."

TROCHYDD MAWR The GREAT NORTHERN DIVER (North Wales) lit. "great diver."

TRODZHEN or EDHNOW-TRODZHAN. Cornish names for the STARLING.

TROELLWR· The NIGHTJAR. (North Wales) lit. "spinner," from its churring note.

TROELLWR BACH (Y)· The GRASSHOPPER-WARBLER. (North Wales) lit "the little spinner," from its song.

TROET A Cornish name for the TURTLE-DOVE; also a Plover.

TRUMPETER SWAN. See *American Trumpeter Swan.*

TRUMPIE: The ARCTIC SKUA. (Orkneys.)

TSHAUHA. A Cornish name for the CHOUGH; also the JACKDAW (?).

TSI-KUK. A Cornish name for the SWALLOW; lit. "house-cuckoo."

TSKEKKER EITHIN. A Cornish name for a Titmouse, or Furzechat.

TUET or TUIT: The LAPWING. (West Yorkshire, Lancashire and Westmorland.) From its cry.

TUFTED DUCK [No. 300]. The name occurs in Willughby (1678) and in all succeeding authors, and is derived from the bird's pendant crest of narrow feathers. Selby calls it "Tufted Pochard," and it also occurs as "Tufted Wigeon."

TUFTED SKART: The SHAG. (Provincial.) From its tuft or crest on the head.

TULIAC: The GREAT SKUA. (Provincial.)

TULLET: The RINGED PLOVER. (Cheshire.)

TUMBLER: The BLACK-HEADED GULL (Redcar, Yorks.)

TURKEY BIRD: The WRYNECK. Because it ruffles the neck-feathers when disturbed.

TURNSTONE [No. 368]. The name occurs in Edwards (pl. 141) as the "Turnstone from Hudson's Bay." Pennant (1766) has "Turnstone" only. The name arises from the bird's habit of turning over small stones, etc., in seeking its food.

TURTLE. Albin gives this as a Bass Rock name for the BLACK GUILLEMOT, and says it is on account of its laying two eggs.

TURTLE-DOVE [No. 348]. From Fr. *tourterelle*, der. from Lat. *Turtur*. The name is found in Chaucer, who speaks of "the wedded turtil with her hearté trewe." It occurs in Turner (1544) as "turtel duve," in Merrett (1667) as "Turtle Dove," and in Willughby as "Turtle-dove." Pennant (1766 ed.) has "The Turtle," while later writers call it the "Common Turtle," but Bewick (1797) and succeeding authors revert to the name Turtle-Dove.

TURTLE-DOVE. A Holy Island (Northumberland) name for the BLACK GUILLEMOT.

TURTUR: The TURTLE-DOVE. (North Wales.)

TWINK: The CHAFFINCH. From its note. Occurs in Montagu.

TWITE [No. 20]. This name, derived from its call-note, is first found in Albin (1738). Willughby, Pennant and other old authors call it the Mountain Linnet. It is sometimes also called Twite Finch (North Yorkshire).

TWO-BARRED CROSSBILL [No 36]. First found in Latham ("Syn " III, p. 108) as White-winged Crossbill. Yarrell calls it European White-winged Crossbill.

TYDIF, TIDIFE, TIDEE, or TYDIE. Ancient names for a Titmouse (see Tit). The first occurs in Chaucer, and may apply to the COAL-TITMOUSE (cf. Newton "Dict. Birds," p. 962, note). Newton also gives Tytyfr.

TYSTIE or TAISTEY · The BLACK GUILLEMOT. (Orkneys and Shetlands.) Newton says it is from Icel. *peisto* Also occurs as Teiste and Taiste

UISEAG (pron. ooshak). A Gaelic name for the SKY-LARK.

ULLAT The BARN-OWL and the TAWNY OWL. (Yorkshire)

UMBER GULL: The immature COMMON GULL. (Hett)

USSEL The BLACKBIRD. (North Yorkshire.) See Ouzel.

UTIIAGE The WHINCHAT. (Shropshire) Swainson thinks it is the same as Utick

UTICK: The WHINCHAT is so called in Middlesex, Nottinghamshire, Shropshire and elsewhere. From its note *u-tick*. Swainson also gives "Tick" simply.

VANNER HAWK: The KESTREL. An equivalent of "fanner."

VAN-WINGED HAWK: The HOBBY. (Hants)

VARE-HEADED WIGEON: The COMMON POCHARD. See "Vare Wigeon."

VARE WIGEON · The female or young male of the SMEW. (North Devonshire.) Montagu says it is from their heads resembling a weasel's, locally called "vare."

VARIEGATED THRUSH WHITE'S THRUSH So called by Macgillivray from Horsfield's name, *T. varius*

VELVERD: The FIELDFARE. (Wiltshire.) A corruption of Fieldfare.

VELVET DUCK: The VELVET SCOTER.

VELVET RUNNER. The WATER-RAIL. (Willughby.)

VELVET SCOTER [No 310]. The name is derived from Willughby and Ray, who, describing it under the name of Aldrovandus's Black Duck, remark that it might be not undeservedly called the Velvet Duck, on account of the softness and delicateness of its feathers. The name Velvet Duck was used by successive writers from Pennant to Montagu. Velvet Scoter seems to occur first in Fleming (1828).

Virginian Colin. An introduced species, not entitled to a place on the British List. The name is found in Macgillivray and Yarrell. It is first recorded in Montagu (Supp.) as American Quail.

VIRGINIAN CUCKOO: The YELLOW-BILLED CUCKOO. (Eyton.)

VIRGINIAN PARTRIDGE: The *Virginian Colin*. (Jenyns.)

WAEG: The KITTIWAKE GULL. (Shetlands.) "Diminutive of (Kitti)wake" (Swainson).

WAGEL or CORNISH WAGEL: The ARCTIC SKUA or the GREAT BLACK-BACKED GULL. Newton remarks that Ray and Willughby got it in 1662 on Godreve Island, near St. Ives. The Arctic Skua seems to have been meant, but they took it to be the young of the Great Black-backed Gull, for which Wagel is still a Yorkshire name.

WAGTAIL: The PIED WAGTAIL generally. The name occurs in the fifteenth century, according to Wright, as *Wagsterd* and *Wagstyrt* (from *steort*=tail). Montagu gives it as a provincial name for the DUNLIN.

WALL BIRD: The SPOTTED FLYCATCHER. (South and east England.)

WALL-CHAT: The STONECHAT (Provincial); the SPOTTED FLYCATCHER (N. Yorks.).

WALLCREEPER [No. 85]. A south European species, which is known to have been taken four times in England. The name occurs first in Merrett's list (1667) as a British species, and also in Willughby, who observes that the bird is *said* to be found in England.

WALL ROBIN: The SPOTTED FLYCATCHER. (Cheshire.)

WARBLER. The name was first used by Pennant ("Gen. Birds," 1773, p. 35) for the birds removed to genus *Sylvia* by Scopoli, from Linnæus's genus *Motacilla*.

WARE-GOOSE: The BRENT GOOSE. (Durham.) So called from its feeding on "ware," which is coarse seaweed thrown up on the beach (A.Sax. *Sǣwār*, lit. sea-weed).

WASHDISH, WASHTAIL, or WASHERWOMAN: The PIED WAGTAIL is locally so called (see Dishwasher). "Warwinckle" in Latham's "Falconry" (1633, vol. II, p. 144) is thought by Newton to apply to the same bird.

WATER BLACKBIRD: The DIPPER. (Yorks., Scotland and Ireland.)

WATER-COLLY: The DIPPER. (Somersetshire) lit "water-blackbird" (see Colly).

WATER CRAKE: The DIPPER (Willughby.) The name is also applied to the SPOTTED CRAKE.

WATER CRAW. The DIPPER. Equivalent of Water-Crow. Occurs in Turner (1544) as the name at Morpeth, Northumberland. Evans says the name is still used in the North of England.

WATER-CROW. A local name for the DIPPER (occurring in Bewick). It is in use in Yorkshire, and Bolam says it is a Border name for the species, and in Scotland often becomes "Wetter-craw." Water-crow is also a Dumfries name for the COOT

WATER-EAGLE. An old Scots name for the OSPREY.

WATER-HEN. An alternative name for the MOORHEN Occurs in Turner, Willughby, and numerous subsequent writers, sometimes as Common Water-hen. According to Rutty, it was used in co. Dublin for the WATER-RAIL.

WATERIE: The PIED WAGTAIL (Forfar.)

WATERIE-WAGTAIL A popular Border name for the PIED WAGTAIL. (Bolam)

WATER JUNKET. A name for the COMMON SANDPIPER. (Swainson.)

WATER-LAEROCK (Water Laik) The COMMON SANDPIPER. (Swainson.)

WATER-LINNET. The MEADOW-PIPIT. (Hett.)

WATER-OUZEL. The DIPPER Occurs under this name in Willughby, and it was the general name for the bird for long after, occurring in Albin, Pennant, Latham, Lewin, Walcott, Donovan and Bewick.

WATER PEGGY. The DIPPER. (Dumfries.)

WATER-PIET, WATER PYET, WATER PYOT, or WATER PIOT. Local names for the DIPPER. Literally the "little water pie." So called from its black-and-white plumage, "piet" being an equivalent to (or diminutive of) "pie" (q.v). In South-west Scotland the name occurs as "Water-pyat." Bewick gives Water-Piot

WATER-PIPIT [No. 70]. This is a close ally of the ROCK-PIPIT, but is an Alpine or mountain species, in place of marine.

WATER-RAIL [No. 459]. The name, from its aquatic predilections, occurs in Willughby (1678) the species being based on the *Rallus aquaticus* of Aldrovandus, of which the name would be a literal translation.

WATER-SPARROW: The REED-BUNTING. (Shropshire.) Occurs in Montagu as a provincial name.

WATER-THRUSH. The DIPPER. (Cornwall)

WATER TIT: The PIED WAGTAIL. (Provincial.)
WATER WAGTAIL: The PIED WAGTAIL. Occurs first in Merrett's list; Turner calls it simply "a wagtale."
WATER WITCH: The STORM-PETREL. (Provincial.)
WATERY PLEEPS· The COMMON SANDPIPER. (Orkneys.)
WATITTY: The PIED WAGTAIL. (Cheshire.)
WATTIE or WATTIE WAGTAIL: The PIED WAGTAIL. (Westmorland.) Wattie is no doubt a form of "Waterie."
WAXEN CHATTERER: The WAXWING. Occurs in Pennant and most other eighteenth century writers to Donovan.
WAXWING [No. 113]. So called from the shafts of some of the wing-feathers being terminated by what looks like a flattened tip of red sealing-wax. It was originally called by Wilughby the Bohemian Chatterer and by Pennant Chatterer in the folio edition (1766), and Waxen Chatterer in the later editions. Selby (1825) calls it Bohemian Waxwing, as also most of the succeeding authors.
WEASE ALLAN: The ARCTIC SKUA. (Orkneys.) Wease is from A.Sax. *was*, moisture.
WEASEL DUCK· The female or immature SMEW. (Northumberland.) From the chestnut and white colour and fur-like texture of the feathers (Bolam). Weasel Duck or Weasel Coot are also Norfolk names.
WEATHER-COCK: The GREEN WOODPECKER. Perhaps eqivalent of Rain-fowl.
WEDGE-TAILED GULL [No. 424] So called from its cuneate tail. Formerly known as Ross's Gull, or Ross's Rosy Gull, after the discoverer, Sir J. C. Ross.
WEE DIVER or WEE DOUKER: The LITTLE GREBE. (Dumfriesshire.)
WEEP: The LAPWING. (Provincial.) From its cry.
WEEPING GUILLEMOT. A local name for the *Ringed* or Bridled *Guillemot* (a variety of the COMMON GUILLEMOT) among the West of Scotland fishermen. (Gray.)
WEET BIRD: The WRYNECK. (Hampshire.) From its cry.
WEKEÉN: The MEADOW-PIPIT. (Kerry.)
WELE· The GREEN WOODPECKER. (Hett.)
WELL PLUM: The COMMON POCHARD. (Provincial.)
WELSH AMBASSADOR. The CUCKOO appears to have been formerly sometimes so called. The allusion is in Middleton's "A Trick to Catch the Old One" (act IV, sc. 5): "This sound is like the Cuckoo, the Welsh Ambassador." It is supposed that this name is an allusion to the annual arrival

of Welshmen in search of summer employment, which probably took place about the time of the Cuckoo's appearance. According to Dyer, however, the Cuckoo is still called "Welsh Ambassador" in Wales.

Western Duck : STELLER'S EIDER. (Gould.)

WESTERN LARGE-BILLED REED-BUNTING [No. 54]. A south-west European species first recorded for the British islands by Mr. Nicoll in 1908.

Western Pochard STELLER'S EIDER. (Selby.)

Wet Bird : The CHAFFINCH. (Rutland and Scotland.) Chambers says it is because its cry syllabled "weet, weet," is thought to foretell rain.

Wet-my-lip or Wet-my-feet. Local names for the QUAIL; the first is a Norfolk and the second a Scots and Irish name.

Wezel Coot. The female or young of the SMEW. (Albin.) From the head resembling that of a weasel. Also spelt Weesel Coot by Pennant. See Vare Wigeon.

Whattie or Whishie : The WHITETHROAT. (East Lothian)

Whaup : The COMMON CURLEW. (Scotland and North England) From its cry. It occurs as Whaap in the Orkneys and Shetlands.

WHEATEAR [No 166, Wheatear; No. 167, Greenland Wheatear] Generally derived from A.Sax. $hwit=$ white, and $ærs=$rump. Newton, however, was inclined to reject this derivation "until it be shewn that such a name ever existed" The name first occurs in the works of Taylor, the "Water Poet" (1654); and in Merrett's list (1667) as "Wheat-ear or White-tail" Willughby, who calls it the "Fallow-Smich," says that in Sussex it is called the Wheatear "because at the time of Wheat harvest they wax very fat," and also White-tail from the colour of the rump He is possibly in error as to the derivation of the word wheatear, as its significance (vide supra) is considered to be similar to the other name of White-tail. The name Wheatear is not used by Turner (1544), who gives the names "clot-burd, smatche, arlyng, and steinchek : " the first indicating the bird's habit of sitting upon clods, the second being an equivalent no doubt of "Chat," the third being a reference to the white rump (from $ærs=$rump and ling, a diminutive) and the fourth being an equivalent to Stonechat. The Greenland Wheatear, a sub-species breeding in Greenland and North-east America, is now known to be a passage-migrant through our islands in spring and autumn.

WHEATSEL BIRD: The male CHAFFINCH. (Norfolk.) So called, according to Gurney, from their congregating in autumn about the season of wheat sowing.

WHEEL-BIRD· The NIGHTJAR. Montagu gives it as a provincial name, and Swainson says it is a Stirling name. From its jarring noise resembling that made by a spinning wheel.

WHEELIEVE: The WILLOW-WARBLER. (Hett.)

WHEETY WHEYBEARD, WHEETIE WHY, WHEYBEARD, WHITTIE BEARD. Provincial names for the WHITETHROAT, because its light-coloured head and neck-feathers stand out so thickly.

WHET-ILE: The GREEN WOODPECKER. (Essex, Herts) From A.Sax. *thwitan*, to cut.

WHEWER: The female WIGEON. (Willughby). Bewick also gives Whim and Pandled Whew, while Pandle Whew is a Norfolk name according to Swainson. Whew is a Northumberland name for the species, said to be derived from the whistling-call of the male.

WHILK . The COMMON SCOTER. (Provincial.)

WHIM· The WIGEON. (See under Whewer.)

WHIMBREL [No. 405]. The name occurs in Willughby (1678). Skeat says it is derived from the bird's cry, resembling "whim."

WHIMBREL CURLEW: The WHIMBREL. (Pennant.)

WHINCHACKER, WHINCHECK, WHIN CLOCHARET. North Country names for the WHINCHAT, of which name they are equivalents.

WHINCHAT [No. 83] So called from its habit of perching on whinbushes, and uttering its monotonous note. syllabled "u-tick" Occurs in Willughby (1678) and most subsequent authors. Macgillivray calls it Whin Bushchat.

WHINDLE and WHEENERD. Two old names for the REDWING, perhaps from the local German *Weindrustle* and *Winsel* (Newton).

WHIN-GREY: The LINNET. (North Ireland.)

WHIN-LINTIE. A Border name for the LINNET. (Lintie= Linnet). Whin-Linnet is also a Scots name.

WHIN SPARROW: The HEDGE-SPARROW. (East Lothian)

WHINYARD: The SHOVELER. (Waterford.) The COMMON POCHARD. (Wexford.) Swainson says whinyard is a name for a knife resembling a Shoveler's bill in shape.

Whip. The SWIFT. (West Riding, Yorkshire.)
Whishey-whey-beard: The WHITETHROAT. So called in many parts of Scotland. (Gray.)
Whishie. The WHITETHROAT. (East Lothian.)
Whisker-bird: The CORN-BUNTING. (Hett.)
WHISKERED TERN [No. 413]. So called from the white stripe running backward from the gape. The name is found in Yarrell. It is the Moustached Tern of Gould ("Birds of Europe," pt. XVIII).
Whistler: The GOLDENEYE and the WIGEON. Also applied to the RING-OUZEL. (Wicklow)
Whistling Duck: The COOT. (Renfrew.)
Whistling Plover The GOLDEN PLOVER. (Norfolk, Renfrew) From its clear whistle. Occurs in Merrett, and Montagu gives it as a provincial name Swainson also applies it to the GREY PLOVER
Whistling Sandpiper. The GREEN SANDPIPER.
Whistling Swan The WHOOPER SWAN. (Selby, Jenyns, Gould.) Used locally in Northumberland.
Whistling Thrush or Whistling Dick A Thames Valley name for the SONG-THRUSH. (Swainson.)
White-and-Dusky Grebe: The SLAVONIAN GREBE. (Pennant.)
White-backed Dove. The ROCK-DOVE (Macgillivray.)
White Baker. The SPOTTED FLYCATCHER. (Provincial.)
White-bellied Swift: The ALPINE SWIFT (Gould.)
WHITE-BILLED NORTHERN DIVER [No 342] A close ally of the GREAT NORTHERN DIVER, but with the bill yellowish-white at all seasons
White-breasted Blackbird. The RING-OUZEL.
White-breasted Warbler. Macgillivray's name for the LESSER WHITETHROAT.
White-breasted Weet-weet. Macgillivray's name for the SPOTTED SANDPIPER.
White-cap. The male REDSTART. (Salop., Yorks) From its white forehead, also a name for the WHITETHROAT.
White Crow: The BLACK-HEADED GULL.
White-eyed Duck: The FERRUGINOUS DUCK is so called by some authors.
White-faced Crow. The ROOK From the bare whitish skin on the face.
White-faced Diver The COOT (Ireland)

WHITE-FACED DUCK : The SCAUP-DUCK. From the broad white band round the base of the bill.

WHITE-FACED GOOSE : The WHITE-FRONTED GOOSE. White-faced Barnacle is also a name for the BARNACLE-GOOSE.

WHITE FINCH or WHITE-WING : The CHAFFINCH.

WHITE-FRONTED GOOSE [No. 275]. The name is first used by Pennant ("Brit. Zoology," fo. ed., 1766) and is derived from the white feathers round the base of the bill and on the forehead. It is the "Laughing Goose" of Edwards.

WHITE-FRONTED REDSTART. Macgillivray's name for the REDSTART.

WHITE GAME or WHITE PARTRIDGE : The PTARMIGAN. (Willughby.)

WHITE GROUSE : The PTARMIGAN. (Bewick.)

WHITE HAWKS. A falconer's term for Hawks of the third year.

WHITE-HEADED CORMORANT : The CORMORANT. (Spring.)

WHITE-HEADED GOOSANDER : The SMEW. (Fleming.) From its white crest.

WHITE-HEADED GULL : The LESSER BLACK-BACKED GULL. (Northumberland.)

WHITE-HEADED HARPY. A name for the MARSH-HARRIER. From its whitish crown.

WHITE-HEADED LONG-TAILED TITMOUSE. See NORTHERN LONG-TAILED TITMOUSE.

WHITE HOOPING OWL, or OWLET or HOWLET : The TAWNY OWL. (Merrett.) Based on the *Ulula aluco* of Aldrovandus (p. 538).

WHITE JERFALCON : The ICELAND FALCON. (Pennant.)

WHITE KITE or WHITE HAWK : The HEN-HARRIER. (Donegal.)

WHITE LARK or WHITE BUNTING. The SNOW-BUNTING. (Cheshire.) White Lark or White-winged Lark are also Norfolk names for the species.

WHITE-LEGGED GOLDFINCH : The GOLDFINCH. After second moult. (Hett.)

WHITE LINTIE : The WHITETHROAT. (Forfar)

WHITE MAA : The HERRING-GULL. (Shetlands.)

WHITE MERGANSER The SMEW. (Devonshire.)

WHITE NUN : The SMEW. (Ireland.) Occurs in Willughby. From the white crest with the black nape suggesting a hood.

WHITE OWL: The BARN-OWL. (Provincial.) Occurs in Sibbald, also Pennant and many later authors. Also called White Hoolet or Howlet.

WHITE PARTRIDGE. A name for the PTARMIGAN.

WHITE-RUMP: The WHEATEAR is so called by Bewick (1797). Still used in Northumberland (Bolam), Cheshire (Coward and Oldham) and Norfolk.

WHITE-RUMPED STONECHAT. The WHEATEAR. (Macgillivray.)

WHITE-RUMPED SWALLOW. The MARTIN. (Macgillivray.)

WHITE-SIDE. The GOLDENEYE. (Westmorland.)

WHITE-SIDED DUCK or DIVER. The TUFTED DUCK. (Armagh.)

WHITE SPOONBILL: The SPOONBILL. (Montagu.)

WHITE-SPOTTED BLUETHROAT [No. 183]. This species gets its name from the white central patch on the blue throat.

WHITE'S THRUSH [No. 154]. The name, given in honour of Gilbert White, of Selborne, occurs in Eyton's "Rarer British Birds" (1836).

WHITE STORK [No. 256]. Occurs as "Stork" in Turner (1544), also in Merrett, who notes it as rare, while the name "White Stork" occurs first in Willughby (1678), who calls it the "common or white Stork." Turner says it is "nowhere to be seen, save as a captive, in our island." This was, however, an error, as the bird has long been known as an irregular visitor in spring to East Anglia, and presumably was, if anything, of more frequent occurrence in Turner's day than at the present time. Turner notes the bird's habit of building upon roofs, or even chimney tops at times in Germany, a habit which, as is well known, prevails at the present day, a Stork building upon the house being regarded in most parts as an honour to the house, and no doubt this explains the former legend that Storks bring the new-born babies to the houses. The Magyars also hold the Stork in great reverence, and say that it must not be hurt. Both in Hungary and Germany old cart wheels are sometimes placed on the chimneys for them to build their nests on. It is said that when this is done the grateful bird leaves as rent a feather the first year, an egg the second year, and a young bird the third. This belief was held by Drayton, who cites.—

> The careful Stork, since Adam wondered at
> For thankfulness to those where he doth breed.

In some parts it was believed that a Stork deserting a homestead was a portent of death. Willughby remarks that

Storks " are said to live only in republics and free States; but this we found by experience to be false, observing them in the Territories of some Princes in Germany. There is a tradition also that they feed and nourish their parents in their old age, when they are unable to seek their own food." The latter belief, it may be remarked, is taken from Pliny.

WHITE-TAIL: The WHEATEAR. (Provincial.) Cotgrave (1611) has "Whittaile."

WHITE-TAILED EAGLE [No. 244] The name occurs in Willughby, who quotes Gaza's name *albicilla* for it (on account of its white tail), which was retained by Linnæus and modern authors. The white tail, however, is only to be found in the adult bird, and does not appear until it is six or seven years old. The immature bird in uniform dark plumage was originally described as a separate species under the name of Sea Eagle (*Falco ossifragus* of Linnæus) This is the "Sea Eagle or Osprey" of Willughby, the Sea Eagle of Pennant (fo. ed., 1766), and of Lewin, Latham, Montagu, etc.

WHITETHROAT [No. 147]. This name, which occurs in Willughby (1678) and most subsequent authors, is derived from the white chin and throat.

WHITE-THROATED BLACKBIRD: The RING-OUZEL.

WHITETHROAT WARBLER: The WHITETHROAT.

WHITE-TOPPED HERON: The NIGHT-HERON. (Hett.)

WHITE WAGTAIL [No. 82]. The name White Wagtail first occurs in Willughby, who also names the species *Motacilla alba*, the distinctness of the PIED WAGTAIL not being recognised until 1832, by Gould. It seems probable that Willughby described an example of the true *M. alba* and not of *M. lugubris*, for he states that the middle of the back "inclines to cinereous" and the white extends on the side of the neck "almost to the wings." The name White Wagtail is of course used by all old British authors for the species now known as the Pied Wagtail. This bird seems to have been regarded as of medicinal value in former times, for Willughby gravely states that "One or two ounces of the powder of this bird put in a pot close-stopt and bak'd in an oven together with the feathers, taken in Saxifrage water, or strong White wine, is said to be good against the Stone, especially that of the kidneys."

WHITE-WALL: The SPOTTED FLYCATCHER. (Northants.)

WHITE WATER WAGTAIL: The PIED WAGTAIL. (Pennant.)

WHITE WHISKEY JOHN. The GREAT GREY SHRIKE From the pure white under-plumage and ashen-grey head and back, and wavering character of its flight (Swainson)

WHITE WIGEON: The SMEW. (Devonshire)

WHITE-WINGED BLACK TERN [No. 414]. The name, arising from the white "shoulder," is found in Yarrell ("Brit. Birds," Supp, 1845). It is the White-winged Tern of Gould.

WHITE-WINGED CROSSBILL. See *American White-winged Crossbill*.

WHITE WINGED LARK [No 57]. So called from the white wing-patch formed by the inner primaries and secondaries being white.

WHITE WREN · The WILLOW-WARBLER. (Cheshire, Scotland.)

WHITTERICK · The COMMON CURLEW. (East Lothian.)

WHITWALL. See WITWOLL.

WHOLE SNIPE: The COMMON SNIPE So called in distinction from the "Half" or JACK SNIPE

WHOOP The BULLFINCH. An equivalent of Hoop.

WHOOPER SWAN [No 271]. This species, so called from its whooping cry, is the common wild Swan of the northern portions of Europe and Asia, which breeds far north and migrates southwards in cold weather It is first described by Willughby (1678) who terms it "a wild Swan, called also an Elk, and in some places a Hooper."

The folk-lore and mythology of northern Europe are rich in legends of the Swan De Kay ("Bird Gods") has shown to what an extent swan-worship prevailed in ancient times. The extent to which it has figured in heraldry alone shows the regard in which it was held in rather later times. The ancient oath on the Swan, still sometimes surviving as "I swan" or "I swanny" is obviously a survival of the ancient swan-worship. It is recorded that Edward I in 1304, on his investiture as a knight, swore an oath on two Swans decorated with gold nets. De Kay says that the expression "I swan" or "it swans to me" meant originally that the speaker had a prophetic feeling that something was going to happen, and that the swan has from time immemorial been a bird of prophecy. The same expression exists in German, "Es schwanet mir," and the literature and folk-lore of Germany are rich in allusions to or legends of the Swan. In fact, the cradle of the ancient Swan-worship and the surviving legends of the bird, as evinced in names of places, stories of swan-maidens, etc., lies in

Central Germany. Frederick II of Brandenburg instituted an Order of the Swan in 1440, and another Order existed at Cleves. The name is a royal one in Bohemia, and the name of the great river Elbe that flows from the confines of that ancient kingdom to the North Sea is itself probably a "swan river," *elbschwan* being a German name for a kind of Swan, while *elb* itself is an equivalent of fairy. In the Norse we find *elptr*, *elftr*, for these birds, which are obviously connected names, while on our eastern coasts "elk" is the name given to a wild Swan. At the mouth of the Elbe are the states of Schleswig-Holstein, formerly a part of the Kingdom of Denmark; and a province in the ancient state of Holsatia was named Stormaria and had for its arms a Swan with its neck encircled by a ducal coronet, which also figures in the ancient arms of the Kings of Denmark (Jonae ab Elvervelt, "De Holsatia," 1592). This province of Stormaria includes among other towns the great modern city of Hamburg, and it appears to have been from this portion of Europe that the invasion of England by the Angles under Ida sailed, landing on the north-east coast of England. For an account of the "swan-coins" of ancient Germany, a curious old work by Christian Schlegel, "De Nummis antiquis Gothanis et Cygneis Dissertatis," may be consulted. An ancient belief was that it was lucky to meet a Swan at sea. On the Island of Rügen in the Baltic it is said to have been credited with bringing the newly-born babies, an office assigned in most parts of Germany to the Stork. The Swan appears several times in the story of the Irish legendary hero Cuchullaind. On one occasion the rescued Princess and her servant follow the hero in the shape of Swans, a story which recalls the tales of Swan-maidens in Danish and German folk-lore. According to a correspondent in the "Athenæum" (vol. III, p. 229), if the Swan flies against the wind, it is a certain indication of a hurricane within twenty-four hours, generally within twelve. A Scottish saying is "When the white Swan visits the Orkneys expect a continued severe winter" (Inwards). A Hampshire superstition is that Swans are generally hatched during a thunderstorm. The same belief is contradicted by Lord Northampton in his "Defensative against the Poyson of Supposed Prophecies" (1583), who says: "It chaunceth sometimes to thunder about that time and season of the yeare when Swannes hatch their young: and yet no doubt it is a paradox of simple men to think that a Swanne cannot hatch without a crack of thunder."

In co Mayo it is believed, according to Swainson, that the souls of virgins remarkable for the purity of their lives were after death enshrined in the form of Swans.

The ancient superstition that Swans sing before their death is alluded to by Pliny among other writers, who tells us he proved it false through his own observation. It may be that this idea originates in the classical belief that Orpheus became a Swan after death, the Swan being, moreover, the bird of Apollo, the god of Music among the Greeks Chaucer, referring to the legend, says —
> But as the Swan, I have herd seyd ful yore
> Ageyns his dethe shall singen his penaunce.

Shakespeare has many allusions to the supposed swan-song.—
> I will play the Swan, and die in music.
> OTHELLO, act v, sc 2
> A Swan-like end, fading in music.
> MERCHANT OF VENICE, act III, sc 2
> And now this pale Swan in her watery nest,
> Begins the sad dirge of her certain ending
> RAPE OF LUCRECE

Although this "death-song" of the Swan has often been deemed to refer to the Mute Swan, there is no doubt that if it were true of any species it would be of the Whooper Swan As regards the Mute Swan, it has long been considered an erroneous belief, yet the bird in life has in the breeding-season a note which Harting describes as " a soft and rather plaintive note, monotonous but not disagreeable. I have often heard it in the spring, when swimming about with its young." There is, however, nothing to show that the Mute Swan was the one to which the swan-song was attributed, and there is much support for the supposition that the wild Whooper Swan is intended. This, although a northern species, comes south in winter, and undoubtedly has a loud and musical note. It has been urged that sometimes when they have delayed their southern journey too long and have been reduced by lack of food, they have been frozen fast to the ice and so have clanged their lives out. Pallas likens the notes of this species to silver bells, and Olafsson says that in the long Polar night it is delightful to hear a flock passing overhead, the mixture of sounds resembling trumpets and violins. Willughby and Ray, who relate, on the authority of Wormius, a similar story of the sweet singing of a flock of wild Swans, remark that the windpipe, reflected in the form of a trumpet, seems to be so contrived by nature for modulating the voice. Colonel Hawker

("Instructions to Young Sportsmen," 8th ed., 1838, p. 261) has set the "Melody of the Wild Swan" (as heard in captivity however) to music as follows:

Allegro, or by Maelzel's metronome, =♩=126.

WIERANGEL or WIERANGLE: The GREAT GREY SHRIKE. Willughby gives it as a North of England name (about the Peak of Derbyshire), and says, on the authority of Gesner, that it is from the German "*Wurchangel*," literally a suffocating angel. Swainson applies it to the RED-BACKED SHRIKE while Nelson and Clarke give Weirangle, Wariangle, Würger, or Worrier, as old Yorks. names for that species.

WIGEON [No. 293]. Occurs in Turner (1544) as "Wigene," and in Merrett (1667) as "Widgeon." Willughby and Ray call it the "Common Wigeon or Whewer," and observe that "the males in this kind at Cambridge are called Wigeons, the females Whewers." Derivation is from Fr. *Vigeon*, from Lat. *Vipio*, according to Newton, but "Vipio" of Pliny is a small Crane.

WIGEON DIVER: The COMMON POCHARD. (Cork Harbour.)

WILD DUCK: The female of the MALLARD. Also an alternative name for the species. Occurs in Merrett's list (1667). Willughby and Ray call it the "Common Wild Duck and Mallard." Most British authors from Pennant onward call it the "Wild Duck." Albin has "Wild Mallard and Wild Duck," which would be the most correct name. It is a saying in the north that—

> When ducks are driving through the burn,
> That night the weather takes a turn.

WILDE LERC or HETH LERK (Turner). Probably the MEADOW-PIPIT, which is still known locally as "Heather Lintie," and frequents such places as Turner describes.

WILD GOOSE. Properly the GREY LAG-GOOSE, but applied to most of the species which visit this country. Fleming's Wild Goose is the BEAN-GOOSE. Barlow (1655) figures a "Wilde Goose," probably the Grey Lag-Goose.

WILD PIGEON: The STOCK-DOVE (Bewick); also the ROCK-DOVE (Shetlands).

Wild Swan: The WHOOPER SWAN. (Pennant.)

Willie Muftie· The WILLOW-WARBLER. (Scotland)

Willock The COMMON GUILLEMOT (Northumberland, Norfolk, Orkneys); the RAZORBILL (Shetlands); the PUFFIN (Kent).

Willow biter· The BLUE TITMOUSE From its nesting-holes being sometimes made in the willow. Newton thinks Billy-biter is a corruption of this name. Also the MARSH-TITMOUSE (Notts)

Willow Lark. The SEDGE-WARBLER. (Pennant.)

Willow Sparrow· The WILLOW-WARBLER. (West Riding, Yorkshire.)

WILLOW-TITMOUSE [No. 98, British Willow-Titmouse; No. 99, Northern Willow-Titmouse]. A close ally of the MARSH-TITMOUSE, first identified as a British bird by Mr. Hellmayr in 1900, although the Continental form (which has been identified once in our own islands) was distinguished as long ago as 1843 by De Selys-Longchamps. In Scotland, the British Willow-Titmouse appears quite to replace the Marsh-Titmouse

WILLOW-WARBLER [No. 122, WILLOW-WARBLER; No 123, Northern Willow-Warbler] Willow-Warbler appears in Yarrell (1843). It occurs in Pennant (1766) as Willow Wren, but by most authors from Edwards to Fleming (1842) it is termed Yellow Wren. Macgillivray calls it the "Willow Woodwren." It is the "*Regulus non cristatus*" of Willughby The Siberian form has been identified in our islands on migration.

Willy The COMMON GUILLEMOT. (Norfolk)

Willy Fisher The COMMON TERN (Forfar); the DIPPER (Teesdale).

Willy Gow· The HERRING-GULL (Scotland.)

Willy Hawkie· The LITTLE GREBE. (Clough, Antrim.)

Willy Whip the Wind· The KESTREL. Given by Gray as found in Don's "Fauna of Forfarshire"

Willy-wicket· The COMMON SANDPIPER. (North England) From its note.

WILSON'S PETREL [No 322] The name is found in Jenyns and in Yarrell (1st ed) and subsequent authors It is named in honour of Wilson the American ornithologist, who first figured it, but without being aware of its distinctness from the STORM-PETREL

WIL-Y-DWR: The DIPPER. (North Wales.) From its frequenting streams; lit. "Water Willy."

WINC. A Welsh name for the CHAFFINCH. From its note.

WIND: The DOTTEREL. (South of England.)

WINDER. A gunner's name for the WIGEON on many parts of our eastern coast. (Hawker.)

WINDHOVER. A very frequent name for the KESTREL (found in Willughby) and arising from its habit of hovering in the air while on the watch for its prey. Pron. "wind-huver." Other names are Windcuffer (Orkneys), Windsucker (Kent), Windbibber (Kent), and Wind-fanner.

WINDLE: The REDWING. (Devonshire.) Rutty gives Windles for co. Dublin. See Wind-Thrush.

WINDLESTRAW or WINNELL STRAW. The WHITETHROAT. (Provincial.) The latter form is a Shropshire name.

WINDOW SWALLOW· The MARTIN. (Bewick.) Also called Window Martin.

WIND-THRUSH: The REDWING. An earlier name for this species found in Merrett and Willughby, and in some later authors to Bewick (1797). It occurs as Wyngthrushe in Turner (1544), the name Redwing being first applied by Willughby, who informs us that "According to Charleton it is called Windthrush because it arrives about the beginning of winter when strong winds blow, by which it is strongly assisted in its passage." Willughby, however, considered the name should be Wine-thrush, being probably borrowed from the German name "Wyntrostel" (or "Vineyard-Thrush"), and in this he is borne out by Turner, who gives "Weingaerdsvogel" as the German name for the species. Swainson gives Wind-Thrush as a Somerset name.

WINNARD: The REDWING. (Cornwall.) See Wind-Thrush.

WINTER BONNET: The COMMON GULL. (Provincial.)

WINTER CROW. The HOODED CROW. (Turner.)

WINTER DUCK: The PINTAIL.

WINTER FAUVETTE: The HEDGE-SPARROW is so called by Bewick (1797).

WINTER MEW or WINTER GULL: The COMMON GULL. (Provincial.) The former name occurs in Pennant.

WINTER UTICK: The STONECHAT. (Cheshire.)

WINTER WAGTAIL: The GREY WAGTAIL. Because found in the South of England in winter.

WITCH: The STORM-PETREL. (Provincial.)

WITCHUCK· The SAND-MARTIN. (Orkneys.)

WITWOLL WITWALL, or WITWALE. The GREAT SPOTTED WOODPECKER is called Witwoll by Willughby. Turner's " Witwol," however, is the GOLDEN ORIOLE. Bewick (1797) gives "Witwall" for the Great Spotted Woodpecker, and Witwale (corruptly Whetile and Woodwale) seems to be properly the GREEN WOODPECKER.

WOH SNATCH (=Wall Snatch) The REDSTART. (Longdendale, Cheshire.)

WOODCHAT SHRIKE [No. 109]. First appears in Ray's "Synopsis Meth Av." (1713) Newton thinks it may be an erroneous rendering of the German name *Wald-Katze*, lit. " Wood-Cat " Occurs in Pennant (1766) and succeeding authors as "Woodchat" simply. Yarrell (1st ed , 1843) calls it Woodchat Shrike. It is the "another sort of Butcher bird" of Willughby and Ray (p 89) and the Red-headed Butcher-bird of Albin.

WOODCHUCK The GREEN WOODPECKER. (Shropshire.)

WOODCOCK [No. 411]. The name is from A.Sax *Wude-coco Wudu-coc* and *Wudu-snite*. " Woodcock " appears in Merrett's list (1667) he remarks that it migrates out of Ireland Turner (1544) spells it " Wod-cok " Willughby, who calls it "Woodcock," says "these are birds of passage coming over into England in Autumn, and departing again in the beginning of the Spring , yet they pair before they go, flying two together, a male and a female," and he adds that " They are said both to come and fly away in a mist " The Woodcock has always been highly esteemed for the delicate flavour of its flesh. The leg especially was commended, in contradistinction to the Partridge's tit-bit which with epicureans was the wing, hence the origin of the old couplet—

If the Partridge had the Woodcock's thigh,
'Twould be the best bird that ever did fly.

Willughby says that in England it is "infamous" for its simplicity or folly, so that the term " Woodcock " is proverbially used for a simple, foolish person

WOODCOCK OWL. A provincial name for the SHORT-EARED OWL. (England and Ireland) Because it comes to us in October, about the time the Woodcock makes its appearance, and departs at the same time as the latter in March. (Montagu). In use in Nottinghamshire and elsewhere.

WOODCOCK PILOT· The GOLDEN-CRESTED WREN. (Yorkshire coast.)

WOODCOCK SNIPE : The GREAT SNIPE. (Ireland.)

WOODCOCK THRUSH : WHITE'S THRUSH is known by this name in Hampshire and elsewhere, partly on account of its frequenting the ground in woodlands, and partly on account of its variegated plumage and fair size.

WOOD-CRACKER : The NUTHATCH. Occurs in Plot's "Oxfordshire" (1677), who says it is an undescribed species, yet it occurs in Turner (1544) under the name of "Nutjobber," and as *Sitta* was described by Aristotle.

WOOD DOVE : The STOCK-DOVE. (Scotland.)

WOOD GROUSE : The CAPERCAILLIE occurs under this name in many older authors (Pennant, Bewick, Montagu, etc.).

WOOD-HACK : The GREEN WOODPECKER. (Lincoln.)

WOOD-KNACKER (=Wood-Knocker) : The GREEN WOODPECKER. (Hampshire.)

WOOD-LARK [No 61]. The name occurs in Turner (1544) as "Wodlerck," and in Merrett as "Wood-Lark," also in Willughby as "Woodlark." Bolam states that Woodlark is also a Scots Border and Cheshire name for the TREE-PIPIT.

'WOOD OWL : The common TAWNY OWL is frequently known by this name.

WOODPECKER. The TREECREEPER. (Ireland, Scotland.)

WOODPIE · The GREAT SPOTTED WOODPECKER (Hampshire, Staffordshire.) So called from its pied plumage (see "Pie"). It is also a Somersetshire name for the GREEN WOODPECKER, according to Swainson.

WOOD-PIGEON. An alternative name for the RING-DOVE; in fact, in rather more general use than the latter, which is rather the written than the spoken name. The name is appropriate, from the bird's partiality to woods, but it is not infrequently used also to denote the STOCK-DOVE, hence tending to confusion, and for this reason the name Ring-Dove is to be preferred, although the authors of the "Hand-List" have chosen Wood-Pigeon. Montagu gives it as a provincial name. Pigeon is from Fr. *Pigeon*. A Dorsetshire superstition is that pigeons' feathers should never be used for beds: folks die hard on them. In Cornwall it is believed that one cannot die easily on a pillow stuffed with wild-birds' feathers.

WOOD QUEST. An old name for the RING-DOVE. (Staffs., Dorsetshire, Ireland). There are several variations— Lyly has Wood Quist : "Methought I saw a stock-dove or wood quist" ("Sapho and Phaon"). In Wiltshire it becomes Quisty, and elsewhere it is Queest (q.v.).

WOOD-SANDPIPER [No. 389]   The name is found in Pennant and succeeding authors to Yarrell.

WOOD SHRIKE. The WOODCHAT SHRIKE. (Fleming.)

WOOD-SPITE or WOOD-SPACK: The GREEN WOODPECKER. (Norfolk, Suffolk.) Occurs in Willughby (1678). The original form of the word seems to be Woodspeight.

WOOD-SUCKER: The GREEN WOODPECKER. (New Forest.)

WOOD THRUSH. The MISTLE-THRUSH   (Dumfries.)

WOOD TITMOUSE· The GOLDEN-CRESTED WREN. Montagu says that this species was so-called in Cornwall. The name also occurs in Willughby, who says it is the GOLDEN-CRESTED WREN.

WOODWALL. The GREEN WOODPECKER. (Somersetshire.)

WOOD-WARBLER [No. 125]. The name is first found as Wood Wren in the Linnean "Trans.," II, p. 245. Up to Fleming (1842) it was generally called Wood Wren, but Yarrell (1843) inserted it under the name of Wood Warbler. It is the Green Wren of Albin, the Yellow Willow Wren of Bewick, the Yellow Woodwren of Macgillivray, and the East Woodhay Warbler of Rennie's ed (1833) of White's Selborne.

WOOD WREN. See WOOD-WARBLER.

WOOFEL   The BLACKBIRD. (Drayton's "Polyolbion.")

WOOLERT   The BARN-OWL. (Salop) A corruption of Howlet

WRAN· The WREN. (In parts of Ireland and Scotland.)

WRANNOCK   The WREN. (Orkneys.)

WRANNY. The WREN. (Cornwall.)

WREN [No. 189, WREN;   No 190, St. Kilda Wren; No. 191, Shetland Wren]. The name "Wren" occurs in Turner (1544), and in Merrett's list (1667). It is from A Sax. *wrænna*, from *wræne*=lascivious, in Dan *vrinsk*=proud, Swedish *vrensk*=uncastrated. How it came to be popularly supposed more recently to be peculiarly feminine is not readily apparent·—

> The Robin and the Wren
> Are God's cock and hen.

is an old and widely-accepted belief, and the idea that the two mate is still seriously held by some uninformed individuals. The same idea is apparent in such names as "Kitty Wren."

An old Irish custom on St. Stephen's Day, and one which has not quite died out, was the "hunting of the Wren" by boys. When captured, it was tied, alive but maimed, to a pole (or, according to Vallancey—"De Reb. Hib.," IV, 13—tied by the leg in the centre of two hoops placed at right angles with one another) and paraded around the neighbourhood, a few doggerel verses being repeated at each house, while a donation was requested, one version being :—

> The wran, the wran, the King of all birds,
> St. Stephen's Day was caught in the furze :
> Come, give us a bumper, or give us a cake,
> Or give us a copper, for Charity's sake.

The proceeding is supposed to have originated through a Wren having at some former time betrayed the Irish to their enemies by tapping on a drum. Yarrell records a somewhat similar practice in Kerry, where the peasantry, on Christmas Day, used to hunt the bird with two sticks, "one to beat the bushes, the other to fling at the bird." Bullock also mentions it as prevalent in the Isle of Man, both on Christmas Eve and St. Stephen's Day, and tells us it was founded on a tradition of a beautiful fairy who lured the male inhabitants to a watery grave in the sea, and who to escape subsequent destruction took the form of a Wren, which form she was supposed to be doomed by a spell to re-assume each succeeding New Year's Day, ultimately perishing by human hands. Waldron records a different custom in the Isle of Man of the killing of a Wren on Christmas Day, which was laid on a bier, carried to the church and buried with the singing of dirges. To my own knowledge this custom of a "Wren hunt" existed in Nottinghamshire also within recent times, the bird being hunted along the hedgerows by boys armed with stones, but I do not recollect that anything definite was done with the bird when killed or maimed.

The before-mentioned allusion to the Wren as the "King of all birds" is perhaps explained by the legend of the birds having agreed to choose as King the one who should soar highest, the place of honour being gained by the Wren, through it having remained on the Eagle's back until the latter had soared to the limit of its power. The Germans, it may be remarked, call the Wren "*Zaunkonig*" or "hedge-king :" the Latin *regulus* however is the GOLDEN-CRESTED WREN. In connexion with this belief in the kingship over other birds, a Twelfth Day custom of parading a caged Wren in Pembrokeshire, with the lines recited, is described in Swainson's "Folklore of British Birds," pp. 36-43 (see also "Notes and Queries," 3rd ser., vol. v, p. 109). O'Curry has recorded that the Wren, like the Raven, was kept domesticated on account of the auguries derived from it, which were employed by the Druids.

An Irish proverb asserts that, "The fox is the cunningest beast in the world barring the Wren."

According to Dalyell the Wren is considered an unlucky token in Scotland, but the Robin a lucky one. That the Wren was formerly considered of medicinal value is shown by Willughby, who writes: " It perfectly cures the stone of the kidneys or bladder (as Aetius writes) being salted and eaten raw, or being burnt in a pot close covered, and the ashes of one whole bird taken at once, either by itself, or with a little Phyllon (a kind of mercury) and Pepper, or lastly being roasted whole, only the feathers plucked off and cast away."

The St. Kilda Wren is a large pale form of the Wren which is confined to the island of St Kilda. It was first described by Seebohm in the "Zoologist," 1884, p. 333. Mr. Hartert has also separated the race inhabiting the Shetland Islands from the typical British Wren.

WRITHE-NECK · The WRYNECK. An equivalent name.

WRITING LARK· The YELLOW BUNTING. (Notts., Yorks, Northants.)

WRITING LINNET: The YELLOW BUNTING. (Longdendale, Cheshire.)

WRITING MASTER The YELLOW-BUNTING (Salop.)

WRYNECK [No. 213]. So called from its peculiar habit of writhing its head and neck. The name occurs in Merrett and in Willughby. Turner (1544) describes the bird under the ancient names of *Iynx* and *Torquilla* (now its generic and specific names) but gives it no English name, considering it to be a form of Woodpecker.

WYPE. The LAPWING. Occurs in the Northumberland Household Book, A.D. 1512. Akin to Swed. *Wipa*, a name for the species.

YAFFLE, YAFFLER, or YAFFIL The GREEN WOODPECKER. So called in Surrey, Sussex, Yorks, and other counties on account of its note, which has been likened to a laugh.

YAPPINGALE or YAPPINGAL: The GREEN WOODPECKER; lit. Bawling singer, from its cry. Yaup in Staffordshire means to bawl, while yap is in fairly general use as indicating a discordant cry, such as that of a puppy. Gal or Gale is probably from A.Sax. *gale*=a singer.

YARN or YERN: The COMMON HERON. (Cheshire.) Probably a corruption of heron.

YARRELL. The adult male RED-BREASTED MERGANSER. (Northumberland.)

YARWHELP, YARDKEEP, or YARWIP: The BAR-TAILED GODWIT. From its cry. Occurs in Willughby. Yarwhelp is also a Norfolk name for the AVOCET; and is apparently applied to denote a point of resemblance to the true Yarwhelp.

YAUP or WHAUP: The AVOCET. (Norfolk). A term equivalent to Curlew. Swainson also gives it as a Renfrew name for the BLUE TITMOUSE.

YDFRAN. The Welsh name for the ROOK; lit. "corn-crow."

YELDRIN: The YELLOW BUNTING in some parts of Scotland.

YELDROCK: The YELLOW BUNTING. (Northumberland, Yorks.)

YELLOW AMMER: The YELLOW BUNTING. (Provincial.) Also Yellow amber or Yellow omber (Salop). Ammer seems to be cognate with Germ. *Ammer*, a Bunting. Swainson thinks it is from A.Sax. *Amore*, a small bird, the prefix "Yellow" referring to the general yellow tint of the plumage. He gives Yellow Amber or Yellow Omber as a Shropshire name.

YELLOW-BILLED CUCKOO [No. 216 American Yellow-billed Cuckoo] Occurs in Yarrell (1st ed.) as Yellow-billed American Cuckoo. This is a North American species recorded as a straggler to the British Islands.

YELLOW-BREASTED BUNTING [No. 46]. A Siberian species having the breast bright yellow, with a chestnut band.

YELLOW-BROWED WARBLER [No. 127]. A Siberian species of Willow Warbler, so called from its pronounced yellowish-white superciliary stripe. It is the Dalmatian Regulus of Gould and Yarrell.

YELLOW BUNTING [No. 43]. Usually known as the Yellow-hammer. The name occurs in Merrett and Willughby as "Yellow-hammer:" Turner (1544) has "Yelow ham." Pennant (1766) calls it Yellow hammer, but in the later editions it appears as Yellow Bunting, as also in the works of most of his successors, Yellow hammer being specified by Montagu as a provincial name. Yarrell (1st ed.) renders it "Yellow Bunting or Yellow Ammer."

In Aberdeenshire, according to "Folklore Journal," there exists the following saying—

>Yallow, yallow, yarlin'
>Drinks a drap o' deevil's-bleed
>Ilka Monday mornin'.

In the West of Scotland (Aird's ' Old Bachelor in the Old Scottish Village ") it becomes—

>Half a puddock, half a toad, half a yellow yorling,
>Cries for a drap o' the deil's bluid every Monday morning

In Yorkshire I believe the saying runs—

>A brock, a toad and a yellow yeorling
>Drink a drop o' the deil's blood
>Every May morning

Chambers gives another Scottish version as—

>Half a puddock, half a toad,
>Half a yellow yorling,
>Drink a drop o' the de'il's bluid
>Every May morning

YELLOW-HAMMER The older name of the YELLOW BUNTING. Synonymous with Yellow Ammer (q v.).

YELLOW-LEGGED GULL. The LESSER BLACK-BACKED GULL. (Fleming.)

YELLOW-LEGGED HERRING-GULL [No. 432]. A Mediterranean species, distinguished by the bright yellow of its tarsi and feet.

YELLOW MOLLY · The YELLOW WAGTAIL. (Hampshire)

YELLOW OWL. The BARN-OWL (Provincial)

YELLOW PLOVER. The GOLDEN PLOVER. (Bewick)

YELLOW POLL or GOLDEN HEAD The male WIGEON. (East Ireland)

YELLOWSHANK [No. 392] So called from its bright yellow tarsi and feet

YELLOW-SHANKED SANDPIPER The immature RUFF Found in Yarrell (1st ed) It is the Yellowshanks of Pennant.

YELLOW THROATED BEE-EATER. Macgillivray's name for the BEE-EATER.

YELLOW WAGTAIL [No. 79]. This species, sometimes called Ray's Wagtail, and named by Bonaparte in 1838 in honour of Ray, was for long considered the same as the Continental BLUE-HEADED WAGTAIL. The Yellow Water-Wagtail of Willughby, Pennant, etc., may therefore be taken as the name of this species. The GREY WAGTAIL is also mis-called the Yellow Wagtail by country people. Thompson gives it as a popular name for this species in Ireland

YELLOW WILLOW WREN: The WOOD-WARBLER. (Bewick.) It is also found in White's Selborne as Yellowish Willow-Wren.

YELLOW WREN: The WILLOW-WARBLER. So called from the prevailing tint of its plumage by many old authors. The name is also applied to the WOOD-WARBLER.

YELLOW YALE or YITE, YELLOW YELDRIN, YELLOW YOWLEY. The YELLOW BUNTING is so called in some parts of Scotland. Yellow Yowley is also a Yorks. name.

YELLOW YOWLING, YELLOW YITE, YORLIN, YIRLIN, YELDROCK, or YELDRIN. Northumberland names for the YELLOW BUNTING.

YELPER. The AVOCET. From its cry. Montagu gives it as a provincial name.

YEORLING: The YELLOW BUNTING. (Berwick.)

YOKEL or YUKEL. The GREEN WOODPECKER. (Provincial.)

YOULRING or YOWLRYNG: The YELLOW BUNTING. Turner (1544) has "Yowlrying," while Sibbald (1684) calls it "Yellow Youlring." Yellow Yoldring or Yoldring is a Yorkshire name.

YSGRAELL, YSGRECHEN. Welsh names for the COMMON TERN. The first signifies "rattle" and the second "screamer," from its harsh cry.

YSGUTHAN. A Welsh name for the RING-DOVE, lit. "cooing bird." Also applied to the STOCK-DOVE and ROCK-DOVE.

YSNITEN. A Welsh name for the COMMON SNIPE; lit. "snipe."

YSWIDW LAS FACH. The BLUE TITMOUSE. (North Wales) lit "little blue tit."

YSWIDW LLWYD FACH: The MARSH-TITMOUSE. (North Wales); lit. "little grey tit."

YSWIDW'R COED: The GREAT TITMOUSE (North Wales) lit. "wood titmouse."

YUCKEL or YOCKEL: The GREEN WOODPECKER. The former is a Wiltshire and the latter a Shropshire name.

ZETHAR. A Cornish name for the "Sea Mew or Gull." (Harting.) Perhaps the COMMON GULL.

FINIS.

A HAND-LIST OF BRITISH BIRDS

By ERNST HARTERT, F. C. R. JOURDAIN, N. F. TICEHURST, and H. F. WITHERBY.

Giving a detailed account of the distribution of each species in the British Isles and a general account of its range abroad.

o o o

Full details of Rare Visitors.   **Full Index.**

o o o

The Nomenclature is revised strictly in accordance with the International Rules of Zoological Nomenclature. . . .

o o o

Demy 8vo - - **7s. 6d. net.**
Special Copies interleaved with Ruled Paper - 10s. net.

o o o

Spectator says :—" Excellent, careful, accurate, laborious and much needed piece of truly scientific work."

LONDON: WITHERBY & CO., 326, High Holborn.

Printed by WITHERBY & Co
at their Printing Press in
Middle Row Place London

MEMORANDA OF ADDITIONAL NAMES

These blank pages are provided for the reader's own notes on names not occurring in this volume

MEMORANDA OF ADDITIONAL NAMES.

MEMORANDA OF ADDITIONAL NAMES.

MEMORANDA OF ADDITIONAL NAMES.

MEMORANDA OF ADDITIONAL NAMES.

MEMORANDA OF ADDITIONAL NAMES.

MEMORANDA OF ADDITIONAL NAMES.

MEMORANDA OF ADDITIONAL NAMES.

MEMORANDA OF ADDITIONAL NAMES

MEMORANDA OF ADDITIONAL NAMES.

MEMORANDA OF ADDITIONAL NAMES.

MEMORANDA OF ADDITIONAL NAMES.

MEMORANDA OF ADDITIONAL NAMES.

MEMORANDA OF ADDITIONAL NAMES.

MEMORANDA OF ADDITIONAL NAMES.